'BRING FURTH THE PAGANTS':
ESSAYS IN EARLY ENGLISH DRAMA
PRESENTED TO ALEXANDRA F. JOHNSTON

Alexandra F. Johnston

EDITED BY DAVID N. KLAUSNER
AND KAREN SAWYER MARSALEK

'Bring furth the pagants':

Essays in Early English Drama
Presented to Alexandra F. Johnston

UNIVERSITY OF TORONTO PRESS
Toronto Buffalo London

© University of Toronto Press Incorporated 2007
Toronto Buffalo London
Printed in Canada

ISBN-13: 978-0-8020-9107-9
ISBN-10: 0-8020-9107-5

STUDIES IN EARLY ENGLISH DRAMA 9
General Editor: J.A.B. Somerset

Printed on acid-free paper

Library and Archives Canada Cataloguing in Publication

'Bring furth the pagants' : essays in early English drama presented to
Alexandra F. Johnston / edited by David N. Klausner and Karen S. Marsalek.

(Studies in early English drama ; 9)
Includes bibliographical references and index.
ISBN-13: 978-0-8020-9107-9
ISBN-10: 0-8020-9107-5

1. English drama – To 1500 – History and criticism.   2. English drama –
Early modern and Elizabethan, – 1500–1600 – History and criticism.
3. Performing arts – England – History.   I. Johnston, Alexandra F., 1939–
II. Klausner, David N.   III. Marsalek, Karen S.   IV. Title: Bring furth the
pagants.   V. Series.

PN2583.B75 2006   790.2′09420902   C2006-904040-0

University of Toronto Press acknowledges the financial assistance to
its publishing program of the Canada Council for the Arts and the
Ontario Arts Council.

University of Toronto Press acknowledges the financial support for
its publishing activities of the Government of Canada through the
Book Publishing Industry Development Program (BPIDP).

Contents

PART TWO: MEDIEVAL PLAYS

PART THREE: RENAISSANCE PLAYS

'BRING FURTH THE PAGANTS':
ESSAYS IN EARLY ENGLISH DRAMA
PRESENTED TO ALEXANDRA F. JOHNSTON

Alexandra Ferguson Johnston

Alexandra Ferguson Johnston was born on 14 July 1939 in Indianapolis, Indiana, the daughter of Alexandra Sherwood and the Rev. Geoffrey Deane Johnston, minister of the Central Presbyterian Church in Brantford, Ontario, during a visit to maternal grandparents. Her American birth gave Sandy dual citizenship when, eventually, that became a legal option, and she was always proud of her American connections. Sandy (whose boundless – bounding? – energy gained her another nickname as well) showed an interest in 'theatrical pursuits' at an early age with the foundation of the neighbourhood Pixie Players at the age of about seven or eight, though no one at that time would likely have guessed the extent to which they would dominate her life. Her organization of local theatricals leaves me with no difficulty imagining Mickey Rooney tearing up to her and shouting, 'Let's put on a play!'

Sandy attended the Brantford public schools; her undergraduate and graduate work was all done at the University of Toronto. She entered the undergraduate class at Victoria College in 1957, where she became part of a close-knit literary crowd, very much under the influence of Northrop Frye. She followed this with an MA in English in 1962, moving on to a PhD which she completed in a brief two years with a thesis entitled 'The Christ Figure in the Four English Cycles' – a phrase about which she might now have some second thoughts. Her supervisor was Father Leonard K. Shook. Sandy spent three years teaching in the Department of English at Queen's University, returning to her alma mater in 1967. She was tenured a mere two years after her appointment, and was promoted to full professor in 1978. Cross-appointments to the Centre for Medieval Studies and the Graduate Centre for Study of Drama involved her in the expanding realms of interdisciplinary teaching. All of Sandy's academic life at the University of Toronto has been spent at Victoria College, and since its founding in 1976 the college has provided a

home (and much more) for the REED project. In 1981 she became the first
woman to hold the rank of college principal on the university's main campus, and she remained principal of Victoria College for ten years, returning
for an encore in 2003–4 as acting principal.

Her research on early English drama took her to York, where her
discovery of the 1433 Mercers' Indenture among the York records led to
both the founding of the project Records of Early English Drama and also
a life-long friendship with Margaret Rogerson (then Dorrell), who was
working on the indenture at roughly the same time.[1] The enthusiasm of
the founding meeting for REED in 1975 was infectious, and (miracu-
lously) has carried on virtually undiminished to the present day. Sandy was
the project's first executive editor, becoming director in 1988, as Sally-Beth
MacLean took over as executive editor. The edition of the York records,
now known as REED 1, which Sandy and Margaret produced, has provided a pilot and test case for the rest of the series; Sandy continued to do
research as editor of the forthcoming collections for Berkshire and
Buckinghamshire, as well as co-editor of the city records for the 2004
Oxford University and City volumes.[2] The story of the early days of the
project is a tribute to both Sandy's energy and determination and the
extraordinary group of people she assembled as advisors, scholars whose
foresight set most of the parameters that guide the project today: David
Galloway, Reg Ingram, Ian Lancashire, Stanley J. Karhl, Anthony Petti,
and Richard Proudfoot, among many others.

It was through the REED project that I first came to know her well.
Around 1978, she suggested to me that I might make a not totally incompetent REED editor, and that a small backwater county like Herefordshire,
in which it was likely that not much ever happened, might be just right for
my talents. She was right about everything except the scale of the project,
and she not only shepherded the research for my first REED volume, but
constantly encouraged my second, far more complex, project. Her inde-
fatigable work for REED has led especially to her acting as the project's
public face. This has involved her not only in the constant raising of
private funds for its completion, but in the writing of an endless series of
grant proposals. It has also formed the primary focus of her published
work, an extraordinary series of more than fifty papers and book chapters,
often deriving from REED's researches, accompanied by her unflagging
attendance at conferences and the presentation of over a hundred papers,
frequently on REED-related subjects. This unfailing presence at meetings
and conferences even led to Sandy's martyring herself as *chauffeur désigné*
to the Worcestershire and Shropshire editors (no names here, please) determined to test every local beer between Kidderminster and Leeds.

Sandy Johnston's participation in the life of the University of Toronto has been extraordinarily varied: teacher and supervisor, college principal, director of a major research project – the list goes on. But this is only a fraction of what has, so far, been a rewardingly full life. She has also been a hands-on theatre person, primarily through her involvement with Poculi Ludique Societas, the university's early-drama-in-performance research project. Those who have not been directly involved in this forty-year adventure will have no idea of the time and energy Sandy has put into it. This has over the years included impersonating the Virgin Mary (an act which just over half a century ago could have got her thrown in jail [at least in England] for 'impersonating a divine personage'), transforming herself regularly into the abbess of a fourteenth-century French convent, and acting as chair of PLS's Board of Directors for as long as I can remember. This labour of love has involved a good deal more than running the occasional meeting: among other things, it has meant regularly signing a thousand fundraising letters (and there is no hyperbole in the number), sewing costumes, and pulling long-stored wagons out from under a pile of raccoon droppings, or out of Victoria College's compost heap where the Judgment wagon (too tall for indoors) was stored.

She has also been heavily involved with the scholarly world of medieval drama beyond the University of Toronto, serving the Medieval and Renaissance Drama Society as vice-president from 1986 to 1990 and as president from 1990 to 1993, and the Société internationale pour l'étude du théâtre médiéval as secretary from 1983 to 1989 and president from 1989 to 1992.

Her honours have been many and varied, including an honorary doctorate of Laws from Queen's University, Kingston, Ontario, in 1984 and a doctorate of Divinity from the Presbyterian College in Montreal in 1991, as well as membership in the Canadian Royal Society (1997) and the presidency of its Academy II, the humanities and social sciences wing. In 2002 she was awarded the University of Toronto's Faculty Award of Excellence in teaching.

As if this weren't enough, Sandy has been active in the work of the Presbyterian Church in Canada, serving as an elder of her congregation since 1973, and as a member of the Assembly of the World Council of Churches from 1991 to 1998. From 1994 to 1997 she served as president of the Canadian Council of Churches. Locally, her ties have always been with the Rosedale Presbyterian Church, where she has long sung in the choir and for many years been Clerk of Sessions for her parish. I should have thought that with all this Sandy would hardly need a hobby, but she is an acknowledged expert in historical embroidery, and her own needlework is nothing short of superb.

Through all of this, Sandy has taught, and her receipt of the University of Toronto's Faculty Award for Teaching in 2002 recognized her as one of the university's most outstanding teachers. I have never sat in one of Sandy's undergraduate classes (though I would love to be a fly on the wall), but we have jointly been on more doctoral supervisory committees than I have had hot dinners, so I have had a first-hand view of her work there. If I, God forbid, were to be a graduate student all over again – a thought which ranks right up there with reliving puberty – I would want Sandy as my supervisor. The care and attention she has invested not only in the dissertations, but also in the lives of her graduate students has provided me over the past decades with a role model, and much of what I know about the real obligations of a supervisor I have learned from her. Her teaching on all levels has been anything but ordinary, and it has always been distinguished by a direct connection with her research: former students tell me of being directed to impersonate pageant wagons in order to map out the route of the York plays, and of being assigned identities of York guildsmen, clergy, and townspeople in order to report on the kinds of drama these people might have seen and their involvement in production and performance.

Sandy retired from full-time teaching in 2004 in order to be able to devote her time more effectively to the completion of the REED project, in particular to the fund-raising that will be essential to the march of big red volumes. Her presence on the campus is, therefore, happily undiminished, and it is clear that her energies will be focused for some time on REED's research. We would all like to wish you, Sandy, a well-deserved rest, but since you have already done enough for several normal lives, we are pretty sure that is not going to happen. Way to go, Tigger!

David Klausner

NOTES

1 The heady story of those early days of REED is told by Sandy herself in 'The Founding of Records of Early English Drama' in *REED in Review: Essays in Celebration of the First Twenty-five Years*, ed. Audrey Douglas and Sally-Beth MacLean (Toronto: University of Toronto Press, 2006), 21–38.
2 John R. Elliott, Jr, Alan Nelson, Diana Wyatt, and A.F. Johnston, eds, *Oxford City and University*, REED (Toronto: University of Toronto Press, 2004).

PART ONE

The Records

Star Turns or Small Companies?

BARBARA D. PALMER

Here is not the place to write the history of the Records of Early English Drama (REED) project, a task which Alexandra F. Johnston justifiably may wish to claim for herself. Here, however, is the place to note, somewhat tongue in cheek, that the title of this tribute describes REED itself as well as the three early drama case studies that follow as the article's content. Most first-generation REED scholars, we of Professor Johnston's vintage, had been reared on the star system, in particular the big three of E.K. Chambers, G.E. Bentley, and John Tucker Murray. Murray's primacy was affirmed by never using his initials, intoning 'John Tucker' with the same sonorous tone that 'Ego sum alpha' leads off the York cycle. Fettered by the anthologies from which we were trying to teach, we vaulted from the Wakefield Master, North Star of a dark age, to Master Shakespeare – and to a host of equally simplistic linear notions about early drama: from minster to marketplace, from London to provincial purgatory, from sacred to secular texts, from rank amateur vagabonds to ranked professional players. As John Wasson wrote, 'It is not hard to believe in a volcano god if one has no facts to account for volcanic eruptions,' his pithy metaphor for those 'early critics [who] could envision grand theories of the development of English drama without being much troubled by facts.'[1]

Also academically trained to follow these comets' tails, Johnston recognized earlier than most that the gas and dust streamers seemed to be missing celestial bodies of hard evidence. Herself a potential star in the ascendant, almost by accident she founded a small company of players when, working in the York Merchant Adventurers' archives, she came across the parchment sheet of the 1433 Mercers' Indenture.[2] After what she describes as a conscience-tussled night, she decided to share 'the single most important document in English medieval stage history' with Margaret Dorrell Rogerson, already working on the York civic records.³ From that nocturnal struggle came not only their co-editorship of the first REED volumes but also the norm of collaboration that has sustained the project since. The records themselves, over the now thirty years of the REED project, have had the nasty habit of whacking egos into shape, of turning stars into small companies. Certainly York did so. Supposed to be the archetype of 'civic Corpus Christi cycles,' it turned out to be the anomaly; and Johnston's own star turn rummaging in the Merchant Adventurers' Archives' Box D63 dims in the small-company constellation of professional staff, talented graduate students, committed volunteers, and field editors whom she brought to share in REED's adventures.

If sheer courage was Johnston's founding gift to REED, asking the uncomfortable question, often at the most awkward time, must be marked her second. Actually, both characteristics fall under the same heading, her blessed inability 'to leave well enough alone.' 'Well enough' seldom is 'good enough' for her relentless, occasionally ill-timed, inquiry. Her former graduate students must be more painfully aware than I that no research really can be called finished if Johnston has found the topic of interest, but I offer one mature example of my own discomfiture over the years. In April 2002 I sat at my kitchen table, proud that my paper for 'The Towneley Plays Reconsidered: A Session in Memory of Martin Stevens' was finished, a month early. I almost forgot that Johnston was sitting opposite, until I heard that familiar voice ask, 'What do "we" know about the Towneleys?' – and heard almost simultaneously, in my own head, the shredding sounds of my erstwhile paper. After her departure one fortuitous Google search (of the Burnley, Lancashire, tourism website) converted the Towneleys from nineteenth-century antiquarian bibliophiles to stridently recusant gentry lawyers, a discovery that only buttressed our long-held mutual conviction that the Towneley manuscript was a Marian *compilatio*, not a fifteenth-century Wakefield guild cycle.⁴

Her own work has not been immune to self-scrutiny and uncomfortable questions. From the 1511 St George play in Bassingbourne, Cambridgeshire, with contributions from twenty-seven neighbouring parishes, the 1526 professionally organized production in Heybridge, Essex, with twenty-three parishes' contributions, and the 1535 Boxford, Suffolk, production with twenty-four parishes, she argues the existence of 'a considerable pool of professional players who toured the countryside under the patronage of local magistrates' – an enormous shift of vision for this scholar of the York cycle.⁵ From 'the play called Corpus Christi,' lintel inscription of early drama studies and mantra of the York records, in 2003 she wrote that 'we now know through the work of REED that Corpus Christi Day held no more special significance for drama than Whitsun or May Day or Midsummer.[6] From her tepid enthusiasm for great household records, which almost led to their being categorically excluded from REED pursuit, she has reformed to the clear-headed explication of a household entertainment that could be untangled only by her own embroidery expertise.[7] And throughout the evolving years, she has remained consistently faithful to the revelations of text and of performance. Granted that sins of omission have formed the REED backbone and shaped us all to notice what is not present, her observations in '"His langage is lorne": The Silent Centre of the York Cycle' nevertheless form a movingly perceptive analysis that should not suffer synoptic abuse here.[8]

Here, on the occasion of Professor Johnston's retirement from full-time teaching and in the honourable REED tradition of not being able to leave well enough alone, the subject I want to revisit is the size, organization, and licensing of travelling companies, itinerant troupes of professional players.[9] 'Itinerant' denotes its root sense of the professional traveller, frequently on a circuit and always for profit, not the vagabond player strolling through hedgerows in hope of unguarded linens and paying audiences. Arguing from REED data for a more flexible counting system, one that can accommodate star turns, small companies, and various configurations within larger companies, to say nothing of somewhat fluid patronage authority, I propose three brief paradigms to illustrate the Johnstonian principle that prefers unanswered questions to unquestioned answers. Before moving to those specific case studies, however, a bit of background on how the size of travelling companies is reflected in the records might be helpful.

Few scholars would contest that from the surviving records we can conclude that companies were small in the fifteenth and early sixteenth centuries. Based on his REED *Devon* volume, John Wasson notes that '[t]he size of the companies varied but was never large before the reign of Elizabeth. Three or four seems to have been the standard size, although two is quite common.'[10] Suzanne Westfall, using the thirty-five Selby Abbey records that specify players' numbers from Glynne Wickham's *Early English Stages*, finds that '[m]ost frequently, the reward was given to a single player.'[11] Her – or rather Wickham's – sample comes from only a fraction of the Selby records, whose slippery entertainment terminology – '*ministrallus, mimus, histrio, ludo, ludus, lusor, iocus, ioculator* ... and (worse-scene scenario) *histrioni ludenti*' – he conflated into 'players.'[12] The whole of the extant Selby Abbey records with unconflated diction suggests not the single itinerant player but, in fact, the title of this paper. Small companies, indeed, but, early on, a tradition of star turns as well: Sir Thomas Darcy's tumbler; Henry VIII's juggler-jester Thomas Brandon (the subject of the first paradigm, below); the duke of Lancaster's *ministrallo pessimo*, John Warst or Worst, whose repeat visits earn him between 18d and 2s regardless of how 'worst' he was.

After the 1572 watershed for those pesky strolling vagabonds, companies grew larger. On that phenomenon scholars agree, but on their numbers G.E. Bentley can play the pre-REED straw man as he claims that 'though there are many hundreds of town records of players' visits, disappointingly few of them record the number of players travelling ... From 1590 to 1607, no numbers are mentioned in the reported [i.e., published] town records. Between 1607 and 1637 nine accounts give the number of players in the visiting troupe as from nine to twenty.'[13] His numbers are wrong, and he also is looking at the wrong sort of records. Civic records do not routinely number players — why should they when there is no individual fiscal grounding, like the paid number of meals or beds? Although economic arrangements vary from town to town, either a civic reward or an audience collection or both seem to have been standard, with the players responsible for their own food and board. Neither do a great household steward's records usually yield players' numbers: his provenance is paying out money in reward from his master or mistress to the group, even if 'the group' is but one.[14]

Had travelling players routinely played at inns, which they did not, and had innkeepers' records survived, which they have not, they might have yielded per capita figures, but the REED project finally seems to have put paid to the myth of provincial inns as playing places.[15] Consequently, the unique extant source for reliable travelling players' numbers may be the great households' pantry stewards' accounts, in the rare instances where those accounts survive. Their survival is rare because they are like yesterday's grocery list, often jotted on whatever scrap of paper is to hand, numerically temporal (cost, quantity, servings, date), and reflective of the household's domestic side, which held little value for our archive-trawling predecessors. Pantry accounts also are notoriously difficult to read, let alone to comprehend without the interdisciplinary assistance of social historians expert in great household management. The diction often is opaque, the spelling quixotic, the foodstuffs mysterious, and the tallying abbreviations ambiguous. Pantry stewards are bean counters, the ancestors of deans, with enormous power in nothing that really seems to matter. Once deciphered, however, pantry stewards' bean-counting compulsions can yield valuable information on travelling practices.

Another approach to travelling companies potentially decipherable from the REED collections is the terminology with which the stewards of records – civic, court, religious, household, pantry – accidentally immortalize travelling players. That terminology may speak to a company's size, organization, and persona – or it may not: the formulae hold marked variation, some of it topical, much of it underdocumented, some conventional, some eccentric, and all too much inexplicable, at present. One bookend of the company-size spectrum is companies performing together, a 'feature of the theatrical business in the 1590s that many theatre historians treat gingerly,' to borrow Roslyn L. Knutson's phrase.[16] At York in April 1593, the Lord Admiral's and Lord Morden's players received 40s total, that November the Lords Ogle's and Darcy's players 20s, and in September 1596 Darby's and Darcy's players 10s. Similar cooperative ventures appear in Cheshire, Leicestershire, the West Riding, and elsewhere, but they are comparatively unusual. Possible reasons behind two companies playing as one may include the size or nature of the performance venue; topical circumstances such as plague, politics, economics, or scheduling conflicts; and, most obviously, increased numbers of available players. Stanley Wells recently speculated that amalgamated companies might offer more boy actors (thus more female roles), and the same speculation might hold for other sorts of histrionic talent.[17]

We all are familiar with companies identified by their patron, but a significant number of entries identifies companies by a player's name: 'players Iohn ledy & his Company,' 'Deshley the player and his Company,' 'mr Kempton & his Company of players,' 'mr Swinerton & his Company of players,' 'Mr Parry & his Compayny of players.' A further group of entries identifies companies by both patron and players: three of the Queen's players, William Smith, John Garland, and John Cowper, 40s to depart York in August 1598 and not to play (a most unhelpful record of how many players arrived); 'mr Bradshawe & his Company the Kinges players,' 10s; 'to Ellis Guest William Elton & Thomas Lovell & others of his Maiesties Revells,' 20s. Whether these individuals are named because they are the licence holders, player-road managers, senior sharers, or star performers invites further research. Equally silent on company size and organization is the Hardwick steward's phrase of choice in the mid-1590s: 'certain of' Lord Ogle's players, Lord Chandos's, Lord Essex's, the Queen's.[18]

The other bookend of the company size spectrum is the unambiguously solo player: 'Mr Parrie one of the King's plaers,' 'To Mr dishley a player,' Adam Gerdler from York 'to act a part in the kt of the burning pestell' at Skipton Castle, and the poignant 10s Doncaster payment to 'j of the kings players' – in June 1642, two months before the 2 September parliamentary order for stage-plays to cease. To analyse the rewards paid these solo players – how much the amounts seem to be determined by quality, quantity, star status, supply-and-demand, or other market factors – awaits another day, except to echo Alan Coman's observation that 'it is strange that the solo performance of one of them, when he played again, received more reward than the whole company did before.'[19] Stranger still, were they knowable, are the circumstances which prescribed their playing alone, as the three paradigms which follow suggest. The first story is that of Thomas Brandon, Henry VIII's 'entertainer.'

The Ubiquitous Brandon

A decade ago, I wrote that Thomas Brandon 'has excited scholarly pursuit through the various REED territories because he is an identifiable individual who is paid certain sums at certain times in certain places: he thus eventually may serve as a prototype to generalize about court and country entertainment patterns.' My own interest had been aroused by Thomas's appearances at Selby Abbey, which took even the abbey founder, Benedict of Auxerre, two tries to find.[20] Tracing Brandon through the published REED volumes at the time, I summarized:

> In the Cambridge REED volumes he appears between 1532 and 1536; is called 'Master Brandon the Kynges Iugguler,' 'Braunden the Kynges Iogular,' and 'Brandon The Kynges Gugeler'; is paid 2s 11d, 6s 4d plus the Cambridge mayor's supper costs of 20d, and 10s 4d including the banquet charges. Presumably Brandon also plied Plymouth, Exeter, Barnstaple, and Dartmouth between 1520 and 1543 – the Devon span of citations to the king's *iocular*, *iugeler*, *iogulator*, *iester* – although Brandon's name occurs only once; his function is pluralized in the 1526 and 1532 Exeter entries to *Iogulatoribus domini Regis* and *the kynges Iugkelers*. He, or they, are paid three to six shillings per entry, presumably per visit. In Worcester Brandon appears by name between 1521 and 1533; he usually receives 3s 4d a performance, is consistently labeled a 'jugler,' and once in 1527 is accompanied by 'his chylde,' who receives 8d 'for tymblyng.' In the forthcoming Shropshire REED volume [published 1994], Brandon sightings are noted five times in Shrewsbury between 1522 and 1538 [twice by name, three times as the king's *ioculator*]. Oddly, the ubiquitous Brandon does not survive in the York records, nor does the Selby term '*joculator*,' although payments are made to jugglers, jesters, and one of 2d to a *iugulatori* of John Nevile in 1448. More

odd is why Brandon should receive 5s one year at Selby and only 16d the next. (173)

An updated table of Brandon sightings from the published REED volumes, the Malone Society *Collections*, and the unpublished West Riding, Derbyshire, and Hampshire collections follows below in Appendix 1. The table is limited to entries that cite Brandon by name, although it could be doubled were references within the time period to 'the king's iogeler,' presumably Brandon, added. On that amplified basis from the published REED and Malone Society volumes, John Southworth extends Brandon's peripatetic career from 1515/16 at Dover to 1542 at Barnstaple.[21] Southworth also wrestles with terminology in trying to determine Brandon's function. Called 'our welbiloued seruᵃnt Thomas Brandon our pleyer' by Henry VIII, Brandon in fact 'was not a member of the royal interlude players, but the King's *joculator*.'[22] Nor was he just a juggler of objects, Southworth argues, but more of a conjurer, and he assumes the 'prestigiator Regis' paid 2s 6d by King's Hall, Cambridge in 1532–3 to be 'Mr Brandon the Kyng*es* Iugguler' paid 10s 4d by the town treasurer the same year.[23] Whether or not Brandon the *jogeler* is Brandon the magician on this particular occasion, he is immortalized as an illusionist through 'Brandon's Pigeon' and as a jester and juggler through his anecdotal run-in with Will Somer.[24]

Clearly Thomas Brandon is a semi-independent itinerant 'star' with multiple entertainment talents. Presumably his base, and his cachet, are the court and the king's patronage, but he seems to have struck an employment balance between home duty and regular travel routes, which fan out in a distant ring road from London to Chichester, Southampton, Worcester, Cambridge, Thetford, and elsewhere, primarily along main highways.[25] Fully half of Brandon's engagements were at religious houses, with the Dissolution most likely dissolving his travels as well. Some of his venues suggest effective networking: Prior William More of Worcester rewarded Brandon at his Crowle and Grimley manors as well as when 'courting' in London; the earl of Rutland seems to have rewarded Brandon both in London and at Belvoir Castle, Lincolnshire; and the visits to Selby Abbey, not a place one stumbles on by accident, may have come about from a monastic manorial liaison.

Even at this unfinished pausing place, Brandon's travels offer up several Johnstonian questions as touring evidence continues to accumulate. First, one has to wonder about the whole nature of fools, or jesters, or *joculatores*, or *jogulers*, in particular their mental capability and performance talents.

Some, Southworth among them, hold most fools to be mature naturals, but exceptions argue otherwise. Their multiple entertainment skills – verbal, physical, conjuring – and their travel circuits suggest at least an economic intelligence. Second, one wonders what having a patron – royal, noble, civic, clerical – means for entertainers' practices. Often, patronage seems to connote what appears on a Fortnum & Mason mustard jar, 'By appointment to her Majesty Queen Elizabeth II' under a seal, in effect the patronage name, livery, and a basic stipend with the expectation that they will cut their own mustard on the road. As REED data mount, civic waits and great household musicians seem to spend almost as much time on the road as they do in residence; the same may be true of court entertainers, in particular trumpeters, drummers, musicians, players, and fools.[26] Finally, one notes the length of Thomas Brandon's travelling career and reflects with admiration on how long he spun out his entertainment value. Lear's fool only made it through three acts; the ubiquitous Brandon juggled and jested and conjured his way through three decades.

The Elusive Disley (Distle, Dishley, Distley)

And so did the elusive Disley, whose star turn has led scholars a merry chase for over a century. At present, the entries to Disley by name (under the variant surname spellings above, and once with Master, but not yet with a Christian name) number twenty-one, from 1601 to 1633, throughout the Midlands and North, from Lancashire to Londesborough, from a low reward of 5s to a high of 30s. John Tucker Murray links Disley to Dudley's players through a 1612 Gawthorpe entry and sees his replacing Richard Bradshaw as Dudley's lead player. Nungezer adds a 1609/10 Gawthorpe entry. Bentley follows Murray but challenges his assumption of Dudley's ongoing patronage, seeing the troupe instead as 'not improbably a local organization, since four of its six appearances are recorded at Gawthorpe Hall, and it is never recorded farther afield than Leicester.' In his REED Lancashire volume, David George finds eleven named Disley appearances starting in 1610. When John Wasson joins the hunt, he is able to add Disley's 1601 performance at Londesborough, the Cliffords' East Riding home, as well as the twist that on 12 March 1617/18 the earl of Shrewsbury was Disley and his company's patron but by 9 September 1619 they were Lord Dudley's players. The table below as Appendix II chronicles this fugitive player's three-decade trail, which nevertheless at this point must conclude with Alan Coman's lament that even though '[b]y 1615/16 a Mr Disley is Dudley's chief player, yet no one has been able to trace him.'[27]

Even if Disley's origins and identity cannot yet be traced, his documented performances to date encourage several significant observations about star turns and small companies. First, over his thirty years of professional playing, Disley seems to have experienced almost all variants of company size and organization. He played alone; he played as the senior sharer or actor-manager of a company with at least two separate noble patrons, one of them twice; he played as the head of his own company; and on two occasions he seems to have played a star turn with other professional troupes. His first decade suggests that the company is his own, although its licensing history is dim until the 1612 Gawthorpe entry links it to 'Lo: dudley his plaeres.' During Christmastide 1608/9, Disley seems to have been a star performer with Lord Monteagle's troupe at Belvoir Castle. On 27 December Monteagle's players are rewarded 30s; on 31 December 'Dishley the player' is given 30s; and on 2 January 1608/9 Dishley the player receives a further 20s. The 'going rate' at great households for much of the late sixteenth and early seventeenth centuries seems to be 10s per play, which would suggest that Monteagle's men played three plays and Dishley put together the equivalent of a five-play gig for the duke of Rutland. In the absence of access to the Belvoir muniments, one can assume only from the dates that both Monteagle's troupe and Disley's were there at the same time.[28]

His second documented appearance as a solo player with someone else's troupe occurs at Dunkenhalgh on 11 June 1625, when he is paid 6s 8d 'the same day' that 20s is 'giuen plaiers being pirrie & his companie.' Why Disley is doing a star turn with William Perry and presumably his Children of the Revels remains a mystery, but their joint engagement reminds us of how much is left to discover about these so-called provincial companies. The elusive Disley is but one paradigm of professional players who made their living on regular circuits of civic and great household engagements, circuits which were simultaneously more calculated and also more flexible than pre-REED scholars allowed. They did not paint themselves into one corner of the country, although they certainly developed preferred routes and venues. Despite Bentley's labelling Disley's troupe 'a local organization,' its documented locale roamed over Lancashire, Cheshire, Warwickshire, Leicestershire, Nottinghamshire, Derbyshire, and Yorkshire, with farther fields probably yet to be discovered as more REED collections appear, particularly the London volumes where an intensively cast net may trap some of these 'provincial' names. Variously characterized as 'actors' companies,' 'provincial players,' 'outlaws,' or 'wandring Rogues,' these players' wayward trails through the records at the very least draw attention to the labyrinthian matter of licensing. Before REED, licensing seemed straightforward: 'the great Act for Restraining Vagabonds of 1572 ... required licensing of all troupes, and confined the power to noblemen only, or to Justices of the Peace ... In 1597, when the Act was renewed with amendments, the Justices lost their power to license, while the nobles, for better security must each put hand and seal to the authorization of players. By now town players had presumably withered away.'[29] Patently unwithered, Disley, Bradshaw, and Perry are a few among the many star players who seem to have adjusted licensing requirements to their own highly flexible practices.

By 12 March 1617/18 Disley and his company were the earl of Shrewsbury's players and eighteen months later they again were Dudley's. That documented shift in patronage attribution allows a glimpse at what may be part of a travelling circuit. Gilbert Talbot, 7th earl of Shrewsbury, died on 8 May 1616, leaving no evidence that either he or his father ever had players.[30] His brother Edward, 8th earl, died without issue on 8 February 1617/18. Since Edward did not inherit players, he well may have assumed patronage of Dudley's troupe, Disley and company, for the earl's brief tenure. If so, then on 6 November 1616 they play at Dunkenhalgh for 6s 8d; the next day they receive the same reward at Gawthorpe. Three weeks later they play Coventry for 5s; ten months later, October 1617, they receive 10s in Nottingham; and two months later they are back in Coventry for 10s. Their departure from Coventry on 20 December perhaps suggests a Christmastide residence with their patron at either Sheffield or, more likely, in London where Edward Talbot dies on 8 February. Three months later on 12 March 1617/18, the Disley troupe is at Londesborough, where the earl of Cumberland gives them a generous 13s 4d not to play, a sum which probably acknowledges the late earl of Shrewsbury's recent death as well as Lenten restraint. When Disley and company returned to Londesborough seventeen months later as Dudley's players, 9 September 1619, Clifford rewards them with 20s for one play, twice the normal amount – but also the last extant record of their actually playing at Londesborough. Their Londesborough welcome in May 1621 yields 11s in gold not to play, and the following 11 February they 'offered to play but were not suffered,' a turn-away that still netted them 10s. Less than three weeks later the troupe was paid 5s not to play in Leicester, while the next year Leicester doubled their dismissal reward to 10s.

Lest the elusive Disley be thought a singular itinerant star, his three-decade playing career is but one that beckons to updated analysis: for this present study, Richard Bradshaw, William Perry, Ellis Guest, or Thomas Swinerton would have provided equally illustrative paradigms of durable professional troupes.[31] Bradshaw first appears under Dudley's imprimature in February 1595/6 but by November 1602 he has been discharged, a record unknown to Murray, who presumes his continuing under Dudley's authority until 1610 and then disappearing until 1630 in Reading. In July 1617, however, Bradshaw and his company are Lord Darby's players, paid 20s 'in reward from my Lord [Clifford] in spit he wold not heare them play' at Skipton Castle. Their seven visits to Dunkenhalgh between 1625 and 1635 simply record them as Bradshaw and his company, but in 1633 they were on trial in Banbury, Oxfordshire 'for allegedly travelling under false letters patent' in Warwickshire and Leicestershire as well.[32]

If Disley and Bradshaw are faintly entrepreneurial in the licensing line, Swinerton and Perry founded a cottage industry by duplicating royal letters patent for spin-off troupes.[33] Ironically, one prototype of their illicit spin-off probably lies in the entirely licit and well-known June 1559 letter from Robert Dudley, 1st earl of Leicester, at Westminster, to Francis Talbot, 5th earl of Shrewsbury, at Sheffield. Dudley asks Talbot that his servants, 'plaiers of interludes, [who] for the same have the Licence of diuerse of my lordis here, vnder ther seales and handis, to plaie in diuerse shires within the realme vnder there aucthorities as maie amplie appear vnto you^r Lordship, by the same licence I haue thought, among the rest, by my Letter to beseche your good Lordshippes conformitie to them Likewise that they maie have you^r hand and seale to ther licence, for the like libertye in yorke shiere.'[34]

This letter is stunning in its implications of original authority with any number of touring sublicences and raises all sorts of questions about extent and duration. Dudley circulated the licence almost like a petition for his London peers to sign, and his players carried it to Shrewsbury, who that June was in Sheffield rather than at his London residence. What toothsome opportunities such a document, junked up with blotched seals and scrawled signatures, must have suggested to the entrepreneurial player ambitious for his own break-away troupe. Likewise, such a licence with its extended authorities may have offered household stewards and town clerks legitimate patronage choices based on near-to-hand geographical or political contexts. Dudley was an upstart twenty-something London courtier, Shrewsbury the august lord president of the Council in the North: Shrewsbury's local sanction may have carried more weight than Dudley's

original London permit. Giv.en how little attention has been paid to licensing practices of these long-lived provincial troupes (and how easily they
have been lumped together as wandering rogues or London impersonators), one might want to be cautious in assuming that the company
patrons named in the records reveal the whole licensing history.

One for the Road

Companies performing together, companies identified by patron, by player
or players, by patron and players, as part of a company, as solo performer,
authentically or enterprisingly licensed – 'all of the above' permutations
occur in one extraordinary cluster of entries from Londesborough, the
Cliffords' East Riding residence. The Clifford family papers, now known
as the Bolton Abbey Manuscripts at Chatsworth, include 273 numbered
pre-1642 Clifford account books, ninety-two of them with entertainment
payments, starting in 1510. Some manuscripts are modest paper-stitched
pamphlets, some 500-page bound volumes. Approximately eighty-five of
them document hundreds of entertainment expenses between 1570 and
1640. With the Hardwick manuscripts, now also at Chatsworth and also
part of the forthcoming West Riding-Derbyshire REED collections, they
constitute the largest continual body of extant information I know of that
documents professional players' visits to provincial great houses.[35]

The cluster of entries, which create a richly informative great house
scenario, comes from two Clifford manuscripts: Bolton Abbey MS 27, a
pantry account book of December 1597 to December 1598; and Bolton
Abbey MS 142, a household account book of Londesborough steward
William Tomlinson from September 1597 through August 1598. Given the
gulf between the manuscript numbers, the story they tell could not be
inferred until the Clifford entries were sorted chronologically. Taken separately, the two account books tell partial and misleading tales; together
they make a semi-coherent narrative which goes like this if one is allowed a
share of inferential whimsy. Beginning on Friday, 24 February and concluding on Thursday, 2 March, the story covers Shrovetide 1597/8. Records
from two of those days – the pantry account for Saturday and the household account for Monday – are reproduced as Appendices 3 and 4; the
relevant entertainment excerpts from the whole week's accounts are transcribed in Appendix 5. What appear to be telesthetic identifications of
otherwise anonymous personnel in fact were laboriously gleaned from
other Clifford manuscripts.[36] Also gleaned was some background on the
abstruse matters of great household management, staff, dining protocols,

and menus requisite to explicate pantry accounts.[37] Household accounts are trustworthy, definitive records of payment. Pantry accounts are selective records of consumption, revealing only who ate certain foods at certain times in certain locations at whose charge.

This particular Londesborough pantry steward kept track of special side dishes ('messes,' 'dishes' of 'butter & egges') for two set meals: the late morning or midday dinner (abbreviated 'd,' 'de,' or 'den') and the early evening supper ('s' or 'sup'). His counting system is not entirely transparent: he seems to distinguish between 'dinners' and 'messes,' which must account for the food but sometimes obscures the number of people eating it. While he usually totals household-in-ordinary 'messes' at the bottom of recto folios, he always identifies the day's 'Straungeres' who take one meal or both ('ds') in either the parlour or hall, as well as the total number of 'messes' they required.[38] Usually he notes to whose authority the messes are accounted – master's, mistress's, steward's hoard ('ho'), 'boardes end,' or the children's nurse. Any exceptions to a pantry steward's individual counting practices flew unnoted below his documented radar, which means that evidence from pantry accounts must be taken *cum grano salis*. That someone was not recorded at dinner or supper suggests but does not prove his absence from the residence. Missing a scheduled formal meal, then as now, can be attributed to illness, attempts to diet, boxed picnics, cold collations, injudicious snacking, food preferences, a good old-fashioned sulk in one's room, or tardiness. When a group of six musicians arrived at Londesborough too late for supper on 6 June 1594, the pantry steward made a singular defensive note in his accounts that they 'had a kidd pie to there supper by my ladies comanedement.'

The present scenario begins on Friday, 24 February 1597/8, with three of the Londesborough household musicians – Richard Laverock's men – in residence as well as John Addeson, who is the Clifford children's dancing master (and a master dancer himself).[39] In time for supper Friday evening John Wilson and two fiddlers arrived from Kirkby Stephen, Westmorland, a rugged winter trek of several days over the Yorkshire dales but a familiar route. Wilson heads a company of between six and nine 'fellowe players' from Kirkby Stephen and Nateby, just south of the Clifford holding at Brough. Although Wilson's troupe turned up nowhere in the REED Westmorland records (nor in any other REED collection to date, including the Cliffords' Skipton Castle accounts), they played at Londesborough in February 1595/6, January 1596/7, December 1597, and on 9–10 February 1597/8, just two weeks before Wilson and his two fiddlers returned for Shrovetide.[40] Wilson himself seems to have held their licence, and he also seems to have had some special talent, like Adam Gerdler, that allowed him to do star turns for the Cliffords as well as lead his small travelling company. By dinnertime Saturday, 25 February, Lord Wharton's men started to trickle in: two on Saturday, six by Sunday, eight by Monday. That they are Wharton's players is likely but not certain. The pantry steward identifies them only as 'my Lord wharton men,' listing 'players' independently, and the corresponding household account records no payment to them. On the other hand, although many of the Wharton household appear throughout the Clifford accounts, only entries to his players record this large number: six of them in February 1594/5, eight in January–February 1598/9, twelve in May 1599, and eight in February 1600/1.

After Saturday's late morning dinner but in sufficient time to set up and perform one play after the early evening supper, twelve of Lord Derby's players arrive. Three players, one of them the company 'player-road manager,' either take supper at Tomlinson's table, the 'steward's board,' or elsewhere in the hall but under the steward's authorization for three messes, side dishes of buttered eggs, in addition to the usual supper fare. At some point, presumably supper, Tomlinson (in his role as 'house manager') and the player-road manager sort out performance requirements: final choice of plays, hall set-up, blocking adjustments, unusual 'business' with actors or properties.[41] By Sunday, 26 February, Londesborough has its full complement of entertainment options, which in a full swell of speculation may top out at twenty-one professional players (twelve of Derby's, eight of Wharton's, and John Wilson), five musicians, and a dancer. Back in the pantry account, Wilson with his two fiddlers and Derby's twelve players eat both dinner and supper. Wharton's men somehow tot up six dinners and two suppers. The Clifford household hears two plays from Derby's players, either one after dinner and one after supper or one before and the other after supper.[42] Addeson, the dancer, stays on.

On Monday, 27 February, the day before Shrove Tuesday, the scene shifts. Although Addeson, Wilson with his two fiddlers, and eight of Wharton's men are there for both dinner and supper, one, several, or all of Derby's players are paid 20s for three plays and leave Londesborough after dinner, presumably late morning. Additionally, in what may be a unique great household entry, they receive 3s 8d for three nights' horseboard. At some point on Monday, in a quintessence of hapless timing, another company of players shows up at Londesborough and claims to be Derby's men. For their pains, the imposters are given 3s 4d but are not allowed to play. On Shrove Tuesday, certainly the presumed apex of the festivities, what Londesborough entertainment there was must have been provided by John Wilson; his two fiddlers; the Clifford musicians if they were still in residence; Wharton's men (if they were players); John Addeson; and, possibly, by part of Derby's men, whose gustatory presence is not documented in the pantry account. By Ash Wednesday, however, at least nine and perhaps eleven of Derby's players are back for dinner, although they are not documented for supper. On Thursday, eight of them eat dinner and the company, 'players being me Lord of Darbies men,' is given 10s prior to its departure. On Friday, 3 March, Londesborough is blessedly black.

Knowing that the season is Shrovetide helps to tease out this opulently bizarre entertainment scenario, although loose threads still dangle. One speculative explication, however, at least makes partial sense of the Shrovetide calendar, the company's fluctuations in size, and the singular 3s 8d payment 'to thomas tomes for ther horssmeayte 3 nyghtes and laiding.' At great houses players normally were paid only when they left, since their reward to some degree reflected the lord's (or lady's) pleasure with the performance. Based on that norm of payment at departure, Derby's men leave Londesborough on Monday with 20s for three plays, return on Wednesday, and leave again on Thursday with another 10s, a schedule which does not easily accommodate Shrovetide.[43] Since Derby's players do not arrive at Londesborough until Saturday, the three-nights' horseboard must have covered Monday, Tuesday, and Wednesday nights when the horse is not stabled at Londesborough. What scans is that one or several of Derby's men go off on Monday to do a Shrove Tuesday star turn elsewhere – an elsewhere which requires a day's travel each way and overnight lodgings. Thomas Tomes, whether a stabler or a player, receives the going rate for horsemeat of one shilling a day, which factors into one horse to carry the players' baggage.[44] Their engagement would seem to be in a town where the players would have to pay for stabling, rather than at a great house where they and their horses would be accommodated, but a search of the published and unpublished town records a day's journey from Londesborough has not yet documented a breakaway from the Derby peloton.

Not illogically, the Derby impersonators fetch up after dinner on Monday hoping to play for the Cliffords on Shrove Tuesday, timing which suggests that they had good intelligence on Derby's Londesborough booking but bad intelligence on the gig's elaborate schedule and the real company's Saturday arrival. The remaining Derby's men, now a small, or at least smaller, company, stay on at Londesborough to play after dinner on Shrove Tuesday, with John Wilson and the fiddlers. Wilson is paid 6s 8d and, with his two musicians, leaves after the performance, perhaps for a nearby second engagement Shrove Tuesday evening. Derby's players, waiting out Ash Wednesday for their colleagues (and the horse) to return, finally leave Londesborough on Thursday, 2 March with another ten shillings, which is either a parting gratuity, payment for a fourth play on Shrove Tuesday, or a correction to Monday's apparent underpayment of 20s for three plays. The payment is cryptic, and it is hardly the only riddle in this speculative construction. The records are silent on who my Lord of Derby's players are, who tried to impersonate them, where they came from before Londesborough, where they went after Londesborough, or what they played when at Londesborough. As Wasson concludes, in some frustration, 'These entries of 1598 confuse the entire issue. As frequently happens, the more we learn, the less we are sure of.'[45]

One factor which these particular entries may articulate, however, flows yet again from Alexandra F. Johnston's blessed inability to leave well enough alone. Based on no prior evidence of which I am aware, her sole response to my conference preview for this top-secret festschrift was that she always had assumed that travelling companies used great houses as home bases. Although by no means certain, that notion of a great house home base would explain why Lord Wharton's men took their meals at Londesborough but were not paid for playing. What is certain, however, is that the Cliffords booked Derby's men for the Shrovetide festivities at Londesborough and they went out of their way to accommodate the players (and their horse). Clearly several groups or types of entertainers – the household musicians, a professional dancer, the lead player from Kirkby Stephen, two Kirkby Stephen musicians, some or all of Derby's dozen players, some or all of Wharton's eight players – in some fashion combined, divided, played together, played separately, came, and went during the week. Clearly the Lords Clifford would not have gone to that sort of trouble and expense for Muriel Bradbrook's 'crowd of pitiable vagabonds who roamed the countryside, their packs filled by a few tattered gaudy garments and a half-dozen thumbed old interludes' nor for what Alan Somerset delightfully terms the 'gaggle of incompetents' in *Histriomastix*.[46] Clearly, Derby's men at Londesborough have richly earned the *Histriomastix* welcome to true players – 'my Lords pleasure, all comers bee bounteously entertaind.' And, clearly, we need to be very cautious in how we count small companies and star turns.

APPENDIX 1: Thomas Brandon, the King's Joguler

Date	Place	Entry	Reward	Notes
1517–18	Chichester, Sussex: St George's Guild accounts	Magistro brandon logeler	2s	
1520–1	Shrewsbury, Shropshire: bailiffs' accounts	Magistro Brandon Joculatori domini Regis	11d [misprint for xl d?]	plus 2d per person from town citizens and 16d on wine
11.10–16. 1521	Worcester: account book Prior William More	kynges joguler Thomas brandon	3s 4d	
2.1–7. 1522/3	Worcester: More account book	Thomas brandon the kynges lugeler	3s 4d	
4.17–23. 1524	Worcester: More account book 'courting' – at court	Thomas the kyngres loguler	3s 4d/ 12d 12d	add-on sums not explained
6.4–10. 1525	Worcester: More account book	thomas brandon the kynges loogler & seruant	3s 8d	
8.19–25. 1526	Worcester: More account book	thomas brandon the kynges loguler	3s 4d	
1526–7	Southampton, Hants: Book of Fines	bramden the kinges gege logeler	5s 4d	
10.6–12. 1527	Grimley, Worcs.: More account book	thomas brandan the kynges logeller to his chylde for tumblyng	3s 4d 8d	
10.4–10. 1528	Worcester: More account book	thomas brandon the kynges logeller	3s 4d	
7.11–17. 1529	Grimley, Worcs: More account book	thomas brandon the Kynçes logeller	3s 4d	
1529–30	Southampton, Hants: Book of Fines	Bramdon the kinges logeler	5s	
1529–30	Thetford, Norfolk: priory register	M Brandon le loguler Domini Reges cum seruo	3s 9d	
11.6–12. 1530	Grimley, Worcs: More account book	thomas brandan the kynges loguller	3s 4d	
1530/1	Thetford, Norfolk: priory register	M Brandon the Kynges locu er	2s	

APPENDIX 1: (concluded)

Date	Place	Entry	Reward	Notes
1530/1	Ipswich, Suffolk: chamberlains' accounts	Mr brandon the Kynges lugler	6s 8d	
1530/1	Belvoir, Lincs, or London	Brandon, jogelar	5s	
1530/1	Belvoir	Brandon, jogeler	3s 8d	
1530–2	Southampton, Hants: Book of Fines	brandon the kynges logler	5s	
9.10–16. 1531	Grimley, Worcs: More account book	thomas brandon the kynges loguler	3s 4d	
1531–2	West Riding, Yorks: Selby Abbey accounts	Magistro Brandon loculatori domini Regis	5s	'hoc anno'
9.15–21. 1532	Crowle, Worcs: More account book	thomas brandon the kynges loguler	3s 4d	
1532–3	Cambridge: town treasurers' books	Mr Brandon the Kynges lugguler	10s 4d	reward & banquet charges in the total
1533	West Riding, Yorks: Selby Abbey accounts	vno locular Magester Brandan	16d	
1533–4	Exeter, Devon: receivers' account rolls	Brendon the kynges luggeler	5s	
1533–4	Southampton, Hants: stewards' accounts	mr brandan king lugler	3s 4d	
5.31–6.6. 1534	Worcester: More account book	thomas brandon the kynges logular	3s 4d	
1534–5	Southampton, Hants: Book of Fines	master Brandon the kynges luggeler	6s 8d	
1534–5	Cambridge: King's Hall accounts	braunden the Kynges logular	2s 11d	
1534–5	Shrewsbury, Shropshire: bailiffs' accounts	Magistro Brandon loculatori Domini Regis	7s 10d	plus 3s 8d bailiffs spent on wine
1535–6	Cambridge: town treasurers' books	Brandon The Kynges Gugeler	6s 8d	
1536–7	Thetford, Norfolk: priory register	M Brandon the Kynges ioguler	3s 4d	

APPENDIX 2: Disley the player and his company*

Date	Place	Players	Reward	Notes
10.3–5.1599	Leicester	Earl of Dudley's players with Earl of Darcy's	10s total	
4.21.1601	**Londesborough**	**deshley & co.**	**13s 3d**	
1601–2	Leicester	Lord Dudley's players	10s	
12.24–5.1604	Leicester	Dudley's players	10s	
6.19.1608	Doncaster	Dudley's players	10s	
12.31.1608	**Belvoir**	**Dishley the player**	**30s**	
1.2.1608/9	Belvoir	Dishley the player	20s	Monteagle's players paid 30s on 12.27.1608
3.13.1609/10	**Gawthorpe**	**Distle & co**	**20s**	**[Lent]**
1.12.1610/11	Londesborough	Lord Dudley's players	40s	
10.7.1612	**Gawthorpe**	**distley & his co. my Lo: dudley his plaeres**	**30s**	
3.4.1612/13	Gawthorpe	Distle & his co.	6s 8d	[Lent]
1613–14	Congleton, Cheshire	Lord Dudley's players	2s 6d	
12.16.1614	Leicester	Lorde Dudlies playors	10s	
Michaelmas 1615/16	Congleton, Cheshire	the Lord Duddleys players	3s 4d	see Coman, REED Newsletter 14: 1
11.6.1616	Dunkenhalgh	Shrewsbury's men	6s 8d	
11.7.1616	**Gawthorpe**	**distle & his co.**	**6s 8d**	
11.27.1616	Coventry	Earl of Shrewsbury's players	5s	
October 1617	Nottingham	the Earle of Shrewsburies plaieres	10s	

APPENDIX 2: (continued)

Date	Place	Players	Reward	Notes
12.20.1617	Coventry	Earl of Shrewsbury's players	10s	
3.12.1617/18	**Londesborough**	**Lo: shrewsbury's players: disley & his co.**	**13s 4d**	**not to play [Lent]**
9.9.1619	Londesborough	Lo: dudley's players: disley & his co.	20s	for one play
11.7.1620	Dunkenhalgh	my Lord Dudleyes men	13s 4d	
1620–1	Leicester	Lord Dudleyes Players	10s	
5.4.1621	**Londesborough**	**dishley & his co.**	**11s in gold**	**not to play**
7.25.1621	**Dunkenhalgh**	**disley & his Companye**	**5s**	
2.11.1621/2	Londesborough	Lo: dudleyes players	10s	'offered to play but were not suffered'
3.2.1621/22	Leicester	a Company of Players beinge the Lord Dudleys Servants	5s	not playing
1623	Leicester	lord dudleyes players	10s	'for the like': i.e., 'that played not'
3.2.1624/5	**Dunkenhalgh**	**disley the player & his co.**	**8s 4d**	**[paid on Ash Wednesday]**
6.11.1625	**Dunkenhalgh**	**disley the plaier**	**6s 8d**	**[apparently with Perry & company]**
3.21.1625/6	**Dunkenhalgh**	**disley the Plaier**	**5s**	**[Lent]**
February 1627/8	**Dunkenhalgh**	**Disley the plaier**	**3s 4d**	**[Shrove Tuesday 2.25.1627/8]**
1627/8	Leicester	Lord Dudley his players	5s	
1628/29	**Leicester**	**Dishley and his ffellowes**	**5s**	

APPENDIX 2: (concluded)

Date	Place	Players	Reward	Notes
12.10.1629	Dunkenhalgh	disley & his co.	6s 8d	
2.19.1629/30	Doncaster	dishley & co.	10s	[Lent]
March or April 1629/30	Dunkenhalgh	Disley the player	10s	for one play [Lent: 10 February–11 April. 1629/30]
9.12.1632	Doncaster	dishley & co.	5s	'not play in the towne'
1633	York	Mr Dishley, a player	15s	

* The twenty-one records which name Disley appear in boldface; eighteen entries to Dudley's or Shrewsbury's players which may or may not be Disley and his company provide equal opportunity speculation on travel patterns.

30   Barbara D. Palmer

Appendix 3: Clifford Pantry Account. Saturday, 25 February 1597/8. Devonshire MSS, Chatsworth: Bolton Abbey MS 27, f. 78. Reproduced by permission of the Duke of Devonshire. Photograph by Ian Fraser-Martin.

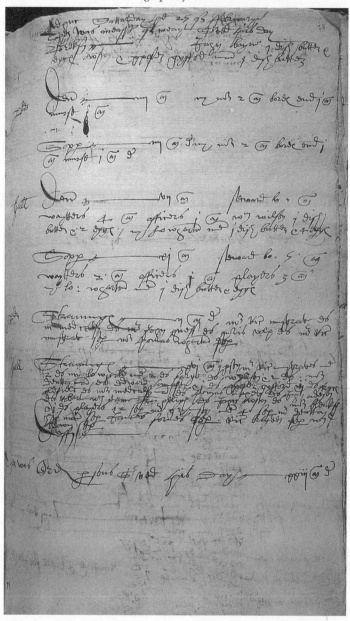

Appendix 4: Clifford Household Account. Monday, 27 February 1597/8. Devonshire MSS, Chatsworth: Bolton Abbey MS 142, f. 13. Reproduced by permission of the Duke of Devonshire. Photograph by Ian Fraser-Martin.

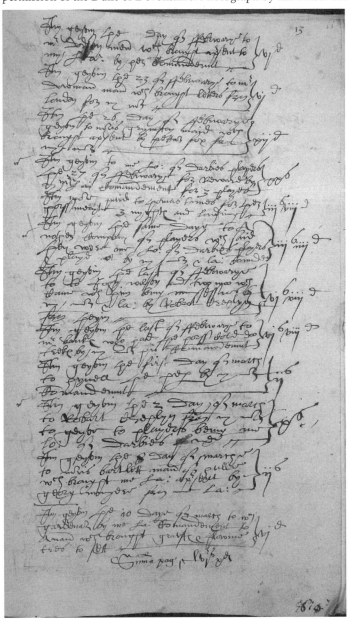

Appendix 5: Shrovetide Entertainers
Londesborough 1597/8

1. Friday, 24 February 1597/8. Bolton Abbey MS 27, f. 77
ffryday the 24 of ffebrwary ...
hall [left margin] Sopper j mess Laverockes men 3 j dish j mess
hall [left margin] Straungeres... willson & 2 fyddlers de? sopper... Iohn
Addeson denner

2. Saturday, 25 February 1597/8. Bolton Abbey MS 27, f. 78
Satarday the 25 of ffebrwarye ... hall [in margin]
denner mr wilson j dish butter & 2 egges my lo: whartones men j dish
butter & 4 egges
Sopper xj messes Steward board 9 messes waytters 2. messes officers j mess
players 3 messes my lo: whartones men j dish butter & egges
hall [in margin] Straungeres ... my lo wharton men 2 ds ... wyllson & 2 ds ...
Iohn adeson ds ... players 12 soppers

3. Sunday, 26 February 1597/8. Bolton Abbey MS 27, f. 79
Sondaye the 26 of ffebuwary ... my Lo wharton men denner mess
hall [in margin] denner ... my Lo wharton men denner mess
hall [in margin] Straungeres ... mr wilson sopper my lo: wharton men 6
denner & 2 sopper ... players 12 ds[?: s a blot] ... wilson & 2 ds ... Iohn
Addeson ds

4. Monday, 27 February 1597/8. Bolton Abbey MS 27, f. 80
mundaye the 27 of ffebrwarye ... my Lo wharton men denner messe
hall [in margin] Straungeres ... my lo wharton men 8 denner [?sop: blot] ...
players 12 denner ... Iohn wilson & 2 ds ... Iohn Addeson ds

5. Monday, 27 February 1597/8. Bolton Abbey MS 142, f. 13
Item geyvin to me Lo: of Darbies players the 27 of ffebrwary for Reward
by my m^r & La: Commandement for 3 playes xx^s

6. Monday, 27 February 1597/8. Bolton Abbey MS 142, f. 13
Item more paid to thomas tomes for ther horssmeayte 3 nyghtes and
laiding iij^s viij^d

7. Monday, 27 February 1597/8. Bolton Abbey MS 142, f. 13
Item geyvin the same daye to A nother Company of players which said

they were me Lo: of darbies players and playd not by my mr & la: Comandement iij^s iiij^d

8. Tuesday, 28 February 1597/8. Bolton Abbey MS 27, f. 81
Tuysday the last daye of ffebrwary ... Iohn wilson & 2 j messe
hall [in margin] Straungeres ... my lo wharton men 7 ds denner & sopper
Iohn Wilson & 2 denner Iohn Addeson denner

9. Tuesday, 28 February 1597/8. Bolton Abbey MS 142, f. 13
Item geyvin the last of ffebrwarye to to [sic] Iohn wilson and too moo
which Came with him being mussessions by my mr & la: by Robart
Creplyn for theym vj^s viij^d

10. Wednesday, 1 March 1597/8. Bolton Abbey MS 27, f. 82
wedenesdaye the first day of march ... hall [margin]
Denner vij messes denner Steward board: 3 messes
players 2 messes waytters j messe j dish butter officers j messe boyes denner
messe ...
hall [margin] Straungeres viij messes j person ... my lo wharton men 7
denner S
... players 9 denner

11. Thursday, 2 March 1597/8. Bolton Abbey MS 27, f. 83
hall [margin] Straungeres ... players 8 denner

12. Thursday, 2 March 1597/8. Bolton Abbey MS 142, f. 13
Item geyvin the 2 day of march to Robart Creplyn from my mr to geyve to
players being me Lo: of Darbies men x^s

NOTES

1 John Wasson, 'Professional Actors in the Middle Ages and Early Renaissance,' *Medieval & Renaissance Drama in England* 1 (New York: AMS Press, 1984): 1.

2 Alexandra F. Johnston and Margaret Rogerson, eds, *York*, REED (Toronto: University of Toronto Press, 1979), 1:55–6.

3 [Alexandra F. Johnston,] History of the PLS, *Poculi Ludique Societas*, January 2004, University of Toronto, 27 June 2004, http://www.chass.utoronto .ca/~plspls/hist.html. Independently, both Johnston and Rogerson were looking for evidence to refute Alan Nelson's computer analysis argument that

the York Cycle could not have been performed on separate wagons in procession. They clearly were successful, but as Johnston notes, 'We were only two of a number of scholars who were working in archives all over Britain discovering new evidence of performance practice. From this group of scholars came [REED].' Her conscience's struggle over whether to share the 1433 Mercers' Indenture with Rogerson was delightfully self-confessed in '"This endenture made in þe feste of Corpus Christi": How REED Came to Be,' International Medieval Congress, Leeds, 8 July 2002.

4 The session, sponsored by the Medieval and Renaissance Drama Society, was presented at the International Congress on Medieval Studies, Kalamazoo, 3 May 2002. For the Towneley *compilatio* argument, see Barbara D. Palmer, '"Towneley Plays" or "Wakefield Cycle" Revisited,' *Comparative Drama* 21 (1987–8): 318–48; repr. in *Drama in the Middle Ages*, ed. Clifford Davidson and John H. Stroupe (New York: AMS Press, 1991), 290–320; 'Corpus Christi "Cycles" in Yorkshire: The Surviving Records,' *Comparative Drama* 27 (1993): 218–31; and the revised product catalyzed by Johnston's curiosity about the Towneleys, 'Recycling "The Wakefield Cycle": The Records,' *Research Opportunities in Renaissance Drama* 41 (2002): 88–130; David Mills, '"The Towneley Plays" or "The Towneley Cycle,"' *Leeds Studies in English* ns 17 (1986): 95–104; and Garrett P.J. Epp, 'The Towneley Plays and the Hazards of Cycling,' *Research Opportunities in Renaissance Drama* 32 (1993): 121–50.

5 Alexandra F. Johnston, 'Parish Playmaking before the Reformation,' in *The Late Medieval Parish*, Harlaxton Medieval Studies 14, ed. Clive Burgess and Eamon Duffy, forthcoming, kindly shared in draft.

6 Johnston, 'The Feast of Corpus Christi in the West Country,' *Early Theatre* 6.1 (2003): 15. Based on his Norfolk, Suffolk, and Devon research John Wasson ventured the same argument that 'perhaps [Corpus Christi plays] were simply plays on various religious subjects presented at Corpus Christi or Whitsun' at the First REED Colloquium in 'Records of Early English Drama: Where They Are and What They Tell Us' (JoAnna Dutka, ed., *REED: Proceedings of the First Colloquium* [Toronto: University of Toronto Press, 1979]), 139.

7 Johnston, '"The Lady of the farme": The Context of Lady Russell's Entertainment of Elizabeth at Bisham, 1592,' *Early Theatre* 5.2 (2002): 71–85.

8 Johnston, '"His langage is lorne": The Silent Centre of the York Cycle,' *Early Theatre* 3 (2000): 185–95.

9 Earlier, briefer versions of this study were prepared for 'Itinerant Playing in the Sixteenth Century,' a session sponsored by the Medieval and Renaissance Drama Society at the International Congress on Medieval Studies, Kalama-

zoo, May 2004; and for Blackfriars Playhouse: The Second Conference, Staunton, Virginia, 22 October 2003.

10 Wasson, 'Professional Actors,' 4.

11 Suzanne R. Westfall, *Patrons and Performance: Early Tudor Household Revels* (Oxford: Oxford University Press, 1990), 125. See also her Appendix A, 'Size of Itinerant Player Troupes,' 210–12.

12 Barbara D. Palmer, 'Early English Northern Entertainment: Patterns and Peculiarities,' *Research Opportunities in Renaissance Drama* 34 (1995): 171. If Wickham was overly cheerful in translating all entertainment terminology as 'players,' surely Wasson was overly morose in writing that 'no definitive study of professional actors in the Middle Ages will ever be possible[:] ... their movements, their patronage, often their very existence are hopelessly obscured by confusion in the Latin terminology' ('Professional Actors,' 1).

13 G.E. Bentley, *The Profession of Player in Shakespeare's Time, 1590–1642* (Princeton: Princeton University Press, 1984), 240. Bentley, following Murray and Chambers, draws the majority of his evidence from printed antiquarian excerpts, which lead him to conclude, 'Unfortunately I have no evidence at all about [touring properties and logistics] except for a few stray references to horses, wagons, and hampers.'

14 Occasionally antiquarians published excerpts from great household records in their local history studies, which in turn made selected entries accessible to Murray, Chambers, and Bentley. Thomas Dunham Whitaker's *Craven* (London: Nichols & Son, 1805) for the Cliffords, earls of Cumberland; and Joseph Hunter's *Hallamshire*, rev. ed. Alfred Gatty (Sheffield: Pawson & Brailsford, 1869) for the Talbots, earls of Shrewsbury, were two of the more popular lodes.

15 Among other fictions, the myth of provincial inns as playing places is discussed at length in my 'Early Modern Mobility: Players, Payments, and Patrons,' *Shakespeare Quarterly* 56. 3 (2005): 259–305. The New Folger Library Shakespeare editors Barbara A. Mowat and Paul Werstine make the same distinction when they write in the series' standardized introduction that '[w]hile surviving records show only a handful of occasions when actors played at inns while on tour, London inns were important playing-places up until the 1590s.' They further note that '[t]he actors of Shakespeare's time are known to have performed plays in a great variety of locations' – royal residences, universities, Inns of Court, private houses, churches, guildhalls. See, for example, *Cymbeline* (New York: Washington Square, 2003), xxxix.

16 Roslyn L. Knutson, *Playing Companies and Commerce in Shakespeare's Time* (Cambridge: Cambridge University Press, 2001), 38–40.

17 Stanley Wells, 'Boys Should Be Girls,' Blackfriars Playhouse: The Second Conference, Staunton, Virginia, 22 October 2003.

18 The York payments are published in Johnston and Rogerson, *York*; the Cheshire and Leicestershire entries are forthcoming in their respective REED collections. I am indebted to Sally-Beth MacLean for allowing me to consult the late Alice Hamilton's extensive work on the Leicestershire collection on deposit at the REED Office in Toronto. Manuscript descriptions, folio numbers, and bibliographic annotation for the West Riding-Derbyshire records cited throughout 'Star Turns or Small Companies?' will be available when the complete collections, co-edited by Barbara D. Palmer and John M. Wasson, have been checked and prepared for REED publication.

19 Alan C. Coman, 'The Congleton Accounts: Further Evidence of Elizabethan and Jacobean Drama in Cheshire,' *REED Newsletter* 14.1 (1989): 5.

20 With the kind permission of editor Peter H. Greenfield, I am cribbing generously from my initial treatment of Brandon in 'Early English Northern Entertainment,' *Research Opposition in Renaissance Drama* 34 (1995): 167–82. Legend tells that in a vision St Germain instructed Benedict to develop a monastic community but 'Benedict misunderstood the visionary Latin place-name to fetch up in the familiar Salisbury instead of the unfamiliar marsh-lands of Selby which St. Germain had intended. He tarried in Salisbury until St. Germain reappeared in a corrective vision which guided Benedict, with the relic of St. Germain's dried finger which he had stolen from Auxerre, to relocate himself in the West Riding' (169).

21 John Southworth, '"Jugler" and Jester,"' *Fools and Jesters at the English Court* (Phoenix Mill, Gloucestershire: Sutton, 1998), 94–9. Likewise, Philip Butterworth, in *Magic on the Early English Stage* (Cambridge: Cambridge University Press, 2005), 8–14, 192, 193, also traces Brandon references as he makes a persusasive argument for medieval 'jugglers' and 'joculators' in fact being 'conjurors.'

22 Anna Jean Mill, ed., 'Dramatic Records of the City of London,' Malone Society *Collections II, Pt. III* (1931), 286–7; the bracketed headnote on Brandon was added by E.K. Chambers.

23 Southworth, '"Jugler" and Jester,' 95, citing Alan H. Nelson, ed., *Cambridge*, REED (Toronto: University of Toronto Press, 1989), 1: 105–11.

24 Southworth, '"Jugler" and Jester,' 96–7, quotes the marvellous illusion of 'Brandons Pigeon' from Reginald Scot's 1584 *Discoverie of Witchcraft*, and Robert Armin's 1600 *Foole upon Foole* anecdote of Will Somer's engineering Thomas's dismissal from Henry's court.

25 Peter H. Greenfield generously provided the five 'named' Brandon entries from his unpublished Hampshire REED collection; he notes that 'there also are [Southampton] payments to the king's juggler, but not identified specifi-

cally as Brandon, in 1518–19, 1521–2, 1523–4, and 1524–5 (on 16 May)'; while in June 1522 and August 1523 'the Kyngse Ioglar' is at the Middleton household in Nottinghamshire. James Stokes also kindly searched his unpublished REED Lincolnshire collection for Brandon but found nothing more than the two payments recorded in H. Maxwell Lyte and W.H. Stevenson, eds, 'Extracts from Household Accounts,' *HMC Report on the Manuscripts of the Duke of Rutland Preserved at Belvoir Castle* (1905), 4: 270. Access to the Belvoir muniments has been denied to scholars since the end of the nineteenth century.

26 Will Somer, Henry VIII's, Edward VI's, and Mary's fool, would seem to be an innocent or natural fool bound to the monarch's side – except for the mystery of his portrait carved within the Haddon Hall dining room window recess, as are the figures of Henry VII and Elizabeth of York. Begun ca. 1500 by Sir Henry Vernon, treasurer to Prince Arthur and husband of Lady Anne Talbot, daughter of the 2nd earl of Shrewsbury, the dining room was finished ca. 1545 by Sir George Vernon. Why Will Somer made a readily recognizable Tudor third portrait may lie in the Vernon papers, now with the inaccessible Belvoir Castle muniments. Somer, like Brandon, may have been known to the Vernons and Manners through their regular trips to London, but he also, like Brandon, may have found his way into the wilds of Derbyshire to Belvoir and Haddon Hall. On Somer's long career as a court fool, see Southworth, 'William Somer,' in *Fools and Jesters*, 70–80; and Suzanne Westfall, 'The Boy Who Would Be King: Court Revels of King Edward VI, 1547–1553,' *Comparative Drama* 35 (2002): 278.

27 John Tucker Murray, *English Dramatic Companies 1558–1642* (1910; New York: Russell & Russell, 1963), 2:42–4; Edwin Nungezer, *A Dictionary of Actors* (New Haven: Yale University Press, 1929), 116; G.E. Bentley, *The Jacobean and Caroline Stage* (Oxford: Clarendon Press, 1941), 2:423; David George, *Lancashire*, REED (Toronto: University of Toronto Press, 1991); John Wasson, 'Elizabethan and Jacobean Touring Companies,' *Theatre Notebook* 42 (1988), 51–2; Coman, 'Congleton accounts,' 7.

28 Lyte and Stevenson, *HMC Report on the Manuscripts of the Duke of Rutland Preserved at Belvoir Castle*, 4:464. Whether Belvoir pantry accounts survive, which presumably would reveal who was in residence when, awaits access to the muniments.

29 M.C. Bradbrook, *The Rise of the Common Player* (London: Chatto & Windus, 1962), 37. Peter Roberts takes Bradbrook to task for confusing the legislation, whose complicated and extenuated provisions he details, but he also stubbornly holds to the notion of strolling players, with no fewer than nine footnotes to E.K. Chambers' *The Elizabethan Stage*. Peter Roberts, 'Elizabethan Players and Minstrels and the Legislation of 1572 against Re-

tainers and Vagabonds,' in *Religion, Culture and Society in Early Modern Britain: Essays in Honour of Patrick Collinson*, ed. Anthony Fletcher and Peter Roberts (Cambridge: Cambridge University Press, 1994), 29–55.

30 Palmer and Wasson have completed the REED fieldwork for both the Shrewsbury and Cavendish collections, which are intertwined through the Talbot-Cavendish marriages; although Gilbert had a bearward and musicians, no reference to his players (or to his father's) yet has surfaced.

31 An efficient initial resource to trace players' names is David J. Kathman, *Biographical Index of English Drama Before 1660*, http://shakespeareauthor ship.com/bd, which he regularly updates as new REED volumes and other studies appear. His article 'Grocers, Goldsmiths, and Drapers: Freemen and Apprentices in the Elizabethan Theater' (*Shakespeare Quarterly* 55.1 [2004]: 1–49) had the salutary effect of convincing me that William Perry was a subject for someone else's separate study.

32 Mark C. Pilkinton, ed., *Bristol*, REED (Toronto: University of Toronto Press, 1997), 297–8, in reference to PRO: SP 16/238/32, which 'documents the trial of the members of Richard Bradshaw's "outlaw" troupe in 1633.'

33 Perry is an admirable piece of work whose inventive approach to licensed playing can be inferred from the following REED volumes: David Galloway, *Norwich 1540–1642* (1984), 143, 151–2, 210–11, 214, 223; Mark C. Pilkinton, *Bristol*, 239; R.W. Ingram, *Coventry* (1981), 394; John M. Wasson, *Devon* (1986), 192–3; Johnston and Rogerson, *York* (1979), 1: 580, 593; David George, *Lancashire* (1991), 193–4, 196, 200, 203, 359; and James M. Gibson, *Kent: Diocese of Canterbury* (2002), 1:294, which stretches Perry's putatively authorized stride into the Fortune.

34 Lambeth Palace Library, Talbot MS 3196, Letter 29.

35 The kindness of the late Duke and the Dowager Duchess of Devonshire, the Trustees of Chatsworth Settlement, and the former Keeper of the Collections Peter Day, whose long-suffering patience with this West Riding-Derbyshire REED project and its co-editors has been tested since 1984, cannot be adequately acknowledged. Thanks also belong to Charles Noble, Keeper of the Devonshire Collection; Andrew Peppitt, archivist; Diane Naylor, former administrative associate; and Hannah Obee, Assistant Keeper of the Collection.

36 One of a REED editor's recurrent nightmares is discovering the name of an entertainer late in the field collection day and then having to retrace the entire muniment trail for overlooked entries to that name: here, the Cliffords' Richard Laverock and John Addison are daunting examples, but they pale when compared to the March 2004 revelation that in 1609 a 'Richard Smith' was one of the earl of Shrewsbury's musicians.

37 The most reliable introductory study still is Felicity Heal, *Hospitality in*

Early Modern England (Oxford: Clarendon Press, 1990). A useful website is *Life in Elizabethan England: A Compendium of Common Knowledge 1558–1603*, ed. Maggie Secara, vers. 7.0, summer 2001, http://ren.dm.net/compendium/home.html. Of help here were Secara's files entitled 'Staffing a Great Household' and 'Dinner at Cowdray House, 1595.' See also Madge Lorwin, *Dining with William Shakespeare* (New York: Atheneum, 1976) for contemporary accounts of English hospitality; an indispensable bibliography of period cookbooks, books of household management, books of manners, travellers' accounts, dietaries, herbals, farming manuals, and legal regulations; and three pages of 'buttered egg' recipes (pp. 251–3). Lorwin notes that Robert May's *The Accomplisht Cook, or the Art and Mystery of Cookery* 'gives more than seventy-five ways of "Dressing Eggs,"' 252.

38 The definition of a 'mess' seems to vary from kitchen to kitchen and can mean a serving of food, a course of dishes, a prepared dish of a specified kind of food, or the quantity of food required to make one dish, as in this pantry steward's 'butter and eggs' or my country grandmother's request 'to go pick a mess of greens for dinner.' Normally a 'mess' served four people, although it also could serve two or three (Felicity Heal, conversation with the author, 11 July 2005).

39 This pantry steward classifies both the household musicians (Laverock and his three men) and also the dancing master (John Addeson) as 'extraordinary' to the Clifford household, thus documenting their presence under 'Strangers.'

40 Peter Greenfield found one reference to the waits of Kirkby Stephen, 5 Nov.–2 Dec. 1614 at Carlisle (Audrey Douglas and Greenfield, eds, *Cumberland/Westmorland/Gloucestershire*, REED [Toronto: University of Toronto Press, 1986], 80), but none to the town's players.

41 Bentley is adamant that 'the administrative affairs of a London company had to be concentrated in the hands of one or two men' because of the 'number, complexity, and interdependence of [business affairs]' but ironically fails to deduce that 'an actor-manager' is even more indispensable for a company on tour, which encounters different performance conditions with each venue, to say nothing of the daily logistics of travel and accommodation. Bentley, *The Profession of Player*, 238.

42 On 5 June 1611 fourteen of Derby's men performed one play after dinner and another after supper. On 8 December 1612 eleven of Lord Monteagle's players performed one play before and the second after supper, which may be approximately the same schedule.

43 See Bentley, *Jacobean and Caroline Stage*, vol. 7, 'Appendix A: Lenten Performances in the Jacobean and Caroline Theatres,' 1–9. As he notes, 'the

restrictions seem to have varied from time to time ... [I]n 1597 [the Admiral's Men] played a good part of the season before Easter ... and in 1592 Lord Strange's men scarcely observed Lent at all ...' (1). That in March 1608/9 the Cliffords turn away Lord Vawse's players because it was Lent and 'therefore not fitting' suggests but does not prove that ten years earlier they would not permit Derby's men to play on Ash Wednesday. The elusive Disley played at Lancashire great houses during Lent, and the Blundell Family Hodgepodge Book records 'A Prologue to a Swoord dance spoaken at Latham Vpon Ash wednesday 1638,' which makes clear that the sword dance is part of 'this carnauall' performed 'this night' (George, *Lancashire*, 184).

44 The shilling-per-horse-per-day rate for the 1590s is abstracted from the Clifford and Cavendish travel accounts, a sum with which William Ingram, 'The Costs of Touring,' *Medieval and Renaissance Drama in England* 6 (1993), agrees: 'in the 1590s a normative charge for a night at a country inn would have been about four pence for hay and litter, and eight pence to a shilling for a bushel of oats' (57). Johnston's generous search of her REED Buckinghamshire collection-in-progress concludes from the Temples of Stowe travel accounts that 'the going rate for horsemeat per horse was 12d in the provinces. By 1607 it was still 12d in the provinces but 13d in the near suburbs of London' (Alexandra F. Johnston, e-mail to the author, 18 Aug. 2003).

45 Wasson, 'Touring Companies,' 54.

46 Bradbrook, *Rise of the Common Player*, 42; and Alan Somerset, '"How chances it they travel?" Provincial Touring, Playing Places, and the King's Men,' *Shakespeare Survey* 47 (Cambridge: Cambridge University Press, 1994), 47.

'Young men will do it': Fun, Disorder, and Good Government in York, 1555; Some Thoughts on House Book 21

PETER MEREDITH

I did not realize what I was in for when, in 1974 in Leeds, I went along with Arthur Cawley to see Sandy Johnston about a new and exciting project. REED was soon to come into the world, and medieval drama was never going to be the same again. As a result, not only was I tangled with REED but with York. Neither is an entanglement that I wish to escape from, and here, Sandy, from the depths of the bramble bush are a couple of tales of York and some thoughts – a small tribute to a great achievement.

House Book 21, one of the books minuting the meetings of the governing body of the city of York, records the statement of a certain William Hosyar made at an examination held on 18 May 1555.[1] In his evidence he said that on Saturday, 11 May, he dropped in at Tristram Litster's house (not by the front door, I imagine; it was clearly a below-stairs visit) to see his mates and have a drink. Shaw was there, Gawyn Bulyman, and George Mann, Tristram Litster's apprentice, and some others. Hosyar was from Lincoln and had been in York five months or so looking for service, but he seems to have spent much of his time courting a (rich?) widow, Agnes Clerk alias Watson. He and his mates had a good time until about 10 o'clock that night when for some inexplicable reason they decided to go and fetch a gridiron of William's that had been left in someone else's house outside the city walls. So William, George, and Gawyn went to Layerthorpe postern to get out, only to find it locked – as, unless very drunk, they must have anticipated. Nobody from the watch was about so they went on to the next gate, Monk Bar, but there was no one there either. Then Gawyn, noticing a light in a house nearby, went in and found all the watch asleep. Seeing a bunch of keys, he took them, found one that opened the wicket-gate, and out they went. William picked up his gridiron, they came back through the wicket-gate and so once more into the city. Yet again inexplicably, they failed to return the keys. It all took about a quarter of an hour. They then went past the house in Petergate belonging to Alderman Gale, one of the wardens of Monk ward and therefore intimately concerned with the security of Monk Bar (but they made no attempt to put themselves right with authority); then on down Stonegate and along Coney Street back to Litster's house. By that time it was not worth going to bed properly, so they lay down in their clothes. The urgency for getting the gridiron seems to have evaporated. All this time Tristram Litster was fast asleep, having gone to bed about 9 o'clock. Later in his evidence, William said that as to the keys, he had never had them in his possession and had advised them to take them to an alderman. George Mann, the only other witness at the hearing, said that they gave him the keys to look after when they got back indoors but he was never advised to take them to an alderman. And anyway the whole business was Hosyar's idea.

In a totally unconnected incident a little under a month later on Sunday, 2 June, Whit Sunday, at around 11 o'clock at night, Christopher Luty and his brother Nicholas arrived at John Mann's house in Stonegate (he and his wife were out of town at the time) and were admitted by the servants. There they remained larking with the maids and servants until 1 or 2 o'clock the following morning. The watch, four of them together with one of the sergeants of the sheriffs, more alert than in May or having woken up to do the rounds or perhaps simply kept up to scratch by the sheriffs' sergeant, at about that time noticed the activity in the house and attempted to enter. They were prevented by those inside, which allowed the Lutys to escape, out at the back and through a next-door property, upsetting some-one, most likely the inhabitants of the next-door house, in the process.[2]

These two unconnected events did not happen in a vacuum. By the beginning of the year 1555, as John North came to the end of his mayor-alty in York, Mary Tudor had been on the throne for a little over eighteen months. In that time she had circumvented an initial attempt to prevent her accession, overcome a serious rebellion, which would have been a lot more serious had the timing of the conspirators been better, and had married a foreigner, no less than King Philip of Spain, son to the erstwhile Holy Roman Emperor. On 3 August 1554 they had been proclaimed in York:

> Phillippe and Mary by the grace of god king and Quene of England Fraunce Naples Jerusalem and Ireland Defenders of the Faith prynces of spayne and Cicilie Archduke of Austria Dukes of Myllayne Burgonde and Brabånd Countes of haspurge Flaunders and Tyroll.[3]

Gaining the approval of parliament for the marriage had not been easy.[4] If Mary had had troubles before, she was likely to have even more now. Moreover the transformation of the country back to a Catholic one was also in progress. Whether greeted with joy, willingness to conform, reluctance, or hostility, it was still change: something more to be concerned about. It is hardly surprising under these circumstances that the majority of communications between the queen and her city of York concerned good government. The first communication which the common clerk (or his deputy) recorded was the proclamation of her succession to the throne, delivered to the citizens of York on 21 and 22 July 1553. In view of Edward VI's bypassing of his half-sisters, Mary and Elizabeth, in favour of Lady Jane Grey, the duke of Northumberland's daughter-in-law, as his successor to the throne, there is, not surprisingly, a considerably assertive tone in Mary's proclamation. Having announced the death of Edward 'our late brother of moste werthy memory wherby the corone imperiall of the realmes of England and Irland with the tytle of France and all other thinges appertening unto the same do most rightfully and lawfully belong unto us,' the proclamation continues:

> we do singnifie unto yow that according to our saied Right and tytle we doo take apon us and be in the just and Lawfull possession of the same not dowbting that all our trewe and Feythfull subjectes will so accompte us, repute us, take us and obey us as theyr naturall and leige soveraigne lady and quene according to the dewties of their alleigeans assuring all our good and Feythfull Subjectes that in their so doing they shall fynd us their benigne and graciose soveraigne lady as other our most noble progenitours have heretofore bene.[5]

The following folio of the House Book, for 7 August, contains the date, notice of the election of William Beckwith as alderman in place of Mr Lenard, and as usual the list of those attending, but it is dominated by the words: 'God save the Queene.' The date, moreover, is given in its fullest form providing an opportunity to give Mary all her titles, in contrast with the previous entry which has no regnal year, and the attendance is amongst the largest in this particular House Book, the mayor and ten aldermen, one chamberlain, and thirteen of the twenty-four, expressing, perhaps, since it is a private record, a warm satisfaction in the accession of the new monarch, or perhaps a desire at least to be seen by one's neighbours as welcoming the new queen.[6] At the end of the month (30 August) a letter of

submission was despatched to the queen assuring her of the devout alle-
giance of the mayor, aldermen, and 'wholle Comonaltie of your gracys
Citie of yorke' and hoping for favourable treatment similar to that received from her predecessors. It is a typically ingratiating letter for the
beginning of a new reign, with perhaps a touch of further eagerness in view
of the uncertainties of July and the implied warnings of Mary's proclamation, but it is also perhaps an expression of satisfaction.[7] The House Book
then drops back into the usual business of the city: fishgarths, taxes,
elections of sheriffs and members of parliament.

The state of something resembling emergency, however, continued; a
situation reflected in the city council's directive of 26 February 1554 :

> Assembled in the Counsell Chambre apon Ousebrig the day & yere abovesayd
> whan & where it was ordered and aggreed by the seyd presens that from this
> day there shalbe at every the foure barres of this Citie watche kept nightly by
> sex discrete liable & honest men in harnesse by discretion of the wardens of
> that warde begynnyng every night at viij of the Clok and soo contynewyng
> unto fyve of the clocke in the mornyng. And every the barres and posternes
> to be all that tyme suerly lokked. And that the iiij[or] officeres in every warde
> with the Constables shall nightly bryng theym to the Wardens and see the
> seyd watch sustainably sett Provyded that the sayd constables and officeres
> shall allowe no unfranchised man to watch withowte consent of the wardens,
> and that all howskepars of this Citie & aswell franchised as unfranchised to
> be chardged with the sayd watch, Except only wydowes, Aldermen & accus-
> tomed otheres.[8]

This directive was itself a response to the queen's letters (prompted by
Wyatt's and Suffolk's rebellions) of 11 and especially 23 February in the
same year:

> our pleasour ys ye shall make a plaine and full certificat to our Right Trustie
> and welbiloved Cosin and Counsellour Therle of Shrewesburie lorde presi-
> dent of oure Counsell establysshed in theis north parties singnifiing therbye
> both the hole noumbre of able men of the saied Countie wyth the names of
> the Capeteynes appointede for the Leading of the same And also what
> nombre of harnesses and Weapones maie be hadd oute of the same Countie
> with a partyculer Declaracion howe many be horsemen howe manie fotemen
> and of theis howe many archers pykes billmen and so of every sorte whiche
> wee requier yow to putt in suche order that they be allwayes Redie uppon
> one howers warning to be ymployed in our service where and when soever

we shall appointe. Praying yowe to use all possible diligence herein and also to geve order that the wattches maie be forth wyth set to be kepte by dyscrete panefull and the most honest men in all places accustomed whereby as ye shall administer unto us Right acceptable service and pleasour soo will we not forgett the same to be consydered towardes yow to your Comfurtes accordinglie.[9]

The context clearly shows that the setting of watches was not something to be taken lightly in 1554. That this was still true in 1555 is shown by the order of the king and queen dated 26 March of that year encouraging local authorities to be more vigilant and strict. Though this order begins as a tightening of religious controls, it extends to potential troublemakers of all kinds:

Item they [justices of the peace] shall charge the constables and fowr or more of the most honest and catholike of every parishe with the ordre of the same paryshe unto whome idle men vacabondes & suche as may be probably suspected shalbe bound to give reconinge how they live and where they shalbe come from tyme to tyme.

Item they shall have ernest regarde to the execution and kepinge of the Statutes against rebelliones vacabondes reteaneres aile howses & for kepinge of the Statute of hew & cry and shall give ordre for kepinge of good & substantiall watches In places convenient the same to beginne the xxth day of Aprill next.

Item assone as any offendares for murdre fellonye or other offences shalbe take the sayd Justices of peace shall cause the matter to be forthewith examined and there of certifie the lord president of our Counsell established in thes northe parties & in hys absens to his vice president & the reste of our Counsell, therto to theintent they may take further ordr therin as the case requieres.[10]

It was against this background that the Hosyar and Luty affairs took place. Given the national government's almost neurotic concern with preparedness and conspicuous security, the first affair was obviously something that had to be taken seriously.

Hosyar was unlucky in his friends, unlucky in his class, unlucky in his timing, and unlucky in not being a native of York. The case was referred to the city recorder for a legal judgment, who in turn took it to the Queen's Council in the North, and the extraordinary whim of fetching a gridiron in the middle of the night ended in his being sentenced to 'be taken as a vacabund and soo to be whypped about the towne at a cart ars And banasshed this cite.' Goodbye to service and the widow. Clearly the mayor and aldermen could not ignore so open a flouting of their authority, but it is interesting, though not surprising, that it is the 'stranger' who is made an example of. No more is said of Bulyman or Mann.[11]

The Lutys were rather more fortunate. They were both of York; they were Christopher, a gentleman, and Nicholas, a goldsmith; and their crime, apparently young men's larks. How were they known to be those who were sporting themselves in John Mann's house? Did one of their erstwhile companions split on them? Or were they recognized in the street by the watch in the course of making their escape? Or did they come along and make a clean breast of it? However it happened their punishment was light. The immediate sentence given on 4 June was for them to be 'commytted to warde to the Shirefes there to remayne unto they have Founde sufficient Suerties to kepe good rule & ordre within this Citie and no moare to goe abrode forth of ther lodgynges aftere undewe tyme of the night.' On 5 June, the following day, they had been accepted as each other's guarantors for 100 shillings, so if they ever were in the sheriffs' ward it was only for a night. They had to behave themselves in future and not go out of their lodgings late at night, or as the mayor's instructions put it, each 'erit bone conversationis et regiminis infra istam Civitatem, Et quod non vagabitur foras ad aliquid temporem noctis post horam nonam inordinate aut suspiciose ad nocumentum etc.'[12] As with the Hosyar incident, it sounds like a case of 'young men will do it.'

These were not the only minor disturbances of 1555. There was trouble at the swearing-in day (3 February) of the mayor, leading to fines and imprisonment. One troublemaker, by report, had been Tristram Litster, the householder who had apparently slept through the Hosyar affair. Whether they ever found out who another reported troublemaker was, the 'one in a blewe cote with an apron abowt him a kydgell under his arm,' is never clear. That he was not recognized may suggest that he was a stranger to York. Was he reported because of the cudgel, or did he actually do something?[13] John Fisher, one of the sheriffs' attorneys, was dismissed for 'disobedient behaviour disquyetyng at tymes the whole court,' 'synyster Counsell,' procuring 'wrongfull sewtes,' 'threatnynges,' 'braggyng ... most lyke a common barrator.'[14] There was riotous breaking of glass windows in the city and search was made for 'one Canon Lait sarvaunt to William Pullayn of Skotton one of the cheyf offendres.'[15] Dr Stephen Tuble, his wife, Alice, his 'laddes,' *and* his children were bound over for offensive behaviour against 'dyverse worshipfull and honest Citizens of this Citie of purpose to cause strife debat and breakyng of the kyng & quenes peace';[16] and all these before the Hosyar and Luty affairs happened. Afterwards, on 10 August, there was gentry trouble between Sir Thomas Metham and Frances Willestrop at a shooting match on Palacroftes (Paynlathes Croftes, an open area to the north of the walls beyond Monk Bar), which the mayor, 'remembring certayne Letters to us directed from the King and Quenes pryvie Counsell,' felt impelled to report to the Council in the North on the same day it happened. And, if that wasn't enough, the butchers were threatening to withhold supplies from the city.[17]

But there were consolations; merrymaking to set against disturbances, entertainment to soak up discontent, or channel exuberance, or simply because it was fun. A letter from the king and queen received on 8 February announced that England had been 'delyvered by aucthorite of the popes holynesse from all sentencys of Interdiction excommunycation and other censures of the Church,' and bonfires were ordered for Sunday, 10 February, Septuagesima, 'accordyngly with rejoysyng and thankes gyvyng to god for his mercyfullnesse nowe and alle tymes.'[18] Corpus Christi was to be celebrated again in full with play and procession as it had been the previous year. St George was to be honoured with his procession, mass, and sermon at St George's Chapel, again as last year. The decking out of the Chamber on Ousebridge for the mayor and his party of aldermen and the lady mayoress and her party at the procession on Whitsun Tuesday was to be again 'as was done the last yere And further that this yere they [the bridgemasters] shall provyde alsoo of white Cuppes, as hath ben used aforetyme.'[19]

Another entertainment of 1555 that has not been given much attention is the fort-holding put on by 'the young men' on Shrove Tuesday, 26 February 1555. We know about it only because the mayor contributed to their costs:

> reward on shrofetuysday
> Item where dyverse the honest yongmen of this Citie on Shrove tewysday last to shewe my lord mayor Aldremen & wholl comonalte of this Cite honest & pleasant pastyme one sort in defendyng a fort & thother in makyng thassault were at chardges in dyvisynge & preparyng the same it is nowe therfor fully consented that they shalle have towardes thair chardges in reward of the Chamber costes tenne shillynges.[20]

This does not sound like a fort-holding on the scale of the birthday celebrations for James I at Stirling where ten shillings would have been a drop in the ocean of just one lot of firework expenses,[21] but in as much as it is a unique event in York it seems worth giving it some consideration. Where did the young men get the idea from? Was it related to the 'dramas' of the tournament, and perhaps instigated by one of the local gentry? Were they, indeed, as White suggests, younger members of the gentry who put on the show?[22] Or was it an offshoot of the St George celebrations? Or did the young men consider such events rather tame, and put this on as a demonstration of how they thought such a celebration should be managed? The ten shillings which the mayor gave to the young men was a contribution to costs, but we do not know what proportion of the total cost that represented and consequently have no idea how elaborate an event it was. Nor do we know where it took place, at what time of day, how it was costumed (if it was), how many were involved, how many watched ('the wholl comonalte'?), or how the assault was organized. We know it was on Shrove Tuesday, which opens up the possibility of a contest between Carnival and Lent, but there is little evidence for these in England. If it was a simple fight over a fort, it could be more like the Shrove Tuesday football matches. But there is no indication of anyone suffering any injury, as they certainly would have done if the contemporary descriptions of football matches are anything to go by.[23] It clearly also had the approval of the authorities, which makes the football analogy an unlikely one. But who instigated it? Was the fort-holding an attempt by the civic government to channel the exuberance of the young men? Certainly it sounds as though it involved a considerable amount of physical energy, and it was rewarded. Was it a result of the general return to a world of celebration or is it a sign of a newly found freedom in the young men? Had such a thing ever happened before? If it had, it may be simply a replay, like the St George celebrations. Or was it entirely new? The only reason that we know anything about it is financial, as is so often the case, and there could have been fort-holdings in the past which, like Yule and Yule's Wife (apart from one appearance) went unrecorded.[24] What is clear is that some young men at least were disporting themselves in a way that their elders approved. It would be nice to know if the Lutys, or William Hosyar, or George Mann, or Gawyn Bulyman were amongst them.

The mayor and council who had to consider the letters from the queen and her ministers were clearly aware of the national situation and their actions were affected by it, but how aware were those involved in these local events and minor disturbances? Indeed, how aware were any of the inhabitants of York who were not involved in its government? Had they actually attended any of the public proclamations of the queen's accession or marriage? Are their actions in any sense a response to them? Does the national set a tone for the regional? A general sense of unrest could lead some to desire control and restraint and others to feel that anything goes. Besides the appearance of the fort-holding, there is another reference in 1555 to a York entertainment little considered in this civic context, the summer game:

> Apon certayne consideracions it is nowe aggreed that all Somergames latly begonne & used within this Citie shalbe forth with dischardged & leaft of for this yere.[25]

There is one other oblique reference to summer games before this one in Anthony Middleton's will, probate 20 June 1520, where he leaves 2s to a 'somergame lyght' in his parish church of St Michael's.[26] Middleton was a merchant made free in 1509–10 and a chamberlain the year before he died.[27] Another reference to summer games in York is the general ban in Archbishop Grindal's register of 1570, but this is not specific to the city of York and includes not only 'sommerr Lordes or ladyes' but also 'lordes of misrule,' 'anye disguised persons or others in christmasse or at may gammes,' 'minstrels morrie dauncers or others at Ryshebearinges,' etc., intruding inappropriately into churches or churchyards.[28] White draws attention to another reference to summer games in 'Articles of Instruccione' from Elizabeth entered in House Book 24 on 30 June 1569:

> And in this behalf also we cannot but admonishe youe to be warr & circunspecte what lycences you geyve to persones to kepe comon somer gammes for we here of some great abuses therein in sundrye partes of ye Realme both that they ar over generall and Lewdnes & ungodlynes commyttid, by the confluence of noumbres and evill disposyd people for lack of the presence of some wise honest & godlie Justices, And officeres, whereof as we shall be further informed so will we provide remedie[29]

Images of Justice Overdone and *Bartholomew Fair* come to mind. The order was something of a rebuke to the city's government for failing to provide certificates to show that previous orders had been implemented. The order may have been sent to many places but it is here specifically addressed to 'the maior Aldermen & Justices of peace within the Citie of york and the liberties of the same.'[30] The banning of summer games in 1555 by the mayor and council of York immediately gives them a prominence in the city itself. No reason is given for the ban beyond the 'Apon certayne consideracions' and it is only for that year. And what does 'latly begonne & used' mean? Are these another reactivated entertainment or are they new? In which case what does Anthony Middleton's bequest relate to? Unlike the fort-holding, summer games perhaps imply a less restricted and less controlled activity of the young.

Does the uncontrolled activity of the two Lutys remind the mayor and his aldermen that the summer games are a potential threat? The entry banning the games follows immediately after the consideration of the case against the Lutys in House Book 21. The entries in the House Books do not of course contain everything that was discussed at council meetings, nor does their proximity in the records necessarily mean that they were juxtaposed in reality. There is no absolute necessity for the two entries to be related, but it is nevertheless interesting that they come together. The Luty escapade was on Whit Sunday and lasted over into Whit Monday morning. There is no description of what went on in John Mann's house beyond the general 'did suspiciously remayne and accompanyd with the maydes & servantes of the seyd Manne unto it was j or ij of the clock of the same night,' but were they in fact celebrating Whitsun, perhaps with a private ale? Or just having a drink, like Hosyar and his friends – but we have seen what that could lead to.

The fort-holding and the ban on the summer games extends the view of entertainment in York under Mary, but like the other events it needs to be seen against a background. Part of the background, that of those in authority, is apparent and is one of national and local unease alongside national and local hopeful expectation. As always the part of the background that is difficult to see is that of the others, the majority, those not in authority. In the early part of Mary's reign the phrase 'Redie upon one howers warning' must have been constantly ringing in the mayors' ears, but there seems also to have been a sense that if one could keep one's head beneath the parapet one would be all right. Was the earl of Shrewsbury provided with the roll of able-bodied men, the 'plaine and full certificat,' that was asked for in 1555 (House Book 21, f.35v)? It seems unlikely that it was 'plaine and full' enough, since further and more pressing requests were made in 1558. This time it was not only those in authority who must have been made aware of the potential dangers. On 4 February a list of 'the most substanciall honest hable men of this citie and Aynstie' appears in the House Book. On 5 February, unusually marked as 'post meridiem' no doubt to indicate that no time was lost in calling a new meeting, the lord lieutenant's commission for a speedy muster was read. On 8 February at the request of the lord lieutenant, the earl of Westmoreland, it was arranged that all men between the ages of sixty and sixteen should muster in 'the old Baille,' the bailey of the old castle in the southeastern corner of the town, by nine o'clock on the following day. The lord lieutenant's requirements were precise and pressing:

> necessarie and expedient to have generall muster and vewe taken of all their highnesses subjectes within ther county of york for the certayne knowlege what hablemen furnished and unfurnished may be had within the same Soo trustyng in your Wisdoms diligens and circumspections in matteres of chardge with your accustomed forthwardnes in thynges by their majesties and their officeres comitted to youre ordre I as there highnesses Lieutente general for the north parties have appoynted yow to be their Comissioners for that purpose within their Citie of york and the Conty of the same And therfor will & requyre you and likewise also auctorise and in the king and quenes majestes names streightly chardge & commande yow that yow callyng before yow with as moche expedicion as ys possible all & every thinhabitantes within the saied citie & Ainstie ye do circumspectly mustre & viewe the same first notyng how many therof be hablemen to serve their highnesses in their warres on horseback or of fote and how many of theym have harnesse & weapones then how many of that nombre be not harnessed nor weaponed declaryng what kynde of harnes they have with the nature of ther weapones And the names of the persones of every sort And in case ye shall apon your saied musters and vewe fynde any person destitute of suche harnes & furnyture as by the customes lawes & statutes of this realme he ought to have ye doo gyve hym & every suche person so bounden & wantyng streyght chardge in the kyng and quenes maiesties behalffes to provide the same ymediately and to thintent that they shall not be remisse in this commission nor thynke it a thyng to be lyghtly passed over as peraventure at certayne tymes yt haith ben Yt shalbe your partes to declare playnly & certaynly unto the gentlemen headmen yemen and otheres mete for the warres that they shalbe appoynted as occasion requireth to serve in ther owne persones and not to be permytted to shefte theymselfes by sendyng of otheres wherfor they must be by yow very earnestly remembred & warned that their preparacion may be accordyngly willyng therin also to considre that as he whoo willingly furnysshed hym self towardes the defence of his prynces honour and Countri whan he ys called deserveth & shall receyve thankes there after Soo contrarywise he that refuseth or withdraweth hymselfe his servantes or tenantes be appoynted to serve must of reason & justice receyt punyshement accordyng to his desertes.[31]

No longer is it simply the governing body of the city that has to cope with the central government's requirements. These are demands that are going to affect everyone's lives. The city is asked to provide two hundred men, double the quantity they claimed to have produced in the past. Where were the 'young men' in all this? Is this what they were hoping for at the time of the fort-holding? Doing something worthy of their spirit and desires? Were they among the 'wylling,' only too ready to be involved in a fight? One of the most difficult things to know is the attitudes of the participants in events. William Hosyar's story is quite fully told but we have no idea really of what sort of man he was. Was he fooling the authorities or was he really looking for service in York? What did he and the others go out that night in May to find? Really a gridiron? Was he, in another manifestation, one of the honest young men involved in the fort-holding, or were they more like the Lutys? And where do the young gentry fit in? Are they typically bored and ready for anything that will liven life up a bit? Is the Corpus Christi Play or the St George Riding one of those things, or are they part of the tedious old world of grown-up authority?

Once in the very early hours of a snowy February in the late 1970s four academics were walking back along Elgin Avenue from a pleasant evening at a friend's house in Toronto when they saw coming out of the front door of an ordinary suburban house a large wardrobe. There seemed to be no human means of propulsion, just a large moving wardrobe. It was a piece of heightened reality. If we had been James Joyce it would have been an epiphany. It was also very funny. Friendly goodnights were exchanged and we walked on. It has stuck in my mind because it was so odd, and so inexplicable in the sense that we had no idea what was going on. It has since seemed to me that this is what sixteenth-century York is like for us in the twenty-first century. We often know the characters and the site and we are excited by the events but from a human point of view we have no idea what is going on. What did John Huntyngton actually do in the production of the Bakers' pageant? Was he merely a getter-together or was he a kind of eighteenth-century actor-manager? And what was he like? He knew and lived near John Langton who was also a baker, who went over the heads of the mayor and council to take the bakers' case to parliament, encroached on public space to enlarge the extent of his property, and must have been a constant thorn in the side of the authorities. Is that what John Huntyngton was like?[32] Thanks to Eileen White we know quite a bit about John Stamper, performer of St George, 'a man of average means, a craftsman, a minor office holder and churchwarden,' but we know nothing about his attitude to his life or to his role.[33] I shall of course be told that that is obvious. How can you know? It nevertheless seems to me important to tell the stories, to draw together the characters where they can be drawn together, to set them against what background there is. William Hosyar and the Luty brothers may never have been involved in any kind of theatrical activity or entertainment but their stories help to add a human dimension to that activity, give us something to test the plays against. These are the kinds of people who had to be pleased or instructed or entertained; they are the kind who might have provided an anti-culture, or they are the kind who stood glumly in the background waiting for something more interesting to turn up.[34]

NOTES

1 House Book 21, York City Archives, ff. 91–1v; see also Angelo Raine, ed., *York Civic Records* 5, Yorkshire Archaeological Society Record Series 110 (1944) (York and London: Herald Printing Works, 1946), 122–4 (hereafter *YCR*). The facts of the story that follows are as in the House Book, the authorial tone is an addition. Only the mayor, William Beckwith, four aldermen, and one sheriff were present at the examination of Hosyar and Mann, which took place a week after the event occurred. Hosyar lived in the house of a shoemaker, 'one Wale' (probably Thomas Wailles, cordyner, made free in 1548–9 [*Freemen's Registers*, 1:268; hereafter *FR*], so he was probably a 'young man' too) and kept company commonly with his host, Mr Farby (senior), Edmund Dobson, and others. No Mr Farby, senior or junior, appears in the Freemen's Registers; Edmund Dobson was a chapman made free, *per patres*, 1551–2 (so also probably a 'young man'; *FR*, 1:271). 'Shaw' is too vague to be identified with any certainty. I take 'Gawyn' to be Bulyman's first name, whereas Raine takes them to be two separate people. He is referred to as 'Mr Bulyman' by Mann in his evidence, but none of the names appears in the appropriate Freemen's Registers. Raine takes 'George man servant to the seyd Lytster' to be 'George man-servant to the seyd Lytster'; that he is George Mann is shown by the marginal heading to his evidence: 'Manne.' He was a draper, made free in 1556–7 and therefore possibly the youngest of the group (*FR*, 1:276). Tristram Litster, draper, whose house they were drinking in and who slept through this particular escapade, was made free in 1539–40 ('Tristanus Lyster,' *FR*, 1:259), *per patres*, so even he may only have been in his late thirties. All references to the Freemen's Registers are to Francis Collins, ed., *The Register of the Freemen of the City of York*, 2 vols, Surtees Society 96 and 102 (Durham: Andrews, 1897 and 1900) (referred to as *FR* 1 and 2).

House Book 21, on which I draw heavily here, covers the period 1552–5, the latter part of Edward VI's reign and the early years of Mary's. I am most grateful to Dr Eileen White for generously allowing me to make use of her transcripts of the sixteenth-century House Books and to Rita Friedman and the staff at York City Archives for their continued friendly assistance. For a wealth of information on York in the late sixteenth century see Eileen Nora White, 'People and Places: The Social and Topographical Context of Drama in York 1554–1609' (unpublished doctoral thesis, University of Leeds, 1984).

For the layout of medieval York see Angelo Raine, *Medieval York: A Topographical Survey Based on Original Sources* (London: John Murray, 1955).

2 House Book 21, f. 93v; see also Raine, *YCR* 5, 124. The judgments on the Lutys appear in Latin on f. 94. They are not in Raine. There are no appropriate Lutys in the Freemen's Registers and no Luty or Lewty appears in the list of 'the most substanciall honest hable men of this citie and Aynstie' (121 from the City and 35 from the Ainsty) made for the lord lieutenant in preparation for war against Scotland in 1558 (House Book 22, ff. 109v–10v). There is a Brian Lewty made free as a notary public in 1516–17, son of William Lewty, tailor (*FR*, 1:238). Brian in turn had a son William who was made free as a tailor in 1548–9 (*FR*, 1:268), but it is not clear what relation, if any, they were to Christopher and Nicholas. There is a William Lewty, blacksmith, made free in 1577–8 (*FR*, 2:18) whose son, George, is made free as a goldsmith in the early seventeenth century. So Lutys/Lewtys were around in York but so far I have found no other references to Christopher and Nicholas.

3 House Book 21, f. 51.

4 Several extracts from the articles relating to their marriage to prevent any possibility of England falling too much under the sway of Spain are carefully entered in House Book 21, ff. 28v–30; see Paul L. Hughes and James F. Larkin, eds, *Tudor Royal Proclamations*, 3 vols (New Haven and London: Yale University Press, 1964–9), 2:21–6, for the full text.

5 House Book 21, f. 4; see also Raine *YCR* 5, 90–1. There are some slight differences between this version and that provided in Hughes and Larkin, *Proclamations*, 2:3.

6 House Book 21, f. 5. Her titles include at this stage 'on earth supreme head of the church of England and Ireland,' which is also included in the first proclamation from Westminster announcing her regnal style (1 October 1553); see Hughes and Larkin, *Proclamations*, 2:12. Attendances vary from as few as three to as many as thirty. Numbers are always high on the election days of the mayor (15 January) and sheriffs (21 September).

7 House Book 21, f. 7; see Raine *YCR* 5, 91–2, for the text of the letter.

8 House Book 21, f. 34; see also Raine *YCR* 5, 102.

9 House Book 21, ff. 35–5v. The queen's letter seems to be dated 25 February and was presumably not received until 26 February when it is recorded in the House Book. It is not entered until after the city's decision to act upon it.

10 House Book 21, ff. 86v-7.

11 House Book 21, f. 91v; see also Raine *YCR* 5, 123–4.

12 House Book 21, ff. 93v–4; he 'shall be of good behaviour and rule within this City, And that he shall not wander out of doors at any time of night after the hour of nine in an irregular or suspicious way to the harm etc.'

13 House Book 21, f. 77; meeting of 18 February 1555. Those informed on are under the heading: 'The names of certayn informed to be of mysrule on the swearynge day.' They are Robert Stainburn, Tristram Litster, the one with the blue coat, William Slater, and Nicholas Milner (spellings of names have been modernized). The names of the informers are also given. This informal keeping of an eye on potential troublemakers anticipates the explicit instructions contained in the king and queen's letter of 26 March, which institutionalize informing: 'Item they [justices of the peace] shall procure to have in every parishe or parte of the shier as nere as may be some one or more honest men secretly instructed to give enformacion of the behaviour of inhabitantes nighe or abought them' (House Book 21, f. 87). The affair of 'mysrule on the swearynge day' rumbled on for some time; see House Book 21, ff. 76–6v, 76av, 77, 78v, 78b–8bv. It was not until St Maure's day 1556 that Robert Stainburn was released from his bond of good behaviour (House Book 21, f. 120).

14 House Book 21, f. 76a; meeting of 18 February 1555. Fisher was readmitted on 23 September as he was said now to live by the law and had married an alderman's daughter (f. 106).

15 House Book 21, f. 80; meeting of 15 March 1555.

16 House Book 21, ff. 88–90v; meetings of 10, 12, and 15 May 1555.

17 House Book 21, f. 100v (Metham/Willestrop incident), f. 100 (the butchers).

18 House Book 21, ff. 74a–4av; see also Raine *YCR* 5, 112–13; meeting of 8 February 1555. Palliser considers the order for bonfires 'coolly arranged.' 'The restoration of suppressed revenues and hospitals was nearer their hearts than the distant concept of papalism.' D.M. Palliser, *Tudor York* (Oxford: Oxford University Press, 1979), 242.

19 House Book 21, f. 85; see also Raine *YCR* 5, 120–1 and Alexandra F. Johnston and Margaret Rogerson eds, *York* REED (Toronto: University of Toronto Press, 1979), 320–1; meeting of 2 April. It is curious that in 1554 Corpus Christi celebrations were ordered on 9 February, and in 1555 on 2 April, nearly two months later. It is true that in 1554 Corpus Christi Day was

almost a month earlier, 24 May as opposed to 13 June in 1555, but even so the order for the celebrations was given a lot earlier in 1554 than in 1555. Possibly the celebrations in 1554 were ordered early because the council was aware that that was what had been done in the past (that is, in Lent; see the *Ordo paginarum* note, Johnston and Rogerson, *York*, 17), but, perhaps more pressingly, because in that year the crafts who brought forth the Marian pageants would presumably have needed notice in order to get going again after the Edwardian break.

In 1554 St George (23 April) and Whitsun (13 May) celebrations were ordered on 20 April. In 1555 they were ordered, with Corpus Christi, on 2 April. Why was George ordered so late in 1554 given that there had probably been an Edwardian break for this celebration too? An afterthought? Was the mayor uncertain about its reception? Preparations must have been very rushed unless they were already going ahead without official notice (see Eileen White's discussion of this point in '"Bryngyng Forth of Saynt George": The St. George Celebrations in York,' *Medieval English Theatre* 3.2 [1981]: 117). And what were the white cups that were ordered for Whitsun Tuesday, which first appear in 1544 (White, 'People and Places,' 479)?

20 House Book 21, f. 79; see also Raine *YCR* 5, 117; not in Johnston and Rogerson, *York*; meeting of 8 March. White mentions it briefly in her thesis, 'People and Places,' 34 and discusses the activities of later 'young men,' 437–40, and Philip Butterworth refers to it in his *Theatre of Fire: Special Effects in Early English and Scottish Theatre* (London: The Society for Theatre Research, 1998), 100.

21 For a full discussion of the celebrations for James and other similar events, see Butterworth, *Theatre of Fire*, 99–128, and his earlier accounts: 'The Baptisme of hir Hienes Darrest Sone in Stirviling,' *Medieval English Theatre* 10.1 (1988): 26–55, and 'Royal Firework Theater: The Fort Holding,' *Research Opportunities in Renaissance Drama* 34 (1995): 145–66.

22 See White, 'People and Places,' 439–40. The meaning of 'honest' is perhaps more one of general approval than White suggests. It is unlikely that the queen in her letter of 23 February 1554 (quoted above) had in mind members of the gentry or wealthy citizens as watchmen.

23 For a discussion of Shrove Tuesday celebration in England, see Ronald Hutton, *The Stations of the Sun: A History of the Ritual Year in Britain* (Oxford: Oxford University Press, 1996), 151–68.

24 Yule and Yule's Wife appear only at the end of their celebratory life in a late Elizabethan broadside and the documents of their suppression, see Johnston and Rogerson, *York*, 359–62 and 368–70.

25 House Book 21, f. 93v; meeting of 4 June; see also White, 'People and Places,' 56. I am grateful to Dr White for drawing my attention to this reference.

26 Johnston and Rogerson, *York*, 219. His church of St Michael's was in Spurriergate at the end of Coney Street where it joins Low Ousegate.

27 *FR*, 1:232, 'Antonius Midilton, merchaunt'; 1:240, '... Anth. Middylton, Mercat ... Camarariis.' An 'Ant. Middilton, merchant' appears again as the father of 'Johannes Middylton' in the *Per Patres* list in 1541–2 (1:261), but this is either a different man or the scribe has forgotten to add '*def[unctus]*' after the name.

28 Johnson and Rogerson, *York*, 358–9.

29 White, 'People and Places,' 63.

30 House Book 24, ff. 145v–6v.

31 House Book 22, ff. 109v–10v (list of able-bodied men), 112–12v (lord lieutenant's commission). The city later reported that there were 520 able-bodied men in the city and aynsty, 200 already furnished with arms and armour (60 bowmen and 140 billmen) and 320 as yet unfurnished (f. 118). This is a far cry from the grudgingly offered 60 men that had been refused by the Lord President of the Council in 1557, and so was later raised to 100 'accordyng to our old custome wherof xl archres and lx billmen' (f. 51v). The 1558 demands seem to have produced a real assessment of what York could offer if pushed.

32 For John Huntyngton, see Johnston and Rogerson, *York*, 294–5 and 320, and White, 'People and Places,' 395–8. For John Langton's presumption, see House Book 21, ff. 13v–14. He is called 'gentleman' in the Freemen's Register (*FR*, 1:248) and he appears in York as a provider of hospitality to the Bakers' company (Johnston and Rogerson, *York*, 286, 288).

33 For John Stamper, see Eileen White, '"Bryngyng Forth of Saynt George,"' 119–20, and 'People and Places,' 374–95. White's thesis contains a number of brief biographies, 373–451.

34 I would have been one of the latter as far as York is concerned had it not been for the arrival in Leeds in 1970 of Margaret Dorrell (now Rogerson) and in 1974, at what later turned out to be the first SITM Colloquium, of Sandy Johnston. Thanks to both of them for giving me so much pleasure – and work.

The Southwest Entertains: Exeter and Local Performance Patronage

SALLY-BETH MACLEAN

The performance landscape of Devon is already familiar, thanks to John Wasson's edition of dramatic records for the county in the REED series.[1] Records of payments for touring entertainments survive at several important boroughs – Ashburton, Barnstaple, Dartmouth, Plymouth, Tavistock and Totnes – and at the cathedral city of Exeter, where the receivers paid the first of many royal household performers in 1361–2.[2]

My focus in this essay will be the period up to 1485, the date of Henry VII's seizure of the throne. The late medieval Exeter accounts store important clues about local culture in the southwest beyond the obvious civic entertainments. Closer analysis of the touring troupes paid by the receivers will reveal a hidden entertainment landscape beyond the towns – the venues belonging to patrons whose performers may have played Exeter on occasion but cannot have ignored seasonal demands for performances at home. My purpose will be to explore who these patrons were, where their families and their interests were based, what political influences may have affected their reception in towns like Exeter, and what architectural evidence survives to indicate the type of playing spaces available at home or on the road in the period.

Before 1485 we do not know much about locally produced entertainment in Devon. The parish accounts available do not yield records of Robin Hood games until later in the century, although Exeter's surprisingly early notice of Robin Hood players in the 1426–7 civic accounts may be evidence that St John's Bow parish was already engaged in this festive custom.[3] There were certainly waits providing music for special events in the civic calendar at Exeter, from at least 1362–3 when the first notice of an annual payment occurs in the records.[4] The Corpus Christi play that has given rise in the past to speculation about cycle drama at Exeter has been analysed in Alexandra Johnston's recent article 'The Feast of Corpus Christi in the West Country.'[5] Situating the play references in the political context of a local dispute between the bishop of Exeter and the city over the jurisdiction of two Exeter parishes – St Stephen's within the Walls and St Sidwell's outside the east gate – she demonstrates that the play was never a cycle produced by craft guilds but rather a smaller production that remained in the hands of the Skinners' guild as an aspect of the ecclesiastical celebrations on the feast of Corpus Christi. The city may have made an attempt to co-opt the production in the early fifteenth century for its own purposes on a different day, but the Skinners, whose confraternal face was the guild of Corpus Christi, resisted successfully, presumably with the support of the bishop and dean of the cathedral. As a possible alternative the city seems to have developed an elaborate May game festivity on the Monday of Whitsuntide.

For the most part the available records suggest that it was performers of one sort or another, touring under the patronage of royalty, nobility, or gentry, who provided the dominant source of entertainment, primarily in Devon boroughs on the main roads.[6] The nature of their performances is mostly obscured by generic, sometimes interchangeable terminology – *administralli, historiones, mimi, ministralli* – although the occasional piper, jester, trumpeter, bearward, and even that remarkable fellow, the king's leopardward, are mentioned specifically.[7] Others have attempted to differentiate the generic terms used in fifteenth-century accounts, but I have come to doubt whether we will ever know when a *histrio, mimus,* or *ministrallus* in that period was performing music, doing acrobatics, juggling, dancing, tale-telling, or performing an interlude on the road.[8] Only when more informative sources such as the earl of Northumberland's 2nd Household Book survive can we speak with any confidence about the types of entertainer under patronage in an individual household.[9]

It is only after the accounts begin to slide into English around 1500 that we meet identifiable players on the road, though what they were playing still remains a mystery. Where they played in the towns is less perplexing. One of the more welcoming venues in Devon would have been the Guildhall at Exeter, located on the same site since the twelfth century though the present structure was largely rebuilt during the second half of the fifteenth century. With its proud late-Elizabethan façade on the High Street, the Guildhall serves even now as a handsome location for formal civic events.[10] What we might consider the principal seat of the mayor was here and this would have been the primary site for civic banquets and other entertainments. In accounting for official rewards for performances the Exeter receivers seldom specify the Guildhall (or any other venue) – their primary interest was in the money spent. Occasionally a locally produced performance event draws special notice of the location: in 1430–1 payment was made 'lusoribus ludentibus Natale Christi in Gihalda coram Maiore & socijs suis' and in 1495–6 'pro quadam lusione facta in Gild Aula Exoniensis coram Maiore & socijs suis.'[11] A 'domus maioris,' presumably the house belonging to the mayor himself rather than an official civic building, also appears from time to time in the accounts linked with performance payments in the fifteenth century.[12]

Barnstaple, which also has medieval performance records, had a guildhall too in our period, though it does not survive.[13] But these are indoor spaces. In the Devon records, and indeed in most other county collections available, there is little evidence that touring troupes with patrons performed outdoors, despite a common assumption that market squares and innyards would have been their usual venues.[14] REED editors have found numerous records of civic-sponsored entertainment for the mayor and other civic officials in English towns before 1558 and, with few exceptions, the venues when recorded are indoors, mostly linked with town authorities.[15]

Robert Tittler has succinctly summed up the key reasons why guild, moot, or town halls functioned as alternative theatres for professional players in provincial towns after 1559 and I would only add that some of these reasons could be extended backward in time as well: 'The format of [this] command performance, following the presentation of credentials and the grant of permission, promised something for everyone. It demonstrated the mayor's authority, while his presence on opening night lent dignity both to himself and the occasion. It provided the players with the official endorsement of the mayor and perhaps some immunity from local harassment. It created the aura of proper decorum appropriate to performance in the town's seat of government, while at the same time relegating the players' activities to that civic space most able to be supervised and controlled. Finally, it allowed town officials to scrutinize the content of the performance, and presumably to forbid "unseemly" ideas from wider expression.'[16]

From the players' viewpoint there could be other advantages as well. The guildhalls frequently offered the most congenial space in town and in some cases, such spaces were comparable in size to the private halls where they played elsewhere in the provinces.[17] Some troupes were also able, literally, to cash in on special relationships between their patrons and the towns concerned. Certainly in the later Tudor period at some locations such as Leicester's guildhall, there was a 'gathering' at the door for members of the audience allowed into the official performance.[18] Control of the

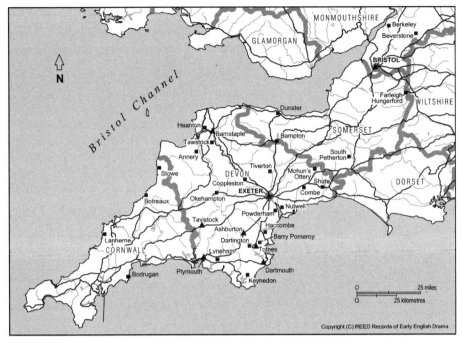

1. Southwestern England, showing performance venues before 1485

gate was then more easily managed at indoor venues and meant guaranteed income beyond the mayor's reward.

But are such civic spaces the whole story? The map (Plate 1) locates the familiar boroughs (indicated by triangles) as well as a sprinkling of squares across the county that deserve to be acknowledged as an integral part of Devon's entertainment landscape. These are the primary residences associated with many of the patrons of the performers who toured the county, residences where we can assume the patron, family, and guests would have enjoyed entertainment at the key festive dates in the seasonal calendar – at Christmas and Shrovetide, for example – as well as at special events such as weddings.[19]

A handful can be highlighted here to illustrate the origins of some of the performers touring Devon, many of whom were more locally based than has yet been fully recognized. The performers may be nameless, but their patrons are not, so we can track their identities, their families, lands, and residences. Approximately half of the patrons in Devon's long list of touring performers up to 1558, and certainly before 1485, were residents of the southwest, mostly Devon and Cornwall. This contrasts strikingly with the performer lists for the other southwestern counties of Cornwall, Somerset, and Bristol. Survival of records plays a part here, of course. Borough and household records for Cornwall, like those for Somerset, are relatively few before the mid-sixteenth century, and Bristol's civic records only begin in 1531.[20] Even so, the number of locally patronized troupes circulating within these counties before 1558 is less than a quarter of those from further afield. So the nobility and gentry of Devon seem to have been more actively engaged in entertainment patronage before that date even though the family papers that might have helped us track their retinues and entertainment expenses for the most part do not survive.

So who were these local patrons? The list is a roll call of the most prominent families in late medieval Devon: the Beaumonts of Combe and Heanton, the Bonvilles of Shute, the Bourchiers of Tawstock, the Carews of Haccombe and Mohun's Ottery, the Courtenays of Tiverton, Oke-hampton, and Powderham, the Dinhams of Nutwell, the Hankefords of Annery, the Holands of Dartington, and more besides. And if the evolution of Exeter's civic festivities in the fifteenth century was affected by political rivalry between the bishop of Exeter and the city burgesses, then we should probably pay attention to other political influences represented by these local touring performers whose patrons held offices or lands in the immediate area.

As we trace the development of Exeter's arts patronage it is worth considering the varied urban motives for welcoming minstrels of local magnates. Rosemary Horrox, in her study of urban patronage in the fifteenth century, has identified some of the goals, even of the most inde-pendent-minded provincial towns, in seeking patronage, ultimately from the Crown though often through intermediaries who could be advocates at court. Two main categories of grant were sought: for financial help (e.g., remission of fee farms, favourable tax assessments) and for increased local autonomy and confirmation of charter rights at the beginning of each reign: 'Towns were therefore in a vulnerable position. They needed con-tinuing royal favour to obtain economic help and preserve their liberties, but their political muscle was slight. Their obvious solution was to find influential supporters who could press their claims at court and generally uphold their interests.'[21] In the early fourteenth century, Exeter was a city of moderate size, ranked about twenty-eighth among English towns ac-cording to taxable wealth.[22] Yet it lay at the hub of the important south-western road network with several important regional functions, as the seat of a wealthy and extensive diocese, administrative centre for the justices of assize, headport for Devon and Cornwall, and occasional military stronghold with its royal castle of Rougemont.[23] Two centuries later Exeter's expansion, largely due to its cloth-making industry, had brought it to sixth place in wealth and third in population size among English towns, well along the path to incorporation as a county in its own right in 1537.[24] It is in this politicized context that we can take a closer look at the patrons of locally based performers.

Before digging deeper into the Exeter records, we should acknowledge the limitations of the primary source, the receivers' accounts. As REED's *Devon* editor, John Wasson, has pointed out, the early rolls for the fourteenth century tend merely to summarize gifts and apart from the early fifteenth century (i.e., before 1440), payments to touring performers may have been made elsewhere: ' [T]he explanation ... may lie in the practice of the receivers in the sixteenth century, when such payments were itemized on separate paper books and only rarely on the parchment rolls. None of these paper books exists for years earlier than 1523, however ...'[25] Perhaps a clue that such might have been the case is the stray cancelled payment to two touring troupes that creeps into the receivers' accounts for 1447–8, during a period of seeming cultural drought when only waits' payments were recorded in the 'gifts and grants' section.[26]

The family recurring most often in the medieval and early Tudor accounts at Exeter was the Courtenays, starting with Edward, 3rd earl of Devon, whose minstrels were first recorded in 1415–16.[27] The fourteenth-century Courtenay earls of Devon have been described as 'rich, powerful and well connected at court – [they] dominated the political life of Devonshire to an extraordinary degree. Theirs was the greatest of local lineages whose influence touched most of the significant members of local political society.'[28] Earl Edward's livery roll of 1384–5 is a rare survival, illustrating that he distributed his livery to 135 men and women, including four minstrels who would have been members of his permanent household.[29] (A fragmentary household roll a few years later records an annual wage of £9 13s 4d for three minstrels.)[30] Earl Edward and his successors had extensive lands in Devon, Cornwall, and Somerset but their principal residence was at Tiverton Castle, little more than ten miles from Exeter. Once an impressive fortification on a steep cliff overlooking the River Exe, the castle has been truncated and domesticated over the centuries. Its north and west wings are now ruinous and the site of the medieval great hall seems likely to have been in the west wing adjacent to the solar block at the southwest corner of the site.[31]

The Courtenay earls had another residence about twenty miles west of

Exeter on the edge of Dartmoor, where there was good hunting to be had
in the forests around Okehampton Castle. The substantial ruin is impres-
sively situated on a rocky spur towering above the Okement Valley, just
off the high road into Cornwall. Here too there would have been entertainment in the great hall when the household was in residence.[32] From
these bases, the entertainers of successive generations of Courtenay earls
made local tours, primarily to Exeter, but also to Barnstaple on the north
coast of Devon and to Plymouth on the south.[33] The family fortunes took
a plunge in the fifteenth century, when their loyalty to the Lancastrian
royalty ultimately led, on and off, to confiscation of estates and violent
death on the battlefield or by execution.[34]

Martin Cherry has traced the Courtenays' gradual decline from their
dominant position as others found favour with the Crown and rival families acquired property and local prestige.[35] Even in the late fourteenth
century Earl Edward experienced some discomfort with the advent of the
earl of Huntingdon, John Holand, Richard II's half brother, who was
granted huge tracts of land in the county and was made admiral in the
west, among other offices, in 1389.[36] Holand was created 1st duke of
Exeter in 1397, a title that later descendants were to hold as well. Successive generations of the Holand family had a magnificent residence at
Dartington Hall, located about twenty-five miles southwest of Exeter and
a couple of miles off the main road into Totnes.

Dartington is one of the outstanding noble residences from the period to
survive, with many of its features intact, rescued from decay in the early
twentieth century by Leonard and Dorothy Elmhirst, a pair of enlightened
philanthropists ably assisted by William Weir, a sensitive architect of the
Arts and Crafts school.[37] Behind the modest entrance stretches a broad
quadrangle with the great hall and separate kitchen range at the south
end.[38] This courtyard (265' × 164') is the largest known in a private
residence before the sixteenth century.

Dartington provides us with a splendid example of the type of residen-
tial performance space that our medieval entertainers would have known,
to be compared with the indoor space in the Guildhall available to them in
Exeter. Entrance to the great hall through a three-storey vaulted porch led
into the screens passage where three arched doorways connected with the
pantry, buttery, and passage to the great kitchen, and a fourth, at the porch
end, led to the stairs giving access to rooms above. The hall is an impressive
room, approximately 69' × 38', undoubtedly innovative in its time, not
least for the placement of the enormous 17' fireplace behind the dais rather
than in the centre or along a side wall of the hall (Plate 2). Tall four-light

2. The great hall (high end) at Dartington. Reproduced from Christopher Hussey, 'Dartington Hall Devon: The Home of an Experiment – II,' *Country Life* 84 (3 September 1938), 229.

windows on both the north and south walls bring plenty of light into the space – what Pevsner describes as the 'weak window tracery' is mid-eighteenth century but otherwise the walls are part of the original late fourteenth-century fabric of John Holand's great hall.[39] The hall was roofless when the Elmhirsts acquired it so what we see today is the five-bay open timber roof replacement, with the screen designed by Weir. The original is known from an 1805 drawing which shows a more elaborate version – to quote Pevsner, 'an experimental stage in the development of the hammerbeam roof, probably just preceding Herland's remarkable technical and aesthetic achievement at Westminster Hall for Richard II (begun 1394).'[40] The medieval entertainment tradition established by the minstrels of the Holand family has not been lost. The hall has been revitalized as a performance and dining space through the Elmhirsts' generous vision – it is still possible to enjoy concerts in that fine acoustic space during the annual Dartington Music Festival.

Admittedly we can only speculate about medieval performance conditions in such halls, as we seldom have specific evidence even of demountable stage construction in either household or civic records. However, if the lord and other members of his family and guests were accustomed to sit at the high end of the hall, on the dais, how likely is it that they would have given pride of place there to mere performers? Alan H. Nelson's research and fortunate discoveries of descriptive documents for later but nonetheless comparable performances in Cambridge college halls suggest that demountable stages were placed near the upper end, but not on the dais.[41] Certainly not at the lower end where the honoured guests would have had to squint to get a view from their otherwise privileged seats at the opposite end. I would suggest that performances in such spaces were mounted with a keen awareness of social hierarchy and that plays especially were more likely staged 'in the round' but towards the upper end so that the host and his chosen companions could have the best view.[42]

To return to Exeter and the political forces at work there in the early fifteenth century, besides the several generations of the Courtenay and Holand families there were other local power-shakers patronizing performers paid by the city receivers. By the late 1420s, the cadet branch of the Courtenay family had risen in prominence and become rivals with the senior Courtenay line, now represented by Earl Edward's grandson, Thomas, still in his minority.[43] Sir Philip Courtenay was based at Powderham Castle, just a few miles south of Exeter. The late fourteenth-century limestone range of Sir Philip Courtenay's original manor house still stands behind the nineteenth-century west entrance tower but the interior has been substantially altered. A remarkable rococo grand staircase was inserted in the upper end of the great hall when it was partitioned in the mid-eighteenth century and both rooms now have a decidedly later character, although the three-arched stone service doorways remain at the former low end of the hall (now called the Marble Hall). Sir Philip, who held numerous local offices between 1427 and 1463 (the date of his death) patronized minstrels who appeared several times at Exeter in the 1430s when he was one of the most influential men in the county.[44] He also counted among his circle the patrons of other performers – a prominent west country landowner, William, Lord Botreaux of Botreaux Castle, near the border on the north coast of Cornwall (now only a mound on the outskirts of Boscastle);[45] Sir William Bonville of Shute in southeast Devon, emerging as another influential political leader in the county with connections through marriage to both the senior and junior branches of the Courtenay family;[46] Sir Nicholas Carew of Haccombe (which does not survive) about seventeen miles south of Exeter;[47] and perhaps most importantly, Sir Walter Hungerford, Sir Philip Courtenay's father-in-law and a major figure at court with strong southwest interests.[48] Lord Hungerford's principal residence was in the neighbouring county of Somerset in the northeast corner at the castle of Farleigh Hungerford, now a tranquil ruin. His minstrels were among the most frequently paid at Exeter in the late 1420s and early 1430s. There was also one female patron represented at Exeter: Margaret, Lady Harington, whose family lived at Hill's Court nearby and whose husband William belonged to another family linked by marriage with the Courtenay earls of Devon.[49]

Also on the entertainment list are two generations of the important Cornish landowners, the Bodrugans of Bodrugan Castle, now only a memory on the south coast; a loyal member of the earl of Devon's affinity, Sir Hugh Lutrell of Dunster Castle, about thirty-five miles north of Exeter, just over the Somerset border;[50] the lord chief justice of England, Sir William Hankeford, and his son, based at Annery on the northwest coast of Devon;[51] the Coplestones, members of the earl of Devon's affinity based at Copleston Hall a few miles northwest of Exeter;[52] and another member of the local gentry, Justice John Hals of Keynedon, south of Exeter and Totnes.[53] From further afield in the southwest came Lord Berkeley's minstrels from Berkeley Castle and Sir Maurice Berkeley's minstrels from Beverstone, both in Gloucestershire, as well as Sir Giles Daubeney's minstrels from Barrington and South Petherton, Somerset.

Not all local patrons were of equal political significance, of course, nor did they retain the same number of minstrels, pipers, or other performers in their households. In the Elizabethan era, civic accounts often reflected the status of such patrons by the level of rewards paid to their touring troupes – a civic ordinance at Chester in 1596, for example, laid out such a template for payments: 20 shillings for the queen's players and a much reduced reward of 6s 8d for those of noblemen.[54] The medieval receivers' accounts at Exeter are not so transparent although they may hint at an emerging system for establishing reward levels that correspond with a patron's status from the perspective of civic authorities. In the earliest years on record, there seems to have been little differentiation in the modest amounts given to performers below the rank of royal: for example, in 1413–14, joint payment of 12d was made to the minstrels of the Hankefords (father and son); Lord Camoys and Richard, brother of the duke of York; the duke of York; the earl of Arundel; and the duke of York (again) and the earl of Salisbury.[55] In one instance 4d was awarded to a single minstrel of the earl of Salisbury, the only specific evidence of a solo performer receiving payment and therefore a possible indication that the other troupes may have numbered three (at 4d each). Only the minstrels of the powerful Thomas Beaufort, earl of Dorset, and lord high admiral of England, rose to the higher reward level of 2s but we might also speculate that he patronized a larger troupe.[56] By contrast, the four minstrels of the king received 3s 4d as well as a breakfast costing 20d.

Two decades later an emerging trend may be detected by calculating the individual reward levels from helpfully specific joint payments to performers from a range of patrons with varying social and political status. The 1432–3 receivers' accounts break down as follows: on a rising scale of reward, which we may equate with the degree of perceived influence, 4d (cancelled) for John Broun, patronized by John Coplestone; 6d each (cancelled) for two minstrels of Lord Botreaux; 8d each to the earl of Warwick's three performers; 8d each for two minstrels of the countess of Westmorland; almost 12d each (from a total reward of 7s) for the largest troupe, eight performers of John of Lancaster, duke of Bedford; 12d each for the two minstrels of the earl of Devon; 12d each for two minstrels of Richard, duke of York; and 20d for a single performer attached to Sir Philip Courtenay's locally ascendant household to be compared with 20d for a single performer of Humphrey of Gloucester, lord protector of the realm and duke of Gloucester.[57]

Some of the visiting troupes that were rewarded, such as those of the ambitious duke of York, had a wider range of travel, but the Devon-based performers seem to have been just that, conservative in their travels, even introverted in their county perspective. Perhaps this is not surprising for some of the lesser nobility, but even the troupes of the powerful Courtenay family were settled in the territory where their patrons' greatest landed interests lay.[58] There is no evidence yet found in the REED collections that they travelled beyond Devon, apart from an isolated appearance of the earl of Devon's minstrels at York in 1449.[59] Only those of the other great magnate family, the Holand dukes of Exeter, ranged more widely, reflecting the broader national interests of their patrons. In the late fourteenth and fifteenth centuries the Holands had lands and offices in many counties as well as residences elsewhere, notably Coldharbour in London. Perhaps the only surprise in their case is that the 1st duke of Exeter chose to build his primary residence so splendidly at Dartington, far from court. There has been some doubt about whether the first duke's heir, another John, spent much time at Dartington.[60] He began a long military career in 1415, just out of his minority, and only came into full possession of his southwestern estates upon his mother's death in 1425. For the next decade, however, his minstrels were among the most frequently and generously rewarded at Exeter and indeed while Holand held the title earl of Huntingdon they can be found only once outside the county of Devon, at Cambridge.[61] This suggests that he may have been in residence at Dartington for periods when he was not abroad although the household accounts that might give solid evidence of his whereabouts do not survive. After Holand regained the dukedom of Exeter in 1443/4 and subsequently assumed the offices of lord high admiral and constable of the Tower, his minstrels can be tracked elsewhere in the West Midlands and as far north as York, a noticeable shift that may be connected with the patron's increasing influence and responsibilities away from his original home. Certainly local recognition of his status had existed in Devon long before, if the payments to his minstrels are any measure.[62]

The story at Barnstaple, where late medieval civic accounts also survive, is much the same, as well as complementary, in covering some years when the Exeter receivers' accounts suppressed their relevant gifts and grants. From 1454 until 1484 the Barnstaple receivers steadily recorded payments to visiting performers in their external expenses section.[63] Locally based troupes patronized by Devon and Cornwall families with residences situated nearby mixed almost equally with the performers from royal or noble households whose lords had broader national interests. Some of the names do not appear on the Exeter list: joining the roll call of influential local landowners are the Beaumonts of Heanton, a few miles to the northeast; the Bourchiers, Lords FitzWarin of Tawstock just south of Barnstaple; the JP John Crocker of Lyneham a few miles east of Plymouth; the Dinhams of Nutwell, a few miles south of Exeter; the Pomerys of Berry Pomeroy near Totnes; John Sapcote of Bampton on the main road from Bridgwater to Barnstaple; and on the north coast of Cornwall, the Arundells of Lanherne and the Grenvilles of Stowe. But the performers of these families have not surfaced in records beyond Devon, however active they may have been in their own region. In a period during which Exeter records run dry, there is also confirmation that some of the familiar families continued their arts patronage: the Bodrugans of Bodrugan; the Bonvilles of Shute (Cecily, Lady Bonville, another female patron); the Courtenays of Powderham; and the Holand dukes of Exeter.

To conclude, the available evidence suggests that before 1485 local cultural activity in the southwest seems to have emanated more from the households of prominent nobility and gentry in the region than from parishes and guilds. Ironically, perhaps, evidence of this performance tradition typically survives in the towns where the patrons' local political interests focused. Two of the Devon patron families belonged to the higher nobility and with a potentially wider sphere of influence, their performance troupes might have been expected to surface in other parts of the country. The Courtenay minstrels, however, seem to have circulated close to home and probably between the several family residences. Of related interest is the evidence that the records for performance payments offer for tracing the diversification of local political influences in Devon as the Courtenay earls gradually lost their supremacy in the fifteenth century, even before the senior branch of the family died out during the War of the Roses. The troupes of the other noble family at the top of the social ladder, the Holand dukes of Exeter, gradually developed a more wide-ranging itinerary, but they had a pre-eminent home performance space in the remarkable hall at Dartington, a great hall of sophisticated design, worthy of comparison with those of the royal court. But whether the venue was the generously proportioned Dartington, the more modest manor house hall of a member of the local gentry like John Coplestone, or the Exeter Guildhall, the playing spaces which can be tracked for these performers were indoor halls, either civic or private, rather than the outdoor venues favoured for ceremonial events sponsored by urban authorities where wider public display had its own civic and economic motives.[64]

NOTES

1 John M. Wasson, ed., *Devon*, REED (Toronto: University of Toronto Press, 1986).
2 Wasson, *Devon*, 70–1. All the boroughs except Tavistock have dramatic records dating from before 1558.
3 See Wasson, *Devon*, 89 for the receivers' payment for a 'lus*um* Robyn Hood.' See also the earlier, somewhat ambiguous reference to the 'lusorib*us* qui

luserunt ante Maij' in 1419 (86). Later in the fifteenth century St John's Bow churchwardens' accounts begin their sporadic record of Robin Hood receipts and expenses (108, 118, 145).

4 Wasson, *Devon*, 71.

5 *Early Theatre* 6.1 (2003), 15–34.

6 Lawrence M. Clopper explores the perhaps surprising lack of evidence for locally produced drama and related large-scale entertainment yielded from REED's survey of dramatic records for many urban centres in his *Drama, Play, and Game: English Festive Culture in the Medieval and Early Modern Period* (Chicago: University of Chicago Press, 2001), especially 113–21.

7 Wasson, *Devon*, 86. See also the section on Patrons and Travelling Companies, 455–529, for the details of itinerant entertainers and their patrons, and for the most comprehensive updating of the data, see the new REED *Patrons and Performances Web Site* (http://link.library.utoronto.ca/reed/).

8 See, for example, Abigail Ann Young's important series of articles drawing on detailed evidence from the REED series: 'Plays and Players: The Latin Terms for Performance,' *REED Newsletter* 9.2 (1984): 56–62, and *REED Newsletter* 10.1 (1985): 9–16, and 'Minstrels and Minstrelsy: Household Retainers or Instrumentalists?' *REED Newsletter* 20.1 (1995): 11–17; and Suzanne R. Westfall, *Patrons and Performance: Early Tudor Household Revels* (Oxford: Clarendon Press, 1990).

9 The evidence in Bodleian Library, MS Eng. Hist. B. 208 is extensively discussed in Westfall, *Patrons and Performance*.

10 See further Bridget Cherry and Nikolaus Pevsner, *Devon*, The Buildings of England (Harmondsworth: Penguin Books, 1989), 401–2; S.R. Blaylock, 'Exeter Guildhall,' *Devon Archaeological Society Proceedings* 48 (1990): 123–78; and H. Lloyd Parry, *The History of the Exeter Guildhall and the Life Within* (Exeter: Exeter County Council, 1936). The Guildhall dates back on the present site to the late twelfth century but it was extensively remodelled in the 1460s and 1480s. Much of the visible fabric dates from this period although the panelling is late sixteenth century. The present measurements of the hall are 66.5′ × 24.9′. Like some other public halls, the Guildhall did not have a minstrels' gallery in the low end in the medieval period – the present gallery is a mid-nineteenth century renovation, so performers from the fourteenth century onwards, if they used the hall, would have entertained on the ground-floor level. As with other venues cited in this essay, fuller architectural details and images are available in the Venues section of the REED *Patrons and Performances Web Site* (cited above in note 7).

11 Wasson, *Devon*, 92.

12 See, for example, two years after the payment to players in the Guildhall, a similar formulation: 'lusorib*us* ludent*ibus* in domo Maioris coram Maiore ex dono xvj d' (Wasson, *Devon*, 93).

13 Barnstaple's first guildhall was built ca. 1350, replaced in 1549 after the town corporation purchased the guildhall of St George the Martyr in the High Street (J.R. Chanter and Thos. Wainwright, *Reprint of the Barnstaple Records* [Barnstaple: A.E. Barnes, 1900], 2:32).

14 See, for example, Peter Happé, *English Drama before Shakespeare* (London and New York: Longman, 1999), 187.

15 For further details, see the REED *Patrons and Performances Web Site* and volumes in the REED series.

16 See Robert Tittler, *Architecture and Power: The Town Hall and the English Urban Community c. 1500–1640* (Oxford: Clarendon Press, 1991), 143–4.

17 See, for example, the detailed comparison of the Common Halls at Norwich and York with Hardwick Hall and Christ Church Oxford in Scott McMillin and Sally-Beth MacLean, *The Queen's Men and Their Plays* (Cambridge: Cambridge University Press, 1998), 71–82.

18 See further McMillin and MacLean, *Queen's Men*, 206, note 16.

19 See C.M. Woolgar, *The Great Household in Late Medieval England* (New Haven and London: Yale University Press, 1999), 26–9, and Westfall, *Patrons and Performance*, passim.

20 There is little evidence of touring professional troupes in Cornwall although numerous local parish dancers and players were on the local routes. The fifteenth- and sixteenth-century borough accounts surviving for Launceston and the badly deteriorated general receivers' accounts for Bodmin have yielded little (see Rosalind Conklin Hays and C.E. McGee/Sally L. Joyce and Evelyn S. Newlyn, eds, *Dorset/Cornwall*, REED (Toronto: University of Toronto Press, 1999), 469–73, 489–95). In Somerset before 1558 the Bridgwater common bailiffs' accounts provide the primary evidence, albeit sporadically, from 1448 onwards (see James Stokes with Robert J. Alexander, eds, *Somerset including Bath*, REED (Toronto: University of Toronto Press, 1996), 1:41–6 and 2:520–1).

21 Rosemary Horrox, 'Urban Patronage and Patrons in the Fifteenth Century,' in *Patronage: The Crown and the Provinces in Later Medieval England*, ed. Ralph A. Griffiths (Gloucester: Alan Sutton Humanities Press, 1981), 147. Horrox notes (148), for example, that Exeter cultivated both the Courtenays and the Bonvilles despite the intensity of their mid-fifteenth-century feud; certainly the rewards to the minstrels of the earls of Devon and of the Bonvilles and their affinity throughout the period are a likely expression of this cultivation.

22 Richard Britnell, 'The Economy of British Towns,' in *The Cambridge Urban History of Britain*, vol. 1. *600–1540*, ed. D.M. Palliser (Cambridge: Cambridge University Press, 2000), 329.

23 For a discussion of the southwestern road network and its connection with touring performance routes, see my essay 'At the End of the Road: An Overview of Southwestern Touring Circuits,' *Early Theatre* 6.2 (2003): 17–32.

24 Jennifer Kermode, 'The Greater Towns 1300–1540,' in *The Cambridge Urban History of Britain*, vol. 1. *600–1540*, ed. D.M. Palliser (Cambridge: Cambridge University Press, 2000), 441. For the process of Exeter's incorporation as a county in its own right, see Joyce Youings, *Early Tudor Exeter: The Founders of the County of the City* (Exeter: University of Exeter Press, 1974).

25 Wasson, *Devon*, xl.

26 Wasson, *Devon*, 98.

27 Wasson, *Devon*, 85.

28 M. Cherry, 'The Courtenay Earls of Devon: The Formation and Disintegration of a Late Medieval Aristocratic Affinity,' *Southern History* 1 (1979): 71.

29 Cherry, 'Courtenay Earls of Devon,' 72, and Wasson, *Devon*, 306.

30 Wasson, *Devon*, 306, for 1389–90.

31 For a nineteenth-century plan showing the remains, with the likely site of the great hall highlighted, see the REED *Patrons and Performances Web Site*, Venues pages for Tiverton.

32 For comparative interest, the hall's measurements are approximately 34' × 23'. The Courtenay earls also had a castle, which does not survive, at Colcombe near the east Devon border.

33 Relevant receivers' accounts do not begin until the last decade of the fifteenth century but the earl of Devon's minstrels are among the first recorded at Plymouth (Wasson, *Devon*, 213).

34 The senior Courtenay line died out in 1471 when Sir John, the 8th earl, died in the Battle of Tewkesbury.

35 Cherry, 'Courtenay Earls of Devon.'

36 Cherry, 'Courtenay Earls of Devon,' 90.

37 See further Anthony Emery, *Dartington Hall* (Oxford: Clarendon Press, 1970) and Victor Bonham-Carter, *Dartington Hall: The Formative Years: 1925–1957* (Dulverton, Somerset: Exmoor Press, 1970).

38 Cherry and Pevsner, *Devon*, 311.

39 Cherry and Pevsner, *Devon*, 312.

40 Cherry and Pevsner, *Devon*, 312. For details of the carpenter Hugh Herland's roof at Westminster Hall, see Simon Bradley and Nikolaus Pevsner, *London 6: Westminster*, The Buildings of England (New Haven and London: Yale University Press, 2003), 230. The 1805 drawing by George Saunders of the

original roof is reproduced in Christopher Hussey's article, 'Dartington Hall Revisited–I,' *Country Life* 145 (23 January 1969), 179, fig. 6.

41 See Alan H. Nelson, *Early Cambridge Theatres: College, University, and Town Stages, 1464–1720* (Cambridge: Cambridge University Press, 1994), 16–60, for full discussion and diagrams of the Queen's and Trinity College hall stages in particular. For a common view of lower end hall staging, see J. Leeds Barroll, Alexander Leggatt, Richard Hosley, and Alvin Kernan, *Revels History of Drama in English*, vol. 3. *1576–1613* (London: Methuen, 1975), 128–30.

42 It is worth noting that in the surviving late sixteenth-century stage sketch of the Swan Theatre in London, the lords' viewing room was above the stage rather than below it. For the sketch, see R.A. Foakes, *Illustrations of the English Stage 1580–1642* (London: Scolar Press, 1985), 52–3.

43 Earl Thomas's struggle to regain the regional dominance that his grandfather, Earl Edward, had enjoyed is discussed in Cherry, 'Courtenay Earls of Devon,' and his 'The Struggle for Power in Mid-Fifteenth-Century Devonshire,' in *Patronage: The Crown and the Provinces in Later Medieval England*, ed. Ralph A. Griffiths (Gloucester: Alan Sutton Humanities Press, 1981), 123–44. His long minority, 1422–33, was followed by the considerable obstacle presented by his mother's residual control of about two-thirds of his estate until her death in 1441 (Cherry, 'Struggle for Power,' 125).

44 See further Cherry, 'Courtenay Earls of Devon,' 92–7, and Josiah C. Wedgwood and Anne D. Holt, *History of Parliament: Biographies of the Members of the Commons House 1439–1509* (London: HMSO, 1936), 229–30.

45 See Cherry, 'Courtenay Earls of Devon,' 96, on the migration of William, 3rd Lord Botreaux into the orbit of Philip Courtenay from the earl of Devon's sphere.

46 Bonville, later created 1st Lord Bonville in 1448/9, had close family links with the Courtenays. His second wife was the daughter of Earl Edward and his daughter wed Sir Philip Courtenay's son William. After his second marriage he was appointed to many royal commissions, eventually becoming steward of the duchy of Cornwall. See further *The House of Commons 1386–1421*, vol. 2, *Members A-D*, ed. J.S. Roskell, Linda Clark, and Carole Rawcliffe, The History of Parliament (Stroud: Alan Sutton, 1992), 284–8, and Cherry, 'Struggle for Power,' 131ff. The service wing of the Bonvilles' unfortified manor house at Shute remains, in a now truncated house characterized by features added in the Tudor period by subsequent owners.

47 Sir Nicholas Carew was also connected with the Courtenays through his wife Joan, the daughter of Sir Hugh Courtenay, second son of Earl Edward. For

the Carews' change in affiliation in the early fifteenth century, see Cherry, 'Courtenay Earls of Devon,' 96–7.

48 See further *The House of Commons 1386–1421*, vol. 3, *Members E–O*, ed. J.S. Roskell, Linda Clark, and Carole Rawcliffe, History of Parliament (Stroud: Alan Sutton, 1992), 446–53, and Cherry, 'Courtenay Earls of Devon,' 93–7. During the period when Sir Walter Hungerford's minstrels were recorded at Exeter, he was chamberlain and chief steward of the duchy of Lancaster estates south of Trent and treasurer of the exchequer, among other offices.

49 William de Harington, 5th Lord Harington, was the brother of John Harington, husband of Earl Edward's daughter Elizabeth. See further the *Complete Peerage* and Cherry, 'Courtenay Earls of Devon,' 96–7.

50 Dunster Castle was substantially renovated in later centuries and in its present form witnesses more to the romantic Gothic aspirations of the mid-Victorians than to its fifteenth-century incarnation. See further G.T. Clark, 'Dunster Castle,' *Archaeological Journal* 36 (1879), 309–20, and Richard Haslam, 'Dunster Castle,' *Country Life* 181 (16 July 1987), 125–7; (23 July 1987), 102–6.

51 Medieval Annery is long gone, its early nineteenth-century replacement demolished in 1958. See further Rosemary Anne Lauder, *Vanished Houses of North Devon* (Callington: Penwell, 1981), 22–32.

52 The Coplestones' hall was near the site of its eighteenth-century replacement but little is known of its architecture.

53 The Hals's cross-wing manor house at Keynedon was rebuilt in the early sixteenth century on the same site (now known as Keynedon Barton): for extensive details, see Robert Waterhouse, 'Keynedon Barton, Sherford, Kingsbridge,' *Proceedings of the Devon Archaeological Society* 58 (2000), 127–200.

Many details of the titles, offices, and properties of all Devon patrons can be found on the REED *Patrons and Performances Web Site*. See further James Whetter, *The Bodrugans: A Study of a Cornish Medieval Knightly Family* (St Austell: Lyfrow Trelyspen, 1995) for Sir William (d. 1441) and Sir Henry (d. 1487) Bodrugan. Both had Devon connections. Sir William was a member of the commission for piracy in the 1430s when his minstrels visited Exeter and Sir Henry's first wife was Joan, daughter of Sir Philip Courtenay of Powderham. Sir Hugh Luttrell, whose mother was a daughter of the 2nd earl of Devon, was a liveried member of the earl of Devon's affinity, appointed joint keeper of the warrens, chases, and parks of the earldom during Earl Thomas's minority in the 1420s (see further *House of Commons 1386–1421*, 3:655–60). For the lawyer John Coplestone (d. 1458), see *House of Commons 1386–1421*,

2:651–3 and Cherry, 'Struggle for Power,' 129; at the time when his minstrel appeared in Exeter, Coplestone was involved as either arbitrator or negotiator in the dispute between the city and the dean and chapter.

54 Lawrence M. Clopper, ed., *Chester*, REED (Toronto: University of Toronto Press, 1979), 184.

55 Wasson, *Devon*, 83–4.

56 Beaufort was to become duke of Exeter in 1416 so it is not surprising that his minstrels continued to find special favour with the Exeter authorities in subsequent years until their patron's death in 1426. See further Wasson, *Devon*, 87–9.

57 Wasson, *Devon*, 93–4.

58 For the territorial grounding of the Courtenays, see further Chris Given-Wilson, *The English Nobility in the Late Middle Ages: The Fourteenth Century Political Community* (London and New York: Routledge and Kegan Paul, 1987), 163–6.

59 Alexandra F. Johnston and Margaret Rogerson, eds, *York*, REED (Toronto: University of Toronto Press, 1979), 1:76.

60 See Emery, *Dartington Hall*, 61, and Michael Stansfield, 'John Holland, Duke of Exeter and Earl of Huntingdon (d. 1447) and the Costs of the Hundred Years War,' in *Profit, Piety and the Professions in Later Medieval England*, ed. Michael Hicks (Gloucester: Alan Sutton, 1990), 110.

61 For details see Wasson, *Devon*, 88, 90, 91, 92, 93, 95, 96, and Alan H. Nelson, ed., *Cambridge*, REED (Toronto: University of Toronto Press, 1989), 1:25.

62 Henry, the 4th duke (1447–61) held numerous offices under Henry VI, chiefly lord high admiral of England from 1445/6 to 1460. His minstrels travelled more widely than those of his predecessors but after he was attainted in 1461 they appeared only once again, in 1462, at Barnstaple, where there were evidently some loyalists to the Lancastrian cause who continued to honour his lapsed title.

63 See Wasson, *Devon*, 30–6. There is also one relevant stray account for 1435–6.

64 For an informed discussion of this subject, see Alexandra F. Johnston, 'The City as Patron: York,' in *Shakespeare and Theatrical Patronage in Early Modern England*, ed. Paul Whitfield White and Suzanne Westfall (Cambridge: Cambridge University Press, 2002), 150–75.

Coming Home: Provincial Gentry Families: Their Performers, Their Great Halls, Their Entertainments, and REED

ALAN SOMERSET

My main title reflects, perhaps a little ironically, upon past REED policy for editors over the question of household records. I recall that when I began research into the records of Shropshire and Staffordshire, editorial forays into household accounts were discouraged unless the collections were held in public repositories. Difficulties over access, lack of cataloguing, poor conditions of preservation, primitive photocopying facilities, and negotiations for permissions – these and other factors were offered as reasons to dissuade one from pursuing privately held household records. And how far could one pursue them, given that many of the more prominent families had residences in more than a single county? An important supposition was that to launch oneself upon these largely uncharted waters would prevent the timely completion of county collections. These policies, warnings, and suppositions came to be questioned, ignored, and finally discarded in favour of whole-hearted seeking after household records as the project has proceeded – REED has indeed 'come home,' and the results have been immensely valuable. One factor that has facilitated this is the growth in the reputation of REED. In early days, a researcher needed patience to explain the relevance of an obscure research project operating from afar ('Canada, you say? I have a brother in Vancouver ...'). Now, even curators of the more obscure local archives and museums as well as of private collections of family accounts are well aware of the project's scope and importance, and this eases access greatly. The information that re-searchers are uncovering in private collections is altering our sense of the social landscape of rural England.

One of the elements that has helped familiarize REED's work has been the REED *Patrons and Performances Web Site* (http://link.library .utoronto.ca/reed). This is now well past the 'pilot' phase, and presents data from a growing variety of county and borough collections. Its final design details are still being refined as we move towards our goal of presenting the full dataset, covering the patron-related entertainers in the first eighteen volumes in the REED series. Still to come after that will be the data in recently published or forthcoming collections (*Sussex*; *Kent: Diocese of Canterbury*; *Oxford*; etc ... oh! the joys of retirement ...). As well, the data about troupes for which no patron was recorded, currently approximately 25 per cent of the total, will need to be incorporated. The website is much more than an index of REED data; reflecting REED's recent enthusiasm for household records, the website research has energetically pursued information not in REED collections, about patrons, their residences, playing companies, and connections The site will also provide capacities to isolate, analyse, and compare data. This essay will reflect on some issues and themes that are arising as this research is continued, first by pursuing a comparative analysis that became possible only through the flexibility and power of the website.

At the time of writing, the database contained the names of 611 patrons, of whom 478 were not 'shadowed' (that is, they appear on the public website). The shadowed ones are available only on our private administrative website while they are being investigated and worked upon, but I have included 'shadowed' data in the analysis here. What is an 'average' patron? My profile of an 'average' patron is gathered by analysis of the numbers of performance events that we have recorded for each patron. The patrons can be further classified as patrons of musicians, patrons of players, etc.; I take it that we are interested in all kinds of theatrical entertainment, so I have used this inclusive category, and will also separate out the numbers for players. Looking at the range of numbers, the distribution of patronage is very uneven. There are at present a total of 478 unshadowed patrons linked to performances in the database; of these, 220 patrons are linked only to single performance records. We may assume that the number of paid performances by these troupes should be larger than the records show (because records are, after all, always incomplete), and further we may assume that the number of records for these troupes will grow as the databases are completed. We may assume a lot of things, of course, but for the present we have to deal with the numbers we have, and those numbers suggest that patronage was widespread but intermittent. A little under 50 per cent of the patrons are found only once. This remains true even if you look at the later period, so it is not true that the singular patrons occur in the fourteenth and fifteenth centuries only, when the records are more sparse and performance activities not as widespread. If we look at the 216 patrons who were born after 1525, 102 of them occur in performance records only once. In fact, confining ourselves to the forty-seven patrons born in 1575 or after, twenty-three of them are likewise singular. The proportion remains approximately the same, across the period: slightly under 50 per cent of patrons are found only once in the records.

We might assume that these 'singular' patrons, from whatever period, are the nobodies of the world of patronage, and it is true that there are some obscure figures among them, persons for whom we can learn no more than the name in the record. But other singular patrons are not obscure – an example is Sir Francis Drake, for whom we have far more details. Probably his musicians accompanied him on his numerous voyages; all we know about them on land is that they apparently are recorded in Plymouth on one occasion. Because the record may not be for a performance the website allows one to pursue further details, to learn that the payment was for a hue and cry, but the musicians presumably got away. An intriguing glimpse at a singular patron, who was hardly an unknown, obscure individual.

On the other hand, there existed some patrons whose names are linked to more than the average number of performances but who are, from the point of view of national importance, public offices, etc., really very obscure. My favourite example (because I am currently editing the REED material in his household records) is Lord Henry Berkeley (1534–1613), who stands eleventh in the count at present, linked to forty-four records of performance, or fifth in the count with thirty-nine records of performance by his players. That is more records than there are for the King's Men, and that number will certainly grow when Berkeley's own household records are factored in. His was a very active troupe, but Berkeley lived a provincial life of obscurity. He lived well beyond his means, held a few minor offices, was involved in extensive litigation to recover the alienated Berkeley properties, was addicted to card-playing (at which he usually lost), and was an avid hunter, all over southern England – his chief interest. His contemporaries nicknamed him 'lord Henry the Harmless'; presumably they did not consult the deer population. Berkeley's life is not recorded in the *Oxford Dictionary of National Biography*.

With Berkeley, let us move now to the other end of the scale, to the 'high-end' patrons whose names occur numerous times in the records of performance events. It is surprising to learn how few there are. Looking at all types of performers, twenty-one patrons are found more than thirty times, and of these only five occur more than sixty-five times. Four of these were monarchs, and the fifth a royal favourite:

Queen Elizabeth (1533–1603): 212 occurrences
King Henry VIII (1491–1547): 184
King Charles I (1600–49): 135
Robert Dudley, earl of Leicester (1532–88): 83
King James I (1566–1625): 66

The rankings and numbers change if one limits consideration to them as patrons of players. Eleven patrons are found more than thirty times, and three, Queen Elizabeth, King Charles, and Robert Dudley occur more than seventy times. Here are the names on the preceding list, reorganized in order of patronage of players:

Queen Elizabeth: 154
King Charles I: 94
Robert Dudley, earl of Leicester: 81
King James I: 37
King Henry VIII: 25

The large changes in the numbers for Henry VIII and James I arise from the numerous appearances by their musicians. The Patrons website, as you see, can significantly augment our store of information about the distribution of early patronage by allowing us to isolate and analyse the data quickly.

Between patrons of performers of numerous events and those many whose players occur only once, what is an average patron? If one looks at all types of performers, the average patron's name is found 6.4 times, whereas if one focuses on patrons linked to players, the average is 7.9 (the reason for the apparent discrepancy is that there are over twice as many 'singular' patrons of non-theatrical performances). Let us look at a sample of these average patrons with six to eight records apiece. I want to look at these 'average' patrons with regard to their family and kinship relationships, their public offices, the geographical range of their companies' performances in relation to the areas of the patrons' influence, and any other information we can glean about their habits that will fill in the 'average' picture. In the course of doing this I will be demonstrating *how* the *Patrons and Performances Web Site* can be used to mine for information about patrons. Everyone is well aware of the new on-line *Oxford Dictionary of National Biography* (if your university subscribes to the site), and how easily biographies can be found, read, and printed out. Our *Patrons and Performances* site, although it presents much information that might be contained in a *DNB* entry, is also capable of presenting information about performance events and (if a patron owned any) about residences and performance venues. As well, it contains information about hundreds of patrons of little national or regional political significance, who never made it into the *DNB*.

Thirteen patrons of players are recorded six, seven, or eight times. Some of these were men whose personal circumstances may explain the paucity of patron records. For example, Thomas Beaufort, duke of Exeter (1377–1426), had minstrels whose records occur on six occasions at Exeter, five of them during his last years when he was in failing health. When he was in his prime, Exeter was away fighting much of the time, from the battle of Shrewsbury in 1403 through the Welsh campaigns against Owen Glendower, the sieges of Harfleur (1415), Rouen (1419), and other French campaigns. No time for minstrelsy. Another exclusion is Ralph Neville, 2nd earl of Westmorland (ca. 1407–84), whose six patronage records all occur before 1449; sometime early in the 1450s he became mentally incompetent, and presumably those who had him in their care dismissed his performing company.

I will look at a selection of six patrons from my list, whose personal circumstances do not preclude continued patronage. Some of these occur early, some later, some are in the *DNB* and others more obscure. What common elements can we detect? I begin with Sir Thomas Denys (1477–1561), whose *DNB* entry describes him as an 'administrator'; this is illuminated by a glance at his eighty-one offices on the website (mostly based in Devon and the southwest) where we see the career of an 'administrator' pass before our eyes. He might have been a model for Justice Shallow, a local bureaucrat whose career was devoted to promulgating the rule of the central government. It is perhaps no surprise, given Denys's connections, that when we retrieve events patronized by his troupe of minstrels, we find that their activities were concentrated on Devon. And there is another significant concentration of activity that we should notice here; all the minstrels' performances occurred between 1530 and 1539, with all but one of them being between 1530 and 1533–4, a single minstrel appearing alone in 1538–9. The records do not cease after 1538–9, nor did Denys; but his name ceases to appear; Sir Thomas Denys was not a lifelong patron, but a short-term one, and one can only wonder why. Next, of higher rank but lesser national importance (not in the *DNB*) is Sir William Compton, earl of Northampton (1572–1630), a Midlands magnate who held a number of offices in that area, many of them no doubt administered by deputies, and one of national importance as a privy councillor from 1629. He lived in a higher style than Sir Thomas Denys (he died £10,000 in debt), and he was patron of a wider variety of entertainers, but only of one kind at a time. Significantly, all the performances are at Coventry, the centre of Compton's influence; the confluence of patronage and influence is again notable. He had players in 1605 and 1608, a bearward on four occasions between 1611–12 and 1615–16, and waits in 1622. One may wonder what Compton, as lord lieutenant of Warwickshire and Coventry, was doing as a patron of players in 1605 and 1610, because such patronage became illegal in 1604 – but Compton had plenty of company among non-royal patrons after 1604. He does not appear to have been a long-term patron to any particular type of performer; again, we can only wonder why. My next example is William Stanley, 3rd Baron Monteagle (1527–81), another 'average' patron, a member of a minor cadet branch of the Stanley family. Perhaps because of the Stanley family's wider connections (as Lords Strange and earls of Derby), William Stanley's troupes' events are a little more widely scattered although they are centred mainly on the north. The pattern of his troupes' activities (if 'pattern' is applicable to such scattered records) reflects that of Sir William Compton: his bearward was rewarded in 1562, 1566, 1567, and 1577, while his players appeared in 1573–4, 1580, and 1581. My next example produces a similarly remarkable concentration: the records of William Bourchier, earl of Bath (1557–1623) are remarkable. He began to become active in public life in the local administration of the southwest when he was in his mid-thirties, filling such offices as JP, lord lieutenant, and recorder from 1584. The events recorded for his players show similar clustering; they are mainly concentrated upon the southwest, Bourchier's centre of influence and residence, and they are also exclusively clustered in his youth, just graduated from Cambridge University, in the period between 1576 and 1578. It is likely that Bourchier was under the jurisdiction of the Court of Wards from his father's death (when he was three) until he attained his majority in 1575; his players begin to appear a year later. But apparently, for some reason, Bourchier decided to give up as a patron of the performing arts before his twenty-first birthday, and so he acted as a patron for only a short time and in a limited locale. Finally, we have a pair of northern barons, father and son: Philip Wharton, 3rd Baron Wharton (1555–1625), and his son Philip, 4th Baron Wharton (1613–96). Both men's activities were centred upon Cumberland and Westmorland, where they both lived at Wharton Hall, presumably a performance venue. The activities of their company of players (I presume it is the same company, passed from father to son) likewise centred upon Cumberland and Westmorland. Again, one wonders why these men, who held offices in the legal administration of the region, were patrons of a company of players when, after all, such patronage was supposedly forbidden by the 1604 Act of Parliament.

What can we conclude from this list of 'average' unremarkable patron activities? These were men of some power and influence, although limited in geographical scope and national importance (only two of the six appear in the *DNB*). They emulated their more powerful and influential betters by becoming patrons of performers, and these their 'average' troupes also operated, usually, within limited areas and sometimes only for limited periods of time. The geographical limitations are easy to explain, while the brevity of these patrons' sponsorship of playing troupes cries out for explanation. Why, to take an example, did Bourchier apparently give up patronage in 1578–9? Did he read John Stockwell's *A Sermon Preached at Paul's Cross* (1578), suddenly see the light, and enrol in a twelve-step program? Or were Bourchier's players perhaps so incompetent that their patron tired of cringing at the reviews? Or perhaps, less facetiously, do we have some evidence here to suggest that patronage of a troupe of players carried financial or other obligations that could make it seem onerous? We cannot know. Whatever may be the answer, the *Patrons and Performances Web Site* has brought forward the evidence that necessitates the question.

The foregoing analysis has immersed us in the lives of obscure, but not insignificant provincial magnates and gentry. A question that has doubtless occurred to many readers, perusing these scattered records of performance, is how these companies made a living? Three to five performance payments, scattered over a number of years, does not provide a steady income! While one might suggest that there existed many other such records, now not extant, in civic collections, this does not provide a sufficient answer, because we cannot safely assume a limitless unknown array of records from a sparse existing scattering of remains. I would like to suggest that an answer might well have been found in the household accounts of provincial families. I want to turn next to another avenue of investigation into such people, to suggest other ways in which their discoverable activities, venues, and connections can yield important information. Anyone who has travelled in England has experienced what have been called 'the stately homes of England' – the imposing castles and palaces of the royal families and the (formerly) very rich aristocrats. A

glance through English history impresses us with the power and prominence of many titled families whose importance in the affairs of the nation
was immense. The Dudleys, earls of Leicester and Warwick, Robert
Devereux, earl of Essex, Henry Herbert, earl of Pembroke, lord president
of the Council in the Marches of Wales, the lord chamberlain, the lord
admiral – these were powerful and influential men, whose entertainers
fulfilled political mandates as they travelled extensively through many
parts of the realm.

   Many of the aristocracy and gentry had spheres of influence far more
minor, but I want to propose that they are of great importance in thinking
about performance activities, and about indoor hall theatres like the
Blackfriars, and its country cousins. By far the majority of families (famous, infamous, and unknown) have left us no surviving records, so we
can say nothing about their activities, whereas, in contrast, we often encounter well-preserved and extensive runs of civic records. Although unfortunate, this is not unusual. Civic records are the collective memory of a
body politic, and their preservation ensures a record of what transpired
during previous administrations. Private household records are of a different nature. Any family that had household servants (particularly a steward) spending family income would expect detailed records to be kept, so
that at the end of the quarter, the half-year, or the year the accounts could
be cast and a clear idea of receipts and expenses gained. But there the
matter, for most families, would end. I expect that few readers will have
preserved cheque books and accounting records from, say, 1995, only a
few years ago (the usual income-tax requirement for preservation of records
is only seven years). When materials like this cease to be important they
are usually discarded because, inherently, they are not of further interest
and they require space for storage. We can only be grateful for those few
families that, for whatever reasons, preserved their family accounting and
other papers.

   I will look here at five minor aristocratic or 'gentry' provincial familes:
the Sheldons of Beoley, Warwickshire; the Newdigates of Arbury,
Warwickshire; the Walmesleys of Dunkenhalgh Hall, Lancashire; the
Puckerings of Priory Park, Warwick; and the Berkeleys of Berkeley Castle,
Gloucestershire, and Caludon Castle, near Coventry.[1] None of these families was of national importance (all well below the radar screens), but all
lived in comfortable obscurity in their family seats. In common, they have
all left household and other accounts, usually written by their stewards,
which tell us much about household activities. All were patrons of entertainers, in some sense. It is not the invariable rule that such families

welcomed troupes of players at their homes – the Sheldons and Newdigates paid musicians only, but paid them in substantial numbers. (The Newdigates enjoyed theatre in London, and purchased many playbooks.) Their household records show that three families (the Walmesleys, Berkeleys, and Puckerings) were active sponsors of performances and regularly welcomed players, and the Berkeleys actively sponsored a troupe of players. I wish to look a little more closely at them, because I think they were representative of many other families whose experiences included going to the theatre in London during visits there, and enjoying drama at home, particularly during festive seasons. The more we learn about such families, the more we realize that performances found in civic records (about which much has already been recorded and written) are just the tip of a much larger iceberg, and that the study of household performance activities is crucial to understanding the whole picture of professional provincial entertainment and of indoor hall performances.

These families all lived in great houses. Three of these survive intact, although perhaps altered by later renovations or changes of use: Dunkenhalgh Hall is now a hotel; Berkeley Castle survives intact as the seat of the Berkeley family; and Arbury Hall, much rebuilt, is the seat of Lord Daventry, descendant of the Newdigates from the seventeenth century. Two houses survive imperfectly or in traces: the ruins of Caludon Castle, on the northeast edge of Coventry, allow one to trace the dimensions of its great hall; and Priory Park, Warwick, can be reconstructed from a few photographs, blueprints, and other materials. One property, Beoley, has vanished without trace – a later house built on the site has been converted into flats, and the property has been subdivided. The surviving houses all had great halls, of roughly comparable size (approximately 55′ × 26′), and were hence of ideal size to use as performance venues. I hope to illustrate that these indoor 'great halls,' ubiquitous in the larger houses of the great and the not-so-great, are of central importance in the architectural history of playing places before 1642, as well as the social history of provincial theatre.

Sir Thomas Walmesley, a Lancashire lawyer knighted in 1603 by King James, lived at Dunkenhalgh Hall with his family until his death in 1642. Twenty-three of his household account books survive, covering the period 1612–54. The hall was partially demolished and much altered in 1799, and as mentioned is now a hotel; it lies eighteen miles northeast, as the crow flies, from the centre of Liverpool. Lord Henry Berkeley did not, alas, live at Berkeley castle, whose impressive great hall has been preserved intact. Lord Henry is known to have visited Berkeley, but because of disputes over succession and the ownership of Berkeley between two branches of the family, Lord Henry used as his principal residence Caludon Castle, eleven miles northeast of the centre of Coventry, on the Leicester road. It is now a ruin, but the size and location of the great hall can be determined from the remains. The Berkeley household accounts, in five books, cover 1593–1612. We may owe their preservation to the inclusion, among the private household details, of extensive records of the many lawsuits that Lord Henry vigorously litigated in his attempts to regain undisputed title to Berkeley Castle. These lawsuits also, significantly, required Lord Henry to often reside at London for significant periods. Of Sir Thomas Puckering, not much remains. He was the son of Sir John Puckering, Queen Elizabeth's attorney-general, and he inherited Priory House, Warwick, at his father's death. The building was demolished in 1925; its great hall was 60′ × 25′, with a ceiling height of eighteen feet. A black-and-white photograph of the hall survives from an estate agent's auction catalogue, taken in 1905.[2] Sir Simon Archer, a Warwickshire antiquarian, was Puckering's executor, which probably accounts for the chance survival among Archer's papers, of Puckering household accounts for one year only, 1620–1. There also survives an estate steward's account for 1619–21, in the Warwick County Record Office.[3] The household book is likely a typical account. We know that Puckering maintained an interest in theatre – in June 1613, a letter to Puckering from Thomas Lorkins carried the news of the fire at the first Globe Theatre (British Library MS Harleian 7002, f. 268); and on 11 January 1637, one Edward Rossingham, presumably a courtier, wrote to Puckering with news from court about a production, by the King's players, of William Cartwright's *The Royal Slave*, revived on Twelfth Night at Hampton Court after its original performance at Oxford before the king and queen the previous summer.[4] This evidence of Puckering's continuing interest in London theatre gossip makes me yearn for more of Puckering's household accounts. But all I can do is yearn.

A hotel, a ruin, a demolished house: why the fuss? The answer is, because of the details conveyed in those accounting records about the range of performance activities by travelling companies. In this brief essay I can only hit a few of the high spots from these rich resources – my transcriptions from the Berkeley account books, for example, extend to over a hundred typed pages. These three men were not just 'provincial' – as mentioned, there is direct evidence that Berkeley and Puckering visited London frequently, and I think it highly likely that Walmesley, being a lawyer, would have travelled there regularly to plead cases. Berkeley was in London twice during 1595, and during both visits he rewarded companies such as the Queen's players, the countess of Warwick's players, the earl of Kent's musicians, and intriguingly, 'a boye yat daunced before your lordship at Sir George Caries,' indicating that Berkeley knew the son of the lord chamberlain.[5] Sir Thomas Puckering visited London in March–April 1620, and he recorded expenses of 1s 10d for going to the Bankside to see the dancing upon the ropes, and of 2s 6d 'in seeing a play for myself, Hicks, and my Footman' (Hicks was Puckering's steward). Upon their returns to their provincial residences, these men spent handsomely on entertainments, and it is reasonable to suggest that their standards were high, set by their experiences in London.

Spend handsomely they did. I can do more than give an outline here, first for Dunkenhalgh. The Walmesley family made, on average, eight to a dozen payments in a typical year, to entertainers of all kinds, usually around the Christmas season. These included waits (companies of professional town musicians) from all over the country; between 1612 and 1636 they rewarded, on fifty-one occasions, eighteen different troupes of players, including five under royal patronage. No play titles are given, but another type of evidence is often found, because many of these are kitchen accounts. A marginal note indicates, in nineteen instances, the length of the players' stay; in eleven of these nineteen, two or more nights are specified.

In the case of Lord Berkeley, I can do no more in the brief compass of this essay than to indicate, by a comparison, the extent of his payments. Between November 1605 and November 1606, Berkeley rewarded entertainers on eighteen occasions, seven of them being companies of players. In the same year, 1606, the city of Coventry made six payments to entertainers, five of them companies of players (including some of the same companies that were rewarded by Berkeley). Apparently Caludon Castle was often a far livelier entertainment centre than the large city to the southwest – this is remarkable because Coventry was, as we know, an extremely active and welcoming venue for professional troupes. The Berkeley records furnish us with the only play title to be found in these accounts: on 1 January 1601 6s 8d was paid 'to my Lord Dudleys players in reward for playing Shores wife.' These records also supply us with numerous payments to Berkeley's 'house' entertainers: musicians, taberer, and players. The musicians and taberer are rewarded regularly from 1593, in the form of both New Year's gifts and performance payments. The amounts spent annually on these entertainers declines after 1597, which is also the year in which 'the players' are first rewarded. Between 1593 and 1605 Berkeley spent approximately £29 on his musicians; a possible reason for their decline is revealed by an entry on 26 July 1605: 'geuen in reward to my Lordes old musicions v s.' From 1597 to 1605 Berkeley spent £14 15s 0d on his players. The impression one gathers from these accounts, then, is of a household passionately devoted to entertainments, a hive of performance activities.

Turning finally to summarize Sir Thomas Puckering's accounts, we are considering a man who, like Sir Thomas Walmesley, did not act as patron to a troupe but who paid large sums to purchase the services of players. A distinction is apparent between three types of Puckering's payments to players. First, unmistakable rewards 'for playing a play in my house' are made on different dates to Lord Dudley's players (20s) and Lady Elizabeth's players (22s), during the Christmas season, 1620–1. Then there are smaller payments, outside the Christmas season, to the prince's players (2 August, 2s 6d), the king and queen of Bohemia's players (27 November, 2s). Perhaps these were payments to go away without playing, or perhaps they were contributions towards a town performance. That the latter may be the case is indicated by two specific instances where the payment was made to 'a company of the King his players offering their service' (23 December, 5s), and to 'the Prince his Players offering their service' (8 January, 2s 6d). The bustle of theatrical activity at Priory House, were it traceable through the records of other years, would materially alter our impression of this small town; this would be even more the case, I suggest, if we were able to add the performance events in the lost records of the Beauchamps and Brookes of Warwick Castle, a few hundred metres to the south.

Many more questions remain to be answered. I have tried to suggest that domestic performances, in the halls of the great and not-so-great, deserve the increased attention that REED is giving to them as it has 'come home.' So also, I suggest, do the playing places in which these performances occurred, the physical circumstances and appearances of which are being recorded on the *Patrons and Performances Web Site*. It is becoming apparent that touring players performed as often, or more often, in such surroundings than they did in public playing places under borough or city sponsorship. Such surroundings involved the players in another set of complex social negotiations which I have already mentioned, and which I will conclude by outlining a little more fully.

One may reasonably speculate about the motives that led these locally prominent men to spend their resources to support the activities of prominent travelling companies (aside, of course, from their philanthropic impulses and aesthetic affection for theatre). Clues are afforded by information contained in these records, which illustrates the need for researchers not to approach the documents with tunnel vision (and incurs the danger of endless fishing expeditions into apparently tangential materials!). Also, what one can find out about the local social relationships of people like Lord Henry Berkeley and Sir Thomas Puckering can be illuminating. To generalize, both these men demonstrate a desire to enhance their positions in the eyes of their local peers and superiors, and to broaden their scopes of influence. Sir Thomas was created a baronet, and set himself the task of becoming prominent socially and politically among the Warwickshire gentry. His social relations included Sir Simon Archer of nearby Stratford-on-Avon, and hence also Sir Simon's extensive social networks. Sir Thomas's political ambitions are demonstrated by his continual efforts to get himself elected as member of Parliament, efforts that led nowhere because Lord Brooke, of Warwick Castle, had other ideas. In the case of Lord Henry Berkeley, I have already mentioned his extensive efforts to regain Berkeley Castle, which necessitated the cultivation of influential people such as Sir George Carey and others. Lord Henry's ambitions to impress others with displays of wealth are also shown by the magnificent funeral procession and ceremony that he lavished upon his first wife at her death.

It is not necessary here to go into further details about the quotidian activities of people like Lord Henry and Sir Thomas, because I trust that my general point is clear; such locally prominent families were jealous of their prestige and anxious to enhance it. Consequently, say, at a performance sponsored and paid for by Sir Thomas Puckering at his home during the Christmas season of 1620, Lord Dudley's players were involved as an expression of that prestige. The idea that such a company, on such an occasion, would offer a cut-down (or cut-rate?) performance tailored to provincial tastes and limitations is, I believe, simply not tenable. Homes, households, lay at the heart of provincial playing, and hence are at the heart of REED's activities.

NOTES

1 The Walmesley family accounts are published in David George, ed., *Lancashire*, REED (Toronto: University of Toronto Press, 1991).
2 The remains of Priory House, after demolition, were transported to Virginia, where they were used to erect a replica house. This was formerly the residence of the Waddell family, but it is now the headquarters and museum of the

Virginia Historical Society. The site of the former great hall of Priory House is now, appropriately, the location of the search room of the Warwick County Record Office.

3 I am indebted to Mr G.M.D. Booth, Senior Archivist, for pointing out this estate steward's book at the WCRO: CR 341/281. Its entries duplicate some of those in the 1620–1 Household Book, but some other entries are unique to it.

4 The letter is preserved as British Library MS Harleian 7000, art. 198, one of eighteen volumes of letters collected by Thomas Baker in the early eighteenth century. The letter is a collection of miscellaneous news, and the news about the play appears approximately halfway down the verso of the sheet (f. 372v).

5 The Berkeley and Puckering records from which these brief extracts are taken will appear in my forthcoming REED volume for Staffordshire/Warwickshire.

Pageantry on London Bridge in the Early Fifteenth Century

CAROLINE M. BARRON

When the Londoners learned of the birth of the future Edward III on 13 November 1312 they assembled in the evening at Guildhall and carolled to show their joy. Then they processed through the streets with flaming torches and 'with trumpets and other minstrelsies.' A holiday was declared, no one worked, many went to St Paul's to give thanks, and after the solemn mass 'they led carols (*menerent la karole*) in the Cathedral to the sound of trumpets' and then all returned home. On the following Monday – 20 November – the mayor and aldermen 'richly costumed' rode to Westminster to make a gift to the king and on returning to the city after dinner 'they went in carols throughout the city all the rest of the day and a great part of the night.'[1] It is clear that these celebrations were relatively spontaneous and informal. But in the course of the fourteenth century the celebration of royal events in the city became more formal and, by the early fifteenth century, it was highly organized.

In these celebrations of royal coronations, weddings, and military triumphs, London Bridge came to play a significant role.[2] For his coronation procession through the city the king usually departed from the Tower of London and rode along Cheapside to Westminster, so London Bridge was not on the route. But when Edward the Black Prince returned victorious from France in 1357 he rode across the bridge.[3] The first clear reference to London Bridge as playing a part in civic ceremonial occurs in 1392 when a reconciliation pageant was staged by the city for Richard II. On this occasion Richard and Anne rode from Wandsworth accompanied by a large civic and religious delegation. The Stonegate at the southern end of the bridge, which marked the city boundary, had been decorated with wooden shields displaying the arms of the king and queen.[4] When they reached the bridge, the royal couple were greeted with speeches and each

was given a fine horse, but there appear to have been no pageants or
singing on this occasion, perhaps to emphasize the contrite rather than
triumphal nature of the event.[5] But the significance of the bridge was
recognized in Richard's demand, the following year, that carved stone
statues of himself and his queen, holding gilded latten sceptres, should be
placed above the Stonegate. Statues of the royal couple were placed beneath large tabernacles, and the ensemble included shields with the arms of
Richard, Anne, and St Edward the Confessor. The statues were painted at
considerable cost, and the surrounding area was plastered and whitened to
show off the statues and shields to better effect. Over £30 was spent on this
embellishment at the king's behest.[6] London Bridge provided three possible sites for pageants or 'events,' although the bridge itself consisted only
of a narrow roadway, almost entirely lined with houses and resting on
nineteen piers. The space at the southern end, where the wide market place
of Southwark high street narrowed to the bridge foot, was sometimes used
for speeches of welcome, but pageants were not constructed there since
there was no appropriate gate or edifice that could be used as a prop. But
the Stonegate, on the second pier, had tall towers and a frontage that could
support musicians, tableaux, and banners of all kinds. At the drawbridge,
on the seventh pier, there was another tower and a small open space which
could also be put to use in the creation of a pageant.[7] So, in due course, the
bridge wardens customarily became responsible for two pageants, one at
the Stonegate and the other at the drawbridge. Apart from the tangible
advantages of the two stone towers serving as appropriate props for pageants, there was the added advantage that the bridge wardens were in
charge of an income independent of the city chamber, which could be
drawn on to pay the not inconsiderable costs of setting up the pageants.

   In considering the pageants on the bridge in the period from 1400 to
1432 we have to bear in mind that we do not have the same material
available for every royal entry. Six entries will be considered here because
we have material about all of them in the surviving records of the London
Bridge House: the coronation of Henry V in November 1413; the welcome for Henry after Agincourt in November 1415; the welcome and
coronation of Catherine of Valois in February 1421; the welcome of the
duke and duchess of Bedford in January 1426; the coronation of Henry VI
in November 1429, and the welcome for Henry VI on his return from his
coronation in Paris in February 1432.[8] It may be worth noting that all of
these events took place in the winter months, which must have added to
the difficulties of those who organized them, and to the discomfort of the
workmen. The choice of such inhospitable times may have been dictated

by the necessities of the campaigning season: in the summer months the king and his nobles had to be away in France, so processions had to take place when there was no fighting to be done.

For only two of these events, however, do we have substantial literary descriptions of the Bridge pageants (1415 and 1432), although it would seem that descriptions of such royal events in the city were in fact compiled and circulated. It is clear that in 1392 Richard Maidstone composed his Latin verse account of the reconciliation pageant for public relations purposes: probably at Richard's behest. Again in 1415 there must have been an official text that was used extensively by the author of the *Gesta* and, less thoroughly, by Adam of Usk and other contemporary chroniclers.[9] The ghost of such a text would seem to lurk behind Thomas of Elmham's account of the coronation celebrations for Catherine of Valois in 1421.[10] In 1432, however, John Carpenter, the common clerk of the city (who may well have been responsible for devising the London pageants on this occasion), wrote a Latin prose account of the pageants created to welcome Henry VI home from Paris, and may well have sent a copy of this to John Lydgate, which he used as the source for his elaborate English poem.[11] As a result of Carpenter's foresight, the 1432 welcome pageant is by far the best documented and best known of the fifteenth-century London pageants.

In addition to these prose or verse descriptions, payments relating to all these Bridge pageants appear in the remarkable series of accounts kept by the wardens of London Bridge.[12] But these also vary. In 1413 and 1415 the various costs of the Bridge pageants are added together from different subsidiary accounts and only the final sum recorded in the weekly payments book.[13] But for the welcome of Catherine of Valois in 1421 the various expenditures related to the pageants are scattered throughout the weekly payments: the first payments occur in the week of 11 January when drinking and other expenses 'about the works on the stone gate' cost 22d, and W. Goos, carver, began his work on 'the head of a Giant for the Bridge against the king's coming' for which he received an initial payment of 18d.[14] The final expenses occur in September when the costs of torches and candles used 'at the coming of the king and queen' were recorded.[15] In between these dates the various costs are recorded intermittently with a crescendo of activity and expense noted in the weeks between 25 January and 1 March, with much night work being paid for in the weeks immediately preceding the procession on 21 February. But for the welcome of the duke of Bedford in 1426, the coronation of Henry VI in 1429, and the welcome of Henry VI in 1432 the Bridge House accounts again record the expenses for the pageants in a block, as if the expenditure on these special events had been accounted for separately and then inserted, when the finances were all tied up, into the main account. So the expenses for the pageant for the duke and duchess of Bedford, which took place on 10 January 1426, were not entered into the accounts until 1 February, and those for Henry VI's welcome on his return from Paris, which took place on 21 February 1432, were entered all together in the accounts in the week of 10 May of that year.[16] The accounts for 1421 provide a great deal of interesting information, but no overall description of the pageant, whereas the later accounting method rehearses the ordinance, or specification, for the pageant, which thus provides a coherent, if brief, description of the Bridge pageants for that event. This is then followed by a brief account of the various expenses, for example, the total costs of the work done by the painters or carpenters, and then these are added up and entered as a block expense.[17]

In the early fifteenth century the total bridge income from rents, tolls, and the Stocks market amounted to some £500 pa.[18] The costs of pageants appear to have varied greatly from just over £8 for the coronation pageant for Henry VI in 1429 to about £80 for the coronation pageant for Catherine of Valois earlier in 1421, as can be seen in this table:

Expenditure of Bridge Wardens on Pageants on London Bridge 1413–32

1413 (Coronation Henry V)	£9	14s	10d19[19]
1415 (Welcome after Agincourt)	£18	12s	11 1/2d[20]
1421 (Coronation Catherine)	c.£80[21]		
1426 (Welcome duke Bedford)	£9	3s	3d[22]
1429 (Coronation Henry VI)	£8	4s	1 1/2d[23]
1432 (Welcome Henry VI)	£28	18s	0 1/2d[24]

The coronation pageant in 1421 appears to have been exceptionally expensive. Its anomalous cost may be due to the fact that the accounts are presented differently on this occasion. Unlike the other five pageants where the particular or subsidiary accounts have been summarized into a single total, in 1421 the costs of the pageant have to be calculated from a multitude of individual costs spread over several weeks in the accounts. There is no single total for the costs of the pageant. It may be that the 1421 pageant *was* exceptionally expensive, but it seems more likely that on the other occasions some of the costs have been absorbed within the weekly accounts and not included in the summary total. If the calculations are correct, in 1421 the costs of the pageant took some 15 per cent of the income of the bridge in that year. Although the bridge estates usually produced more income than was required for the regular maintenance of the bridge, it may be that there is a correlation between the bridge wardens' expenditure on pageants in the early fifteenth century, with a consequent underfunding of maintenance work on the bridge, and the spectacular collapse of the two arches on either side of the Stonegate in January 1437.[25] The elaborate pageantry on London Bridge came at a price.

So, apart from the overall costs, we do not have directly comparable material for the different London Bridge pageants in these years. Although there is a general consistency in the various pageants, and some of the same motifs appear on different occasions, this apparent sameness must, to some extent, have been dictated by the structure of the bridge itself. And it may also be that certain characters, or features, were expected by the crowds, rather as nowadays the attraction of pantomimes lies in the recognition of familiar characters rather than novelties. Certainly on almost every occasion there was a giant standing on top of the Stonegate.[26] In 1415 he was particularly large, and held a great axe in one hand and the keys of the city hung from a baton in his other hand.[27] Moreover on this occasion he was accompanied by his wife, dressed in a red cloak and so large she looked fit to spawn 'giganteos demones.'[28] According to one onlooker, the giant was there 'To teche the Frensshmen curtesye.'[29] But the same giants were not re-used six years later for the welcome of Queen Catherine because the bridge wardens paid William Goos 'kerver' a total of £1 3s 1d for making a new giant's head, which appears to have been able to move so that as the queen arrived it bent its head in obeisance to her.[30] For the welcome of Henry VI in 1432 the giant was clothed in grey Kendal cloth, standing as the king's champion, holding a sword, and bearing the arms of England and France.[31] So although the giants appear quite frequently above the Stonegate, they are not always the same giants.

In the same way, at the drawbridge, there were often constructed two additional towers. In 1415 one supported a lion bearing a lance and the other an antelope (Henry's badge) with the royal arms around its neck.[32] But in 1432 both towers contained antelopes supporting the badges or arms of England and France.[33] In 1426 the two towers were filled with small boys (angels) singing.[34] In the centre of the bridge there seems always to have been some sort of castle or tower structure, made of wood and covered with painted cloth to imitate stone (or white marble and green jasper in 1415). It was around this edifice that the most important, the thematic, pageant was placed. In 1415 the central figure of this pageant was very straightforward: St George dressed in armour with his head bare and crowned with a laurel wreath, as the supernatural hero of the battle to welcome the worldly victor.[35] In 1421 the central figure, in deference to Queen Catherine, was St Petronilla, the supposed daughter of St Peter and the patroness of the Carolingian kings of France.[36] The duke of Bedford was greeted by twelve military figures including Old Testament worthies such as Moses 'dux Hebreorum'; classical heroes such as Hercules and Hector; soldier saints such as Alban; and English heroes such as Henry, 1st duke of Lancaster and John, duke of Bedford, himself.[37] At the Bridge pageant for the coronation of Henry VI, who was eight years old at the time, military figures were jettisoned: instead three girls seated in a tower presented a tableau of a queen holding a sceptre in her hand while her son stood before her holding a crown.[38] Three years later when young Henry returned from France, the pageant presented the figures of Nature, Grace, and Fortune who rose at the king's approach and gave him the gifts of courage and glory, wisdom and understanding, and wealth and honour. But young Henry may have been more entranced by the seven gifts of the Holy Spirit that were given to him in the form of white doves, released over his head by a group of beautifully dressed Virtues.[39]

The construction of the pageants clearly provided work for large numbers of craftsmen. The pageant in 1421 appears to have required nearly 700 days' work (stainers 247, carpenters 240, joiners 79.5, masons 37.5, daubers 30, painters 28, the carver 22, and the plasterer 4.5). In 1426 payments are recorded only to painters/stainers (25 days) and to carpenters (8 days). But in 1432 the painters were most in demand and were paid for 220 days while the stainers were paid for only eighty-seven days and the carpenters for eleven and a half days. Very few of the craftsmen seem to have been employed on more than one occasion although Richard Coyford, stainer, worked for five days on the 1421 pageant and again for three and a half days in 1426.[40] Some of the craftsmen later held office in their crafts: Guy Lincoln, who painted an angel to decorate the tower on the bridge in 1429 was a warden of the Painters' craft in 1441.[41] Roger Aleyn, a stainer who worked on the 1421 pageant, was a warden of his craft in 1428; and Simon Scarlet, one of the stainers of 1432 was warden in 1441.[42] William Hewgynes, stainer, who made and stuffed a lion for the 1421 pageant, was numbered among the 'good men' of the craft in 1431.[43] Many of these craftsmen also supplied materials such as paints, gold and silver foil, paper, wire, cloth, and fur. One would like to know more of Thomas Edward who provided 'ornamentales' (possibly for the little singing boys) at the considerable cost of 66s 8d for the pageant in 1426: perhaps it was his wife, or widow Agnes Edward who, six years later, hired out six cushions, a cloth of gold, and two animals for 2s 6d.[44] There may have been men and women who made a business of hiring out pageant props; Isabel Beauchamp was paid 6s 8d for the hire of eight pairs of angel wings for the pageant in 1421.[45] If she could hire out the wings, she must have envisaged that others could make frequent use of them again later.

It seems that most of the pageants contained written Latin texts. On the Stonegate in 1415 were painted the words 'Civitas Regni Iusticie,' and at the drawbridge tower 'fluminis impetus letificat civitatem dei' (Vulgate Psalm 45:5). St George himself held a scroll that read 'Soli deo honor et gloria.'[46] The names of the twelve worthies who greeted John duke of Bedford in 1426 were written up above their arms to identify them, and the central pageant on this occasion bore the words of the psalm 'Dux itineris fuisti in conspectu eius et Plantasti Radices [eius et implevit terram]' (Vulgate Psalm 79:10). It is clear that this text was chosen in reference to Bedford's badge of a racine or root, which he appears to have used from 1423, soon after he had accepted the regency.[47] It may well have been for this that Thomas Hakon, 'scriptor,' was paid 2s 5d together with a reward of 6s 8d.[48] In 1432 the giant at the Stonegate was girdled with the text 'Inimicos eius induam confusione,' which the author of the Brut chronicle freely interprets as 'And y, the Kynges Champyon, in full myght and power.'[49] At the central pageant the message from Nature, Grace, and Fortune was 'Intende prospere procede et regna' (Vulgate Psalm 44:5). The significance of the gifts from the two groups of Virgins was also indicated by written texts: the gifts of the Holy Spirit came with these words: 'Impleat te Dominus spiritu sapientiae et intellectus, spiritu consilii et fortitudinis, spiritu scientiae et pietatis, et spiritu timoris Domini' (based on Isaiah 11:5) while the seven royal emblems were explained thus: 'Accipe coronam gloriae, sceptrum clementiae, gladium justitiae, pallium prudentiae, scutum fidei, galeam salutis, et vinculum pacis.'[50] There is no suggestion that the Latin texts were also written out in English, but those in the crowd who knew some Latin would doubtless explain the meaning to those around them. It seems that these pageant texts were written in large and bold script, for Lydgate records that they could be read 'withoute a spectacle.'[51]

Perhaps only a comparatively small number would have been able to read and understand the Latin texts that accompanied the pageants, but they could enjoy the visual spectacle and, in addition, there was music. The comparatively informal minstrelsy and carolling of the early fourteenth century appears to have given way to more formal musical performance. There were singers at the bridge when Henry V rode to his coronation in 1413. Two years later when he returned victorious from France, choirs of boys dressed as angels sang the anthem 'Benedictus qui venit in nomine Domini.' On this occasion, liturgical music seems to have been an important feature of many of the pageants around the city. In 1426 Leonello 'cantator' with 'parvulis suis cantantibus' provided the music, and three years later a choir of three clerks and eight boys sang for Henry VI.[52] In 1432 the boys in the choir were divided into two groups of Virgins: one group who gave Henry the gifts of the Holy Spirit and released the doves was dressed in blue tunics decorated with suns, and the other group was dressed in white, spangled with stars.[53] Eleven of the Virgin singers were paid 4d each and three, presumably more experienced singers, received 12d each, so the choir in total cost 6s 8d. However a further 16d was spent on their food.[54] The choirmaster may have been William Holford, who appears in the accounts alongside the singers and was paid 5s as a reward for his labour. William Holford, a clerk in the chapel of St Thomas on London Bridge, was the son of Nicholas Holford, who was the tollkeeper of the bridge as well as one of the chapel clerks.[55] Father and son both lived by their musical talents. Nicholas was paid 3s 1d for various expenses which he had incurred in the preparations for the pageant in 1426.[56] Since in his will, drawn up in 1434, Nicholas described himself as a 'textwriter' he may also have been involved in writing the various scrolls, or in the music, or, perhaps, in the overall design of the 1426 pageant.[57]

The bridge accounts for 1432 also record, following the payments to the singers and the reward to William Holford, the sum of 12d paid to John Steyno[ur], clerk of St Dunstan's [in the East], 'pro factura cantus.' Did he write the words for the song or only the music? Perhaps he acted as the choir master? The song in question must surely have been the 'novum canticum sive carmen' that Carpenter carefully copied into his Latin account of the civic welcome of 1432. It seems very probable that John Carpenter was himself the author of this specially commissioned English song; that John Steynour wrote the music; and that William Holford acted as the choir master and organized the fourteen boys to dance and sing. Let Carpenter's song of welcome provide a fitting conclusion to an essay celebrating one who is herself a mistress of pageants.

Soveraigne lorde to your cite
With alle reverence welcome ye be.

Thanked be Gode of his goodnesse
That you hath kepte from hevynesse
And brought you ayen with gladenesse
Londone your Chambre for to se.

Thanked be ye with alle lowenes
That nought wolde spare youre tendrenes
But put you to travaile and besynes
To worschipe your londe in eche degre.

Wherfor God that ys fulle of myght
Hath holpe you atteyne your right
And crouncd twyes with gemes bright
The piler of worschipe that ye be

Londone be glad with alle thi myght
For God hath sent unto thi sight
Thi lorde thi prince thi kyng by right
Wherfor nowe syng and say with me:

Soveraigne lorde to your cite
With alle reverence welcome ye be.[58]

Appendix: Translation of John Carpenter's
Account of the Pageants on London Bridge in 1432

London Metropolitan Archives, Letter Book K f. 104v; printed in H.T.
Riley ed., *Munimenta Gildhallae Londoniensis: Liber Albus, Liber Custu-
marum et Liber Horn*, 3 vols, Rolls Series 12 (1859–62), 3:459–60.

And then, riding through the middle of the town of Southwark, he came to
the outer boundary of the City, near the Bridge. There a device was made
ready, rather fine, on the middle of which stood a giant of amazing size,
brandishing and thrusting his sword against the enemies of the King's
Majesty, and girdled with this text, 'I shall clothe his enemies in confusion.'
On either side of the giant himself, in the same pageant, were set up two
animals called 'antelopes,' which supported the arms of the kingdoms of
England and France, shining forth like a banner.

On the Bridge itself, indeed, a beautiful structure of remarkable splendour
shone forth. On it three lady empresses sat, glittering in marvellous
splendour, pliant Nature, Grace and Fortune. At the approach of the King
they stood up and gave their own blessed gifts as he went by: that is,
Nature gave him courage and glory, Grace wisdom and understanding,
Fortune wealth and honours. Before their feet they had those words of
David, 'Go on in prosperity, go forward and reign' – as if they were saying,
'Go on in prosperity through Fortune, go forward in long life through
Nature, and reign in goodness through Grace.'

On the right side of this structure stood seven godly Virtues in the guise
of girls, consecrated with golden crowns, and clad in the rays of the sun
over their blue-clad limbs. They, on discovering that the Lord King was
coming, went out to meet him in the outer parts of his 'palace,' showing
him figuratively the seven gifts of the Holy Spirit by releasing seven white
doves, and proclaiming in an inscription, 'May the Lord fill you with the
spirit of wisdom and understanding, the spirit of counsel and courage, the
spirit of knowledge and goodness, and the spirit of the fear of the Lord.'
On the left side also, seven more virgins, pale in milk-white robes, and
shining with stars on their bodies, presented seven royal emblems, listed
similarly on a scroll at their feet: 'Receive the crown of glory, the sceptre of
mercy, the sword of justice, the mantle of prudence, the shield of faith, the
helmet of salvation, and the bond of peace.' And next, all those virgins, as if
with one accord rejoicing in their hearts at the happy arrival of the Lord
King, clapping their hands and dancing for joy, skilfully sang to our King a
new chant or song in the following words: (for the text of the song, see
p. 99)

NOTES

1 H.T. Riley, ed., *Memorials of London and London Life in the XIIIth, XIVth, and XVth Centuries. Being a series of extracts, local, social, and political, from the early archives of the City of London, 1276–1419* (London: Longmans, Green, 1868), 106–7; translated from the Anglo-Norman account in the London Metropolitan Archives [hereafter LMA], Letter Book D f. 168.

2 For a discussion of the role of London Bridge in civic life, see Derek Keene, 'London Bridge and the Identity of the Medieval City,' *Transactions of the London and Middlesex Archaeological Society* 51 (2000): 143–56.

3 Anne Lancashire, *London Civic Theatre: City Drama and Pageantry from Roman Times to 1558* (Cambridge: Cambridge University Press, 2002), 43–50, esp. 44, and 231, note 63.

4 24 August 1392, the bridge wardens paid 13s 4d for the shields, and 1s 8d for a dauber to paint the gate with ochre; LMA, Bridge House Account Roll 11 (CLA/007/FN/01/011), m. 12.

5 David R. Carlson, ed., *Richard of Maidstone, Concordia (The Reconciliation of Richard II with London)* (Kalamazoo, MI: Medieval Institute Publications, 2003), 63–5.

6 For payments on several occasions between 10 May and 20 September 1393, see LMA, Bridge House Account Roll 12 (CLA/007/FN/01/012), mm. 8, 9, 10. The mason/sculptor was Thomas Wrenk/Wreuk who had worked on the alabaster monument of the duchess of Lancaster in St Paul's Cathedral; see John Harvey, *English Medieval Architects: A Biographical Dictionary down to 1550*, rev. ed. (Stroud: Sutton, 1984), 349.

7 Vanessa Harding, 'Pageantry on London Bridge,' in *London Bridge: 2000 Years of a River Crossing*, ed. Bruce Watson, Trevor Brigham, and Tony Dyson (London: Museum of London, 2001), 114–15, and see figs 53, 66, and 67.

8 Lancashire, *Civic Theatre*, chapter 7 and 186–8.

9 F. Taylor and John S. Roskell, eds, *Gesta Henrici Quinti* (Oxford: Clarendon Press, 1975), xxxvii. The existence of what the editors call 'the official programme' makes it less certain that the author of the *Gesta* was in London to witness the welcome for Henry V; even if he was present, it is improbable that he could have seen (and heard) every pageant.

10 Thomas de Elmham, *Vita et Gesta Henrici Quinti Anglorum Regis*, ed. Thomas Hearne (Oxford, 1727), 297–8.

11 H.N. MacCracken, 'King Henry's Triumphal Entry into London: Lydgate's Poem and Carpenter's Letter,' *Archiv für das Studium der neuren Sprachen und Literaturen* 126 (1911): 75–102; Caroline M. Barron, 'The Political

Culture of Medieval London,' in *The Fifteenth Century*, vol. 4. *Political Culture in Late Medieval Britain*, ed. Linda Clark and Christine Carpenter (Woodbridge: Boydell, 2004), 111–33, esp. 118–19.

12 For a description of these records, see Vanessa Harding and Laura Wright, eds, *London Bridge: Selected Accounts and Rentals 1381–1538* (London: London Record Society, 1995), esp. xxiv–xxviii.

13 See notes 19 and 20 below.

14 Harding and Wright, *London Bridge Accounts*, 77.

15 Harding and Wright, *London Bridge Accounts*, 112.

16 See notes 22 and 24 below. For the insertion of the accounts for the coronation of Henry VI in 1429, see note 23 below.

17 The account for the welcome of the duke of Bedford is transcribed in Lancashire, *Civic Theatre*, 198–9.

18 Harding and Wright, *London Bridge Accounts*, xvii-xxi.

19 15 April 1413; LMA, Bridge House Weekly Payments Book, vol. 2 (CLA/007/FN/03/002), p. 26*.

20 14 December 1415; LMA, Bridge House Weekly Payments Book, vol. 2 (CLA/007/FN/03/002), p. 171.

21 Calculated from Harding and Wright, *London Bridge Accounts*, 77–112.

22 1 February 1426; LMA, Bridge House Weekly Payments Book, vol. 3 (CLA/007/FN/03/003), f. 170, printed in Lancashire, *Civic Theatre*, 198–9.

23 29 October 1429; LMA, Bridge House Weekly Payments Book, vol. 3 (CLA/007/FN/03/003), f. 278. If the payment date is correct it would appear that the bridge wardens settled their accounts before the king's coronation procession, which took place on 4–5 November; see Lancashire, *Civic Theatre*, 187 and note 8.

24 10 May 1432; LMA, Bridge House Weekly Payments Book, vol. 4 (CLA/007/FN/03/004), f. 59v–60.

25 Tony Dyson and Bruce Watson, 'London Bridge is broken down,' in *London Bridge: 2000 years*, 128–32.

26 There is evidence for giants at the bridge in 1413, 1415, 1421, and 1432.

27 Taylor and Roskell, *Gesta Henrici Quinti*, 103.

28 C. Given-Wilson, ed., *The Chronicle of Adam Usk 1377–1421* (Oxford: Clarendon Press, 1997), 260–1.

29 The 'Lydgate' poem is printed in Taylor and Roskell, *Gesta Henrici Quinti*, Appendix 4, 191.

30 Harding and Wright, *London Bridge Accounts*, 77– 83. Goos was paid at the rate of 9d a day. The giants (there appear to have been more than one) were dressed and provided with hoops and head armour; Harding and Wright, *London Bridge Accounts*, 86; Elmham, *Vita et Gesta*, 297.

31 F.W.D. Brie, ed., *The Brut or The Chronicles of England*, 2 vols, Early English Text Society, os 131, 136 (1906, 1908), 2:462; see Appendix, 100.
32 Given-Wilson, *Usk*, 260–1; Taylor and Roskell, *Gesta Henrici Quinti*, 104–5.
33 Appendix below, 100.
34 Lancashire, *Civic Theatre*, 198.
35 Taylor and Roskell, *Gesta Henrici Quinti*, 104–5; Given-Wilson, *Usk*, 260–1. After the victory, at Henry's urging, Archbishop Chichele declared St George's Day a 'greater double' feast for general observance; see E.F. Jacob, ed., *The Register of Henry Chichele, Archbishop of Canterbury 1414–1443*, 4 vols, Canterbury and York Society (1938–47), 1:cxliv.
36 The bridge wardens paid 2s for the making of an image of St Petronilla; see Harding and Wright, *London Bridge Accounts*, 99.
37 Lancashire, *Civic Theatre*, 198.
38 LMA, Bridge House Weekly Payments, vol. 3 (CLA/007/FN/03/003), f. 278.
39 Appendix, 100.
40 Harding and Wright, *London Bridge Accounts*, 78; Lancashire, *Civic Theatre*, 198.
41 LMA, Bridge House Weekly Payments, vol. 3 (CLA/007/FN/03/003), f. 278; R. Sharpe ed., *Calendar of Letter Books of the City of London: Letter Book K* (London: John Edward Francis, 1911), 256.
42 Sharpe, *Letter Book K*, 97, 257; Harding and Wright, *London Bridge Accounts*, 83; LMA, Bridge House Weekly Payments, vol. 4 (CLA/007/FN/03/004), f. 59v.
43 Harding and Wright, *London Bridge Accounts*, 83; Sharpe, *Letter Book K*, 121–2.
44 Lancashire, *Civic Theatre*, 199; LMA, Bridge House Weekly Payments, vol. 4 (CLA/007/FN/03/004), f. 60.
45 Harding and Wright, *London Bridge Accounts*, 97.
46 Taylor and Roskell, *Gesta Henrici Quinti*, 105.
47 See Jenny Stratford, *The Bedford Inventories: The Worldly Goods of John, Duke of Bedford, Regent of France (1389–1435)* (London: Society of Antiquaries, 1993), 99–100.
48 Lancashire, *Civic Theatre*, 199.
49 Brie, *Brut*, 2:462.
50 These Latin texts, written out in Carpenter's prose (see Appendix, 100) are also found as side headings in Lydgate's English poem; see A.H. Thomas and I.D. Thornley, eds, *The Great Chronicle of London* (London: G.W. Jones 1938), 158–61.
51 See Thomas and Thornley, *Great Chronicle*, 163.

52 Lancashire, *Civic Theatre*, 199; LMA, Bridge House Weekly Payments, vol. 3 (CLA/007/FN/03/003), f. 278.
53 See Appendix, 100.
54 LMA, Bridge House Weekly Payments, vol. 4 (CLA/007/FN/03/004), f. 60.
55 William Holford was still a chapel clerk in 1461–2; see Harding and Wright, *London Bridge Accounts*, 139
56 Lancashire, *Civic Theatre*, 199.
57 C. Paul Christianson, *A Directory of London Stationers and Book Artisans 1300–1500* (New York: Bibliographical Society of America, 1990), 117–18. In his will Nicholas mentioned two sons, William and Roger. His widow, Alice, drew up her will in 1455 and bequeathed a missal (possibly the work of her late husband) to the chapel on the bridge on condition that her son Nicholas could continue to live in the house she occupied on the bridge for the annual rent of 32s; Guildhall Library, Commissary Wills MS 9171/5, f. 166. For Alice Holford, see *Oxford Dictionary of National Biography*, s.v. 'Women Traders and Artisans in Medieval London.'
58 This song, or poem, deserves recognition in its own right. It has been swallowed up in Lydgate's adaptation, where it has been considerably altered to suit Lydgate's own choice of metre; see Thomas and Thornley, *Great Chronicle*, 162.

> Souverain Lord welcome to youre Citee
> Welcome oure Joye and oure hertes plesaunce
> Welcome oure gladnesse welcome oure suffisaunce
> Welcome welcome right welcome mote ye be
> Syngyng beforne thy Ryall mageste
> We say of herte withoute variaunce
> Souverain lorde welcome welcome ye be
> Maire Citezeins and all the Comonte
> Atte youre home comyng nowe oute of Fraunce
> By grace releved of theire olde grevaunce
> Synge this day with grete solempnyte
> Souverain lorde welcome to youre Citee

The *Ordo paginarum* Revisited, with a Digital Camera

MEG TWYCROSS

The *Ordo paginarum* ('Order of pageants,' a term with ceremonial and religious connotations, as in 'Order of Service') kept by the York civic authorities in the fifteenth and sixteenth centuries is arguably the most important surviving document in the history of medieval English theatre, other than the scripts themselves. It was first compiled in 1415 for the city's official Memorandum Book (A/Y) by the newly elected common clerk Roger Burton,[1] and kept thereafter, conveniently at the back of the book,[2] apparently as a working checklist of the pageants of the York Corpus Christi Play. According to a later marginal annotation, possibly late fifteenth-century, the *Ordo* was to be used by the common clerk as a copy-text for the *sedule* (elsewhere called *billets*) issued annually to the guilds in the first or second week in Lent by the mayor's sergeants-at-mace. These 'schedules' presumably had a quasi-legal status ('you will bring forth your pageant as described, on pain of the forfeitures as laid down'), though by the 1460s/1470s, the time when most of the plays in the Register (what we think of as the York cycle text) were recorded, some of the descriptions are not very exact matches with the pageants they apparently represent.

This list of pageants (ff. 252v–4v) is followed by a list of processional torches and their bearers (f. 254v); a proclamation of the Corpus Christi Play, in English, to be made on the eve of the feast, and mostly concerned with law and order and the (severe) penalties for infringing these (ff. 254v–5r); then a second list of pageants, in two columns, with much shorter descriptions (f. 255r); and another, apparently supplementary, list of torches (f. 255r).

The original scribe of the *Ordo* not only had a very neat hand, he also had a sense of orderly layout. Indeed he seems to have intended a rather impressive document. His page layout was originally spacious. (It is difficult to measure it exactly, as the parchment has become distorted by damp, and damaged along the bottom edge.)[3] Because of the unusual format, it is rather different from the rest of A/Y: he had to manipulate two columns instead of one, so that though he allowed himself a good-sized outer margin and a reasonable gutter[4] – on the rectos quite wide, since it runs alongside his list of the guilds – they were not quite as wide as in most of the rest of the book. In common, however, with the rest of the book, the top margin is narrower but the bottom is quite ample.[5]

The list itself is neatly tabulated. The names of the guilds are arranged down the left-hand side of the page, the descriptions on the right. On the first page, f. 252v (Plate 1), the scribe gave the guilds about 40 per cent of the text area; on the next folio he reduced this to 35 per cent, and then on f. 254r to 28 per cent, but there is still a clear space between them and the edge of the descriptions: this space was later bridged by fork-shaped brackets linking the guild with its pageant.[6] The spacing between items was at least 1½ lines in depth, though they vary according to the number of guild names he had to fit in, and the amount of space he had available as the bottom of the page approached. It appears to have been written freehand, without ruling.[7] Since the text is not right-justified, the right-hand margin of the page is naturally ragged.

It has a carefully flourished heading (up to 'tercio'), written in *littera fracta*, a display version of Anglicana.[8] This is far more elaborate than for any of the other important documents in this section of the A/Y Memorandum Book. The body script is also more than usually formal, written in the *littera acuta* form of Anglicana. It is upright and angular, with a tall double-compartmented **a** and figure-of-8 **g**. The names of the guilds responsible for each pageant are written in a slightly larger script, with elaborated initials. Each pageant description is also given a capitalized initial. Both the guild names and the descriptions are preceded by a paraph. For a civic document, it was visually satisfying and easy to navigate around.

This is far from the impression the *Ordo* gives now. Because it was a working document, it has become a palimpsest. As the ownership and content of the pageants changed, so the list was updated. Alterations, erasures, and insertions have obscured the layout and content, though one can see the ghost of the underlying original. Besides the scrapings-out and rewritings, the bare space around the items gave later writers room to add extra information. (This is probably one of the reasons why the alterations were made on the main *Ordo* and not on the Second List, which is very tightly packed together.) The result is an enticing mess.

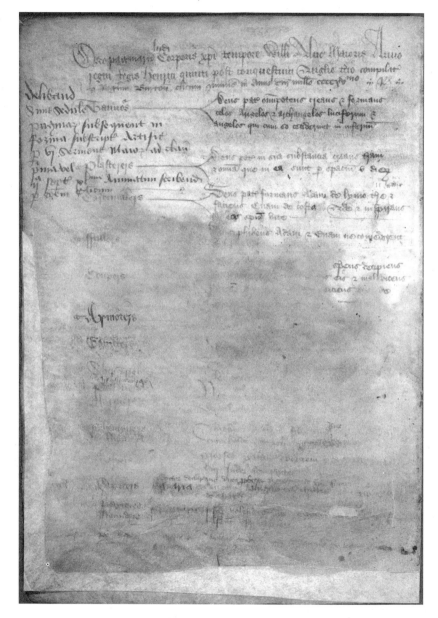

1. York City Archives, A/Y Memorandum Book, f. 252v: beginning of the *Ordo paginarum*. Photo DIAMM, © York City Archives and Meg Twycross.

But what the document has lost in clarity, it has gained as a source of historical information. Scholars have used it to trace the history of the organization of the York cycle throughout the fifteenth and early sixteenth centuries, as pageants changed hands and content was altered.[9] The latest organizational change recorded on the *Ordo*, as noted by Richard Beadle and Peter Meredith in their facsimile,[10] is the guild attribution to the Vestmentmakers who became contributory to the Skinners pageant in 1517.[11] This appears (I am tentative about this) to be in the same hand as made the major alteration to the last paragraph of the proclamation 'to be made on the eve of Corpus Christi' at the top of f. 255r.[12] After that the document seems to have been neglected. It shows, for example, no sign of the amalgamations of the Cardmakers' and the Fullers' pageants in 1529,[13] or the cuts made in the Edwardian reforms of 1548.[14] Perhaps these latter were tactfully disregarded, in the hope that they would go away – as they did, for a brief while, in 1554. Richard Beadle suggests that it was superseded by the Register as the document of record.[15] This is plausible, if we take it that the focus of interest (and penalties) had shifted from the number and type of characters to the actual words, though the 'billetes accustomed' were still being sent out in 1569, for the last recorded performance, and in 1561 the Minstrels describe the content of the play of Herod and the Three Kings, which they have just taken over from the Masons, in terms that echo the *Ordo* almost exactly, another piece of evidence that the *Ordo* was still in use as a source of reference in the mid-sixteenth century.[16]

Less productively, the A/Y Memorandum Book has also suffered rather more than its fair share of the depredations of time, accident, and apparently deliberate vandalism. In her 1885 edition of the *York Mystery Plays*, Lucy Toulmin Smith noted that 'Leaves 243-4-5-6 have all been cut by some destroyer, two of them nearly severed in half.'[17] (There does not seem to be any rhyme or reason for the placement of these slashes, and their date is unknown.)[18] The Ouse flood of 1892[19] soaked the lower half of the manuscript thoroughly, and it was not rescued and dried out in time to prevent considerable damage. As a result, river water has washed out much of the ink in large areas, and parchment already weakened by continuous or deep erasures has turned into holes. These holes and slashes were subsequently reinforced with archivist's brown paper patches, which have hidden all the text underneath them, except where the ink has indefatigably made its way through again (Plate 2).[20] It is not only a mess, it is by far the worst mess of any section of the A/Y Memorandum Book, almost as if it had been singled out by fate to become an editorial nightmare.

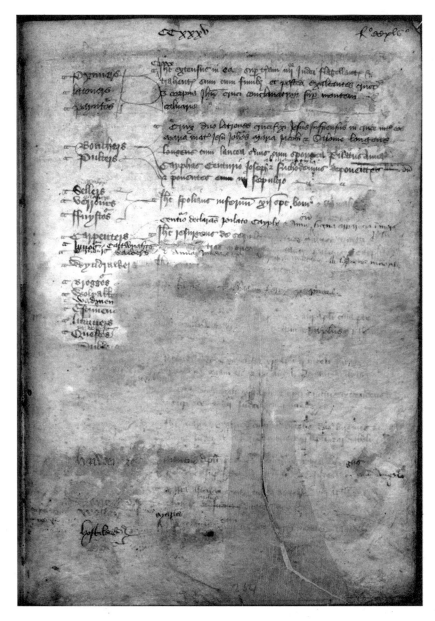

2. York City Archives, A/Y Memorandum Book, f. 254r. Photo DIAMM,
© York City Archives and Meg Twycross.

For subsequent editors, such as the REED duo of Alexandra F. Johnston and Margaret Dorrell Rogerson, recovering the original text has been an archaeological challenge. Fortunately, Lucy Toulmin Smith had transcribed the *Ordo* and the proclamation (though not the lists of torches, or the Second List) for the introduction to her 1885 edition of the *York Plays*,[21] before the 1892 flood and its aftermath. Ultraviolet light has been helpful, and the marks of the quill on the parchment often show up where the ink has been washed away if you tilt the page sideways,[22] but a glance at the REED transcription, which represents the manuscript 'in its present [1979] state of preservation' will show that large gaps remain.[23] The whole of the list of guilds in the bottom half of f. 253v, for example, has vanished under the patch, though occasional ghost words appear insubstantially through the paper, and we know from Toulmin Smith and other sources what they must have been.[24] The bottom corner of f. 253 has been torn off, with any material it might have contained. Judging from the photographs published with the 1983 *Leeds Studies in English* facsimile of the York Register, the general legibility of the manuscript has deteriorated even over the last twenty years.

So given that we have most of the text in printed form, why bother to look at the manuscript again? Precisely because its actual physical state tells a more detailed and complex story than any edition can, no matter how good. The REED edition is scrupulous in signalling alterations and emendations with its standard range of diacritics; but these cannot, even to the most practised reader, give more than a distant sense of the process behind the writing and rewriting. The unskilled may well not notice them at all. Through no fault of its own, because of the medium of print on paper, it presents a misleadingly homogeneous face to the reader.

Besides this, in 2002 the A/Y Memorandum Book was disbound for conservation and rebinding. The York City Archivists took the opportunity to scan certain portions of it, including the *Ordo paginarum*. Having bought copies of the scans, I succumbed to the lure of an old puzzle. The pageant descriptions in the *Ordo* are rather strange. Unlike the concise entries of the Second List (f. 255r), which summarize the content of each pageant – 'Creacio celi et terre, Cain occidens Abel, Temptacio Christi in deserto, Spoliacio inferni' (The Creation of Heaven and Earth, Cain Killing Abel, The Temptation of Christ in the Desert, The Harrowing of Hell), and so forth – the *Ordo* issues a cast list – 'Noe in Arche & vxor eius tres filij Noe cum vxoribus suis cum diuersis animalibus; Maria cum puero Iosep Anna obstetrix cum pullis columbarum Symeon recipiens puerum in vlnas suis & duo filij Symeonis; Ihesus Maria xij apostoli iiij[or] angeli cum tubis & iiij^or cum corona lancea & ij flagellis iiij^or spiritus boni & iiij^or spiritus maligni & vj diaboli' (Noah in the Ark and his wife; three sons of Noah with their wives, with various animals; Mary with the child, Joseph, Anna, a midwife with fledgling doves, Simeon receiving the child in his arms, and two sons of Simeon; Jesus, Mary, 12 apostles, 4 angels with trumpets and 4 with the crown, the spear, and two scourges, 4 Good Souls and 4 Bad Souls, and 6 devils). Sometimes it would be difficult without other evidence (the existence of the play, its place in the list, knowledge of the story and its likely cast) to tell what the pageant was actually about: 'Herodes duo consiliarii iiij^or milites Ihesus & iij Iudei; Ihesus Maria Gabriell cum ij angelis duo virgines & tres Iudei de cognacione Marie viij apostoli & ij diaboli' (Herod, two counsellors, 4 soldiers, Jesus, and 3 Jews; Jesus, Mary, Gabriel with 2 angels, two virgins and three Jews from Mary's kindred, 8 Apostles, and 2 devils).

Usually, however, there is action, but expressed in one or more present participles: 'Abel & Kaym immolantes victimas; Ihesus spolians infernum xij spiritus boni & vj mali; Maria Iohannes Euangelista xij apostoli ij angeli Ihesus ascendens coram eis & iiij^or angeli portans nubem' (Abel and Cain sacrificing their offerings; Jesus harrowing Hell, 12 Good Souls, and 6 Bad [presumably devils?]; Mary, John the Evangelist, 12 apostles, 2 angels, Jesus ascending in their presence, and 4 angels carrying a/the cloud). The characters are apparently fixed in an eternal present. What kind of production can this possibly describe? One has only to compare the *Ordo* with the N-Town or Chester Banns to sense a certain static quality, a snapshot of the action from the play rather than a plot summary. The question begs to be asked: are these descriptions of plays at all? Or could they conceivably be prescriptions for an earlier kind of pageant, groups of costumed characters either posed on a pageant wagon, or marching along the route, similar to the Dublin or Hereford Corpus Christi processions,[25] and familiar from the roughly contemporary pageant processions of the Low Countries?[26]

However, we know that by 1421/2 at least two plays were being joined together so that the populace might more conveniently hear the significant words (*oracula*) of the players, and the amalgamation is described in terms of one guild taking over the *materiam loquelarum*, 'the substance of the speeches,' in the other's pageant.[27] (We should beware of extrapolating from the Paternoster Play, which had a listening audience in 1388/9,[28] to the Corpus Christi Play: they originally served different functions.) A considerable number of the descriptions involve 'speaking' verbs. Have we caught them in 1415 in a sort of halfway house between tableau and play?

We can tell from other documents that the second and third decades of the fifteenth century were a time of drastic change in the organization and content of the Corpus Christi Play. It may possibly mark its expansion into a theatrical event in our sense. The very existence of the *Ordo* suggests that it had reached a stage where some kind of increased control was felt necessary, not merely that a reforming common clerk wanted to have the documents firmly filed in the right place. The fact that the *Ordo*, having been drawn up and pinned down on parchment, immediately began to change shape, shows exactly how revolutionary the next twenty years were.

It seemed to me that if I could reconstruct the original 1415 list on screen I might be closer to answering these questions. Indeed, this was originally going to be the focus of my essay: but this will have to wait now for a later publication. In order to return to the pristine state of the 1415 *Ordo*, I first needed to strip out all the later accretions and deletions. But this of course meant identifying them and, if possible, identifying when they were made and who made them. I became aware of how many more of them there were than most of us had realized. It became even more clear that the nature of the York cycle had changed radically during those crucial two decades. Peter Meredith has discussed in depth the case of the Tilers' pageant and the pageants with which it was amalgamated in 1422:[29] but what about the Bakers', the Butchers', the Spicers', the Carpenters', the Tilethatchers', the Chandlers', and the Curriers' pageants? Major, medium, and minor alterations on the *Ordo* all reflect what could be corresponding changes in performance or even in the nature of the pageants. My attention became focused on the process of alteration and the evidence for it: erasures, overwritings, interpolations, and the different hands at work; and that is what this essay is about.

For this form of manuscript archaeology, the printed edition can only be of limited help. Its diacritics told me that something had been added to the text, but not in whose writing. They pointed out that some material was written over an erasure, but not what had been erased. (I must add hastily here that sometimes it is impossible to ascertain what has been erased, even with the current state of technology.) I took the facsimile down from the shelf. But it was in black and white, which irons out distinctions between erasures and shadows, irregularities in the parchment and intentional ink marks. I needed to look at the manuscript again – which I did. I needed to take it home with me and spend time with it – which is clearly impossible. I needed to enlarge it. I needed to do things to it that would have destroyed the original manuscript. I needed digital photography.

The original scans of the *Ordo* made by York City Archives, though excellent for all ordinary purposes, were not quite detailed enough for the kind of examination I needed to subject them to. I therefore, with the permission of the Archivist, Rita Freedman, went in and acquired some state-of-the-art digital photographs, taken for me by the specialist manuscript photographer for the Digital Image Archive of Medieval Music project (DIAMM).[30]

Digital images have several advantages: though they do not replace work on the original manuscript, they supplement it very usefully. One advantage is that something about having the light source as it were behind the manuscript forces you to notice erasures and changes of ink. In the manuscript, it is possible to see them without being aware of them; on screen they are in your face. How many people have noticed that the famous 1376 entry 'De vno Ten*emento* in quo Tres pagine Corp*oris* Chr*ist*i ponu*ntur per annum*'[31] is written over an erasure in a different ink and different, later, hand, and that the accepted dating of the earliest record of the York cycle is therefore, to say the least, unsafe?

It had become crucial to see as much of the written text as possible. Here the depredations of time, water, and archivists' repairs on the manuscript are particularly frustrating. Lucy Toulmin Smith was a scrupulous palaeographer and noted where she had observed erasures and other alterations before the 1892 flood and subsequent patching. However, she assumed that the main-text hand and the hand that made alterations both belonged to Roger Burton. Her main interest was to establish the original content of the pageants, and so, though she noted in general that 'some of the erasures and alterations were evidently made by Burton himself,' she assumed that this was 'when writing,' and disregarded them in detail. Thus we have no pre-Ouse-flood evidence for them.[32]

Here we are thrown back on what the DIAMM Project has christened 'virtual restoration' by electronic means.[33] It is possible, using various techniques, to recover quite a lot of the vanished text, even through the paper patches. Even if you cannot recover it all, enough of the letter shapes may show up to enable you to determine which hand you are looking at. For example, it seems pretty clear that in the Ironmongers' pageant (*Christ in the House of Simon the Leper*, f. 253r), 'Maria magdalena lavans pedes Iesu lacrimis suis & capillis suis tergens' (Mary Magdalene washing the feet of Jesus with her tears and wiping them with her hair) is a later addition, or at least an alteration. Conversely, the Smiths' 'Ihesus super Pynaculum templi & diabolus temptans eum cum lapidibus & ij angeli administrantes &c' (Jesus on the pinnacle of the temple, and the devil tempting him with stones, and two attendant angels etcetera, f. 253r) seems to be totally original (Plate 3).

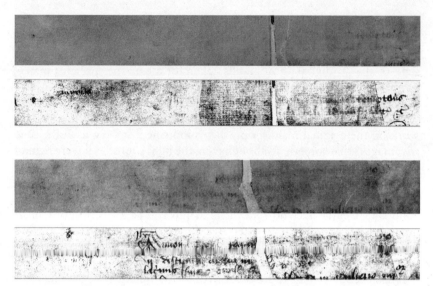

3. York City Archives, A/Y Memorandum Book, f. 253r: Smiths' pageant, *The Temptation of Christ*, unaltered; Ironmongers' pageant, *Christ in the House of Simon the Leper*, altered by Hand B. Photo DIAMM, © York City Archives and Meg Twycross.

One can even sometimes read erasures. It is marginally possible to pick out remnants of ink which have soaked into the parchment even after the eraser's penknife has removed most of it, and enhance them. Minute gradations in UV scans can also sometimes produce at least the ghost of the original, though they have to go through a sequence of processes, since what one is reading there appears to depend on the relative distribution of dark and light pixels. Usually, however, one needs a combination of different techniques: for example, digital enhancement of 'straight' scans, compared with the same area under ultraviolet. It is immensely time-consuming: each minor problem has probably taken me two or three hours, and the major ones several weeks.

However, one major piece has already paid off: I now have a pretty good idea of what was originally written in the last paragraph of the Proclamation, buried under its early-sixteenth-century emendation, and I have published the tentative results in *Medieval English Theatre*.[34] And a minor clarification. In the Second List the pageant of the Raising of Lazarus (*Suscitacio Lazari*, f. 255r) is attributed in Johnston and Rogerson's *York* to the 'Hartshorners.'[35] In fact the ultraviolet scan reveals that the owners are given as 'Hatters Horners.' The imagined *r* is the ascender of the *k* on 'Skynners' underneath, and the abbreviation for *er* after 'Hatt'- is quite clear. The scribe presumably missed out the ampersand for lack of space. This solves the problem of what has always seemed to me a peculiarly restricted commercial activity, and confirms Peter Meredith's inspired guess that 'since Hartshorners is preceded by two capitula instead of the usual one, it may represent a group of crafts rather than a single one.'[36] The 'erased name' on f. 253v is infuriatingly ambiguous: it clearly begins with an *H*, but after that could be either 'Hatters' or 'Horners.' (Moreover there appears to be another name under it and above 'Skynners.') On the whole I rather go for 'Horners,' but this is purely subjective.

Another small but pleasant emendation: the English translation in the Second List of the Bowyers' pageant, *Illusio christi coram Cay[phas]* is not 'perryng,' as suggested in the REED transcription, but, as one might expect, 'poppyng.' As the Soldiers say, 'we schall play popse for þe pages prowe' (play 29 line 355). The next translation looks closer to Beadle and Meredith's suggestion of 'accursyng' rather than REED's 'accunsyng'[37] – it appears to have an *r* in the middle – but I am not yet totally satisfied that I can see what it might be.

For this research, I have found myself working largely on-screen, making transcriptions, annotations, and observations on html pages. The drawback for a paper-based presentation, like this one, is that it is often very difficult to show the minute gradations that I have presented in contrasting colour on-screen in the different medium of a grayscale and necessarily heavily reduced image on paper. The future of publication in manuscript studies seems inexorably to be screen-based – see, for example, the *Beowulf* and Boethius editions.

My major interest in computers and manuscripts so far has been in the teaching of and research into palaeography. Digital images enable the researcher to get in close to the mechanics of writing. With a high resolution scan (these were 850 dpi on an actual-size image) each letter can be magnified to over ten times its actual size without losing definition; in the case of the *Ordo*'s minims, for example, to 20 mm high on screen. The movement of the pen is clearly visible. Not only does it make reading easier, but hands from different pages and even from different manuscripts in different libraries can be anatomized and compared at length. One of the first things that struck me was the difference in the hands involved in the writing of the descriptions, to such an extent that the existence of characteristic letter shapes suggested, even through the paper patches, whether or not an alteration had been made.

It is fairly easy to see that there are two main hands involved in the text on ff. 252v–5r, disregarding the later alterations made at intervals to the guild attributions, and the major early sixteenth-century rewriting of the text of the Proclamation at the top of f. 255r, about which I have written elsewhere.[38] Hand A, whom we have always assumed to be Roger Burton, wrote the heading and text of the original *Ordo*, the first list of torches, and the official proclamation to be read, in English, on the Eve of Corpus Christi from f. 252v to the top of f. 255r. Another hand, Hand B, then wrote what is known as the Second List, which presents all the pageants at a glance. This takes up most of the rest of f. 255r.

Opinion about this second hand has varied: some scholars have thought that it was another scribe, and some that it was Hand A using a less formal script, while some appear to have wavered between the two.[39] Malcolm Parkes, however, believes that it was not the same as Hand A, but

> a second scribe who was probably younger than the first. [In the heading h]e employed a slightly later version of [Anglicana] *Littera acuta*, where *m* was again traced with multiple strokes, but formed with a very shallow clockwise curved movement (instead of the diagonal ones in the handwriting of the first scribe) ... The handwriting of the second scribe in [the Second List] is less consistent, since he was writing more quickly. My attribution of the hand-writing is based on the personal *ductus* of the scribes (the ways in which they wrote – mainly the rhythms which are harder to describe than to see – and the treatment of certain letter forms other than *m*).[40]

✓ Ian Doyle confirms that these two hands are 'quite distinct.'[41] Hand B's preferences include the use of a single-compartmented Secretary letter **a**, and a pointed-apex Secretary **g** with an open tail, which became my touchstone for recognizing his alterations. Doyle also points out his use of 'Secretary final **s**, and the forms of the **I/J**, **f**, and long **s**.' Where Hand A almost always uses the *nomen sacrum* abbreviation 'Ihc' for 'Ih*esu*s,' with a rather elaborate capital **I/J**, Hand B also not infrequently spells 'Iesus' in full with a simple looped head to the **I/J** (Plate 4).

It is easy enough to note the difference between the hands en bloc, but equally easy to miss the fact that the contribution of Hand B to the *Ordo* is quite extensive. (Peter Meredith and Richard Beadle are so far the only people really to remark on them, and that necessarily briefly, though they attribute both hands to Burton.)[42] He rubs, scrapes, overwrites, and makes insertions. Some of his alterations are major, like the scraping out and overwriting as one item of the separate pageants of the Saucemakers

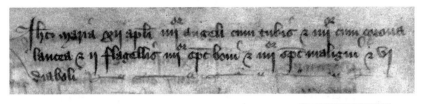

Hand A

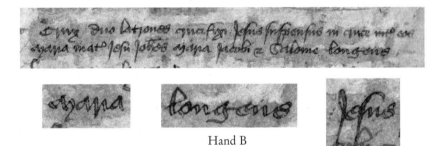

Hand B

4. Hand A compared with Hand B. Photo DIAMM, © York City Archives and Meg Twycross

(*Suicide of Judas*), Tilemakers (*Trial before Pilate*), and Turners, Hairsters, and Bollers (*The Scourging and Crowning with Thorns*), and the total removal of the Millers' pageant (*Dicing for Christ's Garments*) some time during or after 1422.[43] Others are quite small, but reflect at the least a mildly editorial approach to what the *Ordo* was trying to describe. Hand B first appears in the *Ordo* adding a subtitle to the original flourished title:

> Ordo paginar*um* \ludi/ Corporis Chris*ti* tempore Will*elm*i Alne Maioris Anno regni Regis Henrici quinti post conquestum Anglie *ter*cio [HAND A] compila*tus* per Roge*r*um Burton *clericum* co*mmunem* in anno *domini* mill*esim*o ccccxv^mo [HAND B]

Alongside this addition, Burton has set his notarial *signum*: two trefoils flanking the R for '*R*egistravit.'[44]

Hand B has made another alteration to the title: the word 'paginarum' is written over an erasure,[45] and then 'ludi' superscribed. I have spent some time trying to see if anything of the original word underneath 'paginarum' is visible, so far unsuccessfully.[46] It might just, disappointingly, have been 'paginarum' misspelled: but what if it were, for example, 'processionis'?[47]

After this, Hand B seems regularly to have updated and corrected Hand A's original text. At first I thought that some of the alterations were merely cosmetic: where, for example, ink had blotted the original, but that does not seem to be so. A ?later hand has drawn over some of the letters in a darker ink, most noticeably in the Plasterers' pageant, where he has traced over the double-compartmented a favoured by Hand A. It is thus unlikely to have been Hand B, who favours the single-compartmented Secretary a. Lucy Toulmin Smith suggests that this tampering was 'recent' when she saw the manuscript. The same hand with apparently the same ink has been at work in other documents in the Archives, for example Y: A15, the Corpus Christi Indenture of 1432.

But all Hand B's alterations appear to be substantive. Some emend vocabulary: the Cardmakers' 'de costa Ade' (from Adam's rib) seems originally to have been the more unusual 'de costera Ade' (from Adam's side). Others appear to be correcting Hand A's grammar, like the misguided alteration of 'inspirans in eos spiritum vite' (breathing into them the spirit of life), which is biblical and correct,[48] to 'inspirans eos spiritu vite' (inspiring them with the spirit of life).[49] As for the crowd of singing angels which accompany Mary's Coronation, he knows that something has definitely gone wrong with the grammar, but hasn't quite put his finger on the problem: 'cum turba Angelorum cantantes' is unfortunate, but 'cantans' is if possible even worse, and further emendations have disappeared into a mercifully concealing blot.

Some are clarifications, like adding *Isaac* to *Abraham immolans filium suum* (if that is not a later hand), and *ab Aramathia* to the *Ioseph* in the Butchers' and Poulterers' pageant (ditto), or explaining, in the Spurriers' and Lorimers' pageant (*Christ and the Doctors in the Temple*), that 'Ihesus' is in fact a 'puer,' and that 'eorum,' 'eos,' and 'eis' refer to 'Doctores.' Or, in the Scriveners' pageant (*Doubting Thomas*) and the Woolweavers' pageant (*The Assumption*), deciding that 'Thomas de India' was probably too obscure, and altering him to plain 'Thomas apostolus.' He seems to have had serious problems with the nature of the Body of Christ in the Deposition, rejecting 'Ihesum,' and then 'mortuum corpus,' before settling for the 'eum' which he had crossed out in the first place.

Hand B also seems to have had a mild obsession with rearranging the

material according to what he thinks is the focal point: the Painters',
Pinners', and Latoners' pageant (*The Crucifixion*) and the following Butchers' and Poulterers' pageant (*The Death and Deposition*) have both had
their opening words altered to 'Crux' (The Cross); and in the Spicers'
pageant (*The Annunciation*), the Pewterers' and Founders' pageant (*Joseph's
Trouble*), and the Mayor's pageant (*The Coronation*) 'Maria' is pushed to
the head of the cast list, displacing respectively 'Angelus' (Gabriel), 'Iosep,'
and 'Ihesus.' The original 'Mariam' appears in each case to have been
erased, or in the case of the Mayor's pageant, just left there;[50] the Painters'
clearly once read 'Ihesus extensus in cruce,' but Hand B altered it to
'\Crux/ Ihesus extensus in ea.' This produces a curious proleptic syntax:
'*Maria Iosep volens dimittere eam*' (Mary, Joseph wishing to put her
away), '*Crux Ihesus extensus in* ea *super terram*' (The Cross, Jesus stretched
out on it on the ground). It does, I suppose, preserve the list pattern, if one
thinks of the Cross as a character.

   Then there are the alterations which arise from alterations in the actual
performance. Some are small updates as characters are added to the cast
lists: like Herod's son and the messenger in the first Goldsmiths' pageant
(*The Three Kings*, later the Masons'), and, apparently, Mary Magdalene in
the Ironmongers' pageant (*Jesus in the House of Simon the Leper*). But
some of them are major. In early 1422 the Painters and Stainers (*The
Stretching and Nailing to the Cross*) petitioned to combine pageants with
the Pinners and Latoners (*The Raising of the Cross upon Mount Calvary*)
to produce a composite pageant of the Crucifixion of Christ.[51] The result
is recorded at the top of f. 254r: the second pageant has been scraped out,
and the material rewritten as one continuous entry (Plate 5). The Pinners
and Latoners, who kept their pageant wagon, and became the lead guild in
the organization of the pageant, have been moved to the head of the guild
attribution; but Hand B has thriftily recycled the *P* of 'Payntours' so that it
now begins 'Pynners.'[52] Conversely, the 1431 splitting up of the Goldsmiths' entry to show that the first of their pageants has been taken over by
the Masons only needed the insertion of 'Masons' alongside the guild
attribution, and a new paraph to begin the second episode with 'Maria cum
puero ...' The major amalgamation of 1421/2, when the Saucemakers'
(*Suicide of Judas*), Tilemakers' (*Trial before Pilate*), Turners', Hairsters',
and Bollers' (*The Scourging and Crowning with Thorns*), and Millers'
(*Dicing for Christ's Garments*) pageants became one play, *The Condemna-
tion of Christ*, has left its mark across the bottom third of f. 253v and the
top of f. 254r, where the Millers' pageant has been erased, tantalizingly, not
quite completely.[53] The radical scraping and rewriting of the pageants at

5. York City Archives, A/Y Memorandum Book, top of f. 254r: the Millers' pageant erased; the Painters' and Stainers' pageant (*The Stretching and Nailing to the Cross*) combined with the Pinners' and Latoners' pageant (*The Raising of the Cross upon Mount Calvary*) to produce a composite pageant, *The Crucifixion of Christ*; something strange happening to the Butchers' and Poulterers' pageant. Photo DIAMM, © York City Archives and Meg Twycross.

the bottom of f. 253v suggests that the Shearmen (*Via Crucis*) were also affected by the change, though there may have been other reasons. The otherwise unrecorded but pre-Register joining together of the Bakers' *Last Supper* and the Waterleaders' *Washing of Feet* resulted in a major scraping and rewriting, which suggests that the writer was having organizational problems as well as doctrinal difficulty in expressing what the pageant was about. And the Butchers' and Poulterers' pageant, of the *Death and Deposition*, seems to have undergone a refashioning, but with no sign of when this was or what the changes were.

I am very much aware that some of the corrections that I have attributed to Hand B may on further examination turn out to be the work of a Hand C or even a Hand D or E. (Some alterations, such as the addition to the Bowyers' and Fletchers' pageant, *The Buffeting*, are conspicuously later, though it reflects the scene with Peter and the maidservant, which is part of the pageant as we know it, and so must have been before the writing of the Register.) Hand A himself made an alteration at the very beginning: the description of the Tanners' pageant (*The Creation and Fall of the Angels*) has been erased and rewritten a line-space further up. It is written in the same script as the other original entries. But however many hands may eventually turn out to have been involved, it does not change the fact that there are a considerable number of alterations which must, because of their content, have been made anything from seven to seventeen years later than 1415, and the vast majority represent a change, either of content or of ✓ attitude, towards what the list was aiming to describe.

Now comes the shock. Hand A is not Burton. The writing does not match anything written by him in the rest of A/Y or elsewhere, even in the lengthy Chronicle of the Archbishops of York, 'scripta *propria* manu Rogeri de Burton' on ff. 219v–46v of the Memorandum Book (Plate 6).[54] Even at his most formal, Burton writes a cursive, slightly forward-leaning hand with single-compartmented Secretary a, and a pointed-apex Secretary g with an open lower loop.[55] Hand A belongs to a previous generation of scribes. The nearest hand to his that I have so far found is the one that in the Freemen's Register, f. 12r, records Burton's election to the post of common clerk in 1415, the year in which William Alne was elected mayor and the *Ordo* was first drawn up. The Freemen's Register was not only used to record the annual admissions to the freedom of the city, it also recorded the annual election of the mayor, the common clerk, and the *servientes Maioris*, who became the sword- and mace-bearer respectively. These folios, 4r–27v, are not transcribed into the Surtees Society edition.[56] One would imagine that a man would record his own election, but there seems to have been a habit (rather than a tradition) that the outgoing clerk or a deputy wrote the final minute of his reign.[57] I am not capable yet of confirming whether this person was William del Bothe, the previous common clerk, or if he was the one who wrote the *Ordo*. His as are mildly suspect. But Hand A was certainly someone of his scribal generation.[58]

It seems more than likely that Burton was Hand B. Close comparison of word formation in the Chronicle of the Archbishops, and in the entries in the Freemen's Register show without a doubt that he wrote the Second List (which he signed at the end), and it is likely that he wrote the alterations to the Tilers' and the Shearmen's pageants and, for example, the *pastores* alterations in the Tilethatchers' and Chandlers' pageants. The general aspect of most other, shorter, alterations within the time-scale suggests that he wrote them too.[59]

This completely alters the received opinion of what is going on in the *Ordo*. Burton did not write it himself, but commissioned someone else to write it. This is not in itself odd, considering what we know of the role and status of notaries public. Though Burton was an assiduous record keeper in A/Y, other hands besides his are employed in it during his regime. However, he was determined that later users of the list should know that it was he who drew it up, so he added the subtitle with his name and confirmation of the date, and added his notarial *signum* to make sure it was

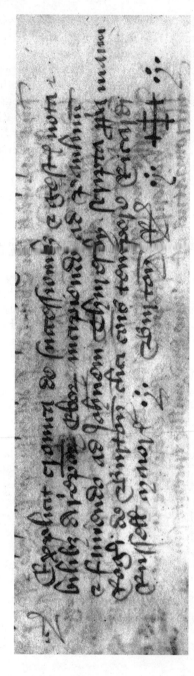

6. [Explicit to the Chronicle of the Archbishops of York] York City Archives A/Z Memorandum Book, f. 246v: *scripta propria manu Rogeri de Burton*. Photo DIAMM, © York City Archives and Meg TwycⅢss.

properly recorded. He does seem, at this stage, to have been insistent that credit should be afforded to him where credit was due. The first thing that he did when taking over the Freemen's Register was to alter his predecessor's account of his election, adding 'notari*us* pu*bli*cus' to his own name. The following year he recorded the exact sum (£7 p.a.) of the fee for himself and his clerk, 'vna*nimi* voce *omnium* nemine reclamante' citing his qualifications as 'cle*ri*cus Ebor*acensis* dioc*esis* auct*oritat*ib*us* ap*ost*olica & imp*er*iali Notarius.'[60] One can only imagine what office politics were when he entered on his twenty-one-year period of office, and what role Hand A played in them. Was he the retiring incumbent, taking on a retirement job? Or was he Burton's own *clericus*? In which case, logic would suggest that if he were the deputy common clerk, and if Burton's deputy common clerk, were, as Sandy Johnston has suggested, William Revetour,[61] here we have Revetour's hand. But I would prefer not to build too many assumptions on such logic without a great deal more detailed research into the hands of York city officials in the early fifteenth century: let us stick with calling him Hand A.

This then raises the question of what Burton meant by *compilatum*. The verb, in both Latin and English, had a wider semantic field in the fourteenth and fifteenth centuries than it does today. In English, it can be used where we would use 'composed' – 'Heere is ended the book of the tales of Caunterbury, compiled by Geffrey Chaucer' – but from the medieval point of view which sees literary composition as the amassing and arrangement of pre-existent material. It looks as if here 'compiled' is used much as in our modern sense, which was also available: 'I haue compiled þis werk of þe sawes of þe foresaide auctores, and of myn owne experience'; Chauliac, quoted *MED* sv *compilen* 2(a). Burton has collected together (and perhaps redrafted) the matter of the billets. These were already being sent out in 1396, when two sheets of parchment were bought for them.[62] Whether he also updated the traditional material (which is well within the standard late medieval meaning of 'compile') we cannot tell; nor what type of draft he supplied to Hand A to copy up. If he had only handed over the tattered original copy-text from 1396 and before, it seems unlikely that he would have claimed to be the compiler of the 1415 list, and the heading states very clearly that this is the list of pageants as they stand 'tempore Will*elmi* Alne Maioris Anno regni Regis Henrici quinti post conquestum Anglie t*er*cio.'

After that, he took over the charge of correcting and updating the list from the original scribe. If some of his corrections seem a bit quibbling, he had the right as common clerk to pull rank. And he had the status and the confidence to alter not only the content of the pageant descriptions, but acclaimed *Mysteries* for the National Theatre. This professional theatre project developed over a number of years, with the first part, *The Passion*, performed in 1977 and the final Creation to Doomsday text directed by Bill Bryden in 1984. Harrison's Yorkshire-accented, working-class play is a condensed cycle based on the York text with additions from the other three surviving series of biblical plays, Chester, Towneley, and N-Town. Harrison's *Mysteries*, provoked by Browne's first York production, have been inspirational in their turn: they have promoted their own view of the characteristics of the mystery play genre and established basic guidelines for other productions. Their influence has been felt back in York itself, where the hard hats and the building-site set used in the Theatre Royal production of 1992 recalled the Bryden interpretation of Harrison's work.

Like Rose's Towneley plays and the Harrison/Bryden *Mysteries*, the four creative works that form the focus of the remainder of this essay have grown out of experience of the York mystery plays. This is not in each case a first-hand experience of the local productions, but one that responds to and projects popular perceptions of the plays in the modern context.

Tony Morris and Barbara Whitehead

Both Tony Morris and Barbara Whitehead have close associations with York and write from an insider's point of view, offering a close-up of the plays in preparation and performance. A performance poet, Morris is York-born and has acted in two Museum Gardens productions.[24] At the time of writing her novel, Whitehead was living in nearby Murton and working in York, where she could undertake the necessary research with relative ease.[25]

Morris's series of poems, *Poet in Residence* (1996), was designed as an artistic documentary. It celebrates the second of the Theatre Royal mystery plays, a condensed cycle that was scripted by Scottish poet Liz Lochhead and directed by John Doyle, then resident director at the theatre. This was a well-publicized production, largely because of the controversy over the choice of a woman, Ruth Ford, to play God the Creator.[26] Much less attention was given to the fact that it was played by the first all-amateur cast since the Edward Taylor production in 1969. Taylor had felt the need to share the role of Christ among three local amateur actors, fearing that a single amateur actor would not have the stamina required to see out the season, but in 1996 local amateur Rory Mulvihill played Christ in the Theatre Royal and exhibited the staying power of any professional.[27]

also their mode, so that they would become much more like descriptions of plays, like, in fact, his Second List. Those made in his hand presumably antedate his final retirement in 1432/3 – though even that is uncertain, as a new common clerk was not sworn in until 1435/6.[63] At some point before 1421/2 he wrote the Second List, perhaps, as Beadle and Meredith suggest, as 'an order of pageants supplementary to the Proclamation, possibly even for the practical purpose of checking their order as they left Toft Green.'[64]

What questions do these discoveries raise (apart from the ones I set out to answer in the first place)? There are a variety of intriguing little problems, such as 'Why were Jesus and the apostles struck out of the Raising of Lazarus?' and 'What else can there possibly have been to erase in the description of the Mayor's pageant of the Coronation of the Virgin?' – 'Ih*esus* coronans Mariam cu*m* turba Angelorum cantants\t/*es*' seems perfectly adequate. But the major ones centre around documents and people.

Much more can and must be done about the hands of scribes in the York records, using digital photography to make close comparisons and identifications. It would be useful to create a database of hands. To advance, we would have to go outside the strictly limited range of documents on early drama. Eventually we might even discover which scribes were responsible for the main text of the York Register. (Peter Meredith has already located the sixteenth-century additions by John Clerke, who also appears in the Bakers' records, now Additional MS 33852 in the British Library.)[65]

There needs to be a lot more work on Roger Burton and his circle: the group of professional functionaries who worked for the city and for the church. Burton was a secular married notary public of the diocese of York;[66] Revetour a cleric in orders who nevertheless worked for the city and made influential friends such as the Boltons and Nicholas Blackburn Senior who got him his chantry post in St William's Ousebridge, next to the council chamber. Sandy Johnston has shown the way with her detailed work on Revetour's will;[67] we need to pursue the ramifications. We tend to think of the city and the church as two separate establishments, but here was a group of men with common professional interests and a common involvement, whether through personal interest or professional duty, in pageantry. What practical effect might this linking of church and city have had on the development of the Corpus Christi Play?

We are unlikely now to find any substantial new documents for York in the REED mode, but this does not mean that there are no new discoveries to be made. We can and must go back and look again at those documents that we have, using all the technological tools at our disposal – which are likely to become yet more helpful as technology progresses. The Heroic

Age of the York records is not over yet; it is just entering its second phase. Dwarfs, maybe, standing on the shoulders of the REED giants, but exciting and new-directional all the same.

NOTES

Plates 1–6 are published by kind permission of the Archivist, York City Archives. I would like to thank Rita Freedman and the staff of York City Archives; Julia Craig-McFeely of the DIAMM Project for arranging for the digital photography and instructing me in the techniques of virtual restoration; Peter Scott for taking the photographs; Malcolm Parkes and Ian Doyle for their expert palaeographical opinions; Pamela M. King, Olga Horner, Lena Etherington, and Muriel Utting, of the York *Doomsday* Project, for energetically discussing and rearranging my argument; Peter Meredith, for lending me the original prints of the A/Y Memorandum Book used in the facsimile, and for making encouraging noises; Rosemary Phizackerley; Ann Rycraft for answering my queries on fifteenth-century York worthies; Andrew Prescott, for helping with notaries public; and David Klausner and Karen Marsalek, for being patient.

 1 Elected 2 Henry V on Saint Blaise's Day (3 February 14/15): York City Archives MS D1 (Freemen's Register), f. 12r. Resigned 3 February 1432/3, having stayed on in the job at the earnest solicitation of the mayor and aldermen ever since his first attempt to resign in 1428, with the proviso that he is doing it of his own free will and is not bound by oath: Freemen's Register, f. 14v. However, no successor was immediately elected, and later notes say that he was common clerk for twenty-one years, which suggests that he did not get away until 1435/6, when Thomas Uldale was formally elected. According to the heading the *Ordo* was drawn up in 3 Henry V (1415/16), confirmed by the subheading as 1415. For an account of Burton, see Richard Beadle and Peter Meredith, *The York Play: A Facsimile of British Library MS Additional 35290, together with a facsimile of the 'Ordo Paginarum' section of the A/Y Memorandum Book* (Leeds: University of Leeds School of English, 1983), lv; hereafter cited as *York Play: Facsimile*.
 2 Originally the A/Y Memorandum Book was in two volumes, the *maior registrum* and the *novum registrum*, with a paper section intended for an index: see Beadle and Meredith, *York Play: Facsimile*, li, and Alexandra F. Johnston and Margaret Rogerson, eds, 2 vols, *York*, REED (Toronto: University of Toronto Press, 1979), 1:xx: hereafter cited as Johnston and Rogerson, *York*. The *Ordo* was written on a series of folios which would originally have been

at the back of the first volume, possibly preceded by a few blank leaves which were later filled up with material dated 1419 and after. This seems to give a terminus ad quem for both the *Ordo* and the Second List; the *Ordo* might just conceivably have been drafted in 1415 on some other document and transferred to the Memorandum Book later. For a collation diagram of this gathering, see *York Play: Facsimile,* li.

3 At this point the folios are about 202–5 mm wide at the top and 290–3 mm deep – slightly narrower than a piece of A4. The written area varies, since the text is not right-justified, and the bottom margin depends on the amount of content to be fitted in, but overall is about 155 mm wide and 245 mm high. These figures vary slightly from the codicological description given in Johnston and Rogerson, *York,* 1:xx, as I made the measurements when the book was disbound: the height measurements were made in the gutter.

4 This is not so visible in the Leeds facsimile, as the manuscript was tightly bound when the black and white photographs were taken, but since it has been disbound, the original layout is much clearer.

5 Dimensions very variable. Outer margin, between 30 and 40 mm on the versos, can be less (down to 15 mm) on the rectos because text block is unjustified. Gutter: on the rectos quite wide, 25 mm to 28 mm, variable on the versos because unjustified. On f. 253r the left margin suddenly narrows (from *Marshalls*) from 28 to 20 mm. Top margin: fairly stable, matching the rest of the A/Y Memorandum Book at about 20 mm to the bottom of the first line. Bottom margin variable, 30 to 35 mm. The rest of this section of the book has outer margins of 45–50 mm, and gutters of 28–30 mm; top margins of 20 mm to top line, and bottom of 45 mm.

6 The forked brackets seem to be an afterthought, as the first one (the Tanners) runs over the paraph mark for the description. Some (e.g., the Chandlers) are purely straight lines. In complicated cases, such as the Goldsmiths, they become a veritable cat's cradle.

7 I can see no ruling on these folios, except for a vertical line on the right hand side of f. 255r, which seems to have come through from the other side. Where there is pricking, it does not, oddly, seem to apply to this particular layout: on f. 252v there is a prick in the middle of the *w* of 'Pewterers,' 50 mm in. This appears to be the original pricking for the rest of this part of the manuscript, totally disregarded for the *Ordo*. There is no attempt to match the text blocks on the recto and verso.

8 I am very grateful to Professor Malcolm Parkes for this information, made in a private communication dated 6 November 2004.

9 See, for example, Martin Stevens and Margaret Dorrell (Rogerson), 'The *Ordo Paginarium* [sic] Gathering of the York A/Y Memorandum Book,'

Modern Philology 72 (1974–5): 45–59; Margaret Dorrell, 'The Mayor of York and the Coronation Pageant,' *Leeds Studies in English* ns 5 (1971): 35–45; Peter Meredith, 'The *Ordo paginarum* and the Development of the York Tilemakers' Pageant,' *Leeds Studies in English* ns 11 (1980): 59–73; Beadle and Meredith, *York Play: Facsimile*, liii–liv; *The York Plays*, ed. Richard Beadle (London: Edward Arnold, 1982), 23–7; and of course Johnston and Rogerson, *York*, passim, especially Appendix 6; 2:657–85. Most of these belong to what might be called the Heroic Age of the York records, when the REED York volumes were in preparation and just published, and attention was focused on the manuscripts.

10 For a detailed and unemotive codicological description of the *Ordo paginarum*, see Beadle and Meredith, *York Play: Facsimile*, li–lix.

11 Johnston and Rogerson, *York*, 214, 215; Beadle and Meredith, *York Play: Facsimile*, liii. As Beadle and Meredith point out, nor do we get any evidence of the later organizational changes, such as the passing over of *Emmaus* to the Sledmen in 1535 (Johnston and Rogerson, *York*, 307), or the Minstrels taking on *Herod and the Kings* from the Masons (Beadle and Meredith refer to this mistakenly as 'the Purification') in 1561 (Johnston and Rogerson, *York*, 334, 337–8). Lucy Toulmin Smith suggested (*York Plays*, xxvi, note 4: see below note 17) that the addition of the Joiners, Cartwrights, Carvers, and Sawyers to the Carpenters and their pageant of the Resurrection must date from 1562 when these trades 'were united,' but Johnston and Rogerson, *York*, 127, shows that this entry dates from 1482 (A/Y, ff. 367v–8r), which would fit the script of the addition.

12 Meg Twycross, 'Forget the 4.30 a.m. Start,' *Medieval English Theatre* 25 (2003): 98–152.

13 Johnston and Rogerson, *York*, 249–50.

14 Johnston and Rogerson, *York*, 291–2.

15 Richard Beadle, Introduction to *York Plays*, 24.

16 Johnston and Rogerson, *York*, 355 (billets accustomed); 338 (Minstrels).

17 *York Plays: The Plays Performed by the Crafts or Mysteries of York on the Day of Corpus Christi in the 14th, 15th, and 16th Centuries*, ed. Lucy Toulmin Smith (Oxford: Clarendon Press, 1885), xix, note 1. She uses the medieval foliation: modern ff. 252, 253, 254, 255. The slashes on ff. 253 and 254 stretch for two-thirds and half of the folio respectively. They might have been the effects of one knife attack on f. 253r, which went through to the following folio, but not as damagingly. The knife cut swerves sharply to the right and then possibly to the right again as it gets towards the bottom of the page – a right-handed criminal? But why should his venom be directed against *The Flight into Egypt* and *The Massacre of the Innocents*?

18 R. Davies, *Extracts from the Municipal Records of the City of York during the Reigns of Edward IV, Edward V, and Richard III* (London: J.B. Nichols, 1843), does not mention them, but then he is not interested in the condition of the manuscript, merely its content.

19 See Stevens and Dorrell, 'The *Ordo Paginarium* Gathering,' 46.

20 See Beadle and Meredith, *York Play: Facsimile,* lv–lvi.

21 *York Plays,* ed. Toulmin Smith, xix–xxvii and xxxiv. Johnston and Rogerson, *York,* footnotes transcriptions where they fill in gaps in what can be seen nowadays. The Second List was published by Davies, *Extracts,* 233–6.

22 See Stevens and Dorrell, 'The *Ordo Paginarium* Gathering,' 46, though my impression is that what one can see are the indentations rather than clean parchment. The marks of the pen are also clearly visible in the facsimile, but we did not succeed in capturing them well enough in our digital scans to be able to do much with them.

23 Transcription in Johnston and Rogerson, *York,* 16–26; explanatory note, 869.

24 There actually seem to be more than even she discerned.

25 For Dublin, see E.K. Chambers, *The Mediaeval Stage,* 2 vols (London: Oxford University Press, 1903), 2:364. For Hereford, see David N. Klausner, ed., *Herefordshire/Worcestershire,* REED (Toronto: University of Toronto Press, 1990), 115–16.

26 See B.A.M. Ramakers, *Spelen en Figuren: Toneelkunst en processiecultuur in Oudenaarde tussen Middeleuwen en Moderne Tijd* (Amsterdam: Amsterdam University Press, 1996); Wim Hüsken, 'The Bruges *Ommegang,*' in *Formes teatrals: Actes del VII Colloqui, Societé Internationale pour l'Étude du Théâtre Médiévale, Gerona, 1992* (Barcelona: SITM, 1996), 77–85; Meg Twycross, 'The Leuven Ommegang and Leuven City Archives,' in *European Medieval Drama 4* (2000): *Selected Papers from the Fourth International Conference on 'Aspects of European Medieval Drama,' Camerino, 5–8 August 1999,* ed. André Lascombes and Sydney Higgins (Turnhout: Brepols, 2001), 77–90.

27 Johnston and Rogerson, *York,* 37–8.

28 Johnston and Rogerson, *York,* 6–7.

29 Meredith, 'The *Ordo paginarum* and the Development of the York Tilemakers' Pageant,' 59–73.

30 For the DIAMM Project, see their website, www.diamm.ac.uk. The A/Y Memorandum Book has recently been disbound for conservation. York City Archives took the opportunity of scanning it. However, the flatbed scanner they used, though it has produced some very good results (especially since it acted as a sort of lightbox), also automatically 'sharpened' the images, removing some of the fine gradations in colour between pixels, reducing their

usefulness for really detailed work. I therefore brought in a specialist manuscript photographer, Peter Scott, from the DIAMM project with their camera to take supplementary digital photographs of the *Ordo paginarum* and various pages from the Freemen's Register. He used a PowerPhase FX camera, taking images as RGB under daylight balanced lighting conditions. This is 'cold light' and does not harm the MS by overheating it. Images were digitized at 850 dpi, and stored as uncompressed TIFs. The copyright in the images resides with York City Archives; DIAMM is licensed to hold copies for archiving purposes; the copyright in the digital restorations belongs to Professor Meg Twycross.

We tried several different approaches: a straight image; raking light, to try and bring up the grooves left by the pen when the ink was washed away; ultraviolet; and a light sheet which cast a glow through the layers of paper of the patch. These techniques were variously successful. Unfortunately, since the light sheet shows the ghosts of the writing on both recto and verso, the original flatbed scans were often more effective in showing up underlying writing. The raking light needed more time than we could give, and the results were disappointingly thin, not much better than the straightforward scans. The ultraviolet was useful, but because of the different pathologies of the water-damaged and undamaged parchments, it needs two different treatments on screen to reveal the writing on the two different areas. The straightforward scans proved eventually to be the most detailed and useful.

31 A/Y Memorandum Book, f. 4v: see Johnston and Rogerson, *York*, 3. I hope to identify the hand, which looks to me at the moment like one which appears later in the Memorandum Book, from the 1390s.

32 *York Plays*, ed. Toulmin Smith, xix, note 1.

33 See website www.diamm.ac.uk for an account of the techniques.

34 See above, note 12.

35 Johnston and Rogerson, *York*, 25.

36 Beadle and Meredith, *York Play: Facsimile*, lii.

37 Johnston and Rogerson, *York*, 26.

38 See above, note 12.

39 Angelo Raine, as reported by Mendal G. Frampton, appears to suggest that the two hands are different, but his comments are ambiguous. Raine is reported as saying that the signature 'Burton' at the bottom of the Second List 'is not in either of the hands of the list proper. That list is in two hands, all the emendations being in one hand and the entries in another ... As to whether any of the three hands is Burton's Mr. Raine does not commit himself. Whether Burton wrote any of the entries, however, the list is later than Burton's 1415 list' (Mendal G. Frampton, 'The Date of the "Wakefield

Master": Bibliographical Evidence,' *PMLA* 53 [1938]: 102, note 79). Either Frampton did not fully understand Raine, or Raine was hedging his bets. Martin Stevens and Margaret Dorrell (Rogerson) appear to subscribe to the theory that Burton wrote both; however, in the REED edition Johnston and Rogerson say of the two Lists: 'The hands are similar though not identical' (*York*, 869, note to 16). Richard Beadle three years later (1982) is cautious: 'If the list is in Roger Burton's hand, then it is not the more formal variety of it which he used for copying the *Ordo*' (*York Plays* 25, note 59). In the facsimile a year later, he and Peter Meredith seem to come down in the 'Burton writing in two styles' camp: 'the script of the Second List is Secretary with Anglicana r, and it is this script which Burton frequently uses for the additions and alterations in the descriptions' (lv).

40 Private communication dated 6 November 2004.
41 Private communication dated 26 November 2004.
42 *York Play: Facsimile*, lv.
43 Johnston and Rogerson, *York*, 37–8. The date of the council meeting which discussed this is cited as 9 Henry V (1421/2). Peter Meredith calls it 1422/3, on the grounds that the alteration would not have taken place before the next Corpus Christi.
44 On notarial *signa*, see C.R. Cheney, *Notaries Public in England in the Thirteenth and Fourteenth Centuries* (Oxford: Clarendon Press, 1972), 108.
45 A happy combination of his characteristic Secretary **a** and **g**.
46 Peter Meredith (*York Play: Facsimile*, liv) suggests that it originally read 'ludi'; but the word is far too short for the space. Malcolm Parkes suggests 'ludorum,' but that does not go along with the usual vocabulary: the 'ludus' is always the cycle as a whole, the pageants are 'pagine.'
47 Peter Meredith points out that the document is called the *Ordo paginarum* elsewhere in A/Y (*York Play: Facsimile*, liv; Johnston and Rogerson, *York*, 11, ostensibly 1399 but in fact a later marginal note); but since this particular reference was made after the *Ordo* had been drawn up, it does not tell us anything about what an earlier document might have been called.
48 Based on Genesis 2:7: Vulgate 'et inspiravit in faciem eius spiraculum vitae'; Douai-Rheims 'breathed into his face the breath of life.' 'Spiraculum' is the direct object; 'faciem' is in the accusative because it follows 'in' meaning 'into.'
49 If the extension of the abbreviation as given in Johnston and Rogerson, *York*, 17 is correct. It could, however, be a blanket abbreviation for 'sp*iritum*.'
50 It is largely underneath the paper patch but is visible through electronic restoration.
51 Johnston and Rogerson, *York*, 37–8.

52 Peter Meredith points this out in *York Play: Facsimile*, liv.

53 See Meredith, 'The *Ordo paginarum* and the Development of the York Tilemakers' Pageant.'

54 F. 246v: 'Explicit cronica de successionib*us* & gestis notabilib*us* Archie-p*is*copor*um* Ebor*acensium* incipiendi ad Paulin*um* & finiendo ad Ioh*an*nem Thuresby scripta p*ro*p*ria* manu Rog*er*i de Burton cleri*ci* comm*un*is tempore Ricardj Russell maior*is* [Signed] ♣ Burton R*egistravit* ♣ ✠ ♣'

55 The 1432 Indenture between the city and the Corpus Christi Guild (York City Archives MS A15) might be in Burton's hand (he notarized it on the bottom); but even though he/the scribe uses double-compartmented **a** and figure-of-eight **g**, the aspect of the script is completely different from that used by Hand A.

56 *Register of the Freemen of the City of York*, ed. Francis Collins, 2 vols, *Surtees Society Publications* 96 (1897 for 1896), and 102 (1900 for 1899).

57 This is not universal, and would not, of course, work if a new clerk was needed because the outgoing clerk had died.

58 A similar hand wrote ff. 142r–3r of the A/Y Memorandum Book (The Weavers' ordinances), dated 1400.

59 Beadle and Meredith rightly say this too (*York Play: Facsimile*, lv), though they assume that he wrote the body of the text as well.

60 For the double title, see Cheney, *Notaries Public*, 85–7.

61 Alexandra F. Johnston, 'William Revetour, Chaplain and Clerk of York, Testator,' in *Essays in Honour of Peter Meredith*, ed. Catherine Batt, *Leeds Studies in English* ns 29 (1998): 153–72.

62 Johnston and Rogerson, *York*, 9: 'Et pro ij pellibus pergameni tempore billarum corporis Christi vj d.' See also 14 (1405).

63 York City Archives MS D1, f. 14v. Later comments add that he served as common clerk for twenty-one years, which would make his clerkship from 1415 to 1436. See also note 1.

64 *York Play: Facsimile*, liii.

65 Peter Meredith, 'John Clerke's Hand in the York Register,' *Leeds Studies in English* ns 12 (1980/1): 245–71.

66 Angelo Raine, *Medieval York* (London: John Murray, 1955), 135; Joan, widow of Roger Burton late common clerk, lived in a dwelling near the old Common Hall in 1446, when plans were drawn up for the building of a new and larger Guildhall (York City Archives MS G16).

67 Johnston, 'William Revetour.'

REED *York*, Volume 3, The 'Revivals'

MARGARET ROGERSON

In accordance with the policy agreed by the founding editorial board, the first collection in the Records of Early English Drama series, the two-volume REED *York*, took the year 1642 as its terminus.[1] In this essay I entertain the notion of a third York volume, one that would take up the story of the local mystery plays in the era of the modern 'revivals' starting with 1951, the year of the Festival of Britain, and extending into the twenty-first century. This is not to propose that the modern records should come together physically between a handsome set of REED-red boards. In fact, in practical terms, such a volume would be impossible because of the quantity of material involved. My aims here are, rather, to draw attention to a hypothetical table of contents for a third volume, and to demonstrate ways in which one particular set of records, four literary documents, challenge the theatre historian.

Modern revival records similar to the published extracts from the medieval and early modern documents relating to theatrical activity in York reside in various repositories: there is no shortage of minute-book notes, cast lists, pageant routes, and financial accounts.[2] There are also distinctly post-medieval forms of documentation: theatre programs and reviews; scholarly articles; newspaper reports; and photographic, sound, and film records. Not all of this material is readily available but a representative cross section is accessible electronically as a virtual archive through the York *Doomsday* Project at Lancaster University, the Illumination Project at the National Centre for Early Music in York, and the website of the York Guilds.[3]

The records that are of primary concern to me here – crime novels by Barbara Whitehead (1988) and Reginald Hill (1990), a collection of poems by Tony Morris (1996), and a play by Peter Gill (2001) – are even more prominent in the public domain.[4] These texts have all appeared in print; Hill's novel has also been adapted for the popular BBC TV Dalziel and Pascoe series; and Gill's play, winner of the Critics' Circle Theatre Award for Best Play in 2002, was premiered by the English Touring Theatre at The Lowry in Salford Quays in 2001, moving then to the Theatre Royal, Bristol, and in 2002 to London, first to The Royal Court Theatre Downstairs and later to The Strand.[5]

These four texts are accessed for reasons besides that of academic enquiry. They therefore reach a much wider audience than other material that would qualify for inclusion in a hypothetical REED *York*, volume 3, and their potential to reflect and to influence popular understanding of the mystery plays of the York revivals, and indirectly their medieval precursors, is considerable. The literary documents considered here offer artistic impressions not only of the York mysteries but also of the mystery play genre as a whole. Readers already familiar with the genre might not always agree with the interpretations of these authors, but novels and plays do not purport to be mirrors of any social or cultural context outside the one that they create for themselves, and so some inaccuracies can be forgiven.

'Revival' Mystery Play Productions: A Background

In the years immediately leading up to the 1979 publication of the York collection, revivals of English medieval theatre, most usually of mystery plays, were an established activity of both academic and community groups worldwide. Performances of single pageants or selections of pageants were common, and productions of Creation to Doomsday cycles were not unknown. In Australia, for example, Diana Large directed a condensed version of the Towneley plays, 'the first performance of a full cycle of medieval mystery plays outside England,' in the Hobart City Hall for the 1972 Festival of Tasmania.[6] In 1975 Jane Oakshott directed a Creation to Doomsday cycle consisting of thirty-six of the York pageants on wagon stages in Leeds as the finale to the centenary celebrations of the university.[7] In 1977 David Parry directed an even more ambitious production of the complete York cycle at the University of Toronto.[8]

By 1979 York itself had well-established local traditions of mystery play revivals. Beginning in 1951 with the production directed by E. Martin Browne, there had been a total of nine fixed-place productions of condensed Creation to Doomsday cycles set against the backdrop of the ruins of St Mary's Abbey in the centrally located Museum Gardens. After a total of twelve productions in the Museum Gardens the plays were taken indoors in 1992. Two productions at the Theatre Royal in 1992 and 1996 were then followed by Gregory Doran's millennium production in the Minster in 2000. Rory Mulvihill, the local actor who played Lucifer in Doran's production, described it as 'the La Scala of mystery plays.'[9] The impact of this high profile event was such that many local people wanted to see future productions of condensed cycles within the Minster's hallowed walls. There are, however, concerns that the Minster might not host another production until 2010 or even later. At the same time, the Museum Gardens site, last used for a fixed-place mystery play production in 1988, remains deeply ingrained in the local consciousness as the 'spiritual home' of the modern revivals.[10] Consequently, the York Mystery Plays Association was formed in 2003 to consider the future. In conjunction with the York City Council this group commissioned a feasibility study to determine whether a production could return to the Museum Gardens in the near future.[11] The outcome of this study was that it is indeed possible but that further discussion is needed before a date can be set.[12]

Alongside the large-scale productions of condensed cycles, there has also been an increasingly strong tradition of processional productions on wagons. In 1954 Browne, who was then involved in his second Museum Gardens production, inaugurated the modern wagon tradition with his pageant play of the Flood performing at two playing places in the streets.[13] The wagon play was designed to provide the public with the option of experiencing, free of charge, something approaching the original performance conditions available to the York guilds, sponsors of the pageants in the Middle Ages. But while the wagon play was envisaged as a demonstration of how things used to be, the Museum Gardens production was unquestionably regarded as the main event. Browne made only modest claims for the experiment: in his view it could not capture the way in which the 'Guilds competed with each other,' although it did have the virtue of conveying a general impression of wagon stages in procession and something of 'the vivacity that can be engendered in their confined space.'[14]

Browne and his successors in the Museum Gardens continued this tradition through to 1988, often with the involvement of local schools, in particular Archbishop Holgate's Grammar School, where the enthusiasm of the Art master, Stewart Lack, ensured a long association with the wagon plays.[15] In 1969 and 1973, when local director Edward Taylor was in charge of the Museum Gardens productions, the wagon tradition was given a colourful embellishment with the invention of the 'River Play.' Noah's Ark with its cast on board took to the waters of the Ouse and the pageant was performed at Marygate Landing and St George's Field. The

1980 Museum Gardens director, Patrick Garland, paid tribute to the medieval performance mode by bringing wagons onto the condensed cycle set for the Nativity, the Passion sequence, and the Harrowing of Hell. In 1988, when the wagon play of the Exodus was performed as an adjunct to Steven Pimlott's Museum Gardens production, a second wagon tradition, driven by academic enquiry, was initiated with a processional production of four pageants under the direction of Meg Twycross of Lancaster University.[16] In 1988 and 1992 Twycross brought outside drama groups to the city, with the additional participation of the local Lords of Misrule, the drama group of the Centre for Medieval Studies at the University of York. The wagon plays were freely available to audiences on a section of the original pageant route.[17] In 1994 another significant development occurred when director Jane Oakshott from Leeds secured a much greater participation of local people for her wagon production, although for safety reasons the original route was off-limits.[18] A follow-up wagon production under Oakshott's direction in 1998 saw the involvement of the surviving York guilds, descendents of the original presenters. Oakshott was thus instrumental in repatriating the York plays in a more thoroughgoing way than had been previously attempted.[19] The process was fully realized in 2002, when local director Mike Tyler steered the guild production of wagon plays through the streets.[20] Tyler followed this production with another success in 2006, and the guilds are now planning for more wagon plays in 2010.

The York revivals have inspired other mystery play productions well beyond the city walls. These are too numerous to consider here apart from noting two instances in which even negative reactions have been creative. The first of these was an academic enterprise orchestrated by Martial Rose, then head of English and Drama at Bretton Hall Teacher Training College. Rose was 'deeply impressed ... bewitched ... fascinated ... and moved' by the 1954 Browne production in the Museum Gardens, but felt that it was 'far from the medieval spirit in which the original performances must have been imbued.'[21] Disturbed by the lack of authenticity of the fixed-place condensed cycle, he was prompted by the York wagon play to mount his 1958 production of the Towneley plays in the grounds of the college, with twenty of the thirty-two episodes performed on a fixed set with the addition of two moveable wagons.[22] Beyond the academy, Yorkshire poet Tony Harrison was annoyed by the 1951 production, partly on the grounds that the northern text had been 'dubbed into posh language.'[23] From this conviction that the plays had been displaced from their original language and from what Harrison perceived as their working-class origins came his

Morris's project spanned three and a half months, during which he took up 'residence' at the theatre to observe the progress of the plays from casting through to performance. The publication of the poems was not just in print form: Morris also gave five performances in the Café Bar at the theatre, accompanying himself on an array of musical instruments ranging from bardic harp to rain stick.[28] These performances were as ephemeral as any live performance, but the printed text remains as a partial record of the poet's own presentation as well as of the 1996 mysteries themselves.

If this scenario could be transported back to the York of the Middle Ages, it would seem to offer the realization of a theatre historian's dream. The York records from that early period do not tell us more than a fraction of what we would like to know and there are no descriptive eye-witness accounts among them; the surviving medieval documents were not written as theatrical records and remain cryptic, awaiting and often defying inter-pretation. But not even Morris's records of theatrical practice are totally transparent. In common with other 'eyewitness' post 1642 documenta-tion, such as video and sound records of revival productions, they tell us more than medieval records can, but they, too, are incomplete and require further contextualization. To some extent Morris's poems, with their focus on the performers and the preparation processes, remain cryptic to outsid-ers and even to local people without first-hand experience in the making of the mysteries.

Morris chose to record particular aspects of his experience in 1996. He describes his role as poet in residence as 'a fly-on-the-wall, at marketing meetings, front of house meetings, backstage, rehearsals, young people's workshops, movement sessions, musical rehearsals, voice training and text study sessions.'[29] In the published poems, he reveals something of the workshops and rehearsals, the development aspect of production that scholars sadly miss in the medieval records. He tells us, for example, that there was 'panting and painting' in the workshops, and describes Catherine Jayes, the musical director, at work:

Cathy, with the water bottle
Perched atop the white piano
Plays alone, working out a melody.   'Cathy of the White Piano,' 19

These are precious details indeed: not only do they give us a sense of the plays in preparation, they also suggest the energy and dedication of those involved. But 'Cathy of the White Piano,' like the other poems in the collection, is not a complete record in itself. For a fuller understanding of the musical component of the production, the researcher will need to look for additional sources of information such as the 1996 theatre program, the script, and sound or video recordings. Actors with a long association with the revivals receive special mention in Morris's work: for example, Hugh Curristan, John Hall, Ian Lucas, and Jenny Burrage-Smith, who had by then played Mary Magdalene in two successive productions:[30]

Jenny, Oh, Jenny,
Is there any other role for you?
...
Someday, Jenny, Oh, Jenny, someday
When you are old and grey
Will they let you play
Mrs. Noah.   'Jenny,' 48

Much of the material in the collection could be classed as theatrical anecdote, but importantly for the historian, the Morris poems also offer commentary on the mystery play genre as a whole:

'I'm waiting for Satan,' says John,
...
Without Satan, temptation's a bore
And Jesus alone can't get on.   'Off Cue,' 21

In this case the local actor playing Satan, Dave Parkinson, was literally 'stuck on a train ... near Manchester' when the director needed him at rehearsal. But while this poem shows the importance of disciplined rehearsals, it also raises the issue of what John D. Cox has termed the 'oppositional role' played by the devil. [31]

The presentation of this opposition is an area where an important distinction between the revivals in condensed format and the original York mysteries becomes apparent. The original cycle plays present an expansive history of God's relationship with humanity. There is a focus in the Old Testament episodes on the rewards of obedience; on affective piety in the Passion sequence; and on the subsequent availability of salvation to the obedient in the final sequence leading up to judgment at Doomsday. The story of the condensed cycles, however, has more emphasis on the conflict between the ultimate representatives of good and evil, the deity and the devil. This conflict was the point of reference for comments by York Festival director Hans Hess in his outline plan for the 1963 festival, for which the condensed mystery plays were to be, as usual, the centrepiece: 'The Mystery Plays are not highly dramatic, and except in human content, remote from the theatre of our time ... The drama will only come to life if the two main parts are in the hands of more than just capable actors, and in my mind the impact of the Plays depends almost wholly on the convincing performance of the two main protagonists. Thus I recommend that once we have found the producer to insist on the two best possible actors for the parts.'[32] By 'best possible actors,' Hess meant 'best possible professional actors.' For him the strength of presentation of the conflict between Christ and Satan was all-important to the success of the plays artistically and, by implication, financially. When Royal Court director William Gaskill accepted responsibility for the 1963 production, professional actors were secured to play a number of key roles including the 'two main parts.' In an innovative move in this year Alan Dobie doubled the roles of God the Father and Christ while Ian McShane played Lucifer.

In the original York text of forty-seven pageant episodes, devils appeared with speaking roles in only six episodes.[33] The presence of evil in the world is established early in the medieval cycle, but after experiencing his own fall and contributing to the fall of Adam and Eve (plays 1 and 5), the Satan/Lucifer figure disappears until the Temptation of Christ (play 22). He then returns briefly in his attempt to stop the Crucifixion by appealing to Pilate's wife (play 30), and is confined to hell in the Harrowing episode (play 37). He thus cannot attend the judgment at Doomsday (play 47) in person, although he is represented by three other devils. The condensed cycle form, however, in an attempt to replicate the structure of more modern plays, prefers a much more visible villain clearly opposed to Christ as hero.

The condensed Creation to Doomsday productions in York have highlighted the opposition between the devil and the deity both in the methods of playing the role and, in some cases, in the process of arranging the episodes for presentation. When scriptwriter Mike Poulton prepared the thirty-seven episode version of the York mystery plays for the millennium production in the Minster, he emphasised the supernatural conflict of good and evil by coalescing the Doomsday and Harrowing of Hell episodes, thus keeping his Lucifer active in opposition for the finale. While this might not make perfect doctrinal sense, it does make good theatrical sense. If Lucifer is seen to be defeated prior to the final moments of the play, some heat goes out of the cosmic battle of good and evil over the fate of humanity.

Scholars are divided in their views as to how the role of the devil was played in the Middle Ages. Cox argues for the 'seriousness of mystery-play devils' and downplays 'the carnival attitudes that are often described as their essential character.'[34] Lesley Wade Soule, conversely, holds with the carnivalesque, arguing that the 'dangerous energy of the character's anger and threat must be converted into the comic energy of the performer.'[35]

Directors of the condensed cycle of mystery plays in York have demonstrated the same difference of opinion. In the Browne production of 1951, for example, professional actor John Van Eyssen played Lucifer with great dignity. The special correspondent for the *Manchester Guardian* declared him 'a very good Prince of Darkness' and commented that 'as with "Paradise Lost," it might be debated who is the real hero of this play-cycle.'[36] Those familiar with the tradition of Milton's Satan, or indeed with other post-medieval devils, such as Marlowe's sophisticated Mephistopheles, could accept the idea of Lucifer as a tragic hero, evil to the core, but essentially dignified. It certainly appears that Van Eyssen was a decorous and totally charming Lucifer, for although the *Yorkshire Gazette* was able to report on 'the robust vigour of the low comedy scenes between the devils,' it was his minions, the little devils, rather than Lucifer who indulged in this kind of activity.[37] With director Browne careful not to offend audience sensibilities in this inaugural production, his choice of Lucifer as the Miltonic hero would appear to have been a wise one.

At the other end of the spectrum, the Lucifer of experienced local amateur actor Rory Mulvihill in 2000 charmed many members of his audience with a very different interpretation of the role. Mulvihill played Lucifer in exaggerated pantomime mode wearing a red jumpsuit that had a tail measuring nineteen feet in length for The Temptation of Adam and Eve episode. As a comic, larger-than-life figure, he made his presence felt on the huge Minster stage. The laughter that invariably greeted his antics helped the audience to take note of him as a contrast to the austere authority of John Hall's God the Father and to the humane warmth of Ray Stevenson's Christ. His bizarre stage business, such as flipping his enormous tail in the Garden of Eden and juggling with bread rolls in The Temptation of Christ episode, drew attention to the dignity and control of his opposite number.

Whether he is serious or comic, it is clear that the directors of the modern condensed mystery play cycles have sought to make a sharp contrast between a strongly drawn villain and an equally strong hero. This accords with the point made by Hess in 1963 and also with Morris's comment in 1996 that 'Jesus alone can't get on.'

Morris concludes his series of poems with 'Epilogue,' in which he offers suggestions about the motives for belonging to what he describes as the 'community / Of hewers for history' (60). Some participants have religious motives, he claims, while others are devoted to the past and to local tradition. The emphasis is on community here, although in other poems in the collection the fellowship is accompanied by the tensions habitually associated with theatrical production:

Once again, Satan is late
Where lateness is a mortal sin.   'Sunday Rehearsal,' 36

Similar motives for participation as well as similar tensions can be seen in Barbara Whitehead's crime novel, *Playing God*. This mystery is set in the context of a Museum Gardens production for which fictional pop star Poison Peters has been imported to play Christ. Whitehead makes use of a number of mystery play 'facts,' not merely as background material inserted for the sake of verisimilitude, but as a means of laying false trails about the identity of the intended victim and composing a list of suspects. While she did not see the plays in 1984, her consultations with director Toby Robertson and her use of sketches and a model of the set provided by the design team have resulted in a careful documentary-style description.[38]

Playing God is the first in Whitehead's tantalizingly entitled crime series, the 'York Cycle of Mysteries,' all of which are set in specific contexts that are clearly identifiable as part of the life of modern York.[39] Some issues that are mentioned routinely in the local press in the lead-up to mystery play productions in York are raised in this novel. These include concerns about blasphemy and possible indecorum; the casting of a professional actor to play Christ; the choice of a local schoolgirl to play the Virgin Mary; technical difficulties associated with the Crucifixion; and the notion of the plays as an expression of, and force for, cohesion within the community. In Whitehead's own estimation, the novel combines 'the threat of evil with the Mystery Plays.'[40] Ultimately this combination leaves a question mark over the 'community feeling' (181) associated with mystery plays, both medieval and modern.

The novel opens with Poison Peters at the railway station, where the welcoming party is not unanimous in its mood. Fans are excited, actors and local dignitaries are bored, and some protestors are vocal: 'a noisy group of fundamentalists ... began to shout "Out with Poison!" and unrolled their banner which said "NO BLASPHEMY"' (17).

Sydney Absolom is one of those opposed to the choice of Peters as Christ: his objections are based on the pop star's sordid reputation for alcohol and women as well as song. An ardent medievalist, however,

Absolom takes on the job of unpaid electrician for the production. The first accident in which Peters is almost electrocuted implies that he is to be the murder victim and sets up Absolom as chief suspect with both a motive and the means to inflict grievous bodily harm. At the beginning of the novel, both Peters and Absolom are possible candidates for the 'evil' that is to be combined with the mystery plays because of the conflict over the casting of the role of Christ, but, as it happens, the evil has nothing directly to do with the plays themselves; it is a pre-existing evil. The production merely provides an opportunity for this evil to be expressed.

The figuratively named 'Poison Peters' is initially suspected of all kinds of iniquity, but turns out to be, in the words of the archbishop of York, a 'clene maiden' (163), and therefore highly suited to the role he has been given.[41] His experience in this role has a profound effect on him, so much so that he starts giving out his autograph as 'Poisson' with the sign of the fish following it, eventually signing with the fish alone (159–63). His family name has biblical overtones and his given name, John, further suggests an apostolic association, especially when his determination to continue his musical career by writing and performing songs about 'reconciliation, and the redeeming power of love' (182) is taken into account.

The securing of a well-known professional to play Christ has always been an important issue for the organizers of the York revivals. While Browne felt he had to take the precaution of keeping his Christ (Joseph O'Connor) and the amateur actor playing God the Father (Noel Shepherd) anonymous in 1951 to preserve decorum, later directors and festival committees have gone to great lengths to place the names of the star performers in the public view as much as possible. Director Patrick Garland, for example, sought the services of Michael York as Christ for the 1980 production. This actor's surname as well as his reputation would have been a major boost to publicity for the plays. When film commitments prevented York's acceptance, Christopher Timothy, a popular TV personality, although a lesser star, whose series 'All Creatures Great and Small' had just come to an end, accepted the role. Publicity then capitalized on Timothy's healing veterinary image as well as playing down the break-up of his marriage and his affair with his 'All Creatures' screen wife, Carol Drinkwater, for fear that this might compromise his portrayal of Christ.

Robert Southwell, the policeman in *Playing God*, asks whether Poison Peters's acceptance of the role means that his career was 'slipping a bit' (12). Local perceptions that the actor playing Christ in York is someone on the way up or on the way down in his career, or between engagements, are thus reflected in this novel. For all their success in the role, the stars who have played Christ in York have not been at the time, at the top of their career, although this has never been articulated in press releases.

The Cross, the central icon of the mystery plays, is another recurring motif in publicity for productions in York. Reports of difficulties in constructing a cross that is both substantial enough to take the weight of the actor playing Christ and light enough for him to carry have been common.[42] In the novel the accident with the cross at rehearsal is a deliberately false clue. The mystery of this accident is easily solved: it was not an intentional evil but the result of the unthinking behaviour of the 'little devils,' who tampered with the mechanism by removing one of its essential parts to use in one of their games.[43]

Publicity for the Museum Gardens productions has also regularly concentrated on the casting of a talented schoolgirl as the Virgin Mary. Around audition time the local press reminds readers that Mary Ure (1951) and Judi Dench (1957) took the role before going on to greater fame.[44] The fortunes of Queen Elizabeth's School prefect, Clare Black, who is the Virgin in *Playing God*, are linked suggestively to those of her illustrious counterparts by the director Bruce Exelby in his futile attempts to seduce her. In the novel the point is partly to exploit the mythology surrounding the role in the context of the York revivals, but more importantly to highlight the evil nature of the director. The central evil of the novel is, of course, the taking of the life of a fellow human being, but there are other evils, like the reprehensible behaviour of the director and the self-interest that comes into play as those associated with the production try to deflect suspicion of murder away from themselves and onto others. These are all evils that negate the spirit of community engendered by the plays. When the murderer is confronted and given the opportunity of surrendering to the police, the crime is seen as a disruption of the 'comradeship, the community feeling' (181) of the mysteries. But for the murderer, community feeling is only to be exploited in so far as it can provide the chance to take personal revenge for old wrongs.

Poison Peters leaves York in much the same way as he arrived, complete with make-up and hair and ready for the photo opportunity, but this time without the protesters. But while normality has been restored, with the plays over and the murders solved, it is clear that this community is not perfect. Theatre historians often extol the virtues of both medieval and modern mystery play productions as examples of community theatre. As in other community theatre contexts, the emphasis is on the positive outcomes of celebrating the identity of an area in its past and present manifestations: harmony, the raising of personal and collective esteem, and 'improved community feeling.'[45] Whitehead reminds us that there is also a dark side.

Reginald Hill

Who is 'playing God' in Whitehead's novel? Is it Thomas Churchyard, who as God the Father looks down from the arches of St Mary's Abbey to survey the history of the world from Creation to Doomsday? Is it Poison Peters, who becomes Christlike by playing Christ? Is it the director, Bruce Exelby, who regards the participants of the York mystery plays as his to command? Or is it the murderer, who is determined to take vengeance? Whatever the answer to the question in the context of *Playing God*, it is clear that the person playing God in Reginald Hill's *Bones and Silence* is Detective-Superintendent Andrew Dalziel.

Fat Andy, made famous by the Dalziel and Pascoe series of novels and the BBC television series based on them, enters this text vomiting into a laundry bucket in his kitchen, scarcely a model of decorum. His colleagues joke about his imitation of the deity, both on- and off-stage, but Dalziel does not consider himself to be 'infallibly perfect' (194) and the novel shows him to be, for all his omniscience, as frail and sometimes even as humble as the next human being.[46]

The mystery plays of Hill's novel, 'an eclectic version ... with a jingoistic concentration on the York and Wakefield cycles' (12), are reminiscent of both condensed cycle and wagon play revivals in York. The Yorkshire city where the novel is set is not named, but there can be no mistaking its likeness to York. There is to be a procession of wagons and the performance itself is to take place at a site that is a clone of the Museum Gardens: 'an expanse of green and pleasant land, dotted with old trees and sinking down in a shallow vallum where remnants of the city's medieval walls could still be seen. More substantial than these ... the ruins of St Bega's Abbey[47] from which had come much of the impetus and, after its closure, some of the material to enlarge the small Anglo-Norman cathedral into a huge Gothic edifice which would hold its own against any in the land' (51).

There are numerous instances in which Hill, like Whitehead, demonstrates a receptiveness to issues regularly associated with the York mysteries in the press. Able to charm policemen, civic dignitaries, and representatives of the church alike, the charismatic director, Eileen Chung, also deals tactfully with protestors who object on principle to 'papish processions and men pretending to be God and Jesus' (112). These qualities certainly put her in the mould of past directors of the York mysteries, but rather than always playing it straight, Hill's flamboyant director frequently takes 'everyone by surprise' (12). At the beginning of the novel she does not place her resident company from the Civil Theatre in the principal roles as Browne did with his professional theatre colleagues in the early Museum Gardens productions. Chung's professionals are stationed in the crowds. Similarly, she avoids the practice of 'importing a middling magnitude telly star to give some commercial clout to Jesus' that has been common in condensed cycle productions in York in more recent years.[48] Hill thus questions some of the revival conventions by having this particular director flaunt them.

Chung is quite aware of the academic concerns regarding authenticity in modern attempts at reviving the ancient mystery plays. As a professional director, however, she is more interested in the impact of her own work for non-academic audiences than with scholarly precision. She is not 'doing any prissy historical reconstruction,' she is 'plugging into the continuum' (167); convinced that the mysteries represent the beginning of 'the modern European theatre' (166), she is determined to have her own place in its ongoing development. Consequently, her production is a mixture of medieval and modern modes: enough of the medieval to signal the origins of the plays, and enough of the modern to keep her present audience interested. Her procession of pageants to the fixed-place performance space is to include a colourful collection of 'medieval' elements: 'music and dancers ... jugglers, tumblers, fire-eaters, fools, flagellants, giants, dwarves, dancing bears, merry monks, cut-price pardoners, knights on horseback, Saracens in chains, [and] nubile Nubians' (49–50). When her tame 'university medievalist' objects, she puts him down sharply: 'Shit, man! This show's for your person-in-the-street. Ask yourself, do they want it authentic, or do they want it *fun*?' (50).

The energetic Chung is full of surprises, the most startling of them being reserved for the very end of the novel, when she is revealed as the author of the series of anonymous suicide-letters that, along with epigraphs from the mystery plays, are used to introduce the sections of the book.[49] The puzzle of the letters is solved when the words of the Temptation of Christ play lead Peter Pascoe and Sergeant Wield to the cathedral tower. Chung is, in a sense, 'playing God' on the tower, but she fails in this role in that, unlike Christ, she succumbs to temptation.

The representatives of good and evil for this fictional mystery play production, God the Father and Lucifer, are chosen from the local community.

To Chung, Philip Swain, descended from a long line of land-owning Swains, 'looks as proud and as prickly as Lucifer' (14), and Dalziel seems 'just about perfect for God' (16). As it happens the good-versus-evil team is more appropriate than even the perspicacious Chung could have envisaged: Dalziel, with his own somewhat bloodshot eyes, witnesses Swain in the act of committing murder and, despite the machinations of both the killer and his legal representatives, eventually brings him to judgment.

As he does so often in his professional life, Dalziel defies his superior officer when he agrees to become a community player. Dan Trimble is not amused that one of his officers intends to 'bring the force into disrepute by letting himself be wheeled round town on a carnival float in his nightgown' (144). There is also disagreement about the tastefulness of Dalziel's casting. Dorothy Horncastle, downtrodden wife of Canon Horncastle, is of the view that 'the image most people have of God' is 'that of a big fat copper who will put everything right' (264). Swain, on the other hand, smarting from the relentless antagonism of this particular 'big fat copper,' tells Dalziel that Chung 'has committed a monstrous blasphemy in casting something as gross as [him] to play the Godhead' (264).

As a policeman, Dalziel is more often than not unorthodox in his procedures and this unorthodoxy could be expected to cross over into his portrayal of 'God Allbloodymighty' (178). Audaciously working class, authoritarian, and often bumptious, he warms to the role and has his own views about how it should be played: 'I've got this grand idea for when I'm talking to Noah' (263). Those who know Dalziel from other books in the series or from Warren Clarke's portrayal of him on television might wonder if he would base his interpretation of the role on the dignified models of the York revival productions. Or would something like Brian Glover's version of the deity in Bill Bryden's production of Tony Harrison's *Mysteries* for the National Theatre be more to his taste?

Harrison worked on the assumption that the medieval guilds were 'the equivalent of the modern trade unions.'[50] This is a point of view that scholars will, quite rightly, dispute. The guilds were, as John Schofield and Alan Vince have stated, much more complex that this, existing 'for a plethora of reasons' and covering 'functions which today might be catered for by clubs and societies (such as the Rotarians or Freemasons), unions, friendly societies, chambers of commerce and others.'[51] This complexity, however, is unlikely to translate readily onto the stage for a generalist audience, and the 'trade union' notion, signalling as it does an image of 'the North,' along with the determined use of the Yorkshire accent, works to repatriate Harrison's *Mysteries* to a somewhat false but colourfully imagined homeland.

Bryden's production of Harrison's play departed from the norm in its casting of Glover as God the Father. Rather than conventional dignity, Bryden was looking for 'down-to-earth and demotically humorous qualities,' and Glover, 'a Yorkshireman who spoke with a strong Yorkshire accent ... represented in his appearance and manner a thoroughly unconventional notion of God.'[52] Hill's Andy Dalziel, likewise unconventional, sometimes clownish, but normally sharp-witted, often vulgar, but also ultimately endearing, could easily fit into Glover's robes.

That Hill had Glover in mind as he wrote Dalziel into the heavenly role seems entirely possible. The comment about the 'grand idea' that Andy has for the Noah episode could even be a reference to a memorable moment in Bryden's production when God descends from heaven, strips off his celestial gown to reveal his work clothes, and 'pauses to pick up a fag-end and stick it behind his ear before giving Noah his instructions on how to build the ark.'[53]

While audiences and theatre critics loved Glover's comic God, some scholars were not amused either by him or by the production as a whole. John R. Elliott Jr, for example, complained that the show was one that starred the 'fork-lift truck' used for God's entrance for *The Creation*, and that it worked 'more through spectacle and gimmickry than through religious impulse.'[54] Darryll Grantley objected to what he saw as excessive comedy in Glover's performance that in his view destroyed the religiosity of the subject matter: 'Making God a stereotype of a working-class figure in order to derive comedy from the incongruity of his being in a position of power is not only insultingly distasteful (though enjoyed by the predominantly middle-class audience) but it also plays havoc with the notion of absolute spiritual authority which forms an important part of the philosophical basis of the Cycle ... the choice between a buffoon-like God and a risible devil can scarcely have much weight.'[55]

Hill readily solves the question of the conflict between God the Father and Lucifer in his policeman versus murderer scenario: the choice between the deceptively 'buffoon-like' detective and the arrogant killer is perfectly clear-cut. But there is a challenge for theatre historians here in the question of an appropriate representation of God the Father in this conflict of good and evil on the stage. I have already mentioned the comic/serious divide in scholarly opinion and modern theatrical practice in the case of Lucifer, but can a similar case be made for his heavenly opponent?

Pageant wagon revivals of the Creation plays can, like Brian Glover's God, work for modern audiences through comedy. In York in 2002, for example, audiences at some of the playing places were able to laugh when a perfectly dignified God had to pause dramatically or even repeat his pronouncements before his behind-the-scenes assistants activated the wonders of Creation that he was describing. Such comic moments affirmed the Brechtian notion that this is a play about the Creation and that this is an actor playing God. The unscripted comedy did not negate the majesty of God's Creation but rather established the distance between the actor and the deity he was representing. As with Glover's working-class God in the Bryden/Harrison *Mysteries*, the recognition that this is an attempt to represent the deity by a human actor goes hand-in-hand with the comedy, but this does not necessarily diminish the statement about 'absolute spiritual authority' that underlies the text.

We can never know how God the Father was presented in the original mystery plays; we can only guess at his authority and dignity as portrayed in the surviving visual arts of the period and through the words of the dramatic texts themselves. But if Martin Stevens was correct in his advice to scholars in 1970 about applying 'the Brechtian aesthetic toward the interpretation of the popular religious drama of the Middle Ages,' we should not be at all concerned if the citizens of medieval York recognized their neighbour under the mask of the godhead or found reason to laugh at his performance.[56]

1963: A Background for Peter Gill and *The York Realist*

Brecht was a major influence on William Gaskill's Museum Gardens mystery plays of 1963. A Brechtian focus on the working class and the underlying opposition between the poor and their rulers was channelled through an emphasis on tyranny and physical cruelty. As noted earlier in this essay, professional actors were placed in the 'two main parts,' God the Father/ Christ and Lucifer. Professionals also filled other (tyrannous and cruel) roles that were pivotal for Gaskill's interpretation: Annas, Caiaphas, Pilate, and the four soldiers of the Crucifixion.[57] One local reviewer commended the callous insensitivities of the Passion sequence: 'Christ is dragged before Pilate (ably played and detachably [*sic*] by Shay Gorman) and the two Jewish high priests thunder out their accusations ... The Crucifixion is carried out with hideous brutality and ghastly competence by the Roman soldiers well played by George Innes, Brian Osborne, Declan Mulholland

and Tim Preece.'[58] The same reviewer was somewhat less impressed by other aspects of the production and complained that Peter's declarations of loyalty to Christ in the Garden of Gethsemene were 'delivered in such a kitchen-sink whine that Christ's admonition to him to cease boasting is meaningless.'

The critic's reference to the 'kitchen-sink whine' was inevitable given Gaskill's recent association with the Royal Court Theatre, the home of 'kitchen sink' drama. By 1963, 'kitchen sink' had made its presence felt. In that year Shakespearean scholar G. Wilson Knight, for example, wrote glowingly of the movement's capacity 'to bring new health to the insane paradoxes of a decaying culture.'[59] According to Knight a large part of the impact of this new theatre was its determined use of dialect that had 'not been attenuated and drained by modern sophistication.'[60] Gaskill himself was later to appreciate the irony that he 'had deliberately lost [his] West Riding accent' during his time at Oxford, not realizing in foresight that the Royal Court was to make its mark on theatre history by promoting 'provincial background[s].'[61]

Also writing in 1963, Martin Browne lamented that when he had contemplated leaving passages of the York mystery plays in 'broad dialect' in his Museum Gardens productions in the 1950s, he 'could not find people to speak them.'[62] He later elaborated on this issue in his autobiography, insisting that 'only a very few of the north-country vowels' were in use in the city and that actors from the countryside, 'mostly employed on the land and rising very early, couldn't face our late hours of performance.'[63]

Gaskill made a more determined effort than any of his predecessors in the Museum Gardens to reinstate a recognizably Yorkshire sound to the local mystery plays. He chose 'professional actors with Yorkshire voices'[64] for the key roles and tried to recruit amateurs who were able to 'use their native Yorkshire accent.'[65] In so doing, he attempted to align the anti-illusion theatrical trend of the present with the medieval theatre, which was, he explained, 'performed by ordinary people, for ordinary people, and ... done in a straightforward way.'[66]

The year 1963 also saw the publication of an important scholarly article by J.W. Robinson in which he focused on eight plays from the Passion sequence in the York cycle, 'all very largely written in true alliterative verse ... and ... all remarkable for the detailed and imaginative realism that has gone into their composition.'[67] Imaginative realism as opposed to illusion was, of course, what the adherents of Brecht in the 1960s most admired. For want of a proper name, Robinson called the author of these plays 'the York Realist.'[68] This was the name adopted by Peter Gill, Gaskill's assistant director in York in 1963, as the title of his award-winning play of 2001/2.[69]

The York Realist

Gill dedicates his play to Gaskill, and while it is fictional rather than autobiographical 'its world contains something of the Gill-Gaskill 1963 collaboration.'[70] The York Realist is set in 'a farm labourer's cottage outside York in the early 1960s' (5); the context is a Museum Gardens production of the mystery plays. The play revolves around a love affair between two young men: John, a middle-class theatre professional from London, who has come to York to work as assistant director for the mysteries, and George, a farm labourer, who has been cast as one of the soldiers at the Crucifixion. While the play is a fiction, it replicates some of the issues associated with Gaskill's 1963 production, with particular emphasis on the Yorkshire dialect. The mystery plays themselves occur off-stage and are revealed to the audience only through what the characters say about them. Their comments reflect on the nature of the medieval originals as well as that of the twentieth-century revivals, and there are also references to the modern professional theatre here, with Gill looking back affectionately to the 'kitchen sink' days of the 1950s and 1960s.[71]

When George stops attending rehearsals his mother suggests that the reason is that it is 'too far for him to go' (24), while George pleads the excuse of 'work and that' as well as the fact that his mother's health needs watching (28). But George has an authentic Yorkshire voice of the kind sought by Gaskill in 1963, and consideration of the demands of his occupation and the difficulties of his residence out-of-town, though they would have been enough to deter Browne in the 1950s, do not prevent assistant director John from trying to draw him back: 'There aren't many people like you in it ... You're so right, you see. You make it sound right' (29).

This is the beginning of an affair that is doomed to failure, and when John returns to the farm to try to persuade George to leave Yorkshire for a life in the London theatre, George is the cruel 'realist' who judges that it cannot work. Sounding right for the mystery plays in York is one thing, but George knows that he 'couldn't learn to speak differently now' and does not want to be a professional 'Northerner as a job' (74). These references to the valorizing of dialect in the theatre of the 1960s serve to emphasise the difficulty of crossing boundaries, whether they be linguistic, geographical, or occupational, rather than to undermine the 'kitchen sink' movement in any way.

Gill makes other observations on the London theatre. There may even be references to himself on some occasions: the director of the fictional mysteries is named Peter and when George reminisces about his time in London with John he mentions the famous 'Sunday Nights' at the Royal Court in the 1960s, where Gill's first play, *The Sleeper's Den*, was performed in 1965: 'I liked most of all that play on a Sunday. That was right good. Nearly a fight there was over that' (73).

Judi Dench as the Virgin in the Museum Gardens mysteries (1957), who goes on to stardom in the professional theatre, is also referred to here. When John tries to persuade George that he could leave the farm, come to London, and earn a living as an actor, George excuses himself by commenting that he is not in the same league as 'the little Quaker lass played the Virgin Mary. She's going to acting school in London' (59).[72]

George's family (his mother, sister Barbara, brother-in-law Arthur, and nephew Jack) attends a performance in the Museum Gardens with Doreen, the local girl who would like to be the woman in George's life. When they return to the cottage they discuss the issue of the 'Northern voices':

MOTHER: It was very Yorkshire, wasn't it? Not that I mind.
DOREEN: All very Yorkshire.
JACK: Jesus Christ wasn't Yorkshire.
ARTHUR: Yes, he was.
MOTHER: No, but you didn't mind.
JACK: I didn't mind. (51)

The complexities of this exchange raise questions about the Yorkshire setting of biblical story and about the insistence of some modern directors on the importance of the Yorkshire dialect for the plays. While the 'Yorkshire voices' were true to the medieval situation, being the dominant mode of speech in the city at the time, a modern audience might be forgiven for finding it somewhat forced at a time when the speech patterns of the local population are more varied. Furthermore, as is evident from the Harrison/ Bryden *Mysteries*, the Yorkshire dialect is now a marker of class as much as of geographical location. But Gill's play questions the working class origins of the mystery plays when John expresses uncertainty about the common perception already mentioned in this essay that the original guild supporters of the pageants were like 'trade unions':

JOHN: That's what they say. I don't know about that. (37)

With telling understatement, Gill raises a number of other questions that a modern audience, both specialist theatre historians and non-specialists, might raise, such as the cutting of the Old Testament episodes:

DOREEN: Couldn't get it in one evening, you see

the emphasis on Noah's wife:

DOREEN: No, she was funny, wasn't she?

and on Pilate's wife:

DOREEN: She was very common, I thought. (45)

Ironically *The Crucifixion* is not one of the plays of the Passion sequence that scholars normally ascribe to the 'York Realist.'[73] It is, however, the focus of Gill's play-within-a-play, and it appears to have impressed him as associate director of the mysteries in 1963.[74] The 'hideous brutality and ghastly competence' achieved by the professional actors playing the soldiers in the Gill-Gaskill production is also ascribed to George by his family:

BARBARA: Our George was cruel in the crucifixion, though.
MOTHER: Too cruel.
ARTHUR: Very real. Very real.
MOTHER: Too cruel for me, I could have punched our George doing that to him. (50)

and later:

MOTHER: You were a cruel bugger, George.
GEORGE: Thanks. (52)

It is clear that, as a farm labourer, George is as foreign to the original mystery plays as was the 'posh language' of the Browne production that offended Tony Harrison:

JACK: Was there a farm labourers' play?
JOHN: It was all done in the town. (37)

The social demographic of the cast of the fictional mysteries also makes George an outsider, despite the fact that he is made to feel welcome:

GEORGE: Jesus is a nice fellow. Well, they all are ... They're all very ... well ... They would be ... Doctors and that. (28–9)

Questions of exclusion from the mystery play revivals can involve audience as well as cast. Writing in 1953, American social philosopher Russell Kirk was delighted that in 1951 York had had 'intelligence and piety sufficient to conjure up the ghost of ... communal faith' and present its first modern mystery play revival.[75] But although he predicted that the city would continue the tradition 'hereafter every five years, and the consequent influence upon belief and art in York' would be 'interesting to observe,' he also claimed that most of the locals were 'bored with religion' and that the audience in 1951 was 'select and generally upper-middle-class' and that 'nine-tenths of the population of modern York ... prefer the carnalities of the cinema and the cheap press.'[76]

As I have argued elsewhere, the mystery plays are an example of 'cultural Christianity,' and religious faith is only one of the factors that might draw actors to participate in them and audiences to watch them.[77] Now, more than fifty years on, and under the influence of Mel Gibson's distinctly carnal and financially successful cinematic venture, *The Passion of the Christ* (2004), we might no longer agree with Kirk that there is widespread hostility to 'religion of any sort,' certainly not when it is allied with the 'carnalities of the cinema.' When *The Passion* was enjoying its box office success in 2004, Easter services also enjoyed record attendances around the world. Perhaps when the York mysteries are next played, there will also be increased interest from a wide social spectrum to participate in the event either as audience or as more involved contributors to the program itself as a result of the Gibson venture.

The Challenges

I began this essay with the proposition that the four literary documents discussed here offer challenges to the theatre historian. Gill's play, perhaps more than the other three works, leaves questions that students and scholars might well feel remain unanswered. Are we sure of how we want to characterize the medieval guilds? Do we envisage these mysteries as Yorkshire fossils or can they be more 'fun' (as Hill's Eileen Chung would put it) if they are updated into the Yorkshire of the present? To what extent are we to imagine the past and understand the present of these community plays as expressing both cohesion and division? While we might not want to go so far as the disruption of community through the extremity of murder, as in Whitehead's *Playing God*, are there other lesser divisions that we should admit to? Whatever the questions that we care to address after reading or seeing these works, one thing that is clear is that they are in a position to influence popular perceptions of the mystery plays as a genre and as such must be of interest to scholars.

NOTES

1 Alexandra F. Johnston and Margaret Rogerson, eds, *York*, REED, 2 vols (Toronto: University of Toronto Press, 1979).
2 The main collections are in the York City Archives and the *Doomsday* Project at Lancaster University.
3 The *Doomsday* Project, directed by Meg Twycross and Pamela King, houses the mystery play archives of E. Martin Browne, the inaugural director of the Museum Gardens mystery plays in York, and his designer Norah Lambourne. Material from these archives is to be published on CD ROM; see: http://www.lancs.ac.uk/users/yorkdoom/emb.htm and http://www.lancs.ac.uk/users/yorkdoom/norah.htm.
   Following the success of the millennium production of the mystery plays in the Minster, the National Centre for Early Music set up a project to collect material on the history of modern productions in the city. This resulted in an on-line York mystery plays' archive, 'Illumination: From Shadow into Light,' available through http://www.ncem.co.uk.
   Records for the 2002 and 2006 wagon productions can be found on the website of the York guilds: http://www.yorkmysteryplays.co.uk.
4 Barbara Whitehead, *Playing God* (London: Quartet, 1988); Reginald Hill, *Bones and Silence* (London: Harper Collins, 1990); Tony Morris, *Poet in Residence, Poems by Tony Morris: The Process and the People of the York Mystery Plays at the Theatre Royal* (Selby, North Yorkshire: Woodman's Press, 1996); and Peter Gill, *The York Realist* (London: Faber, 2001).
5 'Bones and Silence' was televised as episode 10 in the Dalziel and Pascoe series (BBC/Portobello Pictures) starring Warren Clarke (Detective Superintendent Andy Dalziel) and Colin Buchanan (Detective Inspector Peter Pascoe). First aired 18 October 1998, screenplay by Alan Plater.
6 Diana Large, an actor, theatre administrator, and director, who was influential in the theatrical life of Hobart, was teaching at the University of Tasmania at the time. Her cast consisted of a nucleus of eight well-known Australian

professional actors supported by a large number of amateur players. The performance was spread over three nights. See Gillian Winter, 'Diana Large AO,' in *Companion to Theatre In Australia*, ed. Philip Parsons and Victoria Chance (Sydney: Currency Press, 1995), 322–3.

7 Jane Oakshott had recently graduated from the Centre for Medieval Studies at the University of Leeds. She entered the academic debate in the 1970s on fixed-place versus processional staging with her successful practical demonstration of the viability of wagon production. For an account of the 1975 production, see Jane Oakshott and Richard Rastall, 'Town with Gown: The York Cycle of Mystery Plays at Leeds,' in *Towards the Community University: Case Studies of Innovation and Community Service*, ed. David C.B. Teather (London: Kogan Page, 1982), 213–29. Oakshott continued her scholarly engagement with the mystery plays with a 1980 production of the complete Towneley plays in Wakefield, then thought to be its place of origin. This was followed by her 1983 production of the Chester cycle, first at the University of Leeds and later in Chester itself.

8 David Parry was then the Robert Gill Fellow for 1977–8 in the Graduate Centre for Study of Drama at the University of Toronto. The production was organized by a committee chaired by Alexandra Johnston. For an account of this production, see Alexandra F. Johnston, 'The York Cycle: 1977,' *University of Toronto Quarterly* 48.1 (1978): 1–9.

9 Rory Mulvihill, quoted in David Ward, 'Dispute Clouds Future of Mystery Plays,' *Guardian*, 22 September 2003.

10 Mike Laycock, 'Boost for Hopes to Have Plays Outdoors,' *York Evening Press*, 25 August 2003. The 2002 wagon play production used the Museum Gardens for one of their playing stations; see below, note 20.

11 'A New Character Enters Plays Saga,' *York Evening Press*, 29 October 2003.

12 Mike Laycock, 'Further Investigations Needed on Drama Date,' *York Evening Press*, 13 May 2004.

13 In 1954 the first performance began at 6 pm at the west front of the Minster and was then followed by a second performance in Thursday Market, St Sampson's Square, except on market days, when the second performance was in King's Square.

14 E. Martin Browne with Henzie Browne, *Two in One* (Cambridge: Cambridge University Press, 1981), 197–8. Anthony Minghella captures the spirit of competition in his 1983 play *Two Planks and a Passion*. Minghella claims in the introduction to *Plays: One* (London: Methuen, 1992) that he wrote the play 'as an attempt to understand why the medieval Corpus Christi cycle, a collection of apparently innocuous religious plays, aroused so much political intrigue and civic rivalry' (n.p.). This historical play is set in 1392 with a

performance of the plays during a fictional visit of Richard II and Queen Anne. *Two Planks and a Passion* was performed in York in July 1995 by the Settlement Players, directed by mystery plays veteran Dave Parkinson. In the program notes Parkinson comments that the production was attractive 'as a sort of follow up to the Mystery Plays ... with people of York again playing their predecessors from six centuries ago.'

15 In some of the revival years in York, more than one wagon play was staged in conjunction with the Museum Gardens production. *The Flood* was a popular choice: 1954, *The Flood*; 1957, *The Exodus*; 1960, *Christ before the Elders*; 1963, *Abraham and Isaac*; 1966, *The Flood*; 1969, *The Flood* and *The Exodus*; 1973, *The Flood* and *Herod and the Three Kings*; 1976, *The Last Judgment*; 1980, *The Building of the Ark* and *The Flood*; 1984, *The Harrowing of Hell*; 1988, *The Exodus*.

16 Meg Twycross had had considerable experience as a director of medieval plays; see especially her account of her 1977 experiment with simulated pageant wagon performance in 'Playing "The Resurrection,"' in *Medieval Studies for J.A.W. Bennett*, ed. P.L. Heyworth (Oxford: Oxford University Press, 1981), 273–96. In 1988 the four pageants were *The Death of the Virgin*, *The Assumption of the Virgin*, *The Coronation of the Virgin*, and *Doomsday*. They were performed at four stations in Low Petergate, starting at 7 pm on Saturday, 9 July and Sunday, 10 July, the last two days of the York Festival. For a review of the 1988 production, see Alexandra F. Johnston, 'Four *York* Pageants Performed in the Streets of York: July 9, 1988,' *Research Opportunities in Renaissance Drama* 31 (1992): 101–4.

17 In 1992 there were five pageants: *The Crucifixion*, *The Death and Burial of Christ*, *The Harrowing of Hell*, *The Resurrection*, and *Christ's Appearance to Mary Magdalene*. They were performed in Stonegate and Low Petergate, starting at 3 pm on Saturday, 20 June and Sunday, 21 June. For commentary on the 1992 performances, see Meg Twycross, 'The Left-hand-side Theory: A Retraction,' *Medieval English Theatre* 14 (1992): 77–94, and Philip Butterworth, 'The *York Crucifixion*: Actor/Audience Relationship,' *Medieval English Theatre* 14 (1992): 67–76.

18 In 1994 there were nine pageants: *The Building of the Ark*, *Noah and the Flood*, *The Annunciation and Visitation*, *The Nativity*, *The Shepherds*, *The Entry into Jerusalem*, *The Way to Calvary*, *The Resurrection*, and *The Assumption of Mary*. There were five playing places: Dean's Park, King's Square, York Market, St Sampson's Square, and Parliament Street. The performance began at midday on Sunday, 10 July. For an account of the 1994 production, see Richard Rastall, 'The York Cycle,' *Research Opportunities in Renaissance Drama*, 34 (1995), 190–1.

19 In 1998 there were eleven pageants: *Creation to the Fifth Day*, *The Creation*

of Adam and Eve, The Fall of Adam and Eve, The Flight into Egypt, The Temptation of Christ, The Agony in the Garden and the Betrayal of Christ, The Death of Christ, The Harrowing of Hell, The Incredulity of Thomas, The Ascension, and *The Last Judgment.* The playing places were as for 1992 and the performance began at midday on Sunday, 12 July. For an account of the 1998 production, see Jane Oakshott, 'York Guilds' Mystery Plays 1998: The Rebuilding of Dramatic Community,' in *Drama and Community: People and Plays in Medieval Europe,* ed. Alan Hindley (Turnhout: Brepols, 1999), 270–89.

20 In 2002 there were ten pageants: *Creation to the Fifth Day, Noah and the Flood* (with an introduction from *The Building of the Ark*), *Moses and Pharaoh* (i.e. *The Exodus*), *The Angels and Shepherds, The Baptism of Christ, The Woman Taken in Adultery* and *The Raising of Lazarus, The Conspiracy against Jesus, The Death of Christ, The Incredulity of Thomas,* and *The Last Judgment.* The playing places were Dean's Park, Minster South Door, St William's College, King's Square, and the Museum Gardens. The performance began at midday on Sunday, 7 July and Sunday 14 July. For an account of the 2002 production, see Mike Tyler, 'Report by Director,' *Research Opportunities in Renaissance Drama* 42 (2003): 158–61, and Margaret Rogerson, 'Review' in the same volume, 161–9.

21 Letter from Martial Rose, 17 September 1999. Quoted in Philip Butterworth, 'Discipline, Dignity and Beauty: The Wakefield Mystery Plays, Bretton Hall, 1958,' *Leeds Studies in English* ns 32 (2001): 52. Bretton Hall is now part of the University of Leeds.

22 For an account of Rose's 1958 production, see Butterworth, 'Discipline, Dignity and Beauty,' 49–80.

23 Quoted in a press review by Karl Dallas, *Morning Star,* 21 December 1985, in 'Press Reviews,' an appendix to Bernard O'Donoghue, '*The Mysteries*: T.W.'s Revenge,' in *Tony Harrison,* ed. Neil Astley (Newcastle upon Tyne: Bloodaxe Books, 1991), 325.

24 Tony Morris took the role of Annas in 1984 and Cayphas in 1988. His wife, Sue, is also a veteran of the mystery plays (Innkeeper 1988, Percula 1992, Cayphas 1996). I would like to thank both Sue and Tony for discussing their experiences with the plays with me and for giving me access to their extensive mystery play scrapbooks.

25 'It's Murder in York: Inspired Setting for Mystery Writer,' *Thirsk & Easingwold Star,* 29 August 1991.

26 Ruth Ford is a professionally trained local actor and a veteran of the mystery plays. She has gone on to play the First Bad Soul in the Judgment episode in 1998 (wagon plays), Noah's Wife in 2000 (Minster production), and God the Creator in the Judgment episode in 2002 and 2006 (wagon plays). Canon

158   Margaret Rogerson

George Austin's remarks in 1996 about 'political correctness' sparked the
controversy. Hitting back, director John Doyle defended himself against
charges of being 'a pagan and a radical feminist' and gave his own views,
'A God for the Modern Audience,' *Independent*, 29 February 1996.

27 The three actors alternated the roles of Christ, God the Father, and Judas.
Peter Blanshard 'had done some amateur acting,' Gerald Domas was 'a drama
teacher from Pudsey ... [and] a member of the Leeds Proscenium Players,'
and John White 'had played Adam in 1957 and Gabriel in 1960.' See Bernarda
Jaques, 'Ancient Magic Distilled: The Twentieth Century Productions of the
York Mystery Plays,' (unpublished PhD thesis, Tufts University, 1971), 377.

28 The 1996 mystery plays at the theatre ran from 4 June to 30 June. Morris's
performances, 'The Patchwork Poet: Tony Morris,' were presented at various
times during the day on 14, 16, 23, 26, and 28 June.

29 Tony Morris, 'The Mystery of a Poet in Residence: The Art of The Oral,'
Spoken English 30.1 (1997): 16.

30 Jenny Burrage-Smith played the Woman Taken in Adultery in 1988, and
Mary Magdalene in 1992 and 1996, when she also doubled as 'Satan's Snake.'

31 John D. Cox, *The Devil and the Sacred in English Drama, 1350–1642* (Cambridge: Cambridge University Press, 2000), 19.

32 Hans Hess, '1963 Festival Outline,' York City Archives Acc 87:626.

33 An additional devil is indicated by a stage direction at the end of a seventh
episode, The Death of the Virgin. Mary requests that she be spared the horror
of seeing the devil when she dies, but Jesus is firm that the devil must be there,
although he assures her that she will be protected by the angels (ll. 133–4;
154–5). For a list of the appearances of devils in the English biblical plays,
see Cox, *The Devil and the Sacred*, 209–10.

34 Cox, *The Devil and the Sacred*, 23–4.

35 Lesley Wade Soule, 'Performing the Mysteries: Demystification, Story-
Telling and Over-Acting Like the Devil,' *European Medieval Drama* 1 (1996):
148.

36 'Creation to Day of Judgment in an Evening: Mystery Plays Return to York,'
Manchester Guardian, 5 June 1951.

37 'The Powerful Appeal of the Mystery Plays: Outstanding Feature Free from
Sophistication,' *Yorkshire Gazette*, 8 June 1951.

38 The under-stage area, where the first murder is committed, and the mechanism devised for the raising and lowering of the cross, which features in one
of the accidents in the fictional production, were derived from the 1984
design. I visited Barbara Whitehead at her home, The Bronte Birthplace, in
Thornton, a village just outside Bradford, on 12 July 2001. I am most grateful
to her for her generous hospitality and for sharing her thoughts on *Playing
God* and her writing in general.

39 *Death at Dutch House* (1997), for example, features a run-down seventeenth-century house whose impoverished owner is preparing to open it to the public; *The Killings at Barley Hall* (1995) involves the city's archaeological heritage; and the local chocolate industry is the scenario for *Sweet Death, Come Softly* (1992). The other novels so far published in the series are *The Girl with the Red Suspenders* (1990); *The Dean It Was That Died* (1991); *Secrets of the Dead* (1996); and *Dolls Don't Choose* (1998).
     Candace Robb's popular Owen Archer series is also set in York, but this is York of the Middle Ages. The second novel in the series, *The Lady Chapel* (London: Mandarin, 1994), opens in the context of a performance of the mystery plays. The actor playing Christ in the Last Judgment pageant is murdered on Corpus Christi Day and the novel focuses on notions of justice and judgment.

40 Quoted in 'It's Murder in York.'

41 Dashiell Hammett called the generic city of evil in *Red Harvest* (1927) 'Personville' (pronounced Poisonville) The naming of the pop star in *Playing God* could relate to this classic crime novel, with Poison = Person, thus making the actor playing Christ into an everyman figure.

42 For example, a half-hour program on the York mysteries for BBC North, 'The Creation,' made in the lead-up to the millennium production opens with the Crucifixion scene from the play and then switches to Ray Stevenson (Christ) with the pre-production version of the cross. Discussion of the cross recurs throughout the program. Real Life Productions, June 2000.

43 Here Whitehead may have been responding to media accounts of the high-jinks of 'little devils' in the 1980 production who 'had such a good time during the harrowing of Hell that their clubs were confiscated until they had promised to belabour the damned rather more gently,' *Now!* 20 June 1980.

44 Martin Browne makes special mention of Dame Judi's 'progress from attendant angel to Virgin Mary and thence to the top of the professional tree' in his autobiography, *Two in One*, 187.

45 Ann Jellicoe, *Community Plays: How to Put Them On* (London, Methuen, 1987), 257.

46 Dalziel needs the support of his colleagues in solving crimes. The godhead metaphor is completed in this novel when the final suicide-letter of the 'Dark Lady' refers to the 'pretty inspector' (Pascoe) and the 'ugly sergeant' (Wield) as the other two members of the 'Holy Trinity' (382). Peter Pascoe's partnership with Dalziel is summed up in *Death's Jest Book* (London: Harper Collins, 2002): 'He [Dalziel] was aware of his weaknesses, which happily were to some degree Pascoe's strengths ... Sensitivity, intuition, imagination, these were the gifts tossed into the infant Pascoe's cradle which had maybe been crushed in his own by the weightier prezzies of a cast-iron gut and a

sledge-hammer will. No escaping it, Pascoe was a useful, perhaps a necessary complement' (581).

47 St Bega is the saint of Hill's native Cumbria. In the early twelfth century a Benedictine priory dedicated to her was founded at St Bees as a dependency of St Mary's Abbey, York. In the Foreword to *One Small Step* (London: Collins, 1990), Hill places the events of *Bones and Silence* 'quite clearly in 1988' (n.p.) on the grounds of the date given for Trinity Sunday. In this year, Steven Pimlott directed the Museum Gardens mysteries, with Victor Banerjee playing Christ.

48 For example, Christopher Timothy 1980; Robson Green 1992; and Ray Stevenson 2000.

49 Six of the eight parts of the novel have epigraphs from the York cycle, with the other two being provided by Towneley and N-Town.

50 Bernard O'Donoghue, Introduction to *Tony Harrison: Plays One, The Mysteries* (London: Faber, 1999), 7.

51 John Schofield and Alan Vince, *Medieval Towns* (London: Leicester University Press, 1994), 133.

52 Ronnie Mulryne, 'Programme Notes,' in Jason Barnes, '"The Mysteries": Staging and Scenography at the Cottesloe and Elsewhere,' in *The Cottesloe at the National*, ed. Ronnie Mulryne and Margaret Shewring (Stratford: Mulryne & Shewring, 1999), 77.

53 *Morning Star*, 21 December 1985 in 'Press Reviews,' 326.

54 John R. Elliott Jr, 'The Mysteries,' review in *Research Opportunities in Renaissance Drama* 28 (1985): 204.

55 Darryll Grantley, 'The National Theatre's Production of *The Mysteries*: Some Observations,' *Theatre Notebook* 38 (1984): 71.

56 Martin Stevens, 'Illusion and Reality in the Medieval Drama,' *College English* 32.4 (1970): 450.

57 Two of the soldiers doubled in other roles, Brian Osborne doubled as the Poor Man, and Tim Preece as John the Baptist.

58 Vivian C. Brooks, 'Effective New Approach for the York Mystery Plays,' *Yorkshire Evening Press*, 15 June 1963.

59 G. Wilson Knight, 'The Kitchen Sink: On Recent Developments in Drama,' *Encounter* 21.6 (1963): 54.

60 Knight, 'The Kitchen Sink,' 48.

61 'Bill Gaskill' in *At The Royal Court: 25 Years of the English Stage Company*, ed. Richard Findlater (Ambergate, Derbyshire: Amber Lane Press, 1981), 57.

62 E. Martin Browne, 'Producing the Mystery Plays for Modern Audiences,' *Drama Survey* 3.1 (1963): 7.

63 Browne, *Two in One*, 189–90. Although Browne insists that the shepherds

'spoke broad' and whatever dialect was used 'was consciously studied by the actors,' he also 'did not want to cumber actors with the care of learning a dialect: it seemed better to let each speak in his natural way' (190).

64 '"Yorkshire Voices" Sought for Mystery Plays,' *Yorkshire Evening Press*, 1 April 1963.

65 Jacques, 'Ancient Magic Distilled,' 315.

66 '"Yorkshire Voices."'

67 J.W. Robinson, 'The Art of the York Realist,' *Modern Philology* 60.4 (1963): 241–51.

68 Robinson, 'The Art of the York Realist,' 241.

69 Peter Gill, actor, playwright, and director, was appointed as an assistant director at the Royal Court Theatre in the following year, 1964.

70 Peter Gill and Alistair Macaulay, 'Mystery Becomes the Realist,' *Financial Times*, 9 March 2002.

71 Although the setting of the play is the living room, there is a small kitchen leading off it. A sink is visible in the doorway leading to the kitchen, which is referred to a number of times. Gill states that he 'always intended there to be a counter-life in the kitchen beyond the living room,' quoted in 'Mystery Becomes the Realist.'

72 When Judi Dench took the role of the Virgin Mary in 1957 she had already completed three years' training at the Central School of Speech and Drama in London and had been accepted into the Old Vic Company; see John Miller, *Judi Dench, with a Crack in Her Voice: The Biography* (London: Weidenfeld & Nicholson, 1998), 23.

73 Robinson comments that while this play is 'throughout realistic, and contains lines which could have been written by the Realist ... most of the realism is traditional' ('The Art of the York Realist,' 248).

74 Sister Bernarda Jaques records that he 'discovered that the dialogue covering the nailing took just long enough for the soldiers to accomplish it technically' ('Ancient Magic Distilled,' 309).

75 Russell Kirk, 'York and Social Boredom,' *Sewanee Review* 41 (1953): 665.

76 Kirk, 'York and Social Boredom,' 665.

77 'Cultural Christianity' is the term used by Edmund Cusick in 'Religion and Heritage' in *British Cultural Identities*, ed. Mike Storry and Peter Childs (London: Routledge, 1997), 289. See also my discussion in 'Living History: The Modern Mystery Plays in York,' *Research Opportunities in Renaissance Drama* 43 (2004): 1–27.

PART TWO

Medieval Plays

Doubting *Thomas*: 'Womans Witnes' and the Towneley *Thomas Indie*

GARRETT P.J. EPP

The Towneley play *Thomas Indie* is better known for its altered title page than for its contents. A full-colour reproduction of that page, f. 111v of Huntington Manuscript HM 1, serves as the frontispiece for the otherwise monochrome facsimile edition of the manuscript.[1] The twenty-eighth play in this manuscript collection was, like the twenty-sixth play, originally entitled *Resurreccio Domini* (The Lord's Resurrection), but that elaborately rubricated title has been crossed out and *Thomas Indie* (Thomas of India) written in small black letters beside it. The latter title does not seem especially appropriate, given that the play as it stands makes no reference at all to the doubting apostle's legendary evangelization of India; however, it is clearly the title that the scribe intended for this play, which ends eleven folio pages later with the rubric 'Explicit Thomas Indie.' As Thomas himself initially argues regarding the apostolic vision of the wounded but living Christ, things are not necessarily as they seem: like its title, the play as it stands is not as it was originally written, but has been obviously and awkwardly altered. This alteration, more than the apparent change of title, is a textual wound deserving sceptical examination, as it begs important questions regarding the relationships between faith, authority, and gender in late medieval England.

The most recent editors of *The Towneley Plays*, Martin Stevens and A.C. Cawley, state bluntly that the play 'is of course misnamed in that the Thomas episode takes up only a little more than half of its narrative.'[2] However, this is also true of the play's much shorter but notably similar counterpart in York, the only other separate play on this topic, the first half of which likewise dramatizes the appearance of the risen Christ to the other apostles. In Chester and N-Town, the Thomas episode is paired with the appearance on the road to Emmaus to form a single pageant; in York as in Towneley, a separate Emmaus play precedes the Thomas play, and follows an appearance to Mary Magdalene.³ In each case, Thomas explicitly refuses to believe what others, including the audience, have just witnessed onstage. What most distinguishes the Towneley version of the Thomas episode is its discontinuity – a characteristic of the collection as a whole, as well as of some of its parts.⁴ In regard to this particular play, Stevens and Cawley mention what they describe as the 'careless editing of two originally disparate parts' written in different stanza forms;⁵ however, they do not otherwise discuss the individual parts, or the disparities between them. The extant text clearly represents a revision and expansion of an earlier play about the apostle Thomas and his doubts concerning the resurrection of Christ. While the dialogue of that play of Thomas apparently remains essentially intact, its message has been radically altered through the addition of a prologue that centres on an exchange between Mary Magdalene and a highly misogynist apostle Paul. The anachronism of Paul's presence here is unusual even by medieval standards, but has attracted almost no comment since 1859, when none other than John Payne Collier, who had earlier borrowed the manuscript from its owner, Peregrine Edward Towneley, referred to 'the Widkirk Play [sic] ... where St. Paul makes a long harangue against the female sex, which could hardly have belonged to the performance as it was first written and represented.'⁶ Yet the present context of that harangue ultimately offers the audience an extraordinary exception to the antifeminist norm of medieval literature and social hierarchy. In the play as it stands, it is the woman, Mary Magdalene, who, in the face of dogmatic antifeminism, and in contrast to any and all of Christ's chosen male apostles and founders of the church, shows us the way of faith.

Stevens and Cawley usefully summarize the play in relation to its chief biblical source:

> The Towneley version resembles most closely in general outline the gospel narrative of St John, in which Mary Magdalene goes directly to the Apostles, followed by Christ's appearance before the Ten and then, a week later, before the Eleven (with Thomas); see John xx.18–29. Towneley 28, therefore, picks up directly from the end of Play 26, the Resurrection, when Mary Magdalene prepares for her meeting with the apostles. Play 27 [of the Pilgrims to Emmaus] is, consequently, an intruder in the narrative sequence, though some editorial effort seems to have been made to assimilate it.⁷

Yet these modern editors themselves here attempt to make this material seem more unified, and more carefully assimilated into its context, than it really is. Cawley long ago observed that this play was similar to the York Scriveners' more concise Thomas pageant not only in structure but also in the use of specific rhymes and verbal structures, arguing that 'the most obvious differences between Y[ork] and T[owneley] have the appearance of being additions in T to an older play which is more closely represented by Y.'[8] However, all but one of those supposed additions use the same stanza form as the rest of the play; the Magdalene prologue is clearly an addition to a complete and cohesive play, however much that play might differ from any putative sources. The original Thomas play, if only by coincidence, fits the existing Towneley sequence reasonably well; the prologue fits neither that sequence nor, more crucially, the play to which it has been attached.

The original play consists of seventy-three eight-line cross-rhymed stanzas, and has twelve speaking roles: Jesus and the eleven apostles. Peter's lament, which begins this section, was clearly written to begin the play: the speech opens with the exclamation 'Waloway' (65)   much as the York equivalent opens with Peter saying 'Alas' (41:1) – and proceeds to summarize previous events, including his denial of Jesus (Matthew 26:69–75; John 18:15–18, 25–7), an action that is not represented in Towneley, although predicted in the Conspiracy play (20:450–5) and given extended treatment in York (29:87–169). What follows closely resembles at least in outline the York Scriveners' pageant: ten apostles, all but Thomas, mourn Jesus' death; Jesus then enters, rebukes them, and is fed honey and fish before vanishing; Thomas then enters, mourning, and argues with the other apostles before Jesus reenters, restoring Thomas's faith. The narrative thus combines two notably different post-Resurrection Gospel accounts. In Luke 24:33–49, Jesus appears to, and eats with, all eleven apostles along with Luke and Cleophas, shortly after the supper in Emmaus, which is, in that Gospel, his first post-Resurrection appearance. In John 20:19–25, Jesus appears to all but Thomas (that is, to his many disciples, not necessarily just the other ten apostles) the evening after his initial appearance to Mary Magdalene, breathing the Holy Spirit onto them (as in Towneley 28:234 SD) and, as noted by Stevens and Cawley, he appears to Thomas and others only a week later (John 20:26). In Towneley, as in York, the latter interval is elided for dramatic economy.[9] However, the recombined bones of the biblical narratives have been fleshed out in orthodox ways. Even the dual appearance of Jesus to the ten, which occurs both in York and in Towneley and which Cawley has cited as a departure from biblical tradition,[10] is arguably justified by John's Gospel account, in which Jesus twice says 'pax vobis' as if greeting the gathered disciples for the first time (John 20:19, 21).[11] While Cawley rightly praises the York version's 'magnificent economy of words,'[12] the Towneley play is at least consistent: everything is verbally extended or amplified, but nothing new is added to the plot.

That is, nothing is added aside from a completely new and radically different, unbiblical scene: Peter's lament is preceded by that eleven-stanza prologue, written in a different verse form. Apart from a pivotal cross-rhymed quatrain in which Peter explodes with indignation against Mary Magdalene, the prologue uses a six-line tail-rhyme (*rhyme couée*) stanza with varying metre, but mostly aa⁴b³cc⁴b³ – a stanza also used (with similar metrical variance) in the Towneley *Creation, Prophets, Caesar Augustus, Annunciation and Salutation*, and *Crucifixion* plays, but not found in York. Stevens and Cawley oddly assert that this section 'is linked to the Resurrection play by virtue of its stanza form' while noting that the latter play, one of several borrowed from York, actually uses a very different rhyme scheme: aaabab.[13] This tail-rhyme stanza form – the Burns stanza – is also used in the York Scriveners' Thomas pageant, as well as in the York pageants of the *Expulsion from Eden* and *Temptation of Christ*; the same stanza form constitutes about two-thirds of the Towneley *Emmaus* play, which immediately precedes *Thomas Indie*, and all of the infamously misplaced and fragmentary monologue by Judas that fills the last two pages of the manuscript, written in a later hand than that of the main scribe.

What sets this prologue apart, from anything else in York or elsewhere, is less its poetic form than its dramatic content. The only other speaker in this opening section, along with Peter and Mary, is Paul. He is thereby represented as being an apostle, indeed by implication one of the original twelve, long before his famous conversion – the subject of an entire play in the roughly contemporary Digby manuscript,[14] but more importantly a regular feast in the church calendar, and not merely an obscure detail in the biblical narrative. Stevens and Cawley remark only briefly on his unusual presence:

> Although not mentioned as one of the Apostles in the Gospels, Paul is often included in that group on the basis of 1 Cor.xv.9–11. The sequence of speakers indicates that Paul is the second Apostle, Peter being the first. No other Apostle except Thomas is named.[15]

In the cited passage from Paul's letter to the Corinthians, which immediately follows his brief summary of Jesus' post-Resurrection appearances, Paul calls himself the least of the apostles and unworthy even of that designation because of his earlier persecution of the church (1 Cor. 15:9).

Paul's list of the post-Resurrection appearances ends with his own momentous vision of Jesus on the road to Damascus; I have encountered no precedent, medieval or ancient, for including him among the apostles prior to that event. In this inclusion, the play is uniquely perverse.

Peter's prominence here, on the other hand, is obviously unproblematic. Peter is regularly ranked highest among the apostles, and so usually speaks first in medieval dramatic representations of apostolic discourse. The second position is normally reserved for John, who is in any case the second speaker, after Peter, in the York Thomas pageant (and indeed in most other York pageants including three or more apostles), as well as at the Last Supper in the Towneley Conspiracy play – the only other point in any of the Towneley plays where all the onstage apostles are given consecutive speeches. In the Towneley Ascension play, the speaking order is variable: Thomas has the first line in that play, followed by John, then Simon, and then Peter; the next time any number of apostles speak consecutively, Peter speaks first, followed by Andrew and others, while John is silent; following the actual Ascension, the first non-angelic speaker is the Virgin Mary, who addresses John, to whose care she has of course been entrusted at the Crucifixion; John then responds, after which the other apostles speak, starting again with Peter, but followed by Matthew. This sort of variety is unusual; order and rank matter deeply in medieval writing, as in the culture more generally. Even the various unnamed soldiers at the Trial and Crucifixion, in both York and Towneley, as well as in Chester (where they are all 'Jews'), generally speak in numbered order. In the Towneley Lazarus play, Thomas functions as the third (of three) apostles, following Peter and John, although he is the only one of the twelve actually named in the biblical account (John 11:16), John's being the only gospel that ever mentions Thomas by name except as part of a longer list of apostles. In York, any departure from the usual ordering of the first three apostles – Peter, John, then James – has specific textual authority. At the Transfiguration (York 22), for instance, Peter, James, and John speak only in that order, the order in which they are named in the majority of gospel sources for this episode (in both Matt. 17:1 and Mark 9:2, and indeed throughout the Gospel of Mark, but not in Luke 9:28); at the Entry into Jerusalem, the two disciples sent ahead to fetch the donkey, unnamed in all four Gospel accounts, are Peter and Phillip, the latter being the first disciple mentioned after this incident in the Gospel of John (12:20–1).[16]

Towneley is less consistent than York in this respect: where in Luke 22:8, Jesus tells Peter and John – in that order – to prepare the paschal feast, in Towneley (20:338ff) he speaks first with John, and the named order of the two apostles is reversed in what Jesus says. However, this represents a relatively minor deviation from established tradition. The appearance of Paul among the apostles on the day of the resurrection of Jesus is, in contrast, entirely without parallel or precedent, regardless of the speaking order, and its relative impact on the meaning of the pageant as a whole is immense. Commenting on the ten numbered but unnamed apostles in *Thomas Indie*, Stevens and Cawley state:

> Since Paul is an intruder in the list, the remaining eight would have to come from the following list: John, James, Andrew, Phillip, Bartholomew, Matthew, James of Alphaeus, Simon Zelotes, and Jude the brother of James; see Acts i.13. Of these only one of the Jameses and Jude have no speaking parts in two plays. Since Jude Thaddeus did have a speaking part in the Conspiracy and Capture, the only unnamed apostle in the Towneley cycle from among the original twelve is one of the Jameses.[17]

This note is misleading, even aside from its implication that the Towneley plays form a coherent whole that, as Martial Rose once stated regarding the Passion sequence, 'sweeps on in continuous action from play to play and from stage to stage' with a single cast.[18] The number and naming of the apostles varies: 'Iude' is named in the Ascension play (29:437), but Thaddeus or 'Thadee' speaks in the Conspiracy play (20:392); immediately thereafter, either one actor speaks for 'we two Iamys' (20:393), or both Jameses speak together, so both are in some sense present, and named. The note also gives the impression that the 'intruder' Paul is nonetheless supposed to be counted as one of the original apostles, at the expense of another, although this is not the sort of calculation an audience member is likely to make regarding a mostly unnamed group of apostles.

Paul does appear in the Thomas play, proper, but only in name. 'Paulus' speaks three times after the added prologue (in lines 97–104, 313–20, and 473–8, all but the last speech being full stanzas, which is the normal pattern in the play), but is standing in either for an originally unnamed 'Secundus Apostolus,' or specifically for John. All of the lines here ascribed to Paul are preceded by a speech from Peter, and followed by a speech from the anonymous 'Tercius Apostolus,' twice with Thomas intervening. The speaker is neither as prominent nor as distinct a character here as Paul is in the prologue, except that his prayer prompts the first appearance of Jesus. One could perhaps argue that this prayer and divine appearance are intended to evoke or stand in for Paul's eventual conversion on the road to Damascus, but there is little real difference between this prayer and the likewise efficacious requests for comfort uttered by James in York (41:18) or by Andrew in Chester (19:167). Indeed, the prayer represents the speaker as being just another one of the eleven remaining apostles, referring to 'the breede that we eytt [ate]' at the Last Supper (99). The second apostle is surely rechristened 'Paulus' only because of Paul's presence in the newly added prologue.

On the other hand, Peter is not an especially distinctive character in this play, either, following his opening speech. His final speech (457–68) interests me, but for reasons other than character development: it reiterates at length the witness of Luke and Cleophas, the travellers to Emmaus. Whether or not it was ever performed as part of a sequence, the original Thomas play is consistent with the travellers' stated intention at the end of the Towneley Emmaus play to go and 'tell oure brethere all the case' (27:371). However, neither the Thomas play nor the sequence is consistent with the prologue, with its emphasis on the unreliability of the testimony of Mary as a woman: Mary is explicitly not the only one who has previously seen the risen Jesus; moreover, the other witnesses were male.[19] This knowledge alters the force and apparent direction of Peter's long opening speech, and rids it of a certain oddity. If read together with the prologue, rather than as the beginning of a self-contained play, the speech might well appear to be directed against women in general, and Mary Magdalene in particular. Yet all Peter actually says in regard to Mary is

> Sen that Mawdleyn witnes beres
> That Iesus rose from ded,
> Myn ees has letten salt teres,
> On erthe to se hym trede.   (28:69–72)

If not preceded by any denunciations of Mary or her witness, this sounds suspiciously like good faith, combined with longing, not for living proof, but for contact with a living and beloved friend. Even Stevens and Cawley are forced to admit that 'Peter's sudden acceptance of Mary Magdalene's report is inconsistent with his preceding speeches in which he vehemently disputes her claim to have seen Christ.'[20]

This does not mean that Peter's speech is free of misogyny. His second stanza still laments his having denied Jesus 'For drede of womans myght' (78). While he does not directly blame a woman for his own failing, he implies that his unmanly cowardice was all the worse because he feared what a woman might say, rather than what a man might do. This was certainly not the only available interpretation of that event. The fifteenth-century dialogue of *Dives and Pauper* uses Peter's denial to argue against a generalized notion of women as 'þe fendis snaris,' asserting that the woman in question was just doing her job: 'She dede here offys for she was ochyr [usher] & kepere at þe dore, as seith Sent Gregory, & she seyde to hym þat he was on of Cristis disciplis, as she seyde soth, for she was bodyn þat she schulde letyn non of Cristis disciplys entryn.'[21] In the play, in contrast, Peter's misogyny seems to be treated as a non-issue, a statement to be taken at face value. It is never explicitly countered, in word or in deed, in the whole of the Thomas play. On the other hand, if uttered in the presence of Mary Magdalene herself, the statement might seem at least slightly inappropriate. Such a juxtaposition could even encourage the audience to consider the appropriateness of any such totalizing, antifeminist views, by implicitly drawing attention to the divine authority that informs this particular 'womans myght.' However, she is absent, or at least was absent from the original Thomas play. Just prior to Peter's long speech, the first to mention her by name, and after a final protest to Paul that she is telling the truth, Mary Magdalene herself silently vanishes from the text.

In the notes to his translation of the Towneley plays, Martial Rose argues that Mary Magdalene must exit after her last line, despite the lack of any stage direction to that effect: 'She is not present when Jesus appears to the disciples nor when Thomas in turn answers the arguments of the disciples. Had Mary Magdalene been present Thomas would certainly have turned his attention to her in his refutation of the evidence for Jesus' resurrection.'[22] Stevens and Cawley agree, stating, 'Magdalene's exit at this point is supported by later references to her in the third person indicating that she is no longer present.'[23] Still, one might expect the dialogue to contain some comment on her parting, or at least dramatic justification for her exit. While no Gospel text explicitly places Mary Magdalene together with the apostles for any of the post-Resurrection appearances, medieval interpreters sometimes did place her there: Nicholas Love's highly influential *Mirror of the Blessed Life of Jesus Christ*, for instance, includes both Magdalene and Jesus' mother among the disciples at both of the appearances represented here, with and without Thomas.[24] Moreover, the play (unlike the prologue) contains a relatively large number of unusually explicit Latin stage directions,[25] which renders the silence around Mary's apparent departure especially notable.

The apostolic misogyny does not vanish into silence; it simply moves from Paul to Peter and then into the mouth of doubting Thomas, in two speeches that frame the second and final naming of 'The Mawdleyn' (412). In response to the other apostles' attempts to convince him that they have seen Jesus, and his 'bledand' wounds, he tells them, 'Ye ar as women, rad for [afraid of] blood / And lightly oft solaced' (403–4). When one apostle objects that 'gretter care / Myght no synfull wight haue' (409–10) than Mary Magdalene, who has likewise seen Jesus, Thomas is indignant:

> Lo, sich foly with you is,
> Wyse men that shuld be,
> That thus a womans witnes trowys
> Better then that ye se.   (417–20)

Audience awareness that this particular 'womans witnes' is true undercuts the accusation, but not necessarily the misogyny that informs it. Nor do the numerous references to another Mary, Jesus' mother,[26] make a positive difference in this respect: as queen of heaven and eternal virgin, Mary is too easily considered utterly apart from other women, including (or especially) the 'Mawdleyn.' The play itself does not show its audience that women in general are as wise and as trustworthy as men, but clearly indicates that Thomas is wrong about the other apostles: in addition to having the faith that Thomas lacks, the apostles already have all the empirical evidence a reasonable man could require; their witness does not depend on that of a woman, or on 'womanly' fear. It is Thomas, not the apostles, who is being emotional and unreasonable, and thus – in medieval terms – effeminate. Thomas is also effeminate in his elaborate dress, which he casts off at the end of the play; in his very first line he refers to himself as being sorrowful despite seeming 'prowde as pacok' (273). While pride might be considered an acceptably masculine vice, elaborate or overly fashionable clothing is typically denounced as effeminate or sodomitical – one need only recall Chaucer's Pardoner, who 'thoughte he rood al of the newe jet,'[27] or theatrical vice figures such as New Guise in *Mankind* (ca. 1470).[28] Still, in the context of the original play, Thomas's clothing, like his words, at most turns his accusation of effeminacy on himself; it does not erase or undercut his misogyny.

What does undercut the misogyny is the prologue. What is at stake there is precisely the validity of 'womans witnes' or, as Paul twice calls it, 'womans saw' (30, 50). Peter is incredulous of Mary's claim to have seen the resurrected Christ, but it is Paul who lashes out with four full stanzas of misogynist ranting, citing as his authority what is 'wretyn in oure law' (29) and 'In oure bookes' (35). 'As Crist me lowse of syn' (46), he states, women are lawless and irreverent (44–5), full of cunning and guile (32); as 'All manere of men well it wyttyn' (36) they are like apples that are 'full roten inwardly / At the colke within' (42–3). Mary Magdalene may be the archetypal 'fallen woman' of Christian legend, but she is also a saint, 'þe belouede disciples & of þe apostles Apostolesse' according to Love's *Mirror*.[29] Mary Magdalene's importance was greatly enhanced by medieval legend that built on the patristic conflation of Mary from Magdala, from whom Jesus had expelled seven demons according to Luke 8:2, with Mary of Bethany, the sister of Lazarus, who anoints Jesus' feet in John 12:1–8 (in Matt. 26:6–13 and Mark 14:3–9, an unnamed woman from Bethany anoints Jesus' head), and thus with the unnamed 'sinner' who anoints his feet and washes them with her tears in Luke 7:37–50, becoming the very figure of penance. Even without this conflation, however, she is prominent in the Gospels: much like Peter, whenever named together with others (always other women) she is listed first, with the exception of John 19:25, in which she is the last-named of the women present at the Crucifixion – a list that begins with Jesus' mother, who is unmentioned in the parallel list in Mark 15.10, where Magdalene is again the first named. The popular but unscriptural medieval tradition, narrated in Love's *Mirror* and dramatized in the N-Town Passion play, that the first witness to the Resurrection was the Virgin Mary,[30] cannot detract from Mary Magdalene's biblically attested witness. She is telling the truth, and the audience knows it; 'oure books' and Christ himself will attest to it. Paul is simply wrong, and his forceful absolutism is severely undercut. If the misogyny here expressed is unfounded, though endorsed by the very best of authorities, misogyny itself begins to appear untenable. With this prologue in place, the play as a whole takes on a new, very nearly feminist flavour.

This might well be accidental. One might hypothesize that the reviser was attracted by the misogynist statements of the original play, and attempted to bolster them by adding the weighty authority of St Paul. This hypothesis thus posits a reviser oblivious not only to the awkward and unnecessary anachronism of Paul's early presence among the apostles but also to his having undermined his own efforts and opinions from the outset. A second, altogether more attractive hypothesis is that the reviser of this particular play wished to exploit the unexplored contradiction between the stated misogyny and the truth of Mary's witness. The addition would thus represent a calculated attempt to undercut the perceived antifeminist authority of the church itself at its apostolic source. This is an exciting idea for me, personally, given that my own mother's theological training and acknowledged pastoral talents long remained unused due to a continuing distrust of 'womans witnes.' Still it must be admitted that, if the hypothesis is true, the intention has been incompletely and inefficiently carried out. For one thing, the Emmaus reference should have been abandoned, or reference to a disbelieving reception of that witness inserted earlier – after all, both Mark and Luke provide explicit authority for such disbelief. Also, Mary should at least have been mentioned towards the end of the play, if not again given a vocal presence, and 'womans witnes' (re-)affirmed.

This is, incidentally, the way some important gnostic texts handle the same problem: in the last chapter of the Gospel of Mary, Mary Magdalene's lengthy account of private revelations is denounced by Peter, who is then sharply reproved by another apostle, and Mary exonerated; the ending of the very early Gospel of Thomas, aptly enough for my purposes, has Jesus himself admonish Peter for his denunciation of Mary.[31] However, these ancient texts, rediscovered only this past century, were unknown to anyone in the later Middle Ages, and the canonical gospel accounts are often less positive in their treatment of women, and of Mary Magdalene in particular. According to Luke, Mary Magdalene and the other women who visit the tomb are told by angels of the resurrection, and communicate that message to Peter and the other apostles (24:9, 23), but there is no divine appearance to them; clearly disbelieving even the most basic portion of their message, but without a word of denunciation, Peter immediately goes to inspect the empty tomb for himself (24:12).

Another line of Luke's text (24:34), sandwiched between the Emmaus episode and the appearance of Jesus to the eleven, briefly mentions an appearance to Peter. Such an appearance is staged as part of Chester's Resurrection pageant,[32] but is unrepresented within any gospel narrative, and is obviously ignored in the Towneley plays, as it is elsewhere. However, such an appearance is also mentioned by Paul, in 1 Cor. 15:5, as part of the list cited earlier in this paper. That list, like Luke's gospel, does not include any post-Resurrection appearance to Mary Magdalene, or indeed to any women. In her commentary on Luke in *The Women's Bible Commentary*, Jane Schaberg states:

In this Gospel, as in 1 Cor. 15:3–8, there is no appearance to Mary Magdalene or the other women who had been at the cross ... It is impossible to know for sure what traditions were available to Luke ... But since Acts [attributed to the same writer] stresses that only men can witness officially to the resurrection (1:21–26) and lead the Christian community, we can surmise that if Luke had a tradition of an appearance to Mary Magdalene or to another woman, it would have been suppressed in the interests of this perspective on leadership and power, which overarches Luke's entire work.[33]

Men clearly were thought to be the favoured witnesses, at least by both Luke and Paul; a playwright looking to downplay or suppress 'womans witnes' need have looked no further than these writers, while also conveniently suppressing the idea of a separate, previous appearance to Peter. Still, the Gospels were generally read as a coherent, unified whole, and a unified reading or dramatization of the Gospels demands acceptance of any event as prominent as Mary Magdalene's encounter with the risen Jesus. Thus the original play of Thomas accepts the witness of Mary Magdalene as canonical and true, but otherwise treats it much as Luke treats women's witness generally: it is insignificant, at least to anyone other than women. Men apparently need stronger stuff. In the Gospel of John, Mary is famously told not to touch or hold the risen Jesus (the 'noli me tangere' of John 20:17), whereas Thomas is subsequently invited to do exactly that (John 20:27); in Towneley, Jesus' invitation to Thomas (in line 565) is preceded by a general and unbiblical invitation to the other disciples. 'Grope and fele flesh and bone / And fourme of man well-wroght' (133–4).

I suspect that whoever added the Mary prologue realized that there was something wrong in this picture. That there remains something wrong in the picture presented by the revised play should not distract us from what the reviser has actually done, or from the possibility that even the more striking inconsistencies and disjunctures are there by design. If, as I have suggested, the prologue was written to critique institutional and biblical misogyny and antifeminism, Paul's presence there can, or perhaps must, be read as deliberately troubling – a sort of Brechtian *Verfremdungseffekt*, foregrounding biblical disjuncture and incongruity, and deconstructing masculinist authority. Other problems, such as the Emmaus reference, could be seen as an extension of this effect, pushing the audience to reevaluate 'womans witnes' and to question the masculinist witness of biblical and ecclesiastical authority. Of course, this is not what one would generally expect of a medieval text, particularly a religious play text, even aside from any protofeminist subversion. The didacticism is usually explicit, the message clear, but here any plausible message seems to work against itself, and against expectation. Mary Magdalene's presence among the apostles is perhaps unexpected but, unlike Paul's, it is not especially odd, except in juxtaposition with the apostolic questioning of her credentials. Given the unexpected possibility in this juxtaposition of a protofeminist critique, however, one would not expect Mary, as newly valorized exemplum of 'womans witnes,' simply to vanish from the text before the misogynist ranting has ended. In all likelihood, whatever the intentions behind the revision, the revision itself was never completed; on the other hand, since the extant text does not afford Mary an exit, perhaps the reviser envisioned leaving her onstage as a silent witness and rebuke to those who are as convention demands given a voice. In the play as it stands, expectations simply are not met; questions are begged and remain unanswered. Despite the apparent closure effected by Thomas's profession of faith, this text demands of its audience, medieval or modern, an active questioning of authority – textual, dramatic, religious, and cultural. It demands not proof, or faith, but doubt.

NOTES

1 *The Towneley Cycle: A Facsimile of Huntington MS HM 1*, ed. A.C. Cawley and Martin Stevens (San Marino, CA: Huntington Library, 1976). I am indebted to the Huntington Library and its staff for their help in my recent examination of the manuscript, funded in part through an Andrew W. Mellon Fellowship, in preparation of a new student edition of the Towneley plays. All references to the plays in this essay, however, are to the standard two-volume Early English Text Society edition (EETS ss 13–14), also prepared by Martin Stevens and A.C. Cawley, *The Towneley Plays* (London: Oxford University Press, 1994); line numbers are cited parenthetically.

2 Stevens and Cawley, *Towneley Plays*, 617.

3 In the York manuscript, the Emmaus and Thomas pageants are separated by the misplaced Purification pageant, but would have been performed in sequence. See *The York Plays*, ed. Richard Beadle (London: E. Arnold, 1982), *The Chester Mystery Cycle*, ed. R.M. Lumiansky and David Mills, EETS ss 3, 9 (London: Oxford University Press, 1974, 1986), and *The N-town Play, Cotton Vespasian D.8*, ed. Stephen Spector, EETS ss 11, 12 (London: Oxford University Press, 1991); plays and line numbers are hereafter cited parenthetically.

4 I have, along with others, long argued that the Towneley manuscript is not a coherent, performable cycle of pageants, but an eclectic collection of plays and groups of plays arranged in chronological order (*like* a cycle) for a reader; see my 'The Towneley Plays and The Hazards of Cycling,' *Research Opportunities in Renaissance Drama* 32 (1993): 121–50. See also Barbara D. Palmer, 'Recycling "The Wakefield Cycle": The Records,' *Research Opportunities in Renaissance Drama* 41 (2002): 88–130. I first became aware of the problematic nature of *Thomas Indie*, and of the various disconnections between plays, when serving as artistic director for the 1985 Poculi Ludique

Societas production of the Towneley plays in Toronto. A.F. Johnston served both as supervisor for my doctoral dissertation on the York plays, and as dramaturge for the Towneley production, having previously played angel to my devil at the Slaughter of the Innocents in the 1983 PLS production of the Chester plays. My doubts, fears, and inadequacies both as student and as director were regularly overcome by this particular 'womans witnes,' for which I remain eternally thankful.

5 Stevens and Cawley, *Towneley Plays*, 619, notes 69–70.

6 J. Payne Collier, ed. 'The Skryveners' Play, The Incredulity of St. Thomas. From a Manuscript in the Possession of John Sykes, Esq. M.D. of Doncaster,' in *The Camden Miscellany, Volume the Fourth* (Camden Society, 1859), 6.

7 Stevens and Cawley, *Towneley Plays*, 617.

8 A.C. Cawley, 'The Sykes MS of the York Scriveners' Play,' *Leeds Studies in English and Kindred Languages* 7/8 (1952): 68.

9 In N-Town, the entire first appearance of the risen Jesus to the apostles is elided along with that interval, and along with all the apostles other than Peter and Thomas: Luke and Cleophas meet Peter and tell him about the Emmaus appearance; they are then joined by Thomas, who briefly expresses doubts before Jesus himself appears. In Chester's Thomas and Emmaus pageant, the interval is represented by a pause in the action: after the initial appearance of Jesus to the gathered apostles, they meet Thomas, presumably on the street, then return to the wagon stage to lie down; while they are sleeping, Jesus reappears (Chester 19:239 SD: *Tunc ibunt omnes iterum ad mansionem et recumbent. Et subito apparebit Jesus.*).

10 Cawley, 'Sykes,' 68, note 34.

11 The initial stage direction, much like the next (28:120 SD), should read: *Tunc venit Iesus et cantat: 'Pax vobis' et non tardabit* (28:104 SD: Then Jesus comes and sings 'Peace be with you' and he will not stay); that is, he sings, and then vanishes. Stevens and Cawley, like all previous editors of the play, confusingly extend this stage direction by including 'et non tardabit' in the song and adding the first line of the next speech, clearly attributed in the manuscript to the Third Apostle, 'hec est dies quam fecit Dominus' (a quotation from Psalm 117:24, translated in the same speaker's next line), making the song (and action) nonsensical: 'Pax vobis et non tardabit; hec est dies quam fecit Dominus.' They compound the error by adding a lengthy note of explanation that critiques JoAnna Dutka's correct reading of the line (620, note 104 SD) – a reading she got right despite never having seen the manuscript; see Dutka, *Music in the English Mystery Plays*, Early Drama, Art, and Music Reference Series 2 (Kalamazoo MI: Medieval Institute Publications, 1980), 73.

12 Cawley, 'Sykes,' 68, note 34.

13 Stevens and Cawley, *Towneley Plays*, 617.

14 The Digby play, *The Conversion of Saint Paul*, like MS Digby 133 itself, is usually dated to the first quarter of the sixteenth century, with some later additions; see *The Late Medieval Religious Plays of Bodleian MSS. Digby 133 and e Museo 160*, EETS os 283 (Oxford: Oxford University Press, 1982), xxii. Stevens and Cawley state that the Towneley manuscript 'can be dated later than 1475, with a strong possibility that it was written at the turn of the century' (xv), but more recent estimates, including my own, place it well after the first quarter of the sixteenth century – even as late as the Marian period of 1553–8 (Palmer, 'Recycling,' 96).

15 Stevens and Cawley, *Towneley Plays*, 618, note 13.

16 In Chester, the apostle Andrew takes greater precedence than is usual, speaking immediately after Peter both at the Last Supper (15:113) and at the Ascension (20:21), and before any of the other apostles in the Thomas sequence (19:148), although Andrew is not an especially prominent saint in Chester or in any potential sources that I have encountered. Nor is York immune to interesting exceptions: the first disciple to speak at the Last Supper is, uniquely, the non-biblical 'Marcelle myn awne discipill dere' (27:39), presumably based on the legend of St Martial, which turned a third-century bishop of Limoges into a disciple who served at the paschal supper and witnessed the Crucifixion.

17 Stevens and Cawley, *Towneley Plays*, 620–1 note 105.

18 Martial Rose, ed. and transl., *The Wakefield Mystery Plays* (Garden City NY: Doubleday Anchor, 1963), 35.

19 The unnamed disciple who accompanies Cleophas (or Cleopas) on the road to Emmaus is traditionally identified with the evangelist Luke, as in the Towneley Pilgrims play. A few modern commentators have suggested that this disciple might have been identified with Mary, the wife of Clopas (called *Maria Cleopae* in the Vulgate) who stands with the other Maries at the foot of the cross in John 19:25. Most biblical scholars, however, consider the names Cleopas and Clopas, and the figures so named, to be unrelated.

20 Stevens and Cawley, *Towneley Plays*, 619, note for lines 69–70.

21 *Dives and Pauper*, ed. Priscilla Heath Barnum, 2 vols, EETS os 275, 280 (London: Oxford University Press, 1976 and 1980), 6.10.4; 6.11.46–9.

22 Rose, *Wakefield Mystery Plays*, 549.

23 Stevens and Cawley, *Towneley Plays*, 619, note 64.

24 *Nicholas Love's Mirror of the Blessed Life of Jesus Christ*, ed. Michael G. Sargent, Garland Medieval Texts 18 (New York: Garland, 1992), 206, 209.

25 See lines 104, 120, 176, 234, 240, and 296. The final entrance of Jesus (at 560) and the initial entrance of Thomas (273) are marked only by dialogue, but the play's final extant stage direction (296: *hic pergit ad discipulos*) marks the

entrance of Thomas onto the stage, proper, his first lines being delivered
closer to the audience, on the street or in the platea.

26 The Virgin Mary is mentioned at lines 116, 124, 186–7, 243, 345–8, 383, and
598 – mostly by name, and specifically *as* virgin and mother, but only within
the original pageant, not the prologue.

27 The General Prologue, *The Canterbury Tales* I.682; in *The Riverside
Chaucer*, ed. Larry D. Benson (Boston: Houghton Mifflin, 1987).

28 See Epp, 'The Vicious Guise: Effeminacy, Sodomy, and *Mankind*,' in *Becoming Male in the Middle Ages*, ed. Jeffrey Jerome Cohen and Bonnie Wheeler
(New York and London: Garland, 1997), 303–20. Although 'effeminate'
throughout the medieval and early modern periods normally implies an
excessive love of (and hence a likeness to) women, effeminacy is treated as
part of a slippery slope that leads from desiring women to imitating them,
and from sartorial excess to lechery and thence to sodomy.

29 Love, *Mirror*, 206. For a full account of Mary's transformation from biblical
disciple (or 'discipless' – that is, female disciple) to medieval saint and
apostolorum apostola, see Katherine Ludwig Jansen, *The Making of the
Magdalen: Preaching and Devotion in the Later Middle Ages* (Princeton, NJ:
Princeton University Press, 2000).

30 See N-Town 35:89ff, and Spector's note on the play itself on pages 519–20;
cap. l of Love's *Mirror*, which shares significant vocabulary with these plays,
implicitly reveals the lack of biblical evidence for this tradition in its title: 'Of
þe gloriouse resurrexion of oure lorde Jesu & how he first aperede to his
modere as it may be resonably trowede' (193). On the tradition more generally, see Jansen, *Making of the Magdalen*, 59–62, 262–3.

31 For texts and commentary, see *The Complete Gospels: Annotated Scholars
Version*, ed. Robert J. Miller (San Francisco: Harper Collins, 1994). The
Coptic Gospel of Thomas is not to be confused with the infancy narrative
ascribed to Thomas, also included in this volume.

32 Both the Magdalene and Peter episodes are missing from three of the five
Chester cycle manuscripts, but their absence cannot be taken as an indication
that the Chester Skinners ever performed their Resurrection pageant without
these scenes.

33 *The Women's Bible Commentary*, ed. Carol A. Newsom and Sharon H. Ringe
(London and Louisville, KY: SPCK and Westminster/John Knox, 1992), 291.

The Modular Structure of *Wisdom*

DAVID N. KLAUSNER

Almost thirty years ago, Sandy Johnston casually asked me if I might be interested in becoming involved in a new research project digging out in as exhaustive a manner as possible the surviving documentary evidence for performing in late medieval England. She was looking for a researcher to take on the border county of Herefordshire, and the possibility that there might be documents in Welsh had brought my name up. That conversation was the beginning of a long and productive association with the REED project, leading first to the volume for Herefordshire and Worcestershire in 1990, then to the volume for Wales in 2005. It has also led to a long friendship with Sandy, whose casual conversations seem often to have a catalytic effect, as other contributors to this volume have attested. This essay derives from one of them: in the process of editing *Wisdom* for the TEAMS series of teaching editions, I complained to Sandy how odd the play seemed in the context of the surviving drama of the late fifteenth century; in particular, how episodic it was, and how completely its use of source material aligned with these episodes.[1] Sandy's comment, 'It sounds almost modular,' was the seed which led to these present thoughts. Sandy, I offer them to you as a working out of yet another of your insights.

Although *Wisdom* is usually classed as one of the morality plays or, to use more accurately the terminology of the period, 'moral interludes,' it is as different from plays like *The Castle of Perseverance* or *Mankind* as chalk from cheese. In its serious interest in theological, especially Christological, doctrine it is in some ways closer to that most un-English of the moralities, *Everyman*. It has been described as 'undramatic,' a criticism easily disproved by production.[2] Three productions of the play in the past twenty years have helped to rehabilitate it from the assumptions

of non-performing editors: at Winchester Cathedral in 1981, at Trinity
College, Hartford, CT, in 1984, and at the University of Toronto and
Western Michigan University in 1990.[3] Although these productions were
very different in their approaches to the play, they have shown without
question that *Wisdom* does indeed have dramatic virtues.

In this essay I intend to show that *Wisdom*'s construction appears to
have been thought out as a series of modules. I do not intend to prove that
the play is 'modular,' that is, that the playwright intended parts of it to be
replaceable by alternative modules – without an alternative version of the
play that is of course unproveable. I think, however, that I can demonstrate
that there is evidence of 'modular' construction beyond the play's apparent
episodic structure.

Wisdom survives in two texts, a complete version in the Macro manuscript (Folger Library MS V.a.354) and an incomplete one in Bodleian
Digby 133 containing the first 752 lines of the play. Both texts date from
the last two decades of the fifteenth century. Milla Riggio has shown that it
is very likely that the Macro text was copied from Digby.[4] That the play is
constructed of a series of more or less discrete episodes has been noted by
all commentators and most editors; Mark Eccles's EETS edition goes so far
as to divide the play formally into four 'scenes,' which he calls 'Innocence,'
'Temptation,' 'Sinful Life,' and 'Repentance.' Although there is no manuscript justification for such a division, there has been at least a tacit agreement that such a division is sensible. These four sections of the play are
bounded in each case by a significant change of personnel as well as of tone
and manner.

The first section, Eccles's 'Innocence,' is taken up entirely with a
catechetical discussion between the figure of Wisdom and the human soul,
Anima, concerning her true nature. Both manuscripts give elaborately
detailed descriptions of the costuming for both Wisdom and Anima, and a
significant part of the conversation revolves around the symbolism inherent in these costumes. Anima is accompanied by five virgins – her Five
Wits or senses – who frame much of the discussion, singing 'Nigra sum' at
their entrance and 'Tota pulchra es' at their exit with Anima at the end of
the 'scene.' She is also accompanied by her three Mights or Powers, Mind,
Will, and Understanding; their appearance is not indicated by a stage
direction, but it seems certain that they must either follow the Five Wits on
stage (waiting until the end of the plainchant for their lines), or – more
dramatically and rather more likely, avoiding an awkward onstage wait –
appear suddenly at their first speeches:[5]

WYSDOM: Thre myghtys euery Cresten sowll has,
Wyche bethe applyede to þe Trinyte.
MYNDE: All thre here, lo, byfor yowr face!
Mynde.
WYLL: Wyll.
WNDYRSTONDYNGE: Ande Vndyrstondynge, we thre.   (177–80)

This opening section is closed by the recessional exit of everyone on stage, accompanied by the singing of the Five Wits as they leave. The second scene or module, Eccles's 'Temptation,' is bounded by the entrance and exit of Lucifer and consists entirely of his seduction of the three Mights, who appear again after Lucifer has explained his plan to the audience. Convinced by Lucifer to 'go in þe worlde' (501), they exit raucously. Lucifer elaborates on his intentions, and ends the section by carrying off a 'schrewde boy' from the audience (551SD). The third section, demonstrating the three Mights' 'Sinful Life,' begins with the return of Mind, Will, and Understanding. Although there are no stage directions or costume descriptions, it is clear that their fall from grace is indicated by a change of garb. No costume directions accompany their appearances in the first and second sections, but the monastic background to their conversation with Lucifer suggests strongly that they are dressed in monastic habits. In this third section, as each one enters in sequence he comments on his new estate in a manner that indicates his change of clothing. Mind is the most explicit:

Lo, me here in a new aray!   (551)

Will and Understanding follow, each beginning with a line which in the context of Mind's 'new aray' would seem to refer to their garb:

WNDYRSTONDYNGE: Ande haue here one as fresche as yow!   (557)
WYLL: Lo, here on as jolye as ȝe!   (566)

The third section, in which the three Mights demonstrate their newly sinful lives in a series of masque dances, does not come to as neat a conclusion as the first two sections, rounded out with the formal recessional exit of Wisdom and Anima in the first case and the departure of Lucifer with the 'shrewde boy' in the second. At the close of this third section, as the three Mights discuss their future life of fraud and crime,

Wisdom suddenly appears with an injunction to reconsider their present moral state:

O thou Mynde, remembyr the!
Turne þi weys, þou gost amyse.   (873–4)

Although Eccles (and others) have suggested a simple fourfold division, the structure is rather more complex than that; the fourth section, Eccles's 'Repentance,' is made up of three distinct parts or subsections. The first of these includes Wisdom's injunction to the Mights to remember the certainty of their end, followed by the reappearance of Anima, and Wisdom's driving out of the devils who now inhabit her costume. This subsection, like the opening section of the play, ends with a recessional as Anima leads the three Mights off stage. The second subsection consists of Wisdom's sermon to the audience on the subject of the nine things which most please God; it is followed by a conclusion in which Anima, the three Mights, and her Five Wits reappear transfigured. Here again, the divisions of the play are marked by processions and recessions, as well as by an almost complete change of personnel (only Wisdom remaining throughout the section).

This brief recapitulation shows that, although the manuscripts give no indication of the division of the play into distinct episodes, such a division is strongly supported by the text itself. The boundaries between sections one and two, and two and three, are marked by a complete change of personnel on stage; the beginning of section four is indicated by the shock entry of Wisdom into the amoral musings of Mind, Will, and Understanding. My first point, then, is that the play is indeed episodic, the episodes clearly delineated by changes of personnel on stage and often by a formal processional and recessional. Each of these episodes is also distinct in the sources on which it draws, as well as in the nature of the implied audience. Two texts form the primary sources for the first section of the play, Wisdom's commentary to Anima on the nature of the soul. The first of these is an English translation of Heinrich Suso's *Orologium Sapientiae*, which is in turn derived from Suso's earlier vernacular *Büchlein der Ewigen Weisheit*, likely composed in the 1330s. The anonymous English translation of the *Orologium*, entitled *The Seuene Poyntes of Trewe Loue and Euerlastynge Wisdome*, was probably made in the 1390s and survives complete in at least eight manuscripts, with partial texts in a further five. It was printed by Caxton in 1491 in his *Book of Divers Ghostly Matters*

(*STC*: 3305).[6] The *Wisdom* playwright's reliance on the *Orologium* was outlined in detail by Walter K. Smart, who demonstrated that extensive quotation, as well as the use of identical scriptural passages, places the relationship between the two texts beyond question.[7] The first lines of the play will serve as an example (parallels are indicated by boldface):

WYSDOM: Yffe ʒe wyll wet **þe propyrte**
　　　Ande þe resun of my nayme imperyall,
　　　I am clepyde of hem **þat in erthe** be
　　　Euerlastynge Wysdom, to my nobley egalle.　　　(*Wisdom*, 1–4)

Þe maystere, euerlastynge wisdam, seyde: 'ffirst, off þe properte of þe name and þe loue of euerlastynge wisdam, 7 how þe discyple schalle haue hym in felynge of þat loue boþe in beternesse and in swetnesse. ffirst, **if þou wolt wite þe properte and resone of my name,** þou schalt vnderstande þat **I am clepede of hem þat livene in erþe euerlastynge wisdam.** Þe whiche name is most conuenient and best acordynge **to myne nobleye.** (*Seuene Poyntes*, chapter 1)[8]

Especially clear evidence for this relationship is furnished by Anima's request to Wisdom, 'Teche me þe scolys of yowr dyvynyte' (l. 86). The word 'scolys' makes little sense in context here, and was without doubt borrowed from a passage in the *Orologium*, 'where different schools are discussed, and [the word is] transferred to the play without regard to its relevancy.'[9]

The second primary source for this first episode is the *Scala Perfectionis* of Walter Hilton, likely written in the last two decades of the fourteenth century. In particular, the playwright borrowed Hilton's discussion of the nature of the soul to provide the answers to Anima's questions of Wisdom. The correspondence of individual lines is not as close as with the borrowings from the *Orologium*, but the relationship is clear:

ANIMA: In a sowle watt thyngys be
　　　By wyche he hathe hys very knowynge?
WYSDOM: **Tweyn partyes: þe on, sensualyte,**
　　　Wyche ys clepyde þe **flechly felynge.**
　　　The fyve owtewarde **wyttys** to hym be serwynge.
　　　Wan þey be **not rewlyde ordynatly**
　　　The sensualyte þan, wythowte lesynge,
　　　Ys made þe ymage of synne then of hys foly.

The other parte, þat ys clepyde resone,
  Ande þat ys þe ymage of Gode propyrly ...
ANIMA: The doughters of Jerusalem me not lake
  For þis dyrke schadow I bere of humanyte,
That, as þe tabernacull of cedar wythowt yt ys blake
  Ande wythine as þe skyn of Salamone full of bewty.
'Quod fusca sum, nolite considerare me,
  Quia decolorauit me sol Jovis.'   (133–42; 165–70)

For thou shalt understonde that a soule hath **two partyes / That one is called
sensualyte** & that is **flessly felynge** by **the fyve outwarde wyttes /** the
whiche is comon to man & to beest / Of the whiche sensualyte whan it is
ynskylfully and **ynordynatly ruled is made the ymage of synne /** whan it is
not ruled after reason / for thenne is the sensualyte synne. **That other partye
is called reason /** & that is departed in two / In the over partye is lyckened to
a man / for it sholde be mayster and sovereyne **and that is propyrly the
ymage of god** ... That is ye angels of heven that arne **doughters of** the hye
Jerusalem wonder not on me ne dyspyse me not for my blacke **shadowe /**
For though I be **blacke without** by cause of my flesshly kynde as is a **taber-
nacle of cedar /** Nevertheles I am ful fayre **within as the skynne of salomon**
... For so sayth he in another place / **Nolite considerare me quod fusca sum,
quia me decoloravit sol.** (Hilton, *Scala Perfectionis*, Part 2, cap. xiii)[10]

Hilton's treatise (Part 2, cap. xxxi) also contributes the idea of the three
Mights or powers of the soul, Mind, Will, and Understanding, allegorical
concepts for Hilton which are given human personification in the play.
    These two sources provide virtually all the material of the first section of
the play, suggesting a playwright with access to a substantial library with
significant theological holdings. The composition of the play antedates
Caxton's printing of the *Orologium*, so the playwright must have worked
from a manuscript copy. Since the borrowings from the *Orologium* derive
from its English translation, the playwright need not have been fluent in
Latin, but judging from his use of scriptural citation, he was entirely
comfortable with the text of the Vulgate Bible.
    The second part of the play, in which the primary action is the seduction
of the three Mights by Lucifer, also derives closely from Walter Hilton, in
this case from the *Epistle on the Mixed Life*, in which Hilton outlines the
proper relationship between the two poles of religious life, active and
contemplative, explaining that for most a middle ground (*vita mixta*)
incorporating elements both of *vita activa* and *vita contemplativa* is pref-

erable to either extreme.[11] Although the relationship is not as close as with the *Orologium*, Lucifer's arguments in favour of *vita mixta* over *vita contemplativa* clearly represent, as Smart pointed out, 'a summary, with elaborations, of the passages from Hilton.'[12] The arguments put forward (however weakly) by Mind, Will, and Understanding in justification of a contemplative life identify them as contemplatives, and thus provide an unequivocal indication that they are costumed in the habits of one of the contemplative orders. This clear inference is useful, since Mind, Will, and Understanding are the only characters in the play whose dress is not explicitly described in stage directions.

The third part of the play, the three Mights' fall into sin, derives not from a specific written source, but, rather like *Hick Scorner*'s use of the contemporary London crime scene, relies on an understanding of the London underworld, especially as it relates to the practice of law and the system of the courts. In particular, both plays make extensive use of underworld jargon in their descriptions of various modes of fraudulent practice. Following Lucifer's triumphant exit, 'shrewd' boy slung over his shoulder, the three Mights reappear, and their change from monastic habits to gallants' clothing is indicated in their speeches. Each one clarifies the mode of sin which has particularly taken his fancy: Mind is moved to Pride, Understanding to Covetousness, and Will to Lechery. They sing a song, and although neither text nor music survive, it is unlikely to have been sacred in character. It may well have involved the kind of scatological humour (like the 'Crystemes songe' in *Mankind*) that some critics have found lacking in *Wisdom*. The song leads to Understanding's suggestion that they each demonstrate their present state in the world, in effect mirroring the discussion of the true state of the soul in the first part of the play.

> MYNDE: The welfare of þis worlde ys in ws, I ma vowe.
> WNDYRSTONDYNGE: Lett eche man tell hys condycyons howe.
> WYLL: Begynne ye, ande haue at yow,
> For I am aschamyde of ryght nought.   (625–8)

The Mights 'tell' their 'condycyons' by invoking a sequence of three dances, allowing each of them to introduce his followers. Mind presents a dance of 'Mayntennance' (696), in which he is followed by Indignation, Sturdiness, Malice, Hastiness, Wretch, and Discord, accompanied by trumpets. Maintenance is a rather stubborn concept to understand, but essentially involves the financial support – maintenance – of those who will do one's bidding or plead one's case irrespective of the legality of the situation.

Mind's followers are dressed in his livery, sporting lions rampant as their heraldic device, red beards, and carrying warders, all three devices symbolic of aggression. Understanding follows, with a dance of Perjury defined as 'the quest of Holborn,' populated by six jurors: Wrong, Slight, Doubleness, Falseness, Rapine, and Deceit. They are accompanied by a bagpipe, and wear 'hattys of meyntenance,' indicating that they are in someone's pay. Understanding describes their two-faced masks:

> Jorowrs in on hoode beer to facys.
> Fayer speche and falsehede in on space ys.   (718–19)

Finally, Will presents his dance of Lechery, followed by Recklessness, Idleness, Surfeit, Greediness, Spousebreech, and Mistress. They are accompanied by a 'hornepype.' While there is no indication of gender in the first two dances, and we may safely assume that the participants who follow Mind and Understanding are male, Will's dancers are explicitly female: *Here entreth six women in sut, thre dysgysyde as galontys and thre as matrones* ... (752SD). This stage direction has caused a certain amount of puzzlement over the possible situations in which women might be involved in such a performance. The involvement of women in Lechery's dance - not merely as women, but cross-dressed as gallants as well – is clearly intended to be subversive and to indicate specifically the subversive nature of the sin of Lechery.

As a further indication of the fallen state of the three Mights, the dance collapses at this point. The idea of a dance, cosmic or earthly, as a metaphor for order reaches back to Plato, and since the dances of *Wisdom* are representative of the Mights' new-found sins, even that limited order cannot hold.[13] Mind takes umbrage at Will's dismissal of the importance of Maintenance, and chases Will's dancers from the stage.

> WYLL: I sett þe at nought!
> MYNDE: On þat worde I woll tak vengeaunce.
>   Wer vycys be gederyde, euer ys sum myschance.
>   Hurle hens thes harlottys! Here gyse ys of France.
>   Þey xall abey bytterly, by hym þat all wrought!   (764–8)

This third section of the play concludes with a discussion between the three Mights concerning the further exercise of their newly sinful characters. The technical vocabulary of the law courts is evident in their replies to Mind's suggestion that they

> set ... a ordenance
> Off better chevesaunce
> How we may thryve. (786–8)

Understanding will use the courts for direct profit.

> At Westmyster, wythowt varyance,
> Þe nex terme xall me sore avawnce,
> For retornys, for enbraces, for recordaunce.
> Lyghtlyer to get goode kan no man on lyue. (789–92)

Mind will undertake legal manoeuvering with the help of his followers.

> Ande at þe parvyse I wyll be
> A Powlys betwyn to ande thre,
> Wyth a menye folowynge me,
> Entret, juge-partynge, and to-supporte. (793–6)

Will's intentions are more general; for him fornication quickly trumps profit.

> Wen I com lat to þe cyte
> I walke all lanys and weys to myn affynyte;
> And I spede not þer, to þe stews I resort. (798–800)

In order to assist Will in his plan to seduce his 'cosyn Jenet' Mind and Understanding outline how they will provide false testimony against her husband, tying him up in legal complications so that he will wind up in prison.

It seems very likely that a substantial part of this third section of the play would have been very difficult for an audience to follow without some understanding both of the court system and of the jargon of legal manipulation. Understanding's use of legal Latin ('A preuenire facias than haue as tyght,' 855) implies less a fluency in the language than an understanding of legal formulas. The implication of an audience with significant legal competency, perhaps with a number of practising lawyers among them, seems inescapable.[14]

The fourth and final section of the play begins with Wisdom's sudden entry in the midst of the Mights' debauched planning session. Their first reaction is dismissive until Wisdom summons Anima, who appears *in þe most horrybull wyse, fowlere þan a fende* (902SD). As seven small boys dressed as devils run out from beneath Anima's mantle, Mind, Will, and Understanding each in turn confesses his sin and Anima asks for mercy. Wisdom briefly outlines the process of penance through contrition, confession, and satisfaction; as Anima indicates her contrition with her tears the devils disappear. Singing a passage from Lamentations *in þe most lamentabull wyse* (996SD) Anima goes off to Holy Church, followed by her Mights. The process of Anima's absolution is marked on stage by a sermon to the audience, delivered by Wisdom, on the subject of the 'Nine Things which Please God.' The Latin text of the *Novem Virtutes* has been attributed to Richard Rolle, but the attribution is uncertain; several English translations in both prose and verse survive.[15] Wisdom's sermon does not show a clear and direct derivation from any of these English versions and is in fact rather closer to the Latin text. The Nine Things are as follows:

1 Give a penny to the poor.
2 Weep one tear for the Passion.
3 Suffer patiently a word of reproof from your neighbour.
4 Wake one hour for my love.
5 Have pity and compassion on your neighbour.
6 Let not your tongue despise your fellow Christians.
7 Stir not your neighbour to evil.
8 Often pray and ask of me.
9 Love me above all things.

The most striking characteristic of Wisdom's sermon is its lack of immediate relevance to the dramatic action of the play. Wisdom has interrupted the debauchery of the fallen Mights and has demonstrated to them what effect their sinfulness has had on Anima; he has indicated that penance – defined as contrition, confession, and satisfaction – is required to restore Anima to her former beauty, and his sermon is intended dramatically to indicate the period of time during which this penance takes place. But the sermon has nothing to do with penance; in fact, it avoids the primary subject of the play altogether, making no reference to the central sequence of innocence, temptation, fall, penance, and redemption.

Following the sermon, Anima returns accompanied by her Five Wits and the Mights, all wearing crowns, returning the play to its primary concern with penance and redemption.

ANIMA: O Jhesu, þe sune of Vyrgyne Marye,
Full of mercy and compassyon!
My soule ys waschede be thy passyon
  Fro þe synnys cummynge by sensualyte.
A, be the I haue a new resurreccyon.
The lyght of grace I fele in me.   (1067–72)

Anima describes her offence both through her 'inwarde wyttys,' that is the three Mights, and her 'outwarde wyttys,' her Five Wits or bodily senses, noting that her own penance is insufficient for redemption without the grace for which she now asks, 'Yet of myselff I may not satysfye my trespas' (1080). Wisdom replies in the most extraordinarily dramatic moment of the play, likening the pain he feels for Anima's fall into sin to his suffering on the Cross, now remedied through the sacrament of penance. In speeches again derived from Hilton's *Scala Perfectionis*,[16] the three Mights describe their participation in Anima's redemption, and Anima sums up the point of the play,

Nowe ye muí euery soule renewe
In grace, and vycys to eschew,
  Ande so to ende wyth perfeccyon.   (1159–61)

In what ways, then, might we consider *Wisdom* to be composed of a sequence of modules? A 'modular' structure implies that the distinction between its sections is both intentional and is intended to facilitate some sort of movement or replacement, perhaps to satisfy the demands of different audiences. There is no question that the play is episodic; we have already noted that the play divides quite neatly into sections, distinguished by subject matter, rhetoric, and source material as well as by participants. The final section seems to be further divided by the insertion of Wisdom's sermon. These sections, though they have no manuscript support, have been noted by most scholars. I would add that these divisions also indicate a particular kind of audience. The first section, in which the soul and its characteristics are described, represents a general catechesis directed at any Christian audience and derived from a popular treatise of allegorical theology. The second section, derived from a devotional but largely non-allegorical tract, focuses on the arguments in favour of a 'mixed life' – that is a religious life in the world – in contrast to a cloistered, contemplative life. That the arguments for *vita mixta* are placed in the mouth of Lucifer adds an especial tang to them. This discussion seems to be directed particularly towards a cloistered monastic audience, a supposition that is strengthened by the likely costuming of Mind, Will, and Understanding in monastic habits; Lucifer also addresses them as 'Ye fonnyde fathers' (393). The third section of the play could not be more different in the assumptions it makes about the audience. It is essentially a masque of sin in which the three Mights demonstrate their new characters in a series of three set dances. All of this, with the limited exception of Will's new-found interest in lechery, is centred around the legal profession. Understanding becomes Perjury and his followers are false jurors; the plans he makes with Mind following the disruption of the dance are centred entirely around legal manipulation, and all of this is couched in a vocabulary of legal jargon that strongly implies the presence of a significant audience of legal professionals.

There has been little consensus on the likely performance venue and audience for *Wisdom*, and this fact is important to my argument. Gail McMurray Gibson has established the connections of the play with the Abbey of St Edmund at Bury, but there is no evidence of a performance there.[17] Milla Riggio, in her 1984 production, postulated a performance in the Abbot's Palace for a visit by Edward IV in 1474, while Alexandra Johnston has suggested that it might have been written by a monk of Bury for one of the local gentry.[18] J.J. Molloy thought it might have been acted by students at the Inns of Court, and Merle Fifield took it to be a profes-sional piece in the repertoire of a travelling company.[19] E.K. Chambers thought it was a school play.[20] Both the surviving manuscripts of the play unquestionably have strong connections to Bury St Edmund's and to its abbey. It is also not surprising that we have no direct evidence of *Wisdom*'s performance at St Edmund's, given the extreme paucity of abbey records from the fifteenth century.[21] We can, I think, say three things about the audience: they were highly sophisticated, they included some cloistered religious, and they included some in the legal profession. It is unlikely that such an audience could be found anywhere but at the abbey or possibly at the house of a substantial local magnate. The participation of women, certainly in Lechery's dance, and possibly as the 'fyve vyrgynes' who are Anima's Five Wits, implies a highly secularized occasion. A projected visit by Edward IV, such as that proposed by Milla Riggio, would fit the bill, as would any other festive occasion at which the large and wealthy abbey feasted a group of courtiers, friends, and benefactors.

A second 'modular' aspect of the play is the apparent disconnect be-tween the opening and closing portions of the final scene, on the one hand, both of which revolve tightly around the concept of penance and the rituals it involves, and Wisdom's sermon on the other hand. At the beginning of the scene, Wisdom catechizes Anima on the process by which her (Mights') sins may be absolved through penance, and Anima signals the beginning of the process with her tears. In the closing scene, Anima asks for grace of Wisdom, who indicates that her penance and thus her redemption are complete. These two scenes are separated by Wisdom's sermon to the audience. Given the thrust of the rest of the play, we would expect a sermon dealing in some way with the sacrament of penance, and with its efficacy in the redemption of sin. Instead, the sermon deals with the nine things which please God. It might just be possible to link the content of the sermon to Anima's earlier question in the play's first section, 'Wat may I yeue to yowr most plesaunce?' (78), but this seems most unlikely, since Wisdom immediately answers that question, 'Thy clene hert, þi meke obeysance' (81). Could the sermon have been inserted, replacing a previous sermon on the subject of penance, for a specific occasion or a particular audience? Although there is no way to prove such an hypothesis, it would explain the curious imbalance of this last section of the play. It would also assume that the play was performed, and more than once; is there any evidence to suggest this? Though the records of St Edmund's Abbey, scanty as they are, give no hint of any performances of the play, one feature of the Macro manuscript does strongly imply that the play was performed, that it was not 'closet drama,' and possibly that it saw more than one performance. This is the option given in both the Digby and Macro manuscripts of omitting the dances that form the climax of the third section. At l. 685 an annotation in the left margin reads 'va ... ,' followed at l. 784 (in Macro only, since the Digby text ends at l. 752) by '... cat,' indicating the possibility of a cut. The marginal note does not make it clear whether the cut represents what was done in a specific performance or an option which might potentially be followed. It does, however, have two important implications – first, that there was an intention that the play be performed more than once, and second, that different performances of the play might well differ. Omitting the dances, while losing the central 'masque of sin,' would leave the argument of the play intact, and would eliminate the need for eighteen dancers.[22] What we seem to have, then, is a cut-down option for a smaller, less elaborate (and cheaper) production, preserving the argument at the expense of spectacle.

When I speak of the play as modular, I am not suggesting that there may have been other versions intended for different audiences, in which the Mights' fall was described in, say, commercial rather than legal terms. The surviving materials – the two manuscripts of the play and the very limited records of the abbey – make such a thesis ultimately unproveable; however, it does seem certain that the playwright, in constructing his drama of temptation, fall, and redemption, thought structurally in terms of a sequence of discrete and perhaps replaceable 'building blocks' rather than a continuous flow of material. He clearly made conscious changes in the sources he used for each part of the play, as well as in the rhetoric, contrasting the high style of the first and last sections with a mixed style in the second and low style in the third. Thinking about the structure of his play in these terms may well have made it easier for him to insert a new sermon which, though it may have been relevant to an individual performance, is hardly ideal in the context of the whole play.

To summarize, then. *Wisdom* differs in several important ways from other moral interludes. Significant for our purpose are these points: its clear division (though not indicated in either manuscript) into four balanced 'scenes,' each drawing on distinct source material; its provision for the option of omitting the dances and the appearance (in the Macro text) of a sermon for Wisdom whose argument seems incongruent with the context of the play. Taken as a whole, the implication of these is that the playwright consciously built his text as a series of discrete textual entities – modules – in which there was some intentional flexibility for performance. This flexibility may well have been intended to reflect the play's audience on particular occasions. We have seen already that at least two groups, cloistered monastics and lawyers, are implied by the text as it stands. The curiously inappropriate sermon may also reflect an appeal to a specific group of audience members. Though the lack of a performance history for the play does not allow us to go further with this idea, the evidence of the text and the manuscripts does give us more insights into the playwright's method of construction than we have for any other play of the period.

NOTES

1 *Wisdom* and *The Pride of Life* (forthcoming) in TEAching the Middle ageS, published in Kalamazoo, MI, by Western Michigan University Press.
2 '*Wisdom* is too intent on teaching moral virtue to have much concern with dramatic virtues.' Mark Eccles, ed., *The Macro Plays* EETS os 262 (London: Oxford University Press), xxxvi.
3 The Winchester production was directed by John Marshall, the Trinity performance by Milla Cozart Riggio, and the Toronto production by David Klausner.

4 Milla Cozart Riggio, ed., *The Play of Wisdom: Its Texts and Contexts* (New York: AMS Press, 1998), 6–18.

5 All quotations are from the EETS edition and are indicated in the text by line numbers. Stage directions are marked SD with the number of the preceding line.

6 Riggio, *Wisdom*, 25; the English version of the *Orologium* was printed by Karl Horstmann, ed., '*Orologium Sapientiae* or *The Seven Poyntes of Trewe Wisdom*,' *Anglia* 10 (1888), 323–89, from Bodley MS Douce 114. Caxton also based his text on Douce 114.

7 Walter Kay Smart, *Some English and Latin Sources and Parallels for the Morality of Wisdom* (Menasha, WI: George Banta, 1912).

8 Horstmann, '*Orologium*,' 329; bold face mine.

9 Smart, *English and Latin Sources*, 12.

10 Smart, *English and Latin Sources*, 20–1.

11 Karl Horstmann, ed., *Yorkshire Writers: Richard Rolle of Hampole, an English Father of the Church and his Followers* (London: Swan Sonnenschein, 1895), 1:264–92.

12 Smart, *English and Latin Sources*, 27.

13 See James L. Miller, *Measures of Wisdom: The Cosmic Dance in Classical and Christian Antiquity* (Toronto: University of Toronto Press, 1986).

14 Recent work on the understanding of legal procedure among non-lawyers in the increasingly litigious society of late medieval England includes Anthony Musson and W.M. Ormrod, *The Evolution of English Justice: Law, Politics, and Society in the Fourteenth Century* (New York: Macmillan, 1999), and R.H. Helmholz, *The Ius Commune in England: Four Studies* (Oxford: Oxford University Press, 2001).

15 Several versions of the English text are printed by Horstmann, *Yorkshire Writers*, 1:110 and 2:455–6.

16 Smart, *English and Latin Sources*, 21–2.

17 Gail McMurray Gibson, *The Theater of Devotion: East Anglian Drama and Society in the Late Middle Ages* (Chicago: University of Chicago Press, 1989), 108–17.

18 Milla Cozart Riggio, 'The Staging of *Wisdom*,' in *The Wisdom Symposium*, ed. Milla Cozart Riggio (New York: AMS Press, 1986), 13; Alexandra F. Johnston, '*Wisdom* and the Records: Is There a Moral?' in *Wisdom Symposium*, 99–100.

19 J.J. Molloy, *A Theological Interpretation of the Moral Play Wisdom, Who Is Christ* (Washington, DC: Catholic University of America Press, 1952), 84; Merle Fifield, 'The Use of Doubling and Extras in *Wisdom*,' *Ball State University Forum* 6 (1965), 65–8.

20 E.K. Chambers, *The Mediaeval Stage*, 2 vols (Oxford: Oxford University Press, 1903), 2:438.
21 Gibson, *Theater of Devotion*, 121.
22 Doubling the dancers seems to me very unlikely. The play text does not indicate an exit for Maintenance's dancers, but only fifteen lines separate the end of their dance from the entry of Perjury's dancers – hardly enough for the full costume change indicated in the stage directions. Similarly, seventeen lines separate the earliest possible exit for Perjury's dancers from the entry of Lechery's group. The specification in the stage direction that Lechery's dancers are women also strongly suggests an entirely different group.

On Bombshells and Faulty Assumptions: What the Digby *Conversion of Saint Paul* Really Did with the Acts of the Apostles

CHESTER SCOVILLE

Just over twenty years ago, Alexandra F. Johnston described, in a well-remembered conference at the University of Toronto, the academic 'bombshell' that F.M. Salter threw, also at the University of Toronto, thirty years before that.[1] Salter's bombshell was, of course, his revelation that nearly everything scholars knew about the Chester cycle was wrong, and, by implication, that much of what was known about medieval drama in general was also likely to be wrong.[2] This explosion of old myths began a seismic shift in our understanding of medieval drama that has now continued for half a century; and the work of Records of Early English Drama – led by Professor Johnston, and headquartered at the University of Toronto – has kept the pressure on high. The latest earthquake, courtesy of not only Johnston herself but also Barbara Palmer, has been our ability to say, aloud and with conviction, that the 'Wakefield cycle' does not exist,[3] and, if we are really daring, that the Corpus Christi cycle in general does not exist, except in York.[4] Everything we have known continues to be wrong. Standing on this shifting ground is a heady experience, not least because one can never tell what will blow up next.

The Digby *Conversion of Saint Paul* is not the play that first springs to mind when one thinks of this shifting field, and it is an unlikely place, perhaps, to look for the next revelation. The explosions of change have mostly left it untouched; a good deal of what we think about it, when we think about it, is substantially the same as what scholars of a century ago thought about it, when they thought about it. While its cousin in Bodleian MS Digby 133, the other Middle English saint play, *Mary Magdalene*, has got the respect it deserves and has been illuminated anew as a result, *Saint Paul* remains one of the most underrated and least studied of all early English plays. One reason for this neglect is the very assumption that is now teetering on the brink (we may hope) of extinction: the assumption that the norm for English medieval drama is the great civic play cycle. This assumption, as Professor Johnston has noted, 'has proved very hard to eradicate';[5] despite its unwarrantedness, it has coloured all of our subsequent ways of looking at medieval plays; and even now, when the assumption is crumbling, it affects us.

It is salient to note, in fact, that for many decades the benchmark for excellence in early drama was not only the cycle in general but the 'Wakefield cycle' in particular. As all scholars know (or think they know) who have done any casual research on the subject of medieval drama, this was the greatest of all play cycles of medieval England – an improvement on the more primitive but still admirable York cycle, and the work, in large part, of the only genuine genius in Middle English drama, the mysterious Wakefield Master. This shadowy figure is the precursor to Shakespeare's realism, the bridge between the old, static, religionist culture of the Middle Ages and the new, vibrant, humanist culture of the English Renaissance, when the concerns of heaven gave way to real stories about real men.

It is a well-known and compelling tale, and one that is still told, with, to quote Professor Johnston one more time, 'magisterial assurance and no evidence.'[6] The problem with this story, of course, is that it is wrong. While its incorrectness is known to anyone who has gone beyond the casual in their research, the myth remains. It is not harmless, this myth; it has for decades – centuries, by now, actually – had the effect of creating a set of false assumptions that have often blinded us to the evidence before us. It is deeply ironic that the 'Wakefield cycle,' which was supposed, in its move from medieval to Renaissance, to have signalled a preference for hard facts to fantasy, has become in itself the greatest fantasy of its field, distracting us from some of the facts that we have.

In the earliest days of medieval drama studies when this fantasy was taking hold, *The Conversion of Saint Paul* was seen not as a complete work in and of itself, but as a mere fragment – and not a very satisfactory one, either – of a lost and lamented East Anglian whole. The results of the early idée fixe of the cycle are apparent in, for instance, the 1835 comments of Thomas Sharp, who, assuming that all medieval plays were performed on wagons, says, 'Saul ... being mounted, "rydeth forth wt hys svant about the place out of the place," that is, out of the pageant and consequently in the street.'[7] Sharp, in other words, imagined a play in which Saul mounted his horse atop a pageant wagon, and rode the horse from the wagon and into the city street. Admittedly, failure to imagine what was possible on a wagon stage, and what was not, was a general fault of the early scholars who had never seen or performed the plays. Yet it is striking that, given the strength of the old assumption about the universality of cycles and wagons, it was easier for Sharp to believe in a physical impossibility than to see what was actually there.

Furnivall, too, though he rejects the idea that *Saint Paul* was part of a cycle, nonetheless treats it as a wagon play and therefore judges it according to the standards of cycle drama. He also, curiously enough, rearranges the Digby plays in his edition of them; instead of giving them in the manuscript's order (*Saint Paul, Mary Magdalene, Killing of the Children*), he reshuffles them into something like chronological order (*Killing of the Children, Saint Paul, Mary Magdalene*), as if they were episodes – or descendants of episodes – of a lost cycle after all. He also, erroneously, affixes to the Digby plays for the first time the 'play(s)' of *Christ's Burial and Resurrection* from Bodleian MS e Museo 160, as if further to create the illusion of a lost cycle, and states baldly that the only reason he has kept the obviously non-cyclical *Wisdom* in this edition is that he has not yet got his hands on Folger MS V.a.354, the Macro manuscript.[8] Finally, he includes, as an appendix to his introduction, notes on the Chester plays and their sponsorship, further implying that, even if the Digby plays weren't civic 'mystery cycle' plays, they should have been. In all of this fuss, *The Conversion of Saint Paul* gets rather lost. Given that Furnivall is judging its quality by inappropriate standards, it is little wonder that he finds it lacking when he does get around to it.[9]

After Furnivall, the play was largely ignored by scholars. A spattering of articles in the early 1970s dealt with the way in which the play was staged, finally putting to rest the idea of a wagon;[10] and a scholarly edition to replace Furnivall's emerged in 1982.[11] Apart from that, commentary on the play has been limited to a few articles scattered here and there, and very brief mentions in book-length overviews of the field. It is not difficult to see the mischief that has been done. So powerful has the template of the cycle been that for nearly two centuries it was easier to believe in the theory than it was to believe in the possibility of a free-standing, small-scale, complex play of less than 700 lines of verse; and the disbelief has translated in later decades to critical silence.

Yet all Middle English plays, for lack of a better term, must now be re-evaluated. It is now entirely clear, thanks to the long labour of the REED project, that cycle plays were not, in fact, anything like the norm, and that free-standing plays on the scale of *Saint Paul* or smaller were, possibly, more akin to what most medieval dramatic productions in England might have been like. The implications of this understanding are profound, and they have not yet been fully registered, although we are making a good start. A generation ago, O.B. Hardison Jr showed the fallacy of applying evolutionary, biological thinking to the history of early drama, and revealed the profound errors to which such thinking led, even in the greatest of scholars such as E.K. Chambers and Karl Young. But this revelation took years to work through; and in such popular sources as *The Norton Anthology of English Literature* it has still not had its full effect.[12] Similarly, the new understanding of Middle English drama that I have alluded to should reveal to us all the folly of applying Platonic ideals to medieval drama; we cannot assume that there *is* an ideal, or a model, or a unified goal when we look at medieval plays, and we cannot (yet) trust ourselves to have jettisoned completely the assumption that there is one.

In all of this fuss, *The Conversion of Saint Paul* has, again, got rather lost. Our new understandings have not yet resulted in, for instance, a re-evaluation of *Saint Paul*. It is still mostly ignored, and when it is dealt with at all it is still most frequently dismissed as inferior. Yet in the paucity of studies explaining exactly what the play *is*, we surely have not enough perspective to say for certain how successfully (or not) it accomplishes its goals, or even necessarily what those goals are. Most of the evaluative tools we have developed for judging medieval plays with biblical subjects, after all, came into being largely to deal with Corpus Christi cycles, real and imaginary. Since *Saint Paul* has nothing to do with that form, its poor reputation may derive not from any inherent lack, but simply from our long-standing failure to see it for what it actually is.

The Conversion of Saint Paul, unfortunately, also suffers by comparison with its closest neighbour. *Mary Magdalene* has attracted far more and much better attention. There are several reasons for this contrast. First, *Mary Magdalene* is more fashionable in its subject matter: the figure of the Magdalene has in the past decade or so come to represent the suppressed feminine within the Western and Christian traditions, and is therefore a powerful subject for feminist perspectives.[13] Paul, who has been identified by many as the figure most responsible for the suppression in the first place, makes a much less attractive subject. Besides the subject, however, there is also the form: the Digby *Mary Magdalene* is large-scale enough to stand comparison with the cycles, and the presence of characters like the World, the Flesh, and the Devil moves it also closer to both the comedy and the allegory of the morality play; there is therefore a well-developed set of critical tools with which to discuss the play. This is not to discount the excellence of many recent studies of *Mary Magdalene*, especially those by Theresa Coletti,[14] but to note merely that scholars of this play have some advantages deriving from the history of the discipline.

No such luck is available to the prospective scholar of *The Conversion of Saint Paul*. Neither allegorical nor cyclical, neither comical nor grandiose, neither fashionable in subject nor familiar in form, the play stands on its own. We do not even know for sure whether it is one typical example of a lost saint-play tradition in England, or whether it was thoroughly atypical.[15] We have no certain record of its performance.[16] We have, in short, little or no pre-existing framework for it.

When a work of art is inexplicable through the normal means, a common reaction is to dismiss it as crude. The same sort of dismissal was once given to *Mankind*, which has in more recent years gained critical favour. Of course, *Mankind* is indeed crude in its uniquely scatological way. But as many have recently argued, the play's physical crudeness is used in the service of considerable theatrical and intellectual sophistication. It is, no doubt, an advance in scholarship to recognize this. However, *The Conversion of Saint Paul* has yet to shake off its own reputation for crudeness, this time not physical but intellectual. The reputation has scarcely changed in a century. Furnivall again: 'These Digby Mysteries, being poorer than the Towneley, point to the decay of the old religious Drama in England.'[17] Hardin Craig: 'We must not overpraise the Digby Conversion of St. Paul.'[18] Arnold Williams: 'The play, as a dramatic piece, needs some apology.'[19] And the play's most recent editors: 'Our author is apparently confused.'[20] Given this idea and its frequent repetition, it is no wonder that even the best scholars can underestimate the play, even going so far sometimes as to see failures of sophistication that are not actually there.[21]

For instance, the most recent editors of the Digby *Conversion of Saint Paul* state, in their introduction and notes, that the playwright has adapted the story from Acts 9:1–27, and from several other liturgical, traditional, and patristic sources. Insofar as the play deviates from the bare bones of Acts 9, they imply, it represents an account that has been 'expanded and/or misread.'[22] The editors have failed, however, to take into account the skill with which the Digby playwright handles the Acts of the Apostles, particularly the way in which he reconciles the book's three, not one, accounts of Paul's conversion, in chapters 9, 22, and 26.

A key example of this complexity can be seen in the brief, curious, and usually ignored, scene between the two soldiers at 248–61. The playwright in this scene confronts the fact that the accounts in Acts do not agree on what Saul's companions experienced at the moment of his conversion. The account at Acts 9:7 says that 'viri autem illi qui comitabantur cum eo stabant stupefacti' (the men who went in company with him, stood amazed, hearing indeed a voice, but seeing no man).[23] Yet when Paul[24] recounts the same story to the Roman tribune in Jerusalem at Acts 22:9, he declares, 'qui mecum erant lumen quidem viderunt: vocem autem non audierunt eius qui loquebatur mecum' (they that were with me, saw indeed the light: but they heard not the voice of him that spoke with me). Thus, in one part of Acts, Paul's companions hear but do not see, while in another part of Acts, Paul's companions see but do not hear. Still later, when Paul recalls the moment again, this time to Agrippa at Acts 26:14, he recounts the version in Acts 22 but adds the detail that 'omnesque nos cum decidissemus in terram' (we were all fallen down on the ground) when the light shone. Thus the accounts in Acts are not in full agreement on whether Saul only was struck down, or he and his companions.

In sum, the play's biblical sources conflict on the experience of the witnesses to Saul's conversion; yet given that drama must always keep the experience of witnesses and audiences in mind, and must make some concrete decision about what to stage, the Digby playwright has had to make some decisions.[25] But he has not merely chosen Acts 9 and then deviated from it; in fact, his methods and motives are far more complex than they may appear.[26]

The simplest way to harmonize the sources would be to make one soldier hear but not see, and to make the other see but not hear – to have, in other words, one witness from Acts 9 and the other from Acts 22. Yet the Digby playwright does something both more subtle and more traditional than that. Secundus Myles has experienced the version in Acts 22, seeing the light but making no mention of a voice:

> Sertenly thys ly3t was ferefull to see,
>   The sperkys of fyer were very feruent!
> Yt inflamyd so greuosely about þe countre,
>   That, by my trowth, I went we shuld a bene brent!   (255–8)

This rather superficial understanding of the event is in deliberate response, however, to the more thoughtful and complex musings of Primus Myles, who has experienced not merely the version in Acts 9, but also something of the version in Acts 22:

> The wonder grett lythtys þat were so shene
>   Smett hym doune of hys hors to þe grownde,
>   And me thowt that I hard a sounde
> Of won spekyng wyth voyce delectable,
> Whych was to [vs] wonderfull myrable.   (250–4)

Primus Myles does not seem to have fallen down himself as in Acts 26, because he says specifically that the lights smote down *him*, i.e., Saul, not *us*.[27] He has certainly seen the lights as in Acts 22, but, in agreement with Acts 9, did not see a man. Yet also as in Acts 9, he heard a voice, or, more precisely, *a sound of one speaking with voice*; he did not hear the actual words. Let us note at this point a difference of detail between Acts 9 and Acts 22; in the former, Saul's companions hear a voice, while in the latter, they 'heard not the voice of him that spoke.' The Digby playwright has reconciled these two versions by making Primus Myles hear the sound of a voice, but not its words (that this is a traditional interpretation is suggested by its presence in the Douai's footnote for Acts 22:9, though I have not been able to determine its history in greater detail than this). So, Primus Myles's experience is a harmonization of the accounts of Acts 9 and 22, while Secundus Myles's experience is drawn only from Acts 22.

This distinction is inverted, however, during the soldiers' recounting of the scene to Annas and Caiaphas at 36/–80. This time, Primus Myles mentions only the visual aspects of what he saw, mentioning no voice: 'A meruelous lyȝt fro th'element dyd glyde, / Whyche smet doun hym to grunde, both horse and man' (371–2); his interpretation here echoes only Acts 22, and has lost all reference to Acts 9. Meanwhile, Secundus Myles states,

> A swete dulcet voyce spake hym vnto,
> And askyd wherfor he made suche persecucyon
> Ageynst hys dyscyplys, and why he dyd soo.
> He bad hym into Damaske to Ananie goo,
> And ther he shuld reseyue baptym truly   (375–9)

This version echoes Acts 9, but without the traditional interpretation that comes from harmonizing the passage with Acts 22. It also is unexpected from Secundus Myles, who previously made no mention of having heard a voice; suddenly he heard not only the sound of the voice but its sense as well. In other words, whereas Secundus Myles before experienced only Acts 22, he now seems to have experienced only Acts 9. Furthermore, Primus Myles seems to have forgotten Acts 9, and remembers only Acts 22.

It would be easy to suggest, as the play's editors do, that the playwright was simply careless or confused. Certainly it would have been more consistent to maintain Secundus Myles's recollection of Acts 22, and, if the

playwright wished to portray forgetfulness, to make Primus Myles remember only Acts 9. Yet there may be more to the playwright's overall
strategy than meets the eye. For one thing, the play is entirely self-conscious regarding its status as translation and harmonization: so that the
audience is not misled to consider its account authoritative, Poeta notes,
'Whoo lyst to rede þe booke *Actum Appostolorum*, / Ther shall he haue þe
very notycyon' (10–11). Yet if an alert and literate audience member
should go to seek that 'notycyon,' he will encounter three different accounts of Saul's conversion. The situation is not unlike that of a reader of
the four Gospels, who finds, in Chaucer's words, 'that every Evaungelist, /
That telleth us the peyne of Jhesu Crist, / Ne seith nat alle thyng as his
felawe dooth' (VII.943–5).[28] To a medieval Christian, of course, there is
and can be no contradiction between the accounts, for, as Chaucer also put
it, 'nathelees hir sentence is al sooth, / And alle acorden as in hire sentence, /
Al be ther in hir tellyng difference' (VII.946–8). But this brings in the
problem of expressing the common 'sentence' of the multiple accounts,
and that is always tricky.

Eamon Duffy argues that in the late medieval world, Nicholas Love's
Mirror of the Life of Jesu Christ, a translation of the *Meditationes vitae
Christi*, 'went a long way towards satisfying lay eagerness for knowledge
of the Gospels,'[29] and did so by providing a Gospel harmonization with
commentary. Yet the *Meditationes* was fairly confident in its ability to use
scripture as a baseline for meditations that sometimes departed from the
literal sense. 'It is possible,' says the author of the *Meditationes*, 'to contemplate, explain, and understand the Holy Scriptures in as many ways as
we consider necessary, in such a manner as not to contradict the truth ...
Thus when you find it said here, "This was said and done by the Lord
Jesus" ... if it cannot be demonstrated by the Scriptures, you must consider
it only as a requirement of devout contemplation.'[30] This attitude is
untroubling to the late thirteenth-century writer of the *Meditationes*, and
to his original audience, most probably a Poor Clare or community of
Poor Clares.[31] The traditional Catholic attitude about scripture reflected
in the *Meditationes* was, roughly, that the Word was 'too sacred to be
communicated to the "lewed"'[32] directly; rather, it must be mediated and
expanded in order to inculcate the right faith. As such, the boundary
between scripture and commentary could get, sometimes playfully,
blurred.[33]

By the sixteenth century and *The Conversion of Saint Paul*, the task of
translating scripture and expanding on its episodes was much more fraught.
The histories of early Tudor regulations of plays, and of the implications of

the Protestant emphasis on *sola scriptura*, are too complex to go into here; but the newly state-controlled yet increasingly unstable definition of orthodoxy during this period must surely have made any maker of religious drama extremely cautious.[34] It is surely this self-consciousness, and not any generalized unease over the playwright's abilities, that generates such formulaic pleas for the audience's indulgence as, 'as we can, we shall vs redres' (12), 'Here shalbe brefly shewyd, wyth all our besynes' (166), and 'Howbeyt vnable, as I dare speke or say, / The compyler hereof shuld translat veray / So holy a story' (356–8). The task of a 'compyler' (oddly glossed by the play's editors as 'author' rather than as 'compiler') is, after all, not necessarily to smooth out all the rough edges.[35] Here, the playwright has left some inconsistencies in the text, as if to indicate his play's own provisional nature.[36]

The central episode in the play apart from Saul's actual conversion is of course Saul's macaronic sermon at 502–71, and his subsequent arrest and escape. The play's editors state that the sermon is supposed to be an illustration of Acts 9:20, 'in synagogis praedicabat Iesum quoniam hic est Filius Dei' (he preached Jesus in the synagogues, that he is the Son of God).[37] Yet the subject of the sermon is neither Christological nor Trinitarian, but penitential: it is an exposition of the Seven Deadly Sins and their remedies. This has been cited by some as one more example of the playwright's confusion. Yet the playwright is not at all confused; instead, he is making another conscious decision regarding harmonization. In focusing on the Seven Deadly Sins, Saul's sermon is surely an illustration not of Acts 9:20 but of Acts 26:20:

sed his qui sunt Damasci primum et Hierosolymis
et in omnem regionem Iudaeae et gentibus adnuntiabam
ut paenitentiam agerent et converterentur ad Deum
digna paenitentiae opera facientes.

But to them first that are at Damascus, and at Jerusalem,
and unto all the country of Judea, and to the Gentiles
did I preach, that they should do penance, and turn to God,
doing works worthy of penance.

The evidence for this is strengthened by the fact that only in Acts 26 is Saul immediately arrested following his sermon (Acts 26:21, 'me ... conprehensum' [having apprehended me]). And indeed, Saul is arrested immediately after his sermon by the Servus Sacerdotum, at lines 572–92, rather than some time after, as specified in Acts 9:23. Yet, when the Servus Sacerdotum does arrest Saul, his speech is an echo of what is said by 'omnes qui audiebant' (all that heard him) at Acts 9:21:

> Whate, ys not thys Saule þat toke hys vyage
> Into Jerusalem, the dyscyplys to oppresse?
> Bounde, he wold bryng them, yf ony dyd rage
> Vpon Cryst – þys was hys processe –
> To þe pryncys of prestys, he sayde, dowtles.   (572–6)

This closely paraphrases the account at Acts 9, in which Saul's enemies say,

> Nonne hic est qui expugnabat in Hierusalem eos qui invocabant nomen istud et huc ad hoc venit ut vinctos illos duceret ad principes sacerdotum?

> Is not this he who persecuted in Jerusalem those that called upon this name: and came hither for that intent, that he might carry them bound to the chief priests? (Acts 9:21)

Again, one might argue that the author is confused, but it is far more plausible that, on the contrary, he is harmonizing his sources both skilfully and deliberately, wishing to leave nothing out and taking advantage of all that he finds.

Finally, Saul's escape, freed as he is by an angel, certainly derives principally from Acts 22. Yet even there, the playwright adapts from other sources within Acts. Acts 22:17–21 specifies that Saul was visited by another vision of Jesus, while in a trance in the temple in Jerusalem; yet for the playwright to introduce such a set and yet another appearance of God would surely have been theatrically clumsy at this point. Additionally, the source at Acts 22 does not specify much about the details of the appearance, specifying only that Jesus tells Saul,

> Festina et exi velociter ex Hierusalem: quoniam non recipient testimonium tuum de me ... Vade, quoniam ego in nationes longe mittam te.

> Make haste, and get thee quickly out of Jerusalem; because they will not receive thy testimony concerning me ... Go, for unto the Gentiles afar off, will I send thee (Acts 22:18, 21).

Important though this passage is to Paul's history, as it is the point at which he receives his commission to the Gentiles, it does not provide a satisfactory ending to the play, lacking as it does any obvious visual cues and opening up a new storyline rather than closing down an old one.

However, the playwright has other sources from which to borrow at this point, such as Acts 5:17–21, 8:26, 10:3–7, 16:23–9, and 27:23, in which angels intervene as rescuers for Peter, Paul, and other apostles and disciples; and such Old Testament sources as 1 Kings 19:5, Daniel 3:19–28, and the whole of the Book of Tobit, in which angels serve a similar function. The playwright may have felt that, at this point, it was reasonable and dramatically effective, in the words again of the *Meditationes*, 'to contemplate, explain, and understand the Holy Scriptures in as many ways as we consider necessary, in such a manner as not to contradict the truth.'[38] Yet, as if again unsure of the ethics of doing such a thing in a sixteenth-century context, the play cuts the scene short, omitting the potentially dramatic escape by basket over the wall, and concluding with a further reference to scripture and 'Besechyng yow all, of hye and low degre, / Owur sympylnes to hold excusyd and lycens, / That of retoryk haue non intellygens' (658–60).

This discussion does not pretend to be a complete overview of all that might be said concerning *The Conversion of Saint Paul*. It does not even pretend to be remarkably original; much of what I have said here is a mere expansion of what I have noted elsewhere. But it is intended to make a few fairly basic points – none of which are original either, but all of which need to be made repeatedly in this ever-shifting field. First, the Digby *Conversion of Saint Paul*, like many another early English play, is subtler and more complex than is generally recognized, and deserves more and better attention than it has received in the past. Second, the assumption of crudeness or lack of knowledge or ability on the part of the playwright should be a last critical resort; it is better by far to presume our own ignorance than to presume that of the text we are studying. Third, and most importantly, the best way to see this play, and many another early English play, is with a microscope – that is, to avoid as much as possible the old, compelling, but wrong ideas about Corpus Christi plays, cycle drama, in fact the very notion of any overarching norm into which early English plays can be said to fit; overarching theories of this kind tend to make the plays themselves, the very objects of study, vanish.

In summation, the REED project has made it possible for scholars in the field of early English drama to realize that '[o]nly when we fully assimilate the wide diversity of possible types of performance within our critical discourse will we be able to understand clearly the drama of late medieval and early modern England.'[39] But in order to see what those possible types were in the first place, we must re-examine not only the records that have been found, but also the texts, including *The Conversion of Saint Paul,* that we have always had to hand but perhaps never looked at through the right lenses before. In this case, the possible type seems to be a saint play which, in focusing on the moment of conversion in a context of religious upheaval, and in harmonizing varied scriptural sources into a single account at a time when any handling of scripture was dangerous, self-consciously and skilfully keeps itself from coming to too firm and closed an interpretation. It is, in short, a self-conscious, guarded play of intelligence and piety in a dangerous time.

NOTES

1 Alexandra F. Johnston, 'The *York Cycle* and the *Chester Cycle:* What Do the Records Tell Us?' in *Editing Early English Drama: Special Problems and New Directions. Papers Given at the Nineteenth Annual Conference on Editorial Problems, University of Toronto, 4–5 November 1983,* ed. A.F. Johnston (New York: AMS Press, 1987), 121–43.

2 F.M. Salter, *Medieval Drama in Chester* (Toronto: University of Toronto Press, 1954).

3 Barbara D. Palmer, 'Recycling "The Wakefield Cycle": The Records,' *Research Opportunities in Renaissance Drama* 41 (2002): 88–130; Garrett P.J. Epp, 'The Towneley Plays and the Hazards of Cycling,' *Research Opportunities in Renaissance Drama* 32 (1993): 121–50.

4 The early pioneer was John Wasson, 'Records of Early English Drama: Where They Are and What They Tell Us,' in *Records of Early English Drama: Proceedings of the First Colloquium,* ed. JoAnna Dutka (Toronto: University of Toronto Press, 1979), 128–44. See also Alexandra F. Johnston, 'What If No Texts Survived? External Evidence for Early English Drama,' in *Contexts for Early English Drama,* ed. Marianne G. Briscoe and John C. Coldewey (Bloomington, IN: Indiana University Press, 1989), 1–19, and Alexandra F. Johnston, 'The Feast of Corpus Christi in the West Country,' *Early Theatre* 6.1 (2003): 15–34.

5 Johnston, 'Feast of Corpus Christi,' 15.

6 Johnston, 'Feast of Corpus Christi,' 16.

7 Thomas Sharp, ed., *Ancient Mysteries from the Digby Manuscripts* (Edinburgh: Abbotsford Club, 1835), iv.

8 F.J. Furnivall, ed., *The Digby Plays with an Incomplete 'Morality' of Wisdom, Who Is Christ,* EETS es 70 (London: Oxford University Press, 1896), xiii.

9 Furnivall, *Digby Plays* xviii–xxix.

10 Mary del Villar, 'The Staging of *The Conversion of Saint Paul*,' *Theatre Notebook* 25 (1970–1): 64–8; Glynne Wickham, 'The Staging of Saint Plays in England,' in *The Medieval Drama*, ed. Sandro Sticca (Albany: State University of New York Press, 1972), 99–119; Raymond J. Pentzell, 'The Medieval Theatre in the Streets,' *Theatre Survey* 14 (1973): 1–21.

11 Donald C. Baker, John L. Murphy, and Louis B. Hall Jr, eds, *The Late Medieval Religious Plays of Bodleian MSS. Digby 133 and e Museo 160*, EETS os 283 (London: Oxford University Press, 1982).

12 See Barbara Palmer's remarks, 'Recycling,' 110–11, note 11.

13 See, for example, Susan Haskins, *Mary Magdalen: Myth and Metaphor* (London: HarperCollins, 1993).

14 See Theresa Coletti, '*Paupertas est donum Dei*: Hagiography, Lay Religion, and the Economics of Salvation in the Digby *Mary Magdalene*,' *Speculum* 76 (2001): 337–78, and 'The Design of the Digby Play of *Mary Magdalene*,' *Studies in Philology* 76 (1979): 313–33; at the time of writing I have not yet seen her book, *Mary Magdalene and the Drama of Saints* (Philadelphia: University of Pennsylvania Press, 2004).

15 Clifford Davidson, in 'The Middle English Saint Play and Its Iconography,' suggests that *Saint Paul* 'represents a rich theatrical genre,' but also notes how varied that genre may have been and how little evidence for it remains. See *The Saint Play in Medieval Europe*, ed. Clifford Davidson, EDAM Monograph Series 8 (Kalamazoo, MI: Medieval Institute Publications, 1986), 105.

16 John C. Coldewey has argued that the Digby plays may have been performed at Chelmsford in 1562; however, he notes that the totality of the evidence 'does not force us to conclude' that it was so, and no further evidence for this or other specific performances has yet been discovered. See 'The Digby Plays and the Chelmsford Records,' *Research Opportunities in Renaissance Drama* 18 (1975): 103–21.

17 Furnivall, *Digby Plays*, viii.

18 Hardin Craig, *English Religious Drama of the Middle Ages* (Oxford: Clarendon Press, 1955), 313.

19 Arnold Williams, *The Drama of Medieval England* (East Lansing: Michigan State University Press, 1961), 164.

20 Baker, Murphy, and Hall, *Late Medieval Religious Plays*, xxiii.

21 Despite his importance to the history of the field, I would not, however, include Craig among 'the best' scholars, at least not when it comes to this play. His remarks, a lengthy iteration of what I have quoted, are without a doubt the least perceptive commentary ever written on *The Conversion of Saint Paul*, from every angle, and should be avoided entirely.

22 Baker, Murphy, and Hall, *Late Medieval Religious Plays*, xxii–xxiv, 195–7. All
    citations of the play refer to this edition, and will be by line number. The
    editors are not alone in reading the play's treatment of scripture so casually;
    even so great a scholar as Arnold Williams says merely that the play 'follows
    the scriptural story rather closely' (*Drama of Medieval England*, 163, my
    emphasis).
23 Biblical citations in English are to the Douay, in Latin to the Vulgate; for
    the latter, I have used *Biblia sacra vulgata iuxta vulgatam versionem*, ed.
    B. Fischer et al., 4th ed. (Stuttgart: Deutsche Bibelgesellschaft, 1994), but
    have amended its minimal punctuation to bring it in line with the Douay.
24 He is called Saul before Acts 13:8 and Paul after; it is possible that a new
    source for Acts begins at this verse. See *The New Oxford Annotated Bible
    with the Apocrypha*, RSV, ed. Herbert G. May and Bruce M. Metzger (New
    York: Oxford University Press, 1977), 1337, note 9.
25 I use the term 'the Digby playwright' guardedly, and for lack of a better. I do
    not mean to imply common authorship between *Saint Paul* and the other
    plays of the manuscript, or to ignore the different layers of revision in *Saint
    Paul* itself. For purposes of the present argument, however, I shall not be
    considering those later revisions (the scene with Belial and Mercury, and the
    '*Daunce*' stage directions), but only what appears to be the original play,
    which must, after all, have been written originally by someone.
26 Some of what is said here has also been said in my *Saints and the Audience in
    Middle English Biblical Drama* (Toronto: University of Toronto Press, 2004),
    81–105, but the present discussion is more detailed in the area of source
    harmonization.
27 Indeed, the stage direction specifies that Saul falls off of his horse, but says
    nothing about what happens to the soldiers; 182 SD.
28 F.N. Robinson, ed., *The Works of Geoffrey Chaucer*, 2nd ed. (Boston:
    Houghton, 1957).
29 Eamon Duffy, *The Stripping of the Altars: Traditional Religion in England
    1400–1580* (New Haven: Yale University Press, 1992), 79.
30 *Meditations on the Life of Christ*, ed. Isa Ragusa and Rosalie B. Green, trans.
    Isa Ragusa (Princeton: Princeton University Press, 1961), 5.
31 Ragusa and Green, *Meditations*, xxvii.
32 Duffy, *Stripping of the Altars*, 217–18.
33 Janette Dillon, *Language and Stage in Medieval and Renaissance England*
    (Cambridge: Cambridge University Press, 1998), 5–13.
34 See Dillon, *Language and Stage*, 82–7, Duffy, *Stripping of the Altars*, 482.
35 A review of the history of the word 'compile' reveals that it is related both to
    the concept of loose collection and of translation; compare Wynken de

Worde in 1531, 'Yf I had them compyled in one treatyse,' and Caxton in 1483, 'His passyon bede compyled out of greek in to latyn' (*OED*, 'compile.' V. I.1 and 4).

36 This self-consciousness may also explain the play's Latinate diction, which a number of critics have charged inhibits the play's clarity. But surely, in a politically fraught time, the appearance of Latinate obscurity, embodied in a humble, harmlessly stuffy Poeta, could have been a guard against accusations of heterodoxy and rabble-rousing. The play's avoidance of 'plain speaking' may also be a way of avoiding the appearance of dogmatism. 'Within ideology, plainness becomes a sign of truth. Thus the language of plainness can in turn be appropriated by any authority that presents itself as truth-telling.' See Simon Shepherd, *Marlowe and the Politics of the Elizabethan Theatre* (Brighton: Harvester, 1986), 13, quoted in Dillon, *Language and State*, 79. The language of obscurity may be harder to grasp. Yet even here, the play plays both sides of the fence, salting its Latinate language with traditional humility topoi, describing itself as 'lackyng lyttural scyens' (657) and apologizing for 'all our besynes' (166). Such topoi are, of course, to be found in writers from Cicero to Chaucer, and must not be taken as an actual index of quality.

37 Baker, Murphy, and Hall, *Late Medieval Religious Plays*, 196, note 502.

38 Ragusa and Green, *Meditations*, 5.

39 Johnston, 'Feast of Corpus Christi,' 29.

Some Theological Issues in Chester's Plays

DAVID MILLS

A Spectrum of Belief

On 30 May 1575 the assembly at Chester voted by 33 votes to 12 that the Whitsun plays were 'meet to be plaied' at midsummer. On the face of it, this was a perverse, not to say dangerous, decision. When the plays had last been performed, at Whitsun in 1572, there had been considerable controversy. An annalist reported that 'manye of the Cittie were sore against the setting forthe therof' and another pointed out that 'an Inhibition was sent from the Archbishop to stay them but it Came too late.'[1] So soon after the unsuccessful northern rising of 1569 and the excommunication of Queen Elizabeth in 1570, the 1572 production looks decidedly ill-advised. Moreover, we know from other sources that the 1572 opposition was led by a group of clergymen in Chester headed by the returned Genevan exile Christopher Goodman, who had informed the archbishop of York in advance of the intention to stage the plays and of the objections to them.[2]

Goodman also used the pulpit to attack the 1575 resolution and drafted a letter of protest to the mayor, Sir John Savage, which in the event he did not send. Again an injunction was obtained from the archbishop 'procured. by some precise Cittizins,' according to an annalist evidently unsympathetic to the objections.[3] 'Precise' here suggests that these citizens were regarded as Puritans. The term 'Puritan' is, however, a broad brush, and if we are to understand the objections to the plays and the decision of 1575, we need to consider in more detail the spectrum of belief in Chester.

There was a strand in radical Protestantism that was resolutely opposed to theatrical performance of most kinds. William Perkins, the influential Puritan theologian, itemizes his general objections to what he terms 'common playes which are in use in the world,' as representing human vices 'for the causing of mirth and pastime' and because of cross-dressing.[4] But Perkins has a special objection to religious plays, which deserves to be quoted in full:

> *Recreation may not be in the use of holy things*; that is, in the use of the word, Sacraments, prayer, or in any act of religion. For these things are sacred and divine, they doe stand by Gods expresse commandement, & may not be applyed to any common or vulgar use. For this cause it is wel provided, that the Pageants, which have beene used in sundrie cities of this land, are put downe; because they were nothing else, but either the whole, or part of, the historie of the Bible turned into a Play. And therefore the lesse to be allowed, considering that the more holy the matter is which they represent. the more unholy are the playes themselves. Again, all such jests, as are framed out of the phrases and sentences of the Scripture, are abuses of holy things, and therefore carefully to be avoided. The common saying may teach us this much, *It is no safe course to play with holy things*.[5]

We hear the same argument in less measured tones at the end of the description of Chester's plays in David Rogers' 1609 'Brevary of Chester History':

> And we haue all cause to power out our prayers before god that neither wee. nor our posterities after us. may neuar see the like Abomination of Desolation. with suche a Clowde of Ignorance to defile with so highe a hand. the most sacred scriptures of god.[6]

For such, there could be no case whatsoever for plays based on biblical material.

But holding 'Puritan' beliefs did not necessarily entail such an antitheatrical stance. As M.M. Knappen says: 'The Puritan attitude toward dramatic productions was ... moderate at first. Bale wrote religious dramas, and he had Puritan imitators as late as the 1570s. Calvin allowed the production of a biblical play at Geneva.'[7] And Christopher Goodman, at least in his official stance, similarly adopted a less absolutist view. In 1572 he, together with Robert Rogerson (possibly Robert Rogers, archdeacon of Chester) and John Lane, wrote to the archbishop of York to complain that, despite a letter from York forbidding the production, the plays were going ahead. The letter states:

my humble request with my brethren & fellow ministers of this City, who now are present to joyn with me in the same, is unto your *Grace* & your council, that in the name of the Lord Iesus your wisdoms may take such order with the said plays, as by your authority they may either be corrected, allowed, & authorized (if god by any such indirect means will have his gospell furthered where ordinary preaching wanteth not) or els by the same your authority utterly defaced & abolished for ever as pastimes unfitt for this time & Christian commonwealths.[8]

Goodman here suggests that the issue centres upon the legality of the performance rather than its subject. Although doubtful of the value of their production, he leaves open the possibility that the scrutineers might consider that the gospel could be furthered by the plays. Unlike the Breviary author or his source, therefore, he does not condemn the plays because of their biblical subject matter but because they are propaganda for the superstitions of the former unreformed church and hence a rallying point for rebellion.

Goodman entertained suspicions of Sir John Savage's motives in promoting the production, which were doubtless fed by the fact that Sir John stood at the conservative end of the religious spectrum. Though Cheshire was not a hotbed of recusancy, as Lancashire was perceived to be, the local aristocracy were perceived to be either passive conformists or crypto-Catholics, in particular the leading local families of Derbies and the Savages; and the bishop of Chester, William Downham, was known to be lax in his pursuit of recusants in his diocese.[9] John Hanky, the mayor in 1572, had, by Goodman's account, enlisted the support of the earl of Derby. The Stanleys had a history of recusant support. The previous earl had remained under suspicion of plotting a rebellion, and in 1569 his two sons were committed to the Tower on suspicion of plotting the rescue and promotion of Mary, queen of Scots. Haigh comments that the earl's 'household was a nest of conservatives and plotters.'[10] Nevertheless, he was appointed head of the Ecclesiastical Commission. Goodman himself was appointed to the commission in 1567 following a purge of some of its conservative and recusant members, and would be aware of the ineffectiveness of the commission under Thomas Stanley's leadership. Henry Stanley, who succeeded his father in 1572, was described by the Spanish ambassador as 'a passionate heretic.'[11] The Savage family was also under suspicion. Sir John Savage is listed as 'cold' in a Puritan note of the religious commitment of gentry of the diocese in ca. 1579–80.[12]

But suspicion of the mayor's motives did not lead Goodman to condemn the plays outright. In an earlier letter of 1572 he had said:

> albeit the same [i.e., the plays] have neither been perused nor allowed according as by her Majesty in those cases it is provided ... [their production] giveth great comfort to the rebellious papist, & some greater occasions of assembling & conference than their intentions well considered is at this present meet to be admitted.[13]

In his draft letter of 1575 to Mayor Savage, he similarly seems to imply that there might be occasion and purpose suitable for a production:

> Yf we were freed from all thes plagues, and all necessarie workes abowt this Citie [tobe] done. yf wickednes & sin were suppressed, & disolute persons broght to good order. Yf the Citie were so hable to cast away so moche monie as by occasion of thes plays wilbe vainely wasted, or elles coulde not bestow it better: than myght you seme to haue som pretence & leasure to play.[14]

Goodman could be said to be exercising his responsibility as a Puritan cleric, seeking to protect the populace from error but keen to promote the gospel by legitimate means. Frank Luttmer comments: 'From the perspective of Puritan preachers, the battle over village greens and Sabbaths was primarily a defensive one. The culture of the ungodly was not only an offence to God. It destroyed souls.'[15] Goodman's attitude could have encouraged supporters of the plays to assume that the objection lay rather with the unbiblical or 'unorthodox' material within the text than with the biblical subject matter. If the material could be shown to be godly, presumably all would be well. Perhaps with this possibility in mind, the council, in its resolution of 1575 authorizing the midsummer production, added to its decision the condition that 'they shall be sett furth in the best fayssion with such reformacion as mr maior with his advice shall think meet & convenient.'[16] We cannot know whether this was Savage's concession to enable the resolution to pass, or a prudent disclaimer on the part of the assembly.

Certainly in Chester some Anglican clerics of an ascetic temper may have been sympathetic to the plays. One example – though there is no evidence of his involvement in the revising the text – would be Canon James Miller, rector of St Michael's Church in Chester and precentor at the cathedral. Miller oversaw and largely wrote the latest extant manuscript of the Chester plays in 1607. This, as Bob Lumiansky and I noted, is a scholarly reconstruction of the text which is best described as an edition. It also includes the only piece of musical score for the plays, a setting of the Angels' song from the Shepherds' Play, which the Later Banns single out as a special feature. Miller's will is that of an austere Christian, asking to be buried without pomp. But it also asks for burial at the west end of the cathedral where some of his predecessors as precentors were buried. He had what was evidently an extensive library of service books, histories, and music. Anglicans such as Miller would have the necessary sympathy for the plays, the theological knowledge, and the grasp of the position of the objectors, to advise the mayor on an acceptable revision of the text.[17]

Revising the Cycle

Goodman's letter of 11 June 1572 to the archbishop of York acknowledges what is also clear from the extant manuscripts – that the text of the plays was not stable and had been revised on numerous occasions.

> For albeit divers have gone about the correction of the same at sundry times & mended divers things, yet hath it not been done by such as are by authority allowed, nor the same their corrections viewed & approved according to order, nor yet so played for the most part as they have been corrected.[18]

His comment that these revisions had 'mended divers things' suggests that there had been some responsiveness to the changing political and religious climate over the years. That in turn may have persuaded Goodman that, however unlikely it might seem, there might be scope for a revised play cycle to become an acceptable vehicle for the reformed faith, though such a revision would have to be carried out 'by such as are by authority allowed' and would need to be supplemented by a close control of the actual performance to ensure that the text was played as written.

This rolling program of revision makes it impossible to determine the date(s) or status of the texts that make up our extant manuscripts. We can, however, gain some sense of what was in the 1572 text from the list of 'absurdities' in the plays that Goodman and his supporters submitted in 1572 to the archbishop of York. 'Absurdities' is a somewhat restrained word, particularly for Goodman, and covers theologically unacceptable material, such as the Purgatory references in *The Last Judgment*; non-scriptural material, such as the Octavian and Sibyl episode in *The Nativity* or the return of Enoch and Elijah in *Antichrist*; and inappropriate representation, such as the comic presentation of the shepherds 'who by the

Scriptures seem to be honest men.' That much of this material is in our extant text suggests either that that text was not the one used in 1575, or that the revision took little notice of the detail of Goodman's complaints. The play division in Goodman's list is not that of our extant text.

Although the mayor was required to take personal responsibility for 'reforming' the 1575 text, it seems unlikely that any large-scale revision could have taken place between 11 May and 23 June 1575. The production had been prepared for Whitsun when plague threatened the city, and part of the thinking of the council in agreeing to the rescheduling as the threat of plague receded may have been that considerable investment had already been made by the companies. To both revise the text thoroughly and rehearse the new text would probably have been impracticable. Annalists, speaking of the production, refer only to the omission of certain plays; e.g., 'leauinge others vnplaied which were thought might not be Iustified for the superstition that was in them.'[19]

The most probable candidates for omission, on the evidence of the present text, are the final group of plays, plays 22–4, *The Prophets of Antichrist*, *Antichrist*, and *The Last Judgment*. The first two are based largely upon non-biblical sources, while the last play, as Goodman pointed out in 1572, contained 'Purgatory affirmed, preaching of merits of man. The divell speaking Latin, & setteth forth invocation of Saints.'[20]

The Late Banns, which do not describe the content of the text as we have it, defensively draw attention to the insecure foundations of this group by their comments on play 21, *Pentecost*:

This of the oulde and newe testamente to ende all the storye
which oure author meaneth at this tyme to have in playe ...
And after those ended, yet dothe not the author staye.

(Late Banns, 165–6, 169)[21]

These lines continue the tendency throughout these Banns to separate scriptural from non-scriptural material and focus the responsibility upon the 'author.'

Who is 'oure author'? Implicitly, one might imagine that it is the supposed original author, Ranulf Higden, whose role in creating the text is celebrated in the opening lines of these Banns. But 'meaneth' has present reference, and we must therefore conclude that 'oure author' is the latest reviser of the text. But is 'oure author' the same person as 'the author' of line 169? Is a distinction being made between what is now being performed and what was in an earlier text but has now been omitted? Does 'at this tyme' imply that at another time more of the 'storye' was 'in playe,' and/or that more might be played on a future occasion? However we answer these questions, these Banns firmly mark off the last three plays as a distinct group and make them prime candidates for omission.

On the other hand, the case of Andrew Tailer, 'Tailer vsinge the occupacion of Diers' might suggest that play 23 was performed, since he refused to pay the Dyers 'for the charges in the setting furth of their parte and pagent of the plaies' sett furth and plaied in this Citie at midsoomer laste past.'[22] He was committed to prison and was eventually released when two other citizens, John Banester and Edmund Gamull, paid on his behalf. Andrew's action is often taken as a religious objection, but there is no justification for that assumption. While there are several alternative reasons – lack of money, a protest as a tailor against assessment with the Dyers – it is at least possible that he objected to being assessed for the costs in preparing a play which in the event was not performed. All that can be said is that if plays of superstitious content were not to be performed, *Antichrist* would fall under that head.

Meeting 'Genevan' Objections

It is, however, possible to discern a pattern of revision in the plays that reflects an informed response to the Protestant theology of Puritans such as Goodman, which had developed among the English exiles in Geneva during Mary's reign. One aspect of this, which I have discussed elsewhere, is the emphasis upon covenant theology in the cycle.[23] This appears across the cycle, in plays 2, 4, 5, and 15 and reflects the Puritan view of the elect of God, those with whom God has made a covenant. Initially, this represented the Jews, but the cycle shows how that covenant passed to the Gentiles.

The Genevan exiles took their authority entirely from the word of God. For them the Bible was a prescription for life, both spiritual and secular, and it was therefore essential that it should be not only widely available but properly interpreted by those gifted with faith. A result of this priority was the production in exile of a new Bible, the so-called Geneva Bible, which was published in 1560, although the New Testament had appeared separately in 1557. The Geneva Bible was by far the most popular translation of the Bible in the later Tudor period. By the seventeenth century there had been over 120 editions of that Bible, compared with twenty-two for the Bishops' Bible of 1560 and seven for the Great Bible. Conjoined with the Genevan Service Order, the Genevan Bible remained the major vehicle for the dissemination of Puritan theology in England, to the dismay of the Anglican Reformers.

The aim of the Geneva translators was to produce a reader-friendly Bible which would direct the reader's interpretation to a right reading. Among the many innovative reader aids of the Bible were margin notes, in all some 300,000 words, which directed the interpretation of the text, and prefatory introductions to each book. We may detect a similar directive and interpretative concern in the Chester plays where the dramatic equivalent of such margin notes are the explications within from 'historical' characters within the plays and the interventions of a 'contemporary' Expositor who directs the audience's reading of the events they have witnessed, a directive device that also has precedent from earlier Protestant drama in John Bale's use of a Prolocutor.[24] This purposeful didacticism, whose most immediate model lay in the didactic *Stanzaic Life of Christ*, on which the cycle draws, determines the comparative lack of 'human interest' in Chester's text. Whereas York and Towneley evidence concerns how men should behave, in Chester the focus is directed upon what men should believe. Holiness takes precedent over righteousness in the cycle.

Justification by Faith

Play 4, *Abraham*, may perhaps indicate how the emphasis of the cycle may have shifted in revision. Here we have two plays – our Chester version and that in the Book of Brome. It seems now generally agreed that the Brome play represents an earlier version of the Chester text, but focuses entirely upon the interaction of Abraham and Isaac as the patriarch struggles to carry out God's harsh command. The main differences in Chester take the form of two significant 'additions' – a term I use for convenience only – at the beginning and a change in the final audience address. Neither of the two opening additions appears in the other cycles.

The first dramatizes the meeting of Abraham and Lot with Melchizedek after Lot's rescue from the four kings; this is interpreted as a figure of the Eucharist and of tithing. The episode is interpreted by St Paul in the Epistle to the Hebrews and the Geneva Bible glosses Hebrews 9:13 as 'The Leuitical Priest offers beasts bloude: but Christ the true & eternal Priest offered his owne blode, which was most holy and pure; the Leuitical Priest offered yerely, and therfore dyd only represent the true holynes; but Christ by one only sacrifice hath made holy for euer all they that beleue.'[25] Chester's Expositor glosses:

In the owld lawe, without leasinge,
when these too good men were livinge,
of beastes were there offringe
and eke there sacramente.
But synce Christe dyed one roode-tree,
in bred and wyne his death remenber wee;
And at his laste supper our mandee
was his commandemente.   (121–8)[26]

Geneva also glosses Hebrews 7:6: 'The Leuites receaued tythes of their
brethren but Melchisadec of Abraham the patriarch, therfore his priesthode
is more excellent then the Leuitical' (365b) and Chester's Expositor glosses:

And teathinges-makinge, as you seene here,
of Abraham begonnen were.
Therfore to God hee was full deare,
and soe were both too.

By Abraham understand I maye
the Father of heaven, in good faye:
Melchysadecke a pryest to his paye
to minister that sacramente.   (133–40)

Though Chester is not adopting the wording of the Genevan glosses, their
shared aim is to point to a priesthood separate from the Levitical.
Melchizedec served the reformers as a sign of a superior priesthood sepa-
rate from that of the latter-day Levites, the Roman Catholics. To the alert
Puritan of the 1570s, the episode had resonances even beyond those of the
Expositor's account.

Baptism

Chester's cycle uniquely among the four extant English compilations lacks
a play of the baptism of Christ. Other series of plays dramatize this
episode as the authority for the sacrament of baptism, and also use it as the
motivation for the Temptation; the devil, hearing the voice of God desig-
nating Jesus as his Son at the baptism, resolves to test his identity through
temptation. Significantly, John the Baptist appears among the patriarchs in
Chester's *Harrowing of Hell* and refers to his baptism of Christ (play 17,

57–72), which may suggest that a baptism play in an earlier version of the
cycle was subsequently removed. The Church of St John in Chester is
dedicated to the Baptist and the remains of a wall painting of the Baptist in
the wilderness can still be seen.[27] *Also Shyol...*
Chester does, however, include as its second addition to the Abraham
play God's injunction to Abraham to be circumcised and henceforth 'eyche
man-chylde one the eyght daye' (177). Circumcision is the mark of the elect:

> Whoesoe cyrcumcysed not ys
> forsaken shalbe with mee iwys.   (181–2)

> for therby knowe thou maye
> thy folke from other men.   (187–8)

The Expositor expressly refers to this act as 'an sacrament / in the ould
lawe' (195–6) and a precursor of baptism:

> But when Christe dyed away hit went,
> and then beganne baptysme   (199–200)

thereby replacing the obvious link between the sacrament and Christ's
baptism by the evolution of Old Law into New with the Passion of Christ.
While this evolution had been a commonplace of patristic writers, it
assumed new force during the Reformation as the central issue for the
Anabaptists, who regarded the New Testament as having the higher authority. Their views were opposed by both Anglican and Puritan factions;
Martin Bucer, for example, 'argues for a continuity, albeit not a total
continuity, of rites and ceremonies between the Old and the New Testament,' the point made by our play.[28] As their name suggests, a defining
feature of the Anabaptists was their position on infant baptism, 'Infant
baptism was regarded as without warrant in Scripture, contrary to [the
Anabaptists'] principle of voluntary action in religion, an invention of the
devil, and chief source of the corruption of the Church and of its subjec-
tion to the State,'[29] which denies continuity from infant circumcision.
Compare Article 27 of the Anglican Articles of Religion, designed to
counter this view: 'The Baptism of young Children is in any wise to be
retained in the Church, as most agreeable with the institution of Christ.'[30]
Within the context of the play, the immediate appearance of Isaac as a
young boy visually reinforces the point.

The Prophetic Role

The reading of the Nativity prophecies to Herod in play 8, 'The Three Kings occurs only in Chester, where the prophecies are explicitly attributed by speaker and verse, and explained. The Doctor lists Jacob, Daniel, Micah, Isaiah, and David. This stress upon prophetic fulfilment is paralleled by the 1557 Genevan preface to the Epistle to the Hebrews, which lists the prophets of Christ's coming. On the Nativity, it cites Isaiah, Jacob, and David; on the Passion, Isaiah and Zachariah; on the Resurrection, Isaiah, Jeremiah, and Zachariah. It also, under Jacob, indicates that the prophecy is validated by the fact that Herod is not Jewish, which is taken up under the same prophet by Chester:

> for kinge Herode that is nowe rayninge
> is noe Jewe borne nor of that progenye,
> but a stranger by the Romans made there kinge.   (277–9)

Finally, Herod makes a significant comparison in Chester between himself and the tyrannical Athaliah (332–5), who had the royal children murdered to secure her power (2 Kings 11:1) but was subsequently killed (2 Chron. 23:12–15). She was a traditional figure for Herod, but only in Chester among our biblical plays is the comparison made. Athaliah had become, for the exiles, also a figure for Queen Mary and as such the name would have strong political resonance for someone like Goodman.

The Eucharist

Central theologically to the cycle is the signification of the Eucharist. The Late Banns stress the importance of Christ's words in play 15, The Last Supper:

> And howe Criste our Savioure at his laste supper
> gave his bodye and bloode for redemtion of us all,
> yow Bakers see that with the same wordes you utter
> as Criste himselfe spake them, to be a memorall
> of that deathe and passion which in playe after ensue shall.
> (Late Banns, 131–5)

Unlike York, Chester has a further disquisition upon the Eucharist by Christ on his resurrection, indicating that the redemption required both the Passion and the Resurrection together and that it is at that point that the Eucharist becomes fully effectual. The speech is marked out from the rest of the cycle by a stanza-form found nowhere else in the plays.

In 1572 Goodman found in this second speech the key evidence of unreformed theology in the cycle, and quotes the offending lines:

> 17 The words. And therto a full ryche messe, in bred myn one bodie, & that bred I you gyve, your wyked lyffe to amend, becomen is my fleshe, throgh wordes 5 betwyxt the prestes handes.[31]

Our extant text reads:

> And that bread that I you give,
> your wicked life to amend,
> becomes my fleshe through your beleeffe
> and doth release your synfull band.   (*Resurrection*, 174–7)

The requirement of faith on behalf of the receiver is common to Protestant and Catholic alike, and the speech goes on to stress that the reception of the Eucharist while in a state of sin results in damnation. But the 1572 lines quoted by Goodman make no reference to the active role of faith in making the Eucharist effectual. Instead, the bread becomes the body and blood of Christ through the words of consecration by the ordained priest and the spiritual power is inherent in the element itself. The element is transubstantiated to the body of Christ.

For the Reformer, there is no 'Real Presence' in the Roman Catholic sense and the Eucharist is not a re-enactment of Christ's sacrifice. The insistence in the Late Banns on using the exact words of Christ at the Last Supper may perhaps indicate that there was at some time in the history of the text a more elaborate explanation such as is found in the N-Town plays. The key to the latter is Mark 14:22: 'Jesus took bread, and blessed, and brake it,' which the Geneva Bible promptly explains: 'To blesse is here taken onely to gyue thankes, as S. Luk and Paul interpreted, and Marke also speaking of the Cup' (82). Tyndale had put it more bluntly: 'Here it is manifest that Christ consecrated no bread, but delivered it to his disiples, and bade them eat it.'[32]

Play 4 reveals a similarly careful interpretation of Melchizedek's gifts. In the Geneva Bible, the bread and wine which he gives to Abraham are defined as 'For Abram and his soldiors refection and not to offer sacrifice.'[33] Though the play text assigns a figural significance to the gifts, it firmly stresses the commemorative aspect of the Eucharist:

> But synce Christe dyed one roode-tree,
> in bred and wyne his death *remenber* wee ...
> Melchysadecke, a pryest to his paye
> to minister that sacramente
> that Christe ordayned the foresayde daye
> in bred and wyne to *honour* him aye.   (Play 4, 125–6, 139–42; my italics)

There are two indications that this interpretation may not always have been the one played. The Later Banns sternly warn the Barbers and Wax-Chandlers:

> The offeringe of Melchesadecke of bread and wine
> and the preservation thereof sett in youre playe.
> Suffer yow not in enye poynte the storye to decaye.   (82–4)

What might have preceded the extant version is perhaps indicated by the reading offered by the *Stanzaic Life of Christ*, a recognized source for sections of the cycle:

> And for hit shuld after bifalle
> Goddes body made to be
> of bred & wyn to saue vs alle,
> therfore the two offret he ...
> And Goddis body & blode ye sene
> of brede & wyn sithen Crist vs wan.   (2413–16; 2419–20)

Given this care, it seems surprising that Chester appears to affirm the inherent power of the consecrated bread in the *Antichrist* play, where Elijah uses it to expose the devils:

> Have here breadd both too.
> But I must blesse yt or yt goe,
> that the fyend, mankyndes foe,
> on hit have no power.   (565–8)

The play continues by attributing a spiritual radiance to the bread which the devils cannot look upon. In Bale's *King Johan* this belief in the power of the consecrated bread is envisaged by Dissimulation as a consequence of the coming of Usurped Power: 'Holy water and breade shall dryve awaye the devyll' (1003).[34] This with other details in the *Antichrist* play make it a very strong candidate for omission in 1575 on the grounds of its superstitious content.

For the Reformer, Christ is present in the sacrament. Christ's physical body, glorified, has ascended to heaven and remains there, but his spiritual being is uncircumscribed and universal. His presence within the sacrament is therefore a spiritual presence effected by the faith of the believer, not a 'real' presence effected by the words of the priest. The Geneva gloss on Luke 22:19 reads: 'The bread is a true signe, & an assured testimonie that the body of Iesus Christe is gyue*n* for the nourriture of our soules, likewise the wyne signifieth that his blood is our drincke to refreshe & quicken vs euerlastingly' (137). Dan Danner explains the glosses further: 'The bread and wine were signs of Christ's body and blood and not only pointed to these realities but guaranteed a sacramental or spiritual presence of the Lord's body and blood to nurture and refresh the faithful. The marginalia stop short of explicitly mentioning the partaking of the elements by faith or the mysterious work of the Holy Spirit, although both are clearly implied.'[35] Thus the small changes to the lines that offended Goodman encapsulate the centrality of the faith of the recipient and the continuing presence of Christ in the sacrament. Whoever wrote the lines had a firm grasp of the precise theological implications of his words.

Redemption

One objection to *The Last Judgment* that Goodman does not raise is the image of the bleeding Christ. The image suggested to the Reformers that Christ's sacrifice was ongoing and not final. As Christ says:

> For my body ys all torent
> with othes false always fervent;
> noe lymme on mee but yt is lent
> from head right to the heele.
>
> ...
>
> Behould nowe, all men! Looke on mee
> and see my blood freshe owt flee
> that I bleede on roode-tree
> for your salvatyon.   (417–20, 425–8)

Glossing Hebrews 10:19–20: 'Having therefore, brethren, boldness to

enter into the holiest by the blood of Jesus, By a new and living way, which
he hath consecrated for us, through the veil, that is to say his flesh,' the
Geneva Bible says: 'The bloude of Christ is alwayes fresh and lyuely
before the father to sprincle and quicken vs' (370). In *The Ascension* Christ
speaks in similar terms:

> Theise droppes nowe with good intent
> to my Father I will present ...
> For theise causes, leeve yee mee,
> the droppes I shedd on roode-tree.
> All freshe [Hm fleshe] shall reserved bee
> ever, tyll the laste daye.   (137–8, 149–52)

The blood is a token of Christ's redemption of mankind and a validation of
his justice in the Last Judgment. The play makes it clear that the blood
refers to the blood-stained body and clothing (121–4), and the long explication (125–52) seems designed to deflect alternative readings of the bleeding Christ.

The remission of sins is an article of faith, voiced in the Pentecost play
by Simon:

> And I beleeve, with devotyon,
> of synne to have remission
> through Christes blood and Passion,
> and heaven when I am dead.   (347–50)

But in 1572 Goodman found a different version: 'Simons words. And I
beleve with devotion, of syn to have remission, throgh penance & contrition, & heven whan I am dead.'[36] The redeeming sacramental power of
penance placed the church in a mediating position between the sinner and
Christ. The objection was evidently taken on board by the reviser before
the 1575 production, if not the 1572 performance, and Christ as the sole
redeemer through the Passion is firmly stated.

The End of the Plays

When in 1575 Mayor Savage was summoned before the Privy Council
after the performance, the charge was that the production was his sole
initiative and that it imposed needless costs on the citizens. The defence is
that the production was a customary event and was staged for the benefit

and profit of the citizens.[37] The content or revision of the plays seems not to have been at issue. Although one annalist unhelpfully comments that the plays were 'to the misliking of manye' and another refers to them as 'ye popish playes,' Randle Holme, the Chester herald and antiquarian, says that the production was 'to the great dislike of many because the playe was in on part of the Citty.'[38] Some critics have suggested that the failure of the cathedral authorities to provide a barrel of beer for the players in 1575 as they had in 1572 is a sign of ecclesiastical disapproval; but if the plays were not performed at the Abbey Gate as in the past, there would have been no cause to make that provision there.

It seems significant that the charge was one of the wastage of public money rather than the content of the plays or their potential as a rallying point for anti-establishment opposition. While this may have been a political move on the part of the Privy Council, it may also suggest that the text of the plays and arrangements for their revision were not the focus of the council's concern. The corrections to the text and performance may not have satisfied Goodman, who maintained in 1575 in a letter to the mayor that he finally decided not to send, that 'they contene suche absurd matter and doctrine, a<.> nether standeth with godes word nor the religion which you professe, nor the laws of this realme,' but they seem to have defused more moderate objections within the city and perhaps beyond.[39]

NOTES

1 L.M. Clopper, ed., *Chester*, REED (Toronto: University of Toronto Press, 1979), 103–4, 97.
2 See David Mills, '"Some Precise Cittizins": Puritan Objections to Chester's Plays,' in *Essays in Honour of Peter Meredith, Leeds Studies in English*, ed. Catherine Batt, ns 29 (1998): 219–34. On Goodman, see Jane A. Dawson, 'The Early Career of Christopher Goodman and the Development of English Protestant Thought' (doctoral thesis, University of Durham, 1978).
3 Chester City and County Archive, CR/60/83 (1574–5), f. 13r.
4 *William Perkins, 1558–1602: English Puritanist: His Pioneer Works on Casuistry: 'A Discourse of Conscience' and 'The Whole Treatise of Cases of Conscience,'* ed. Thomas F. Merrill (Nieuwkouf, Netherlands: B. de Graaf, 1966), 218.
5 *William Perkins*, 217–18.
6 Clopper, *Chester*, 252.

7 M.M. Knappen, *Tudor Puritanism: A Chapter in the History of Idealism* (Chicago: University of Chicago Press, 1939), 439.

8 Denbigh Record Office, Ruthin, Plas Power MSS, DD/PP/839 (11 June 1572), pp. 120–1.

9 K.R. Wark, *Elizabethan Recusancy in Cheshire*, Chetham Society, series 3, 19 (Manchester: Chetham Society, 1971), 12–20.

10 Christopher Haigh, *Reformation and Resistance in Tudor Lancashire* (Cambridge: Cambridge University Press, 1975), 213, 253–4.

11 Haigh, *Reformation and Resistance*, 259.

12 Cited in Wark, *Elizabethan Recusancy*, 51–3.

13 Denbigh Record Office, Ruthin, Plas Power MSS, DD/PP/839 (10 May 1572), p. 119.

14 Denbigh Record Office, Plas Power MSS DD/PP/843.

15 Frank Luttmer, 'Persecutors, Tempters and Vassals of the Devil: The Unregenerate in Puritan Practical Divinity,' *Journal of Ecclesiastical History* 51 (2000): 46–7.

16 Clopper, *Chester*, 104.

17 On Miller, see R.M. Lumiansky and David Mills, *The Chester Mystery Cycle: Essays and Documents* (Chapel Hill, NC: University of North Carolina Press, 1983), 71–6; David Mills, 'James Miller: The Will of a Chester Scribe,' *REED Newsletter* 9.1 (1984): 11-13.

18 Denbigh Record Office, Ruthin, Plas Power MSS, DD/PP/839, pp. 120–1.

19 Clopper, *Chester*, 110; see also Chester City and County Archives, CR/469/542, f. 30v.

20 Denbigh Record Office, Ruthin, Plas Power MSS, DD/PP/839, p. 122.

21 Banns quotations from Lumiansky and Mills, *Chester Mystery Cycle: Essays and Documents*, 285–93.

22 Clopper, *Chester*, 111–12.

23 David Mills, 'Chester's Covenant Theology,' in *Porci ante Margaritam: Essays in Honour of Meg Twycross, Leeds Studies in English* (2001): 1–14.

24 Texts in Peter Happé, ed., *The Complete Plays of John Bale*, 2 vols. Tudor Interludes Series (Cambridge: D.S. Brewer, 1985–6). Happé comments that the Prolocutor 'is perhaps parallel to the use of narrator in York 12, and the Expositor in Chester 5' (1:12).

25 Quotations from *The New Testament of our Lord and Saviour Jesus Christ: A Facsimile Reprint of the Celebrated Genevan Testament M.D. LVII* (London, n.d.), 24.

26 R.M. Lumiansky and David Mills, eds, *The Chester Mystery Cycle*, 2 vols, EETS ss 3, 9 (Oxford: Oxford University Press, 1974, 1986).

27 See Sally-Beth MacLean, *Chester Art: A Subject List of Extant and Lost Art Including Items Relevant to Early Drama*, Early Drama, Art, and Music Reference Series 3 (Kalamazoo, MI: Medieval Institute Publications, 1982), 33–4.

28 Irena Backus, 'Church, Communion and Community in Bucer's Commentary on the Gospel of John,' in *Martin Bucer: Reforming Church and Community*, ed. D.F. Wright (Cambridge: Cambridge University Press, 1994), 65. John Bale attacks the sect in *King Johan* (2532, 2680–1)

29 James Hastings, ed., *Encyclopaedia of Religion and Ethics* (Edinburgh: T. & T. Clark, 1908–26), 1:410 col. b.

30 E. Tyrrell Green, *The Thirty-nine Articles and the Age of the Reformation* (London: W. Gardner, Darton, [1896]), 206–16, esp. 214–15.

31 See note 13.

32 'The Supper of Our Lord,' in *William Tyndale: An Answer to Sir Thomas More's Dialogue, The Supper of Our Lord, William Tracy's Testament Expounded*, ed. Henry Walter (Cambridge: Parker Society, 1850), 241.

33 *The Geneva Bible: A Facsimile of the 1560 Edition*, introduction by Lloyd E. Berry (Madison, WI: University of Wisconsin Press, 1969), Genesis 14:18, note.

34 Happé, *Plays of John Bale*, 1:55; Peter Marshall, 'Forgery and Miracles in the Reign of Henry VIII,' *Past and Present* 178 (February 2003): 39–73, evidences the exposure of forged relics and miracles in the 1530s and shows how more radical reformers developed an analogy to the 'false miracle' of transubstantiation.

35 Dan G. Danner, *Pilgrimage to Puritanism: History and Theology of the Marian Exiles at Geneva, 1555 to 1560* (New York: P. Lang, 1999), 127–8.

36 See note 13.

37 Clopper, *Chester*, 112–17.

38 Clopper, *Chester*, 109–10.

39 Denbigh Record Office, Ruthin, Plas Power MSS, DD/PP/843.

The Role of the Presenter in
Medieval Drama

K. JANET RITCH

Prologue

It has been fashionable for the past forty years or so to interpret medieval theatre by way of a Brechtian dramaturgy. Those who do so are justified by artistic licence far more readily than by the medieval paradigm that they are attempting to interpret. Although the fashion may be on the wane in 2006, Brechtian notions still cling to certain aspects of our understanding of the medieval stage. This study focuses upon the double-faced Janus of medieval theatre, the liminal presenter, who stands poised upon the threshold between fact and fiction, reality and illusion, history and contemporary society at the entrance to many a medieval play. Like any door, the presenter's technique may open wide in a warm and welcoming way, or obstruct in a cool and uncomfortable manner. The former represents the ideal that the medieval prologue strove to attain, while the latter might easily comprise one of Brecht's well-known alienation effects.

On the surface, nevertheless, there is a resemblance between the theatrical styles advocated by Bertolt Brecht and those in use in the Middle Ages; they all share in common techniques which are thought to alienate the actor from his own role as well as the audience from the action on stage. These techniques include masks, allegorical characters, episodic narratives, and the above-mentioned presenter, all features, to varying degrees, of medieval morality plays and biblical dramas, which are consequently defined as 'presentational rather than realistic.'[1] Brecht's presentational or epic theatre, where the actor narrates his part, is anti-illusionistic and anti-Aristotelian in that it deliberately blocks any empathy in the audience for the dramatis personae.[2] In his *Short Description of a New Technique of Acting which Produces an Alienation Effect* of 1940, Brecht wrote that the 'first condition for the achievement of the A-effect is that the actor must invest what he has to show with a definite gest of showing ... That being so, it is possible for the actor in principle to address the audience directly.'[3] Direct addresses to the medieval audience are often (but not exclusively) made by some sort of presenter figure who is thought to break all theatrical illusion in this way. The following study begins with this 'first condition' and the start of most plays; it examines presenters in English and continental biblical plays, and related forms of address to the audience, in order to ascertain how they may function in a very anti-Brechtian manner in the late Middle Ages. Finally, it expands the analysis to other literary works of the Middle Ages and relates the theatrical usages to these exterior ones in order to illuminate the expectations and effects of dramatic prologues within this tradition. Setting aside the very complex issue of theatrical image, this study necessarily highlights the text and its oral presentation.

Definitions

Despite the wide variety of speech headings associated with the individual presenter, he is often named merely Expositor or Prologue. Prologue suggests the opening presentation, whereas Expositor denotes the interpretation of the action. 'Presenter' is preferred here, nevertheless, because some of these figures do not appear at the beginning of the play, and many of them also convert to Epilogues at the end. The character who addresses the audience directly at both ends of the production may often represent fundamentally the same figure, even when the speech heading changes. Neither do all of these figures expound, as an 'expositor' should, with equivalent degrees of moral, figurative, or typological interpretation. Finally, the generic term 'presenter' both allows for cross-Channel comparisons, and forces a reconsideration of whether medieval religious drama can be characterized and distinguished as presentational in the Brechtian sense. This study excludes all Banns, Proclamations, and any other pre-performance advertisements (such as the French *monstre*); it focuses instead upon presenters from the late Middle Ages that survive in French and English biblical plays that present salvation history, whether in cycles from Genesis to the Apocalypse, Passion plays, or shorter sequences to the same salvific end.

One could argue that all plays are presentational by definition, insofar as they involve impersonation before an audience. This definition is a compromise between those of Karl Young and Lynette Muir.[4] Other dramatic elements which may contribute to the impersonation (or mimesis), such as props, set, and dialogue, are only accidents attached, in varying degrees, to the two essentials: impersonation and audience. Within these terms, presenters who address the audience directly might be considered extratheatrical or metatheatrical, since they are said to set aside their impersonation during the direct address, thereby alienating the audience from the action as much as themselves from their role. Martin Stevens, in particular, considered the Expositor an 'alienating' technique within the ludic nature of medieval drama.[5] Ralph Blasting was influenced by this theory enough to allow for an effect of both 'momentary scepticism and contemplation' at once, caused by the presenter self-consciously drawing attention to the presentation at a distance from the signified reality. Although he explains the simultaneity of scepticism and contemplation as a paradox, Blasting opts for the presenter's affirmation of a higher reality, on account of the Real Presence of Christ in the Host staged throughout the German *Künzelsauer Fronleichnamspiel* (1479) with which he was concerned.[6] His ultimate rebuttal of the supposed alienation effect is significant but limited to those plays that were performed in association with the Feast of Corpus Christi, a celebration in honour of the Host. In England, only one of the four extant manuscript traditions of biblical plays, the York cycle, was consistently associated with this feast day, having been performed annually on the Feast of Corpus Christi for almost two hundred years.[7] In fact, the N-Town plays and the Chester cycle employ an individual presenter far more often than the York cycle. In France, while the majority of plays were associated with Pentecost, if there was any liturgical occasion for them at all, most of them seem, from the texts, to have been introduced by a presenter. On the basis of the broader and more fully documented evidence of the French tradition, this study argues that no medieval audience of any French or English biblical play would stand back in 'momentary scepticism' to re-examine the primary assumptions of their faith, since the presenter's role was more or less homogeneous with both the play and the cultural ethos of the time.

Of the two lengthy studies of the presenter, one by David Carnahan on what he names the 'prologuist' in French drama up to the fifteenth century and the other by Jörg Fichte on 'expository voices' in German and English medieval drama, the former provides the most comprehensive definition of his subject.[8] The prologuist is the person who delivers the introductory speech, either 'the author ... a member of the company or a priest, not a member of the company, for the purpose of fixing the attention of the audience, of giving them an understanding of the plot, and of serving as a vehicle for the apologies and explanations of the author.'[9] Both Carnahan and Fichte find the origin of this figure not in the classical chorus, but in introductory forms of Latin liturgical drama. Carnahan remarks upon biblical and liturgical echoes in the prologues and some irregular prologues: double prologues in six of the eighty-seven French plays that he studied, direct addresses to royalty in the audience, or a general speech used both as an introduction and as part of the ensuing dialogue. Double prologues occur when one prologue introduces the entire sequence of episodes to be performed and another focuses upon the initial episode, normally the first day in the French tradition. Graham Runnalls, citing Carnahan, has summarized the topoi usually found in prologues as prayers for the audience, invocations for God's help with the performance, summaries of the action, at times even descriptions of the theatre and the set, affirmations of the text's authorization by ecclesiastical authorities, the *captatio benevolentiae,* and excuses if the actors perform badly or forget their lines, etc.[10] The 'etc.' here includes the celebrated topos of calling for silence, equivalent to the hortative *silete* in Latin, which came to signify a musical interlude in the German and French Passion plays.[11] In other terms, presenters perform a stage-manager function, a didactic role as interpreter of the theology actualized by the plays, or an edificational role to create 'a pious mood.'[12] In all these forms, the direct address to the audience 'is normally regarded as a feature of a 'naïve' dramaturgy' in origin, which, according to Carnahan, becomes more apologetic as the plays become increasingly secular.[13] In sum, the presenter effects a kind of rite of passage from audience to impersonations and from contemporary reality to the actualization of a certain historical understanding or of some even more remote spiritual reality, as a mediator between episodes (separated by minutes, days, or years), between the play and the audience, and between all involved and God.

All of these features are prevalent in medieval theatre in general, but certain assumptions must be tested against new editions and research in the field. The considerations to be examined within the late medieval tradition include the following:

1 the degree of the presenter's integration
2 the English tradition in comparison with the French
3 the actual profession in real life of the individuals who normally pronounced these prologues
4 the uniqueness of the topoi listed above to this presentational figure in medieval drama

The wide variety of uses to which the presenter was put, either simultaneously or successively, functioned in any case on many levels at once. As with every symbol, artistic or literary device, the application of the role of presenter may be effective to varying degrees.

Degree of Integration in the Role of the Presenter

Both Carnahan and Fichte agree that the only suitable prototype for the presenter, prologue, or expositor in medieval drama must be found in the daily assigned reading (*lectio*) of the Latin liturgy used to introduce the *Visitatio sepulchri* and the *Ludus pastorum*, the earliest forms of Christian drama. Since the *lector* was generally the priest, Fichte identifies him as the first expositor.[14] Discussion of the suitability of a liturgical choir or a classical chorus for such an introductory role has also competed for attention, however, especially in German criticism. Since the English Renaissance has further muddied the waters, as epitomized by Shakespeare's marriage of the medieval prologue with the received notion of the classical chorus, some clarification on this issue would be helpful.

The Greek tragic chorus never functioned as a prologue, but entered singing the *parodos* (choral entrance song) after at least one opening speech. Euripides, for example, employs two distinct forms of prologues, which Carnahan would consider irregular.[15] The first kind is given by a figure totally extraneous to the action who never appears on stage again. For example, Aphrodite pronounces almost sixty lines at the beginning of Euripides' *Hippolytus* and then disappears. She introduces herself and recommends that men worship her, then justifies the action she is about to take against Hippolytus for failing to do just that. She then informs her audience of precisely the steps she has already taken to exact her revenge and foretells how she will bring her action to a satisfactory conclusion. By the end of the play, all her predictions are fulfilled. An alternate pattern is best exemplified by Dionysus in the *Bacchae*, who explains his desire for revenge and the manner in which he will exact it.[16] In this case, however, he does not disappear from the plot, but remains as a disguised agent within it. In both cases, the prologues begin with an I-identifier, recapitulate significant past events whose influence is still to be felt, and orient the audience to the set and plot, the latter being, according to Aristotle, the most significant feature of tragedy. Consequently, the classical chorus functions as a mediator, much as the medieval presenter does, but never as a prologue.

The second pattern employed by Euripides matches both the irregular prologue identified by Carnahan as integral to the ensuing dialogue, and the usage of some English biblical plays. Although God in the latter does not immediately lay out all his plans leading up to Doomsday, he does introduce himself and present his intentions in the initial plays dealing with the Creation. All four of the English biblical plays – the York and Chester cycles, the Towneley and N-Town plays – commence with some variation of 'Ego sum alpha et oo / primus et novissimus' (Chester 1.1–2), first in Latin, then translated as 'I am gracyus and grete, god withoutyn begynnyng' (York 1.1).[17] In subsequent episodes, God appears in the person of Christ, whereas the prevailing self-introductions, used as openers, pertain mainly to the enemies of Jesus, including the devil. York's Caiaphas, for example, addresses his audience like a true prologuist:

> Pees, bewshers, I bid no jangelyng ȝe make,
>   And sese sone of youre sawes, & se what I saye,
> And trewe tente vnto me þis tyme þat ȝe take,
>   For I am a lorde lerned lelly in youre lay;
>
> By connyng of clergy and casting of witte
>   Full wisely my wordis I welde at my will,
> So semely in seete me semys for to sitte,
>   And þe lawe for to lerne you and lede it by skill.   (29.1–8)

Not only does he request silence, but he also demands that his audience stop talking and pay attention, because he is a man of learning who can read and write ('connyng of clergy') and interpret the law ('lerned lelly in youre lay') to them ('þe lawe for to lerne you'). His immediate audience, whom he addresses as 'bewshers' (*beaux sires*), are four soldiers (*milites*) and his fellow high priest, Annas, but the same address embraces just as well the wider audience, whose attention he must attract for the play to be heard and its message received. This is a conventional opening for the northern plays that lend themselves to blustery characters paradoxically screaming for silence.

Five other pageants in York and five in Towneley open with a similar demand for peace. But of the five pairs of pageants that are shared to varying degrees between the York and Towneley plays, only one opens with such a demand; Towneley 8 reproduces a parallel passage from York 11 with minor variants.[18] Pilate accounts for four of these ten openings, with Pharaoh, Herod, Caiaphas, Rex, Primus miles, and Jesus contributing to the rest. All parody the power wielded by those who are puffed up with their own self-importance, except for Jesus' 'Pees be both be day and nyght / Vntill þis house and till all þat is here ' (York 27.1–2). This last is anomalous in that it opens the scene for the Last Supper with only four lines, in which Jesus passes a spiritual peace, rather than appealing for attention. Two other openings in Towneley and four others in York demand attention and silence with addresses to the audience as 'Poure bewsheris' (York 19), 'seniours' (York 36), 'Lordingis' (York 38) and 'Man on molde' (York 37). In this last case, the double play of citizens as actors on the pageant wagons and as audience is particularly significant as Jesus addresses them all as men and women on earth, both audience and actors, in their fragile and fallen human condition. All are consequently implicated in the collective will to salvation against the prevailing temptations.

Like Dionysus, none of these presenters stands outside the action; on the contrary, they all actually control it. The majority explain their actions to some degree, state explicitly what they are doing or intend to do, threaten punishments (aimed, by implication, at the audience as well as the other characters on stage), and claim attention through bombastic speech. Furthermore, in both the Greek and the Christian culture the audience already knew the plot. One assumes that they wanted to hear it again for the comfort of cultural continuity, and possibly for new interpretations of the old events. In Greek tragedy, the interpretation is provided by the individual playwright; in the York cycle, where basically the same plays were repeated year after year, the local actors who were familiar to the citizens of York must have provided the interest through the quality of their performance.

Rather than offering any suggestion that Euripides could have influenced the English biblical plays directly, given the blockage in textual transmission and considerable linguistic barrier between the two traditions, a stronger case can be made for the common exigencies of an open-air performance to crowds whose attention might easily stray. Greek amphitheatres were built with marvellous acoustics, but the wagons on which both the York and Chester plays were performed were pulled into differing locations that were not all sympathetic to resonating sound. When a station at which the wagon stopped was within a narrow street, the actors' voices would bounce off the walls, but in an open square or field, there was no such advantage. Such introductory techniques were entirely reasonable for pre-technological societies without amplification systems, lighting effects, or mixed media. In practice, an introductory presentation of the self, theme, setting, and plot proved to be effective theatre in both the classical and the medieval traditions.

English Practice

Hans-Jürgen Diller has described in great detail the wide variety of addresses to the audience made by all characters of every social standing in English biblical plays. In contrast, presenters who remain aloof from the action, the so-called extratheatrical characters, are rare.[19] Whereas Alexandra F. Johnston has calculated that 77 per cent of the forty-eight episodes in the York cycle begin with a significant opening statement, as discussed above, there is only one extratheatrical prologue in the entire cycle, pronounced in 144 lines by a 'Doctour' introducing *The Annunciation.* Johnston notes especially this presenter's style of recapitulation (from Genesis), 'a familiar pedagogical trait used by countless teachers and preachers.'[20] To this anomaly may be added one other Doctor, who opens the interpolated *Assumption of Mary* in the N-Town manuscript; a 'Contemplacio' who appears in the *Mary Play* and introduces *Passion Play II* from the same N-Town manuscript; a complex expositor in the Chester cycle, who rides a horse (*equitando*) from his first appearance in the fourth pageant and seems to assume a variety of names; and finally a most interesting Appendix in *The Resurrection of Our Lord.* Excluding the latter, these presenters stand out as exceptional in the context of an average of forty plays in each of the four recorded traditions.[21]

Curiously, all of these figures are implicated in various kinds of revisions or additions to original material, not precisely datable. The one prologue in the York cycle is an older form that was replaced in the actual performance by an unrecorded one sometime in the sixteenth century. A belated note in the right margin identifies the presenter as 'Doctor.' Subsequently (it seems), the same scribe added: 'this matter is newly mayde / whereof we have no Coppy.'[22] The marginalia can be dated by the 'very distinctive hand' of John Clerke, who was responsible for comparing the Register copy with performances between 1535 and 1569.[23] Even the earliest possible date for this remark places it within the turmoil of the English Reformation when the speech of the prologuist might well have been revised in an apologetic vein. Yet its position right before *The Annunciation* is most significant, since the transition from Old to New Testaments is often highlighted through dramatization of material, concerning a procession of prophets (*Ordo prophetarum*) or a Parliament of Heaven (*Procès de paradis*), which originated in sermons. In the old prologue of 144 lines, the Doctor first addresses God, then cites the various prophets who foretell the advent of Christ (Amos, Isaiah, Joel, and John the Baptist) with

Latin quotations at regular intervals, supplemented by accounts of Old Testament events that prefigure the salvific role of Jesus and underline the purity of Mary, his mother. It is no coincidence that the one prologuist in the *York* cycle highlights this pivotal juncture between the old and new dispensations in a variation upon the *Ordo prophetarum*. Whereas *York* has recourse to a presenter, both *Towneley* and *N-Town* dedicate entire plays (i.e., *The Play of the Prophets*, Towneley 7; *Jesse Root*, N-Town 7) to dramatizing the same transition. The Chester cycle attempts to enliven such static mises en scène by foregrounding one prophet, Balaam, and the interpretation of him by another Doctor-Presenter. While the action may be livelier in this latter biblical play, the theological transition to the New Testament is far less effective.

The Doctor and Contemplacio in the late fifteenth-century N-Town play are analogous to the one presenter in York.[24] The Doctor in *The Assumption*, while citing among his sources primarily the *Legenda aurea*, recapitulates a biography of Mary from her miraculous conception to her death, and ends with a polite request for attentive silence. Contemplacio is more interesting, however, since his ongoing commentary from prologue to epilogue of the *Mary Play* provides the foundation for the dramatic demonstration of his words, like the skeleton that the dramatic action fleshes out. Functionally, Contemplacio's appearances at regular intervals between episodes act as a rhetorical *transitio* in the dramatic action. His first intervention is typical of his procedure. He begins with a recapitulation of what has just been dramatized, 'Sovereynes, 3e han sen shewyd 3ow before, / Of Joachym and Anne' (ll. 254–5) and moves the action forward three years to Mary's presentation at the temple: 'And as a childe of thre 3ere age here she xal appere' (l. 262), concluding with a request for silence. In his next appearance, he effects a similar transition of eleven years to Mary's betrothal at fourteen years of age. Just before the final episode in which Mary visits Elizabeth, Contemplacio narrates the omitted details which lead up to this visit. Two of his interventions are most notable: his introduction to the Parliament of Heaven and the epilogue. Contemplacio's recapitulation before the Parliament of Heaven turns in lamentation back 4,604 years to man's fall from grace, before supplicating God for mercy in the name of two prophets, Ysaie and Jeremye. Like the Doctor in York, Contemplacio becomes the mouthpiece for the prophets instead of allowing them to speak for themselves.[25] The epilogue recapitulates aetiological explanations for the Magnificat and the Angelus (the Ave of the rosary), which were previously dramatized by a personified Angelus after Mary's presentation at the temple, and by her visit to Elizabeth. Peter Meredith posits that the naming of Contemplacio at the opening to the second Passion play in the same manuscript represents a borrowing from *The Mary Play* sequence in order to create a sense of uniformity throughout the N-Town manuscript. This last manifestation of Contemplacio in the second Passion play is accompanied by a stage direction describing him as *an exposytour in doctorys wede*. Clothed as a conventional expositor or doctor, he reminds the audience of the previous performance of 'last зere.'[26] Again, Contemplacio's role has more to do with narration and *transitio* (the transition from one playlet to another) than deep theological expositions, although the latter are not entirely negligible. A number of clues indicate that both *The Mary Play* and *The Assumption* are late additions to the N-Town manuscript (BL: Cotton Vespasian D. VIII), itself a compilation.[27]

The complex and obscure manuscript tradition of the Chester cycle encompasses eight fragments and cyclic manuscripts, of which two very minor fragments might date from the late fifteenth century. Lumiansky and Mills chose as their base text the earliest complete cyclic manuscript of five, Huntington MS Hm of 1591.[28] Apparently, the *originalis* (master copy) of the complete cycle, dating from 1422, was lost in 1568. Between 1568 and 1572, therefore, the various companies in Chester who owned copies of the individual plays that they were responsible for performing paid scribes to make a new master copy of the surviving texts. In 1575, however, Sir John Savage was instructed to 'make any changes that were doctrinally necessary.'[29] Other evidence confirms that the original material was modified at this time to suit the Protestant context of the late sixteenth century.

Within the five pageants in which the Chester Expositor figure appears (4, 5, 6, 12, and 22), there is some continuity of style and presentation, albeit with a proliferation of speech headings, all fulfilling aspects of the presenter's role. The first pageant, 'The Barbers Playe' of Abraham, opens with Preco demanding 'All peace, lordinges that bine presente' (4.1), and 'rowme and space' (4.7) for Abraham, the new centre of attention. This is the stage-manager function of the presenter, even if 'preco' actually signifies 'preacher' in medieval Latin.[30] After announcing that the play begins 'in worshippe of the Trynitie' (4.10), he names himself 'Goobett-on-the-Greene' (4.13), a self-identification which is more in line with God, Pilate, Herod, and the like than with the usual prologuist. In any case, by the time that Expositor appears on his horse (4.113), Goobett is gone. At Expositor's final appearance in the same pageant, he is also identified as 'the Docter,' a speech heading which carries over to play 5.[31] In play 4, Expositor/Docter, in turn, loses the last word to Messenger who directs the crowd to make room for Balack with stage-managerial aplomb. Whereas the Huntington MS uses the Doctor sparingly in play 5, a later 1607 manuscript (Harley 2124) representing the same episode restores 'Expositor' as the speech heading (nine times) for another interpretation of the *Ordo prophetarum*. Back in the 1591 manuscript, the sixth play, on the Nativity, again employs a Preco and a Nuntius, not so much as expositors as characters; it is now Nuntius who fills the typical stage-manager function of making room for the play (6.177 ff.), while Preco is called both 'boye' and 'bedell' (6.250, 269) by Octavianus, who dispatches him to make an announcement (as a real *nuntius* would) within the action of the plot. Expositor concludes by providing a link between the Nativity play and the next episode on the Sibyl. Preco appears again as a full character in his own right in play 10, *The Slaughter of the Innocents*, where Herod now names him 'prettye Pratte, my messsingere' (10.41). In the twelfth play, *Doctor* preaches a three-point sermon against gluttony, vainglory, and avarice after the three temptations of Christ. In play 22 on Antichrist's prophets, Expositor's commentary matches the style of the *Ordo prophetarum* (play 5) found in the 1607 manuscript. Consequently, the functional roles of a presenter are not clearly demarcated as extratheatrical in these Chester plays. Although some scholars protest that Preco and Nuntius/Messenger are named precisely to convert them from presenters to full-fledged characters, they still perform the stage-manager/transitional function, while not being hermetically sealed off from the action. Conversely, Expositor and the Doctor, fundamentally the same character, constitute the only interpreter of the plays to the audience. Perhaps Preco originally shared this function, but lost it in the course of the revisions.

Most notably, Expositor in the Chester cycle is more likely to appear as an epiloguist expounding upon the typological significance of the past episode for salvation history than as a prologuist. Occasionally, he narrates omitted action, but if he interprets the action, he does this *after* it has just occurred. The best example occurs when Melchisedek presents a cup of wine and some bread to Abraham as a gift. Expositor expounds the figurative significance of Melchisedek's gifts for the 'unlearned' (4.115) in the audience, as types for the Eucharist that Christ will proffer to mankind in the New Testament. Several more interventions in the same play draw out further significance in the story of Abraham and Isaac; i.e., circumcision is interpreted as a type for baptism (4.189–200) and the obedience of Isaac to his father Abraham as a type for that of Jesus to God (4.460–75). This afterword or final-word style continues in even more baroque detail in play 22 when Expositor interprets the prophecies of Ezechial, Zacharias,

Daniel, and John the Evangelist *after* each specific prophecy, before concluding with the Fifteen Last Signs. Here, the transition from Pentecost to Apocalypse functions along the lines of the *Ordo prophetarum*. Transposed to future time, the prophecies must now impress upon the audience the necessity of being prepared for an imminent Second Coming and Last Judgment. Like *The Mary Play*, Chester plays 4–6 and 12 are all composite plays with several parts. Although Fichte concludes that the English presenter's primary purpose is to create smooth transitions, he still allows for a thematic objective as well, to unite the parts into one continuous *Heilsgeschichte*.[32] This quest for thematic unity has more to do with the literary compilation of a composite text than any theatrical considerations and the resultant didacticism is rather heavy-handed.

Karen Sawyer's scholarship has shed light upon the odd name of the presenter in *The Resurrection of Our Lord*, Appendix, a character similar to the Chester Expositor. Her argument builds upon the research of Alexandra Johnston, which documented a popular parish tradition involving Easter plays on the Burial and Resurrection of Christ in the Thames Valley between 1507 and 1538.[33] These records suggest that the commonest form of Easter Resurrection play in England maintained 'close connections with' the rhythm of Easter liturgical practice.[34] It is such free-standing biblical plays, rather than complete cycles, which should now be considered the English norm for early religious theatre. Within this historical context, Sawyer is able to demonstrate convincingly that what is generally regarded as a sixteenth-century Protestant play (Folger Library MS V.b 192) is actually a reworked version of a conservative Catholic extra-liturgical play, possibly revised between 1543 and 1547.[35] To this end, Appendix is appended, as it were, to the Catholic tradition.

The Protestant revisions are primarily doctrinal, the revised theology being expressed in one long sermon preached by Christ at Emmaus, and in the speeches of Appendix. Unfortunately, the manuscript is fragmented, lacking leaves which would probably have contained a prologue and epilogue at the extreme ends of each of the two days of the play. The first day seems to end with an epilogue, although missing leaves interrupt Appendix's speech after the first ten lines. The next day picks up in the midst of a resurrection appearance of Jesus to Peter. Given the provocative nature of some of Appendix's attacks upon the clergy and contemporary acts of censorship, at least in the archdiocese of York after the Reformation, these missing parts may have contained commentary offensive to the established church.[36] For example, the first intervention by Appendix draws a parallel between the Pharisees (called Bishoppes) and the Doctors of his own time

242   K. Janet Ritch

who attempt to dissuade the laity from reading the scriptures for themselves (l.262).[37] Appendix implies that the bishops of his day are suppressing the truth to the same degree as the high priests and Pharisees in Christ's time, who bribed the soldiers to hush up the Resurrection. Since Appendix even reverses the charge of heresy upon these Doctors and the elite who can read but do not, and then encourages the general laity to read for themselves, one must question Appendix's function as a conventional Doctor (of Theology). His confrontational attitude contrasts sharply with the traditional *doctor theologiae* in York, who customarily preached a sermon on the day following the Feast of Corpus Christi in order to free the feast day itself for the performance of the York cycle.[38] More fittingly, Sawyer associates Appendix with Zwinglian theology and a reformist appropriation of Erasmian ideals.[39]

Like the Chester Expositor, Appendix interprets (or, to be more precise, re-interprets) the episode that has just taken place, but rarely effects transitions, as if he only faced backwards. In other words, Appendix employs the same 'afterword' style as the Chester Expositor. To move the play forward, Appendix tags one line onto the end of his speech, such as 'Nowe marke the progression of the resurrection' (Sawyer, 'Resurrection,' l. 271), 'and soe I nowe commytt you, to the rest which shalbe played' (l. 527) and 'Nowe I will kepe you noe longer. / ffrom ye rest of ye matter' (l. 971). The stage-manager functions of crowd control and cries for silence are almost entirely lacking. In one case, Appendix is defending the power of prayer 'to make Christ tarrye with vs' (l. 965). Previously, he had defended the truth of the Resurrection and Christ's less canonical appearance to Peter. Subsequently, he will explain the 'naturall bodie, after resurrection' (l. 1034). In this way, Appendix is more of an apologist, in the theological sense, than a prologuist or any other kind of presenter. His function thus confirms Carnahan's assertion that the apologetic function of a presenter becomes more pronounced as the tradition develops. Nevertheless, whereas the supposed secularization of the plays in France is thought to account for the phenomenon there, it is the Protestant Reformation in England that best explains the presenter's conversion to apologist. Appendix, like the Chester Expositor, belabours the dramatic action by doubling back in heavy-handed apologetics.

The surviving presenters in the English biblical plays are rather sparse; the majority may well be re-formed replacements for earlier Prologues and Expositors, a modus operandi that the loss of the *originalis* in Chester invites, that the marginalia in the York Register suggests (without supplying the revised text), and that *The Resurrection of Our Lord* confirms. The limited use of such a figure in fifteenth-century biblical plays suggests that, far from constituting the most primitive portion of a composite play or a symptom of 'naive dramaturgy,' these figures were actually added or further developed to bolster intellectual apologies as the Reformation proceeded. Ironically, the number and variety of Shakespeare's presenters, like the neoclassic Choruses in *Romeo and Juliet* and *Henry V*, along with Time in *The Winter's Tale*, and the mock-medieval Gower, the avatar of Chaucer's contemporary in *Pericles*, surpass those of the medieval English biblical plays, at least as far as the records go. Even the presiding deities who present the classical plays of Euripides can hardly be considered naive; rather, they represent an effective staging technique for attracting attention, much as in the York cycle. As far as the extratheatrical speech headings are concerned, Contemplacio strongly suggests a teleological aim to inspire contemplation. Since the Doctors in both N-Town and York function similarly, along the lines of a preacher, this mystical aim for actors and audience alike is effective insofar as it does not put up any barriers, in the form of scepticism, to the collective will to salvation. Nevertheless, the presenter of the English tradition was used most often as a structural device for effecting transitions, especially when disparate episodes were being assembled, re-assembled, or re-interpreted into a composite manuscript.

French Practice

In sharp contrast to the English tradition, the usage of presenters in French analogues is far more systematic, even as it is far more developed with respect to *Heilsgeschichte* or broad theological themes. The function of the French presenter follows a fairly uniform pattern throughout a great many more surviving play texts. Six of the most significant and complete examples represent the usage in the later Middle Ages. Independently, Graham A. Runnalls and Jean-Pierre Bordier have reached an authoritative agreement on the historical context of each of these texts to which the following descriptions adhere.[40]

The two French texts to have originated in the fourteenth century establish patterns which persist into the late Middle Ages. Consistently, the prologues assume the form of a thematic sermon with citations of the theme in Latin and *auctoritates*, divisions of the argument, developments, and exhortations for the whole community to pray together. The epilogues are usually shorter and less systematic. The earliest text is *La Passion de*

Semur, whose composition may date from the beginning of the fourteenth century, although the colophon to the manuscript is dated 1488.[41] The play's division into two days allows salvation history to embrace the period extending from Creation up until the Temptation of Christ in one day; the second covers the public ministry of Jesus, his death, and its aftermath up until his resurrection appearance to Thomas. Each of the two days in this manuscript is introduced by a prologuist who speaks between 150 and 200 lines. The manuscript's opening is defective, but the speech heading for the prologuist of the second day is 'Predicator' (preacher), an attribution which, according to Bordier, was added at a late date.[42] Although the first full statement of the theme (identified later as 'Nunciate ...') is missing in the first prologue, the second prologue displays the full form of a proper sermon on the theme 'Magnus Dominus' with two distinctions. The epilogue to the first day, also lacking a speech heading, is spoken by the messenger (*nuntius* again), who blesses the company before dismissing them. The Parisian manuscript that Runnalls entitles *Le Mystère de la Passion Nostre Seigneur* (also known as the *Mystère Sainte-Geneviève*) has a terminus ante quem of 1440, but a composition dated closer to 1380. Its 4,500 lines belong to one day of performance embracing Christ's Passion and Resurrection. An untitled prologue begins with a sermon text, 'Deus in adjutorium,' taken from Psalm 69. An unmarked epilogue is pronounced by Centurïon, who addresses the audience as *vous,* but then identifies himself with them for the *Te Deum* and closing benediction.[43] The preachers who might be defined as extratheatrical characters introducing the action are never entirely distinct from the intratheatrical characters who conclude these early plays. All address the audience directly.

To these earlier plays may be added the *Mystère de la Résurrection,* performed in Angers in 1456, consisting of nearly 20,000 lines divided into three days of performance. Each day opens with an unidentified presenter pronouncing a sermon, explicitly named, with a different theme in each case. The opening one of 245 lines is the most complex since it introduces the 'Thema pro dictis tribus diebus,' which consists of the three articles of the Creed concerning Christ's Descent into Hell, Resurrection, and Ascension.[44] Every prologue to each of the three days opens with the 'thema' for the day in Latin, leads the whole company (actors and audience) in praying the Pater noster and Ave Maria, and returns to the Latin theme with a translation and amplifications, in a manner similar to the two earlier plays. The first prologue exemplifies the fifteenth-century devotional tone and identifies the presenter with the audience:

Supplicacion et priere
A Dieu Nostre Seigneur et Pere
Qu'il *nous* doint grace de jouer
Ce present jeu pour le louer
Et *nous* pardoint tous les mesfaiz
Qu'*avons* penséz et ditz et faiz,
Et qu'il *nous* doint salvacion
Par le merite et passion
De son seul filz et par sa grace,
Si que le *voyons* face a face.[45]

(Supplication and prayer to God our Lord and Father, that he may give us
grace to play this present play in order to praise him; and that he may
pardon all the misdeeds that we have thought and said and done; and that
he may give us salvation by the merit and passion of his only son, and by
his grace, so that we may see him face to face.)

The *nous* in the first instance clearly signifies the actors themselves, but
subsequently encompasses the entire gathering, so that the plea for forgiveness is made to God on behalf of all. After these homiletic openings, in
all three cases a declaration of the plot about to unfold ensues. Finally, each
of the first two days concludes with a much shorter address to the audience
of about eight lines, reminding the audience to return the next day for
more. Closure of the complete performance is achieved by the traditional
singing of the Te Deum laudamus.

There is a certain ambiguity, however, concerning the identity of the
presenter of the two Epilogues in the Angers *Mystère de la Résurrection*.
At the end of the initial sermon, two further speeches are recorded in
advance of the action to follow: the first to invite the audience to dine mid-
way; the second to provide closure to the whole day's play, as if the same
Prologue were responsible for them all. Yet when one reads fully to the
end of the first day, an alternate ending is provided, to be pronounced, as
the stage directions inform us, by the '*predicator seu ille qui portat
prothocollum*' (the preacher or he who carries the master copy).[46] An
analogous speech at the conclusion of the second day is headed 'Portitor
Libri.'[47] The Presenter in the first instance seems to be assigned to perform
the ensuing stage-manager functions (as both preacher and book carrier),
but then distinguished as one or the other in the second instance, and
finally superseded by the book carrier by the end of the second day.

Supporting documentation for the lost *Mystère de la Passion*, performed at Châteaudun in 1510, itemizes six gold crowns paid to François Souef for having taught a woman to play Mary Magdalene and for having 'servy de protocolle et porté le livre tous les jours que on a joué ledit mistere.'[48] The miniature of Jean Fouquet, which illustrates a saint's play entitled 'Martyrdom of Saint Apollonia' in the *Livre d'Heures d'Étienne Chevalier*, is thought to reveal such a *protocolle* at work with his baton in the midst of a round theatre, conducting the performance.[49] Without entering into any debate over the referent of the baton wielder in Étienne Chevalier's *Book of Hours*, we must note the overlap in the speech headings between a priest and a book carrier.[50] The latter is just as likely to function as a prompter as a stage manager.

The family of plays identified by Runnalls as Arras-Gréban-Michel-Valenciennes formed a tradition that thrived from 1430 to 1553. The first three texts in this list all claim identifiable authors, in sharp contrast to the anonymity of their predecessors and the English tradition. All three were designed for a four-day performance of between 25,000 and 30,000 lines. The earliest of these great Passion plays is the *Mystère de la Passion d'Arras*, which was very likely written by Eustache Mercadé (ca.1380–1440) for performance in Arras or an urban centre in the vicinity.[51] The entire play focuses upon the life of Jesus from the Annunciation to Pentecost, although the popular Parliament in Heaven, set outside historical time, frames this plot like a pair of bookends. Mercadé states his opening and closing themes at the very beginning; 'A summo celo egressio ejus et occursus ejus usque ad summum ejus' (Psalm 19:6) is translated by the Preacher and divided into two parts to distinguish the descending grace of God ('A summo celo egressio ejus') from the final Ascension ('occursus ejus usque ad summum ejus') for application to both ends of the four days:

Du souverain de tous les cieulx
Venra Dieu en nature humaine,
Puis apres vray homme et vray dieux
S'en rira en son hault demaine

(From the highest of all the heavens, God will come in human form; then true man and very God, he will laugh it off afterwards in his high domain)[52]

The same two themes are recapitulated in the epilogue, which likewise constitutes, rather unusually for France, a closing sermon. Reminiscent of Troilus after Criseyde's betrayal in Chaucer's portrayal of their affair, God sits laughing in heaven after performing the double movement of grace (descending and ascending), as demonstrated by the entire *Passion*.

Each of the four days in the Arras text, except the second, opens with a prologuist identified as 'Le Prescheur.' Every Preacher develops a sermon on a theme given in Latin, repeated twice, with a translation in French only after the second statement of the subject. Usually the Preacher states the *auctoritas* for his interpretation at this point as well. In place of the Preacher on the second day, this same homiletic opening is performed by John the Baptist, a fully integrated character, on the theme *Pentitentiam agite*.[53] Finally, the Preacher concludes each day, apart from the second, with a much shorter transitional reminder of the next day's play, in a fashion similar to that described for the 'Portitor Libri' at Angers. In order to bring the second day to closure, Pilate and the First Jew of Jerusalem discuss the need to dine, while deferring the sentence of Jesus until the following day – a clever double play between the action on stage and in the audience. The exceptional second day, consequently, proves to be most significant through the simplicity of the substitution of John the Baptist for the so-called extratheatrical Preacher. If an embedded sermon by a fully intratheatrical character causes neither disruption nor cognitive dissonance, why should the regular prologuist delivering a sermon in similar fashion cause any disruptive scepticism?

Arnoul Gréban borrowed the structure of the Arras *Passion* with some innovations, but few, if any, textual echoes. His text is preserved in eight deluxe manuscripts, the earliest dating from 1457. However, its composition is usually ascribed to ca. 1450 because the aldermen of Abbeville bought a copy of it in 1452 for a performance there. Although the introduction to this entire *mystère* is identified by Carnahan as a double prologue, it is far more complicated than that.[54] Before the prologue to the first day of the play proper, there is an Old Testament sequence of four short episodes, entitled by the editor 'Lucifer's Rebellion,' 'The Fall of Adam and Eve,' 'Cain's Crime,' and the 'Death of Adam.'[55] When the first day's play finally opens with a substantial prologue of over 200 lines, a sermon on the text 'Veni ad liberandum nos,' it introduces a Parliament of Heaven, which in turn acts as a kind of introduction to the Annunciation. The four initial episodes, most of which begin with their own Prologue, are still considered one prologue to the main prologue of the first day. The second day deals with Christ's ministry. The third deals with the Crucifixion; the fourth with the Resurrection. With one exception, every day begins with an unidentified prologuist pronouncing a sermon with its own distinct theme based on a Latin quotation with repetitions, then translations and citations of authoritative sources, in the same manner as all former prologuists. Only the third day opens with a transitional prologue recapitulating the action of the previous day before foretelling that to come. What Gréban adds to his prologues, beyond those of Arras, is an opening prayer that ends with an invitation to say the rosary – Ave Maria - in every case. This is a pattern found likewise in the early *Passion de Semur*. All four days of Gréban's play end with a short transitional address to the audience as usual, but in the first three cases it is pronounced by 'l'Acteur.' The last twenty-seven lines, containing a plea for forgiveness under the oxymoronic title of *Prologue Final et Total*, conclude traditionally with the Te Deum. Unfortunately, the double meaning of 'Acteur' as both author and actor contributes to another unresolved ambiguity.[56]

Jean Michel proves to be the most original reviser. No manuscript of the text survives, but the fact that *Le Mystère de la Passion* it was published seventeen times in Paris from 1486 to 1542 attests to the popularity of the play. Characteristic of Michel's formal style is his focus upon an even shorter period of salvation history that eliminates both the Creation and Fall and the Resurrection. The entire play opens with a 'Prologue Capital' in the established form of a sermon and ends with a brief 'Prologue Final' of seven lines encouraging everyone to hold Christ's Passion in remembrance ('la passion de Jesuschrist, / ayons en recordacion').[57] The introductory sermon of 888 lines is so lengthy that it may have been intended only for the reading public buying the printed editions rather than for performance. Nevertheless, the format follows the general pattern set by Mercadé and Gréban. Michel's prologuist states the theme right away, 'Verbum caro factum est' (John 1:14), followed immediately by a loose translation and an invocation to Mary with the Ave Maria. After a restatement of the theme, he makes a division into four parts for each word in the Latin text. Within these divisions, there are further distinctions. The discussion generally revolves around the mysteries of the Trinity and Incarnation with the last word 'est' being related to the eternity and self-sufficiency of God. The word 'factum' is underdeveloped in the sermon, since it is to be portrayed extensively by the play:

En ensuyvant l'ordre promis,
le tiers mot du tesme premis,
c'est *factum*, denotant en somme
les fais de Jesus en tant que homme ...

(Following the promised order, the third word of the theme put forward is *factum*, basically denoting the deeds of Jesus as a man ...)[58]

Perhaps a clearer indication that this first sermon was optional during performance is the actual opening of the first day with a second formal sermon by John the Baptist on 'Parate viam Domini' (Matt. 3:3), involving a repetition of the theme and division into two parts. Less faithful to the Gospels, less learned and less rhetorical than his predecessor, in his own time period Michel nevertheless surpassed Gréban in the popular imagination.[59] Popular does not necessarily mean secular, however, since the 'Prologue Capital' still takes the form of a sermon, and there is no dearth of homiletic and theological material throughout.

In sum, these exemplary plays follow an established pattern of presentation as prologue and epilogue at the outer ends of the production and often between days. Since it may function primarily to effect the transition to the next day and is easily performed by a fully intratheatrical character, closure is not as systematic as the *ouverture*. All addresses to the audience as *vous* (plural) are complemented by an oscillating first person singular and plural pronoun. Even when the presenter uses *nous* instead of *je*, he may mean 'we the company of actors' as opposed to 'you who have assembled to experience the performance.' But this use of *nous* slides in and out of total identification between actors and audience alike, especially when the presenter is addressing supplications to God. If the prologuist is named specifically, it is usually as a Preacher ('Predicator' in Semur; 'Prescheur' in the Arras *Passion*). Unspecified prologues can safely be accredited to the same figure, since all the introductory presenters preach an opening sermon in more or less canonical form: presentation of the theme in Latin, a brief invocation to Mary, restatement of the theme with development in French, and a closing prayer.[60]

It is not safe to assume that the same extratheatrical figure closes the play as opens it, since closure in these plays is assigned variously to the 'Portitor Libri' (Angers *Résurrection*), 'Le Messaigier' (*Passion de Semur*), or the 'Acteur' (Gréban's *Mystère de la Passion*). Like the Messenger (4.484 ff.) and Preco in the Chester cycle, these figures never pronounce a sermon. They mainly inform the audience that the play has momentarily ended, to be resumed after the mid-day meal or on the following day. Sometimes, nevertheless, introductory and closing functions can be performed by characters fully integrated into the plot, such as John the Baptist (Arras *Passion*), Centurïon (*Passion de Sainte-Geneviève*), and the imaginative dialogue at the end of Mercadé's second day. The only *Passion* clearly opened and closed by the Preacher, so named consistently in the speech headings, is the *Mystère de la Passion* from Arras.

In contrast to the sporadic outbursts of presenters in the English tradition, the regularity of the French tradition is quite striking. While all the

French prologuists preach thematic sermons, the tone of these homilies is never really apologetic (in the theological sense), just as no such preacher (doctor or expositor) ever employs the afterword style of the Chester cycle and *The Resurrection of Our Lord*. Endings are usually pragmatic rather than expository, promoting transitions, whether by intra- or extratheatrical characters. Jean Michel, in particular, uses techniques for grabbing the attention of his audience most resembling those found in the York cycle. One wonders if the English plays were ever as uniform and consistent before the Reformation as the French *mystères*.

The Actual Profession of the French Presenter

English scholars have understandably assumed, without much concrete evidence, that the clergy of the Middle Ages wrote and possibly performed the biblical plays. Both external documentation and the extant texts themselves are scant in comparison with the French tradition, whose medieval theatre was less subject to the iconoclastic impulses and censorship of Protestant reformers. In this light, the French records serve to better elucidate the possible complexities of interaction between author, priest, stage manager, prompter, and actor.[61]

Given the predominant use of presenters as prologuists in the French tradition, it is no wonder that David Carnahan entitled his survey *The Prologue*. Within this context, he felt no obligation to distinguish the prologuists from those who pronounced the epilogues, nor resolve the question of whether the author, or an actor, or a priest 'not a member of the company' (i.e., metatheatrical) pronounced the prologue. To dismiss the first immediately, it seems unlikely that the author would be present to pronounce his own prologues. The three French authors, whose names are known, very rapidly lost control of their texts. Mercadé's overriding conception was borrowed more successfully by Gréban, and Gréban, in turn, was overshadowed by Michel. Perhaps these authors were present at the first performance of their own particular versions of the *Passion*, but it seems unlikely that the last two authors, at least, could keep up with subsequent performances. Gréban was working in Paris, for example, when his *mystère* was performed in Abbeville, and in Italy when his two days, incorporated into Michel's *Passion*, were performed in Paris in 1490 and 1498.[62] Michel himself was in Angers at the time of these earlier performances and was actually dead when the last Parisian performance of his text took place in 1507. Furthermore, continuations of their work performed throughout the first half of the sixteenth century owe the majority of their material to the latter two authors; i.e., performances in Amiens (1500), Mons (1501), Amboise (1507), Châteaudun (1510), and Valenciennes (1547, 1549). Finally, the three authors are quite exceptional in the celebrity that has become attached to their names. For the majority of performances throughout France, the names of the authors are not known. Sometimes the scribe who copied or compiled a manuscript is known, as in the case of Jehan Floichot, whose status as either scribe or author of the *Passion of Semur* remains ambiguous. French theatre historians like Raymond Lebègue, Maurice Acarie, Madeleine Lazard, and Graham A. Runnalls have adopted the term *fatiste* (maker of the text) in place of our modern notion of a unique author, in order to leave as indeterminate the precise degree of authorship between that of an originator and a pure scribe (*copiste*).[63] Just as authors are often indistinguishable from scribes, so priests are not necessarily distinguishable from either authors or actors. In the final analysis, the author, the priest, and the actor, whether separate or all rolled into one, were far less significant than the Catholic tradition that accounted for the texts in the first place. Every contributor to the performance was conscious of participating in a tradition that was far greater than him- or (more rarely) herself. In this light, the prologuist is less likely to express the voice of the individual author than a collective persona, *nous*, whose referent is the whole Catholic tradition of the living and the dead.

More recently, Charles Mazouer has reversed Carnahan's assumption that the priestly Prologue was responsible for the epilogue in favour of the *protocolle* performing the prologue. He interprets the role of the book carrier as that of an impresario or presider, who would direct the special effects, act as prompter, and open the play with a sermon. Mazouer assumes not only that the same person pronounced the epilogue as the prologue, but that this *meneur de jeu* was as 'omniprésent sur la scène' as God.[64] The iconography in Jehan Fouquet's miniature, discussed above, supports this interpretation. But do the texts? In those selected for this survey, the name of the prologuist usually changes when the day arrives at its end. Sermons are preached most often by Preachers, but stage business and crowd control is usually handled by the actors, messengers, or a 'Portitor Libri.' A change in the name of a speech heading could signify a modification in function rather than a change in character. The priest preaching the opening sermon might well be functioning simultaneously as the *meneur de jeu*, especially when there is evidence to suggest that the latter controlled both the text and the production, as both director and stage manager.[65] In any case, the priest's sacramental status would be more likely to prevail over a secular *meneur de jeu* for the prologue-sermon.

Supportive documentation from the region around northern France might shed light on the question of whether a priest (preacher) or lay actor pronounced the prologue. In 1925, Gustave Cohen published the director's copy of the eight-day 1501 performance of the Mons Passion play, which remains a rich mine of information. The actual play text in this case was borrowed from Amiens after a successful four-day performance there of the previous year. In Amiens, the players had performed mornings and afternoons; this schedule was distilled by the aldermen of Mons into eight half days of performance. Among the documentation discovered in the Archives Communales de Mons in 1856 was a *Livre des Prologues* which specifies all the opening and closing presentations (all called prologues) for the eight days of performance, plus six more to be inserted between the principal episodes of the first day. Almost all of these prologues were newly composed material for the expanded performance in Mons. The first day opened with eighty-four lines borrowed from the prologue to Michel's *Mystère de la Passion,* supplemented with sixty-five lines of a more local flavour; the second and third prologues of the first day are drawn from Gréban.[66] Cohen published an abridged version of these prologues in a style similar to the *Abregiet* (first and last lines only) of the director's copy. The opening is worth quoting again:

Le Predicateur
tenant mode de docteur, sus quelque montignete
ou en kayere de verité, et de là ne bougera jusques
tous les prologues par lui proferéz ...

(The Preacher in the style of a teacher of church doctrine, upon some small dias or in a pulpit of truth; and he will not budge from there until all the prologues have been pronounced by him ...)[67]

In other words, as Graham Runnalls points out, the prologuist appears on stage dressed as a learned preacher for the entire eight days of performance. But the evidence does not end there. Turning to the first day of the *Abregiet* itself, the same 'Prologuer' is listed with the name of the actor who played him, one 'Sire Gille le Naing, prestre.'[68] Consequently, at Mons at least, a priest seems to have pronounced not only the introductory prologue, but all further transitional prologues up to and including the

'Prologue Final.' In this famous case, the prologuist was definitely a priest, presiding omnipresently over the entire performance.

Moreover, the clergy were generally involved as full-fledged actors as well as presenters. Sire Gille le Naing is not the only priest involved in the production; 'sire Jehan de Bruxelles, prêtre' took over the role of God from 'Maistre Jehan de Neelle,' a bachelor in theology of the Franciscan Order whose real preaching, he complained, suffered because he was spending all his time learning his lines. Another cleric, Messire Maisnart, canon of Saint-Germain in Mons, played the lighter role of Mary Magdalene.[69] At Amboise, the priest was paid 8 'livres Tournois' to play Jesus.[70] Cohen himself comments that 'habitués à la parole, à la "mémorisation" et à la récitation de leurs sermons, ils étaient les mieux préparés à assumer les tâches les plus lourdes.'[71] Even in the sixteenth century, this period of so-called secularization, the total involvement of the clergy is unequivocal. These clergy did not present the plays to the less-learned, looking down in a patronizing way; they shared the sins of the secular world by participating on the same level as the amateur actors.

The evidence for a certain uniformity in the French tradition of prologues and epilogues, as well as clerical involvement, is bolstered by newly published material from Lille, thanks to Alan E. Knight, the editor of the Wolfenbüttel manuscript.[72] In Lille, a dramatic competition evolved in conjunction with, not a Corpus Christi procession, but a Marian procession instituted by Marguerite de Flandre in 1270. The dramatic tradition was fully developed by 1431, to last on and off until 1565. The short plays usually average around 500 lines, open with 'Prologue' and end with a similarly unimaginative speech heading, 'La Fin.' As in the *mystères* of Gréban, Michel, and Mons, the semantic range of the prologue is not restricted to the etymological roots of the word in Greek ($\pi\rho\acute{o}$ + $\lambda o\gamma o\varsigma$, literally 'foreword'), but applies throughout the play. Most surprisingly, from the evidence of one of the earliest *mystères* of the Lille collection, *Elijah's Transportation to Heaven* (*L'enlèvement d'Élie au ciel*) which has no prologue or epilogue of any kind, it appears that the presenter, far from being the most primitive portion of a 'naive dramaturgy,' was a later addition to this tradition.[73]

At Lille, the role of the Prologue is best explained as structural, since these dramatized verse translations (in the medieval sense) necessitate much clipping and trimming to fit the ungainly biblical narratives, especially Old Testament ones, into the restricted space on top of a pageant wagon. Even the initial prologue has more of a structural function than a thematic one; the Lille tradition has not engendered thematic sermons for presenters. Intermediary prologues often apologize directly to the audience for excluding part of the biblical narrative in order to advance the plot. All the prologues commonly cite a biblical or exegetical source for the play, provide background to the narrative, and foretell the plot, occasionally with a moral lesson. The procedure of 'La Fin' is often similar in reverse, by supplying any further information required to bring about closure to the plot and drawing a moral lesson. This 'Fin' may also cite a source and close with a prayer on behalf of all. It seems most likely that all these presentations to the audience are made by the same actor.

These prologues, especially the initial ones, furnish quite a lot of contextual information, including about ten references to clerical involvement in both the composition and performance of the plays. On one notable occasion, the initial prologuist is even identified as 'Le Prescheur' (play 8). On other occasions, the prologues refer to one or more clerics who have chosen the biblical source of the play, and sometimes associate themselves with those who made the selections by using the pronoun *nous*. As Knight points out, the very short prologue to the play *David et Bethsabée* (play 24) suggests that the clerics themselves are going to perform the entire play.[74] Further allusions to the Latin texts of their sources likewise necessitate clerical involvement and suggest that the authors, and perhaps some or most of the performers, were trained at the collegiate church of Saint-Pierre, the only school that taught Latin in Lille.[75] As in the episodic English tradition, these preachers were probably less dependent upon a prompter ('Portitor Libri') than the ones previously discussed, because of the relative brevity of the plays. However, the strong suggestion that priest-presenters overlapped with clerical actors and authors confirms clerical involvement in these aspects of the performance.

In light of the clerical involvement in the authorship, presentation, and performance of the northern French plays, it seems likely that the English clergy followed suit, at least in the same pre-Reformation ecclesiastical system. Speech headings in the English plays, like the Doctor (of Theology) in both Chester and York, the N-Town Contemplacio 'in doctorys wede,' and possibly Preco at one time, suggest this. Whether or not the northern French tradition has implications for the English practice, the evidence for productions in Mons and Lille suggests that the clergy performed both extra- and intratheatrical roles without any apparent cause for self-consciousness. In a sense, the daily roles of the priest in real life demanded that he represent the redeemer in a kind of imitation that he could never set aside. This reality would not change on the medieval stage.

The priest's aim in addressing the audience in performance would never have been to attract attention to himself or deliberately distract it, since the shared goal was the Catholic will to salvation for the community. The priests were unlikely even to be conscious of creating illusion; they aimed at a higher reality and significance to life. In this theatrical tradition, where illusion was not an end in itself, there was no purpose in breaking it to alienate the audience.

The Uniqueness of the Presenter to Medieval Theatre

Prologues were a feature of all communal, oral performance, and 'drama was but one extreme of [the entire] spectrum of methods of presentation of literary material.'[76] On Runnall's list of such presentational genres are the chansons de geste, which were declaimed, lyric poems performed to accompaniment, and romances recited for living audiences. The long prologues to the chansons de geste, as Daniel Poirion has described them, confronted their audiences with a façade-like majesty as familiar, imposing, and awesome as that of the Gothic cathedral.[77] This list could be supplemented by the Vitae, the short legends of the saints in verse form that were sung in churches or monastic refectories on the relevant feast days or recited on pilgrimages or in any public space by jongleurs or clerici vagantes from as early as the twelfth century.[78] Their formulaic prologues, appealing for silence and attention, claiming the absolute veracity of their sources, and blessing the audience greatly resemble those proclaimed in their dramatic analogues. Since Brian Stock coined the term 'textual communities' to describe the complex interplay between the litterati and illitterati in the Middle Ages, scholars have developed the idea that the texts were often performed orally for the benefit of the community. This process became most complex when the reader interpreted a Latin text into the vernacular for a popular audience, as also occurred, in like circumstances, with sermons.[79]

Two factors might account for the ubiquity of the prologue in medieval literature. The first is the use of rhetorical textbooks in the schools that required opening addresses to the audience within a strict set of textual divisions; these texts were written by authors ranging from Roman antiquity, like Cicero and the anonymous author of the Rhetorica ad Herennium, to Isidore of Seville and John of Garland. The second factor is the necessity to couch old stories, familiar to all, in a new light. Whether they named it exordium, proemium, proem, or prologue, all the manuals on rhetoric advised orators, poets, or other authors to open with a direct address to prepare the listener's (or reader's) mind to be attentive and well-disposed. The brief summary of the case and promise of new and unusual material in the classic exordium gave rise to the propensity for laying out the plot in advance. To the same end, preachers stated the theme for their sacred sermons.[80]

Sermons were delivered orally on a great variety of occasions and committed to written form for diverse reasons. Monastic sermons, for example, could be delivered in the refectory or in the chapter house, or communicated through letters or treatises.[81] Consequently, all sermons cannot be considered liturgical in the strict sense, that is, linked to a *lectio* for a Sunday or feast day specified by the liturgical calendar. The Latin term *sermo*, as opposed to its Greek equivalent (from which the term homily derives), was originally a common word for any speech or discourse. It follows that some early lectures delivered in the incipient universities were also classified as sermons and that some of these became traditional there on formal occasions. Furthermore, collections of patristic sermons from the twelfth and thirteenth centuries were studied as models on campus as they had been in the monastic schools, whereas newly composed sermons in such a setting fell under the influence of scholasticism and its formal disputation. It is the latter university or thematic sermon that is most relevant to the presenters in the French *mystère*. Thematic preaching was based upon a scriptural text or quotation from a patristic authority called a *thema*, which was first pronounced in Latin and then translated into the vernacular.[82] One Aquinas tract in regular use in France advised the preacher to take his theme from the Bible. The quotation was to be neither too short nor too long, but to be complete in meaning and fit for oral delivery. This theme had always to be pronounced first in Latin, then translated into the vernacular in precisely the same style as found in both the English and French plays. Remarkably, none of the English presenters preaches a truly thematic sermon, although the Chester Doctor in the twelfth play on the Temptation of Christ comes the closest to it by citing St Gregory and making a thematic division for the three sins of Adam prefiguring the three temptations of Christ. However, even here, there is no Latin *thema* and translation, in conformity with the lack of explicit references to either sermons or themes in the discourse of the other English presenters. The French Prologues, on the other hand, all preach thematic sermons, regularly making explicit references to their speeches as sermons and their topics as themes.

It is difficult to account for the difference in taste between the homiletic Prologues in France and the less formal exegeses of the English presenters.

The controlling influence of the Faculty of Theology in Paris may have played some part in preserving the thematic sermon in France. When Jean Vitrier (d. 1516), for example, attempted to break with the thematic tradition, the Faculty of Theology prohibited him from preaching for three years and later confined him to a convent.[83] In England, the licensing of preachers and the translation of the Bible were topical issues throughout the fourteenth century. Already in 1281, the Council of the Province of Canterbury had promulgated Canon 9, the *Ignorantia sacerdotum* of Archbishop Pecham, which restricted unbeneficed clergy (parish priests and chaplains) from preaching anything but the catechism: the Creed, the Ten Commandments, the seven sacraments, virtues and vices. The theological content of Contemplacio in the N-Town *Mary Play*, which is particularly catechetical, might be connected to such scruples, although his Pater noster and Ave Maria, just as popular in the French *mystères*, were not required by the canon.[84] In 1407, Arundel's Constitutions reiterated this restriction and prohibited translation of even short citations from the Bible. The latter prohibition was difficult to enforce, since the embittered preachers side-stepped it by translating their texts orally for their immediate public, leaving no trace of it in written form.[85] The biblical plays, nevertheless, exhibit no such inhibitions with respect to short citations from the Latin Vulgate in the manuscripts. Marianne Briscoe holds that the homiletic content and style of these plays could have been readily adopted by anyone, regardless of whether they were licensed to preach or not.[86] Both content and style are less formal than those found in the French analogues. It is true that John Clerke was monitoring the content of the plays in sixteenth-century York, but he represented the civic authorities, not a theological institution. In contrast, the involvement of the clergy in the authorship, presentation, and oversight of the Lille and Mons plays exemplifies the high level of ecclesiastical control in the French tradition. Therefore, ecclesiastical supervision of the biblical plays seems to have been more relaxed in England than in France, as reflected in the texts of the respective presenters.

Until the Reformation, the curriculum on homiletics was practically a fixed canon. The sermon collections that circulated served not only as models for imitation but also as a practical resource. With no concept of plagiarism, preachers saw nothing wrong with re-using the great works of past preachers.[87] The popularity and accessibility of the classical sermons would account for local imitators and interpreters of the Advent homily by St Bernard, which inspired the dramatized Parliament of Heaven, and the pseudo-Augustinian sermon, which gave rise to the *Ordo prophetarum*, both commonly dramatized to effect the significant transition between the Old and New Testaments.[88] The Chester Expositor's predilection for typology and figurative interpretation best suits this medieval paradigm and suggests that his contributions to five plays are the decaying remnants of a practice dating from pre-Reformation times. Nevertheless, the entire homiletic tradition was called into question at the Reformation. In 1542 Bishop Bonner of London warned the clergy under his authority to 'rehearse no sermons made by other men within this two or three hundred years.'[89] In France, from 1535 onwards the scholastic or thematic sermon was threatened with extinction; by 1550 it was dead.[90] The French *mystères* seem to have died with it, at least in Paris where the people were not only more literate, but also more tightly controlled by both the Faculty of Theology and the Parliament of Paris. In rural areas, the Catholic tradition was more tenacious.

Despite their differences, the oral delivery of sermons in both France and England rivalled and often complemented the popularity of the biblical plays. At the end of the Middle Ages in France, Passion sermons were particularly popular, perhaps as a direct result of the dramatized *Mystères de la Passion*.[91] Likewise in England, preaching was considered popular entertainment, as much under the Tudors as previously.[92] The very fact that the York plays, performed on the Feast of Corpus Christi, won out over the sermon, which was preached *in crastino* of the feast day, suggests that the two genres were linked closely together. Chaucer's Wife of Bath bears satirical witness to the same ethos when her 'housbonde was at Londoun al that Lente [giving her] the bettre leyser for to pleye, / and for to se, and eek for to be seye.'[93] In her own rather overbearing Prologue, she goes on to list the entertainments she sought:

> Therefore I made my visitaciouns
> To vigiles and to processiouns,
> To prechyng eek, and to thise pilgrimages,
> To pleyes of myracles, and to mariages ...   (ll. 555–8)

The 'prechyng' that the Wife of Bath frequented ought to be equated with the 'pleyes of myracles' she enjoyed as popular entertainment. This tradition, popular in both France and England, enjoyed a continuity which only the Reformation would disrupt.

Within the local parish church, the common people would have been most accustomed to listening to sermons, where they still faced many barriers to full participation in the Mass. When one considers that the medieval liturgy was still conducted in Latin, that the words of consecration that the priest pronounced in the Mass were spoken to God at the altar with his back to the congregation, and that, before the English Reformation and the Council of Trent (1545–63), the public's view was likely blocked by a rood screen, one appreciates better the sense of inclusion that the people must have experienced when the priest finally faced the congregation and addressed them in their own language in front of the rood screen.[94] This liturgical sermon broke down barriers rather than erecting them. Consequently, a presenter, prologue, epilogue, or intermediary commentator, dressed in 'doctour's wedes' to pronounce a sermon would arouse the same engagement, interest, and sense of inclusion as that evoked by the preacher of the parish church. In both cases, the veil of mystery was lifted to admit a fuller comprehension of the Christian truth.

In this light, the actor or priest playing a priest was hardly metatheatrical. These presenters, introductory or explanatory figures, constituted the foundation upon which the plays were built. Priests were not only the first expositors; they were likely the last as well, at least in France. They never had to set aside their impersonation to address the audience since, in many cases, as priests in real life they were already what they were impersonating and, in any case, the actor most fittingly furthered the impersonation when, as a priest, he addressed the audience directly. Janus-like, the presenters effected transitions between awkward episodes or disparate material from various sources, with one head foreseeing the coming plot and the other interpreting what had just occurred. As seen above, the structural function of effecting transitions was the one preferred for the official presenter in the English biblical plays. The foreword-looking head in this metaphor would seem to be Catholic, whereas the backward-looking afterword style is Protestant. Distanced from their traditional roles, both Appendix and the Chester Expositor were themselves alienated by the Reformation from the affective piety (and effective theatre) of the late Middle Ages. The warm and welcoming introduction to the French *mystères* recoils to an 'afterword' distance in these Protestant revisions.

We can safely assume that sermons were as popular in England as in France and the Netherlands, but the English plays seem to have escaped close ecclesiastical surveillance, as the middle-class merchants of the later Middle Ages assumed control of them. In the French *mystères*, the evidence for ecclesiastical creation, control, and participation is overwhelming in comparison. Furthermore, these French- and Latin-speaking clerics were often, if not connected with a university or some such institution of higher learning, then controlled by one. Such a situation would account for the university or thematic sermons found in all of the French plays (apart from Lille) from the early fourteenth century onwards. When every facet of public lifestyle, in both sacred and secular society, was already highly theatrical, it is difficult to imagine space for anything extra-theatrical.

Epilogue

Medieval culture was a richly interwoven tapestry of overlapping genres. The late medieval biblical plays were replete with prayers like the Ave Maria or the Pater noster, and the catechetical or thematic sermon. The continental evidence strongly suggests that priests played themselves and other characters, even while writing, directing, and stage managing the plays. The more standard practice on the continent might have been reflected in England before the Reformation, yet diversity must also have been the rule everywhere. Without further documentary evidence, such ambiguities as those between actor and author, or scribe, priest and player cannot be definitively resolved. Authors, nevertheless, never wrote these plays in the modern sense, but merely dramatized the biblical and theological traditions with which their audiences were already fully conversant. Within the range of functions ascribed to the presenter in the French tradition, the opening speech which explicated the mysteries was more significant than any other, since it constituted the end (the alpha and omega) at which their productions aimed. The whole purpose of the performance was to reduce the distance between itself and the signified reality, to reconcile the community to God rather than alienate it further. In the Catholic context before 1550, the presenter who opened with a sermon or aided transitions was unlikely to cause any member of the audience to recoil in momentary scepticism.

   Like the ghosts of Freud and Marx, the spirit of Bertolt Brecht continues to brood upon the waters. In 1989, Michel Mourlet wrote in his *Thaumaturgie du théâtre ou l'anti-Brecht* that after forty years and despite much opposition, the currency of Brecht had become permanent in France.[95] Influenced by documentary films as much as by Chinese theatre, Brecht's Alienation Effect sought to reveal the written dramatic 'script as of a different conceptual order than the theater event containing it.'[96] Placed in such simple terms, Brecht's purpose is totally incompatible with the ethos of the Middle Ages in which ritual and theatre, the secular and the sacred, orality and literacy, the stage and everyday reality were fully intertwined. The world needs such community and continuity in place of exclusive boundaries and alienation.

NOTES

I would like to express my gratitude to Alexandra F. Johnston for initiating me into the mysteries of medieval drama, and to members of the Northrop Frye Centre at Victoria College, University of Toronto, to JoAnna Dutka, and to the two patient editors of this volume, David Klausner and especially Karen Sawyer Marsalek, for offering valuable advice.

1 John R. Elliott Jr, *Playing God: Medieval Mysteries on the Modern Stage* (Toronto: University of Toronto Press, 1989), 127; Robert Potter, *The English Morality Play: Origins, History and Influence of a Dramatic Tradition* (London and Boston: Routledge and Kegan Paul, 1975), 32ff.

2 Hans-Jürgen Diller, *The Middle English Mystery Play: A Study in Dramatic Speech and Form* (1973; Cambridge: Cambridge University Press, 1992), 112. Brecht classed medieval with classical theatre, since both 'alienated [their] characters by making them wear human or animal masks,' but admitted that the 'social aim of these old devices were entirely different from our own' (John Willett, *Brecht on Theatre: The Development of an Aesthetic* [1957; London: Methuen, 1964], 'Short Organon,' sect. 42, 192).

3 Brecht uses his own term *Verfremdungseffekt* in this tract, originally written in 1940 but not published until 1951 (Willett, *Brecht on Theatre*, 147).

4 It is remarkable that scholarship cannot arrive at a working definition for what distinguishes drama from the liturgy, or from other forms of play or literary genres. My own preference is for this compromise between Karl Young's definition (*The Drama of the Medieval Church* [Oxford: Oxford University Press, 1933], 80 ff.), and that of Lynette Muir (*The Biblical Drama of Medieval Europe* [Cambridge: Cambridge University Press, 1995], 4) quoting Richard Southern, *The Seven Ages of the Theatre*. Southern reduced the theatre, similarly, to two essentials: 'the Player and the Audience' (Muir, *Biblical Drama*, 181, note 13). Cf. also Diller, *Middle English Mystery Play*, 9, who thought in similar terms.

5 Martin Stevens, 'Illusion and Reality in Medieval Drama,' *College English* 32 (1971): 454; cited by Ralph J. Blasting, 'Metatheatrical Elements in the *Künzelsauer Fronleichnamsspiel*,' *Momentum Dramaticum*, ed. Linda Dietrick (Waterloo: University of Waterloo Press, 1989), 98.

6 Blasting, 'Metatheatrical Elements,' 93–5.

7 Alexandra F. Johnston, 'The Feast of Corpus Christi in the West Country,' *Early Theatre* 6.1 (2003): 15–18, Alexandra F. Johnston and Margaret Rogerson, eds, *York*, REED (Toronto: University of Toronto Press, 1979), 1:xv, citing BL Add MS 35290 and Lucy Toulmin Smith, the initial editor of

The York Plays.

8 David Hobart Carnahan, *The Prologue in the Old French and Provençal Mystery* (New York: Haskell House, 1966); Jörg O. Fichte, *Expository Voices in Medieval Drama: Essays on the Mode and Function of Dramatic Exposition*, Erlanger Beiträge zur Sprach- und Kunstwissenschaft 53 (Nürnberg: Hans Carl, 1975).

9 Carnahan, *Prologue*, 7.

10 Graham A. Runnalls, *Les mystères dans les provinces françaises (en Savoie et en Poitou, – Amiens et à Reims)* (Paris: Honoré Champion, 2003), 14 (my translation).

11 Carnahan, *Prologue*, 9.

12 Diller, *Middle English Mystery Play*, 16.

13 Carnahan, *Prologue*, 9; Diller, *Middle English Mystery Play*, 121.

14 Carnahan, *Prologue*, 7; Fichte, *Expository Voices*, 77.

15 Simon Goldhill, 'The Language of Tragedy: Rhetoric and Communication,' in *The Cambridge Companion to Greek Tragedy*, ed. P.E. Easterling (Cambridge: Cambridge University Press, 1997), 128; Carnahan *Prologue*, 105–7.

16 Euripides, *Bacchae*, tr. David Kovaks (Cambridge, MA: Harvard University Press, 2002), 13.

17 All quotations by pageant and line numbers are from R.M. Lumiansky and David Mills, eds, *The Chester Mystery Cycle*, vol. 1, EETS ss 3 (London: Oxford University Press, 1974), and Richard Beadle, ed., *The York Plays* (London: Edward Arnold, 1982).

18 Martin Stevens and A.C. Cawley, eds, *The Towneley Plays*, vol. 1, EETS ss 13 (London: Oxford University Press, 1994), xxvii. Evidence of an indenture in the Mercers' Pageant Documents for 27 February 1454, in letters laying out the conditions by which the parish clerk of Leeds and two citizens of York could produce York's Judgment Play (*domysday*), suggests that similar indentures were drawn up for all five borrowings in the *Towneley* plays from York (Johnston and Rogerson, *York*, 1:87).

19 Fichte, *Expository Voices*, 98.

20 Alexandra F. Johnston, 'The York Corpus Christi Play: A Dramatic Structure Based on Performance Practice,' in *The Theatre in the Middle Ages*, ed. Herman Braet, Johan Nowé, Gilbert Tournoy (Leuven: Leuven University Press, 1985), 369.

21 I am passing over the *Poeta* who plays a conventional role in the Digby *Killing of the Children* and *The Conversion of St Paul* since these are single episodes or saint's plays rather than sequences analagous to the French Passion plays which I am considering. Likewise, the Doctor who pronounces

the epilogue to the Brome *Sacrifice of Isaac*, with a rather shocking interpretation, is also omitted from this discussion. In any case, the latter's afterword function does not differ from that of the Chester Expositor.

22 *The York Play: A Facsimile of British Library MS Additional 35290*, with introductions by Richard Beadle, Peter Meredith, and Richard Rastall. Leeds Texts and Monographs, Medieval Drama Facsimiles 7 (Leeds: University of Leeds Press, 1983), xxxiv–xxxv and f. 44.

23 Beadle, *York Plays*, xxxiii.

24 Peter Meredith, *Mary Play from the N-Town Manuscript* (London: Longman, 1987), ll. 529–52; cf. also Muir, *Biblical Drama*, 176.

25 Peter Meredith believes that Contemplacio's prayer 'absorbed' the former speeches of the two prophets (*Mary Play*, 4–5).

26 Peter Meredith, ed., *The Passion Play From the N-Town Manuscript* (London: Longman, 1990), 89 and 193, note 1SD.

27 N-Town's *Assumption of the Virgin* is written on an interpolated quire in association with a sixteenth-century hand (K.S. Block, *Ludus Coventriae* [London: Oxford University Press, 1922], 354); Meredith, Introduction to *The Mary Play*, 1–5; Stephen Spector, ed., *The N-Town Play: Cotton MS Vespasian D.8*, 2 vols. EETS ss 11–12 (Oxford: Oxford University Press, 1991), 1:xxi, 2:527.

28 Lumiansky and Mills, *Chester Cycle*, ix–xxxiii.

29 David Mills, *Recycling the Cycle: The City of Chester and Its Whitsun Plays* (Toronto: University of Toronto Press, 1998), 180–4; Alexandra F. Johnston, 'Cycle Drama in the Sixteenth Century: Texts and Contexts,' *Early Drama to 1600, Acta* 13 (1985): 3.

30 The use of 'preco' with the meaning 'preacher' is attested as early as the eighth century (R.E. Latham, *Revised Medieval Latin Word-List from British and Irish Sources*, The British Academy (London: Oxford University Press, 1965), 365.

31 Lumiansky and Mills, *Chester Cycle*, play 4.459/60 and 475/76 (where / indicates stage directions between lines).

32 Fichte, *Expository Voices*, 117–19.

33 Karen Sawyer (Marsalek), '*The Resurrection of Our Lord*: A Study and Dual-Text Edition' (PhD dissertation, University of Toronto, 2001), 19, citing documents in the Oxfordshire Archives.

34 Alexandra F. Johnston, 'The Emerging Pattern of the Easter Play in England,' *Medieval English Theatre* 20 (1998): 19.

35 Karen Sawyer Marsalek, '"Doctrine Evangelicall" and Erasmus's Paraphrases in *The Resurrection of Our Lord*,' in *Tudor Drama Before Shakespeare, 1485–1590: New Directions for Research, Criticism and Pedagogy*, ed. Lloyd Ed-

ward Kermode, Jason Scott-Warren, and Martine Van Elk (New York: Palgrave Macmillan, 2004) 54–7; cf. also Sawyer, 'Resurrection,' 54 and note 53; 123–5.

36 Stevens and Cawley, *Towneley Plays*, xviii.

37 Sawyer cites an analogous Annas, dressed 'after a busshop of þe hoold lawe' in *Passion Play I* from N-Town (play 26 in Block, *Ludus Coventriae*, 230, cited by Sawyer, 'Resurrection,' 149), but the correlation between those in charge of the synagogue and the doctors of the synagogue with whom Jesus disputes as a child is much more common (cf. York 20, Chester 11, Towneley 18, and others cited by Lumiansky and Mills, *Chester Cycle*, 2:160–1). Since the same N-Town manuscript features an 'Episcopus' (bishop) of the synagogue in three other plays, two from *The Mary Play* (plays 9–10) and play 14, *The Trial of Mary and Joseph*, the authors of N-Town and *The Resurrection of Our Lord* are remarkable in sharing this high priest-bishop analogy. However, Appendix's application of it appears most pejorative.

38 'Et solut. cuidem doctori Theologie pro uncolumn quemdam sermonem in Crastino festi corporis christi ut in precedentibus,' translated by Abigail Young as 'And paid to a certain doctor of theology preaching a certain sermon on the day after the feast of Corpus Christi as in preceding [years]' (City Chamberlains Rolls Y: C5: 1, 1501, in Johnston and Rogerson, *York*, 1:188 and 2:800).

39 Marsalek, 'Doctrine Evangelicall,' 37–41.

40 Cf. Jean-Pierre Bordier, *Le Jeu de la Passion: Le message chrétien et le théâtre français (XIIIe–XVIe s.)* (Paris: Honoré Champion, 1998), 36–43; Graham A. Runnalls, 'Les Mystères de la Passion en langue française: tentative de classement,' *Romania* 114 (1996):479–92.

41 Lynette Muir, ed. *La Passion de Semur*, Leeds Medieval Studies 3 (Leeds: University of Leeds Press, 1981), 269.

42 Bordier, *Jeu de la Passion*, 76, note 1.

43 Graham A. Runnalls, ed. *Le Mystère de la Passion Nostre Seigneur du manuscrit 1131 de la Bibliothèque Sainte-Geneviève* (Geneva: Librairie Droz, 1974), 266, ll. 4461–77.

44 Pierre Servet, ed., *Le Mystère de la Résurrection: Angers (1456)*, 2 vols (Geneva: Librairie Droz, 1993), 1:82.

45 Servet, *Mystère*, 1:23–32. I have highlighted the words which indicate the first person plural perspective. Unless specified, all translations are my own.

46 Servet, *Mystère*, 1:302. The Latin term *proto-* (or *protho-*) *collum* meant 'original document' (Latham, *Medieval Latin Word-List*, 379) and the master copy of the play text was called the 'original' in both English (as noted at Chester) and French documentation. Nicolas Le Roux, for example, drew up

the original of the *Passion* played in Amiens in 1500, which was loaned to Mons for their 1501 production of the same. See Graham A. Runnalls, 'La Passion de Mons (1501): Étude sur le texte et sur ses rapports avec la Passion d'Amiens (1500),' *Revue Belge de Philologie et d'Histoire* 80 (2002): 1151–5.

47 Servet, *Mystère*, 2:685.

48 Marcel Couturier and Graham A. Runnalls, eds, *Compte du Mystère de la Passion: Châteaudun 1510*, ([Chartres:] Société archéologique d'Eure-et-Loir [1991]), 42; Graham A. Runnalls, *Études sur les mystères* (Paris: Honoré Champion, 1998), 395.

49 Germain Bazin, *Jean Fouquet: Le Livre d'Heures d'Étienne Chevalier* (Paris: Éditions Somogy, 1990), 112–13.

50 Gordon Kipling called this traditional interpretation of the miniature into question in 1997, evoking Graham Runnalls' defence, as polite spokesperson for French scholarship, and his own rebuttal (*Medieval English Theatre* 19 (1997): 26–120). In light of all the documentary evidence, it seems highly unlikely that a French miniaturist like Jean Fouquet would be more familiar with the remote Roman theatrical tradition, which he could only know through books (as Kipling demonstrates), than with the vibrant French tradition which was playing itself out all around him.

51 Bordier arrives at this conclusion after a detailed examination of all the criticism relating to Mercadé's authorship (*Jeu de la Passion*, 41 and note 81).

52 Jules-Marie Richard, ed. *Le Mystère de la Passion: texte du manuscrit 697 de la Bibliothèque d'Arras* (Arras: Imprimérie de la Société du Pas-de-Calais, 1891), ll. 50–1; 61–2; 24,879–82.

53 Richard, *Mystère de la Passion*, 76.

54 Carnahan, *Prologue*, 94.

55 Omer Jodogne, ed., *Le Mystère de la Passion d'Arnoul Gréban* (Brussels: Palais des Académies, 1965), 1:13–31.

56 The ambiguity derives from a confusion in Latin between *auctor* and *actor* (Albert Dauzat, *Dictionnaire Étymologique de la langue française* [Paris: Librairie Larousse, 1938], 10); Charles Mazouer warns his readers that 'acteur désigne l'auteur d'un livre en général' (*Le théâtre français du Moyen Âge* [Paris: Sedes, 1998], 164).

57 Jean Michel, *Le Mystère de la Passion (Angers 1486)*, ed. Omer Jodogne (Gembloux: Éditions J. Duculot S.A., 1959), ll. 29,922–3.

58 Michel, *Mystère de la Passion*, ll. 727–30.

59 Omer Jodogne, '*Mystère de la Passion*, de Jean Michel,' in *Dictionnaire des lettres françaises: Le Moyen Age* (Paris: Fayard, 1964), 1042.

60 Bordier, *Jeu de la Passion*, 76.

61 In England, guildsmen seem to have performed most of the roles. The most

notable exception is the Chester wives who were responsible for the Assumption play. Lawrence M. Clopper, *Chester*, REED (Toronto: University of Toronto Press, 1979), 23, 27.

62 Elisabeth Lalou, 'Arnoul Gréban,' in *Dictionnaire des lettres françaises: Le Moyen Age* (Paris: Fayard, 1964), 93.
63 Raymond Lebègue, *La Tragédie religieuse en France: les débuts (1514–73)* (Paris: Librairie Ancienne Honoré Champion, 1929), 5, note 8; Runnalls defines the *fatiste* in common with scribes as 'souvent un simple compilateur ou bien un des membres d'une équippe … responsable du texte' (*Études*, 46); see also Maurice Accarie, *Le théâtre sacré de la fin du Moyen Age: étude sur le sens moral de la 'Passion' de Jean Michel* (Geneva: Librairie Droz, 1979), and Madeleine Lazard, *Le théâtre en France au XVIe siècle* (Paris: Presses Universitaires de France, 1980).
64 Mazouer, *Le théâtre français*, 162.
65 Carnahan, *Prologue*, 90; Runnalls, *Études*, 77–8.
66 Runnalls, 'La Passion de Mons (1501),' 1143–88, esp. 1147 and 1171.
67 Gustave Cohen, *Livre de conduite du régisseur et le compte des dépenses pour le Mystère de la Passion joué à Mons en 1501* (Paris: Librarie Istra, 1925), 457. The term *docteur* is defined for the time period as a man who teaches, especially an 'homme qui enseigne la doctrine du Christ' (Edmond Huguet, ed. *Dictionnaire de la langue française du seizième siècle*, 7 vols [Paris: Librairie Ancienne Honoré Champion, 1925–67], 3: 236).
68 Cohen, *Livre de conduite*, 7.
69 Cohen, *Livre de conduite*, lxxi.
70 Couturier and Runnalls, *Compte du Mystère*, 79.
71 Cohen, *Livre de conduite*, civ.
72 Alan E. Knight, ed. *Les Mystères de la procession de Lille*, 3 of 5 vols, Textes Littéraires Français 535, 554, 569 (Geneva: Droz, 2001–4).
73 Knight, *Mystères de Lille*, 3:167.
74 Knight, *Mystères de Lille*, 1:74–6.
75 Knight, *Mystères de Lille*, 1:77.
76 Runnalls, *Études*, 367; cf. also Natalie Zemon Davis, *Society and Culture in Early Modern France* (Stanford, CA: Stanford University Press, 1965), 200.
77 Daniel Poirion, 'Chanson de geste,' in *Dictionnaire des lettres françaises*, 241.
78 Paul John Jones, *Prologue and Epilogue in Old French Lives of Saints before 1400* (Philadelphia: University of Pennsylvania Press, 1933), 12–20.
79 Brian Stock, *The Oral Implications of Literacy: Written Language and Models of Interpretation in the Eleventh and Twelfth Centuries* (Princeton, NJ: Princeton University Press, 1983), 522–7.

80 W.A. Davenport, *Chaucer and His English Contemporaries: Prologue and Tale in* The Canterbury Tales (New York: St Martin's Press, 1998), 8–13.

81 Beverly Mayne Kienzle, ed., *The Sermon*, Typologie des Sources du Moyen Âge Occidental, fasc. 81–3 (Turnhout: Brepols, 2000), 271–3; cf. also Bruce L. Venarde, ed. *Robert of Arbrissel: A Medieval Religious Life* (Washington: Catholic University of America Press, 2003), 68–90.

82 Marianne G. Briscoe, *Artes praedicandi*, Typologie des Sources du Moyen Âge Occidental (Turnhout: Brepols, 1992), 22. The short protheme that introduced the theme in fifteenth- and sixteenth-century sermons (Jelle Koopmans, ed. *Quatre sermons joyeux* [Geneva: Librairie Droz, 1984], 16–17) is not in evidence in any of the French or English biblical plays.

83 Larissa Taylor, 'French Sermons, 1215–1535,' in *The Sermon*, ed. Beverly Mayne Kienzle (Turnhout: Brepols, 2000), 712–13.

84 Patrick J. Horner, 'Benedictines and Preaching in *Pastoralia* in Late Medieval England: A Preliminary Inquiry,' in *Medieval Monastic Preaching*, ed. Carolyn Muessig (Leiden: Brill, 1998), 282–9.

85 H.L. Spencer, 'Middle English Sermons,' in *The Sermon*, ed. Beverly Mayne Kienzle (Turnhout: Brepols, 2000), 621–2.

86 Marianne G. Briscoe, 'Preaching and Medieval English Drama,' in *Contexts for Early English Drama*, ed. M.G. Briscoe and J. Coldewey (Bloomington, IN: Indiana University Press, 1989), 154.

87 Taylor, 'French Sermons,' 716.

88 Peter Meredith and Lynette Muir, 'The Trial in Heaven in the *Eerste Bliscap* and Other European Plays,' *Dutch Crossing* 22 (1984): 84–92; Fichte, *Expository Voices*, 77–96; Oscar Cargill, *Drama and Liturgy* (New York: Columbia University Press, 1930), 70–90.

89 Spencer, 'Middle English Sermons,' in *The Sermon*, 597.

90 Taylor, 'French Sermons,' 712, 753.

91 Taylor, 'French Sermons,' 723.

92 Briscoe, 'Preaching,' 154.

93 Geoffrey Chaucer, 'The Wife of Bath's Prologue,' ll. 550–2, in *The Works of Geoffrey Chaucer*, 2nd ed., ed. F.N. Robinson (Boston: Houghton Mifflin, 1961), 81.

94 Cf. K. Janet Ritch, 'Le rôle du jubé dans la *Résurrection de Jésus Christ*, pièce de Maître Eloy Du Mont,' *Memini* 3 (1999): 157. Richard Kieckhefer mentions Eric Gill moving the altar down in 1940 (*Theology in Stone: Church Architecture from Byzantium to Berkeley* [Oxford: Oxford University Press, 2004], 80), but the majority of altars were repositioned after the Second Vatican Council in the second half of the century. In this light, Hans-Jürgen

Diller is mistaken to assume that the priest in a medieval church generally faced the congregation (Diller, *Middle English Mystery Play*, 17).

95 Michel Mourlet, *Thaumaturgie du théâtre ou l'anti-Brecht* (Paris: Éditions Loris Talmart, 1989), 43.

96 Richard Schechner, *Performance Theory*, rev. ed. (New York: Routledge, 2003), 72.

PART THREE

Renaissance Plays

'Awake your faith': English Resurrection Drama and *The Winter's Tale*

KAREN SAWYER MARSALEK

In the final scene of *The Winter's Tale*, the hush that falls on Leontes and the other courtiers when they view Hermione's statue pleases Paulina; 'I like your silence;' she remarks; 'it the more shows off / Your wonder' (5.3.21–2).[1] Academic fascination with this moment would probably please Paulina less, for rather than wondering in silence, we continue to ask what it can tell us about early modern intersections of religious belief and theatre. Two sites of scholarly interest concern me in this essay: the play's use of motifs from biblical drama and its provocative animation of a devotional image. Approaches to the first topic have generally focused on the so-called mystery cycles, and have fallen out of fashion somewhat as scholars probe the latter issue, the scene's flirtation with idolatry and 'superstition' (5.3.43).[2]

I want to inflect our understanding of the statue scene with a wider perspective on the Resurrection play tradition, a perspective that Alexandra F. Johnston's work has made available. By unearthing new performance records and analysing the collective documentary evidence together with nine surviving play texts, Professor Johnston has demonstrated that the English Resurrection play was a long-standing and central, if under-recognized, feature of the English theatrical landscape.[3] The genre encompasses not only pageants from the familiar cycle plays of Chester, York, and Coventry, but also free-standing plays that were part of the rich and varied theatrical activity in English parishes, households, schools, and cities.[4] Furthermore, its popularity and flexibility encouraged early Tudor writers to re-imagine it for humanist and Protestant purposes. As a result, the English Resurrection play boasts 'the longest history of any vernacular biblical plays from the medieval and early modern period,' flourishing in England from the twelfth to the sixteenth century.[5]

272 Karen Sawyer Marsalek

This larger perspective affords a richer understanding of the theatrical tradition embedded in the statue scene. Readings of Hermione's reanimation often set devotional practices and theatre in opposition, an approach that can shortchange the theatrical vitality and conscious artifice that mark the Resurrection play genre.[6] Furthermore, while the spectacular elements of the scene are often understood as exclusively Catholic, we should remember that the genre had already been absorbed by reformist playwrights.[7] Analysing the statue scene as a metadramatic resurrection play staged by Paulina can lead us to a more nuanced reading of its iconoclastic implications. If we see Leontes only as a spectator, Paulina's exhortation 'It is required / You do awake your faith' may suggest that faith can make an image move or lead one to accept an illusion as truth (5.3.94–5). However, if we see Leontes as an unwitting actor in the play Paulina is staging, the context of her charge also shifts. His faith is required not to raise Hermione or to be fooled by a false resurrection, but to recognize and accept her as already risen.

A brief outline of the breadth and contours of the Resurrection play tradition, necessarily indebted to Professor Johnston's scholarship, establishes the auspices and episodic structure that inform Shakespeare's dramaturgy here. It also highlights the position of the Resurrection play in both Catholic and reformist discourses. Since the statue scene has been described in terms of religious ritual, the relationships between Easter liturgy and vernacular Resurrection plays are a useful starting point.

Paradramatic Liturgy and Ritual

Shaping the structures and emphases of the English Resurrection play are components of the Holy Week liturgy documented first in the tenth-century *Regularis Concordia*. These paradramatic ceremonies took place over three days. In the *depositio* on Good Friday the priest placed the cross in a sepulchre, either a temporary structure or a permanent part of the church architecture built into the north wall of the chancel.[8] Monks kept vigil by the sepulchre until just before Matins on Easter Sunday when the *elevatio* took place: the cross was removed from the sepulchre, often secretly, and then carried in procession to the high altar.[9] While these two ceremonies symbolized Christ's burial and the Resurrection moment, the actions still accompanied the established liturgical antiphons. However, the *Visitatio sepulchri*, performed during Easter Matins, developed from a trope, that is, from new dialogue added to the authorized liturgy, and it involved impersonation of biblical figures.[10] Monks portrayed the three

Maries, walking towards the sepulchre '*pedetemptim ad similitudinem querentium quid*' (haltingly, in the manner of seeking for something), while a fourth, who had slipped in quietly to sit by the sepulchre, represented the angel and asked 'Quem queritis?' (Whom do you seek?).[11] At the trio's reply 'Ihesum Nazarenum,' the angel proclaimed the Resurrection and commanded the women to announce this news to others. Further developments of the *Visitatio* included the women's testimony to Peter and John, or Christ's appearance to Mary Magdalene.[12] Post-Resurrection appearances of Christ on the road to Emmaus and in the upper room to Thomas were represented on the continent in a trope for Easter Monday vespers, the *Peregrini*, though no examples appear in English liturgies.

English vernacular dramas of the Resurrection incorporated the same episodes, and coexisted with liturgical and paradramatic Easter ceremonies well into the sixteenth century. The sepulchre vigil, which had become a practice in parishes as well as monasteries, was one of the last ceremonies to disappear as the English church was purged of 'popish' rites; until the reign of Edward VI, parishes were still providing fire and refreshment for those who 'watched' the sepulchre until Easter morning. Some churches reinstated the rite under Mary, and the 1565 injunctions for Coventry and Lichfield suggest some persistence in its observance.[13] Later, in a 1570 translation of Thomas Kirchmeyer's *Regnum Papisticum* (1553), Barnabe Googe mocked the idolatry of the *depositio* and *elevatio*. Along with these rituals, he described dramatic Easter performances:

> In some place solemne sightes and showes, & Pageants fayre are playd,
> With sundrie sortes of maskers braue, in straunge attire arayd,
> As where the Maries three doe meete, the sepulchre to see,
> And Iohn with Peter swiftly runnes, before him there to bee.
> These things are done with iesture such, and with so pleasaunt game,
> That euen the grauest men that liue, would laughe to see the same.[14]

The content of these 'Pageants fayre' recalls the 'Quem quaeritis' or 'Visitatio sepulchri' and related tropes, but they are instead separate events played by 'maskers braue' in costumes rather than by the priests, or 'shauen sort,' that Googe names as liturgical participants.[15] Though Googe was translating a German cleric's description, many of his English readers would have been familiar with such performances through a large and important strand of the English Resurrection play tradition – the extra-liturgical Easter week play.

Extra-liturgical Easter Week Plays

Surviving texts and records of English Resurrection plays fall into two broad categories, outlined by Johnston.[16] The first category consists of Easter or Easter week plays independent of the liturgy that retained the episodic content of the 'visitatio sepulchri' and 'peregrini' tropes. The Easter sepulchre may have been a backdrop, or even a set piece for these performances; Pamela Sheingorn reports that a temporary wooden sepulchre structure could be 'hung with richly colored cloths' which 'created an enclosure, possibly large enough for a person to enter.'[17] From the documentary evidence we know that these seasonal productions also took advantage of theatrical elements such as costume pieces, wigs, temporary stages, and special effects. Another kind of resurrection play is not tied to the Easter celebration; this kind of play adds a depiction of the Resurrection itself, as well as other material from the Gospel narratives, to the traditional liturgical episodes. In this category belong the plays from the York and Chester cycles, the N-Town and Towneley manuscripts, and Nicholas Grimald's Latin tragicomedy *Christus Redivivus* (ca. 1540).[18] However, the two categories of resurrection plays do not correspond to the chronological order of their dramatic records and extant texts, a fact that reveals the error of an evolutionary approach to the genre. For example, the thirteenth-century *Shrewsbury Fragments* fall into the first category of Easter week plays, but so do the sixteenth-century dramas of *Christ's Burial* and *Christ's Resurrection* in Bodley e Museo 160.[19] Composed sometime after 1518, the latter plays were 'to be played, on part on Gud Friday afternone, and þe other part opon Ester Day after the resurrection in the morowe.'[20] The reformist *The Resurrection of Our Lord* (ca. 1547) also seems to be an Easter week text, divided into 'The First Dayes Playe' and 'The Seconde Dayes Playe,' though its content extends beyond traditional liturgical episodes.[21]

Though it is often difficult to distinguish whether a play was part of the liturgy or not, the Easter Resurrection play, notes Johnston, 'is associated exclusively with worshipping communities – religious houses, secular households that kept chapels, and parishes.'[22] Such communities included Lichfield, Lincoln, and Wells Cathedrals, which staged episodes baséd on the 'visitatio' and 'peregrini' tropes during the twelfth, fourteenth, and fifteenth centuries, respectively.[23] The chapel of Magdalen College, Oxford, invested in costumes, wigs, and props for Easter plays during the late fifteenth and early sixteenth centuries.[24] Household statutes for Henry Percy, the 5th earl of Northumberland (1478–1527) require the earl's twenty-eight chapel personnel to present the 'Play of Ressurection upon Estur-Day in the Mornynge.'[25] Finally, Easter plays were both a devotional activity and a source of income for English parishes, particularly in the sixteenth century. Performances took place in Devon (1494–5),[26] Somerset (ca. 1503–4),[27] Sussex (1522–3, 1525–6),[28] and in the Thames valley, an area rich in records of Resurrection drama, as Johnston and Sally-Beth MacLean have demonstrated.[29] Four parishes in that region report a total of ten Eastertide performances between 1507 and 1539. Evidence for special effects of lightning shows that several of these parishes dramatized the Resurrection moment as well as the traditional liturgical episodes.[30] Automata were the focus of one yearly performance not far from the Thames valley; in the village of Witney, priests decided to raise money by staging 'the hole Action of the Resurrection' in a puppet show, with figures representing '*Christe*, the Watchmen, *Marie*, and others,' an event that was recalled with distaste by Elizabethan author William Lambarde as 'Popishe Maumetrie' from 'the Dayes of ceremonial religion.'[31]

Despite Lambarde's characterization of this Resurrection play, some worshipping communities seem to have adapted their Easter plays in response to the changing religious climate. At St Laurence, Reading, the churchwardens paid one Master Labourne twice for his work on their Resurrection play: first in 1533–4 for 'refourmyng' it, and two years later for recopying the book.[32] At least one stage of revision is indicated here, and possibly two, during the early pangs of the first Henrician reformation. The reformist play *The Resurrection of Our Lord* may also spring from the parish or private chapel tradition; its didactic speeches include passages based on Nicholas Udall's translation of Erasmus's *Paraphrases* (completed 1546, published 1549). The play's reviser continued to amplify the evangelical tone of that Erasmian source, weaving reformist views on vernacular scripture, the Eucharist, and the existence of ghosts into the fabric of the Easter drama.[33]

Other Resurrection Plays

Reformist revisions to Easter week plays should not surprise us, since the surviving texts and records of the Chester, York, and Coventry cycles also reveal citizens' efforts to retain their biblical drama despite shifts in religious policy. Within these larger dramatic sequences, the second type of Resurrection play appears, relocated from its traditional performance time of Easter week to a Corpus Christi, Whitsun, or even midsummer performance. These large-scale productions usually took place under civic or other secular auspices rather than in a parish, cathedral, or chapel,[34] and their Resurrection plays dramatize not only the liturgical episodes, but also the conspiratorial cover-up arranged by the high priests, sepulchre guards, and sometimes Pilate. Scholars more frequently note the influence of these plays on *The Winter's Tale*, since their performance extended between five and twenty years into the reign of Elizabeth. York presented its Corpus Christi play until 1569, having prohibited its most Mariological pageants under Edward and Elizabeth, and its citizens continued to press Archbishop Grindal for permission to stage the pageants as late as 1580. Chester's plays survived to 1575, though the last staging omitted some plays 'wh*i*ch were thought might not be Iustified for the supe*r*stition that was in them.'[35] Coventry's Corpus Christi play, the pride of a strongly reformist city, saw its last production only four years later in 1579. Michael O'Connell argues:

> To those who sponsored and performed them   and presumably to a major-ity of those who watched them – the plays were not 'late medieval,' perhaps not even necessarily Catholic ... the overall reluctance to give them up and the attempts at revision, even if too little and too late, suggest that what they represented in cultural and political terms was something a good deal more complex than a simple Catholic-or-Protestant alternative.[36]

The same may be said of the Resurrection play tradition that intersects with this civic drama.

That such plays were 'vital cultural practices' (in O'Connell's term) is apparent not only from evidence of revision and persistence in perfor-mance, but also from new sixteenth-century compositions on the subject. Reformer John Bale composed a mini-cycle, now lost, of eight plays on the ministry, Passion, and Resurrection of Christ.[37] Around 1540 at Brasenose College, Oxford, Nicholas Grimald eschewed the cycle format but re-tained its wider range of Resurrection episodes and characters in his hu-manist play *Christus Redivivus*.[38] Writing in Latin, Grimald grafted the Easter narrative, post-Resurrection appearances, and the Great Commis-sion onto a classical five-act structure. Bale praised Grimald for teaching 'that our salvation is alone in Jesus the Saviour,'[39] a teaching which comes from Christ's own lips at the end of the play:

(si fieri possit) unusquilibet
Me mortuum sibi, me rediuiuum sibi putet.
Nihil opus erit, uetustas ceremonias,
Aut uictimas retinere, aut sacrificia.

[If it be that anyone believe I died for him and lived again for him, there shall be no need of old-time ceremonies, or observing burnt offerings and sacrifices.] (210–11)

Neither Matt. 28:19–20 nor Mark 16:15, the biblical sources for Christ's charge, contain any reference to Jewish rituals and law; the repudiation of outdated 'ceremonias' and 'sacrificia' added by Grimald constitutes an attack on the Mass and good works. These dead practices are contrasted with 'uiuida ... fide,' living faith, which alone assures one's salvation (210–11).

Along with its determinedly reformist bent, the humanist emphases of *Christus Redivivus* distinguish it within the Resurrection play tradition. Grimald characterizes the soldiers as 'milites gloriosi' who invoke Hercules, Pollux, and Mars along with Jehovah, and portrays the high priest as personally counselled by the fury Alecto (138–47, 194–5, 182–9). Moreover, as in *The Winter's Tale*, an oracle is a byword for truth: Mary Magdalene requests that the apostles trust her joyous report, 'hæc ut folia Sibyllæ credite,' as they would a Sybilline oracle (176–7). The layers of classical, Catholic, and reformist references in *Christus Redivivus* confirm the flexibility of the Resurrection play genre, and presage its complex effects in the statue scene of Shakespeare's romance.

Paulina's Resurrection Play

The plays discussed above, of course, do not incorporate a human actor as a 'living' statue, and in this respect their dramaturgy differs significantly from that of the last scene of *The Winter's Tale*. However, Shakespeare prepares us for the slippage between static image and Resurrection drama with the description of the statue in 5.2. There a gentleman of the court informs us of a marvellous statue of Hermione which has been 'many years in doing, and now newly performed by that rare Italian master Giulio Romano' (5.2.94–5). Leonard Barkan finds similarities between this description of a statue and the language used to hype stage plays, and suggests that Hermione is only '*performed*, in the sense of *perfected*' when she moves and speaks – when she is transformed through theatre.[40] The language of the description also opens up space for another reading of 5.3, where we see not only the newly created and perfected statue, but also a 'newly performed' version of a dramatic genre that has also been 'many years in doing.'

Given the varied auspices of Resurrection play performances in England, and the regular connections between auspices and episodic content, the location and season of events in *The Winter's Tale* 5.3 take on additional significance. Though scholars have analysed Hermione's return to life in conjunction with the biblical play versions of the Resurrection, the scene's physical and temporal settings recall instead the free-standing Easter dramas performed by worshipping communities. The statue stands in a place of devotional activity; rather than displaying Hermione's image in her art gallery, Paulina 'keep[s] it / Lonely, apart' in a 'chapel' (17–18, 86). Her term establishes an environment for the Catholic veneration of images, as Julia Reinhard Lupton has argued,[41] but just as importantly, it sets the stage for an extra-liturgical Easter play. Like the earl of Northumberland, Paulina has a household chapel which she uses to present a resurrection. In the 'discovery space' at the Globe or Blackfriars, Hermione's curtained environs would resemble the Easter sepulchre structure in church architecture. A stage property of a tomb, altar, or canopy like those owned by the Admiral's Men in 1598 would reinforce the impression of ecclesiastical space.[42] The play's cycle of mourning and reconciliation, winter and spring, also parallels the structure of the church calendar, where a vigil separates Good Friday observances from the joyous performances of Easter week. At least one production of *The Winter's Tale* capitalized on this liturgical aptness, for the King's Men presented it at court on Easter Tuesday, 1618.[43]

Interactions between characters also draw on Resurrection play dramaturgy. Both Darryll Grantley and Cynthia Marshall compare Leontes and the other onlookers to the holy women in the *Visitatio sepulchri* episode and, more specifically, link Leontes' experience to Mary Magdalene's individual post-Resurrection encounter with Christ. Paulina's repeated cautions against touching the statue remind both critics of Christ's warning 'noli me tangere,' and Marshall argues that Leontes' penitent reactions to the statue resemble Mary Magdalene's speeches before her encounter with Christ in the Towneley resurrection play (26/429–46).[44] Parallels also exist in the York Resurrection pageant (38/270–87) and in the Bodley e Museo *Christ's Resurrection*, where Mary Magdalene continues to grieve even after she has heard from the angel, a result of the authors' Gospel harmonization. In *Christ's Resurrection*, the Magdalene sees herself as remiss in 'dewty' and 'diligence' because she did not keep watch through the night at the sepulchre. Had she 'waytid wisely with humble affiance,' she would have been rewarded with a sight of the Resurrection (204–9). Her pilgrimage to the tomb prompts her remorse and contemplation much as the sight of Hermione's statue awakens new love and grief in Leontes.

Yet more telling are the similarities between Leontes and Peter, who grieves at the sepulchre in three sixteenth-century Resurrection plays: the Bodley e Museo *Christ's Resurrection*, the Chester play, and *The Resurrection of Our Lord*. Peter's failings are greater than those of Mary Magdalene, since he has repeatedly denied Christ. He models contrition in *Christ's Resurrection* through a lengthy monologue. Entering *'flens amare'* (weeping bitterly), he laments his lack of steadfastness:

> Fulle of wo may I bee, sorowfulle and pensyve,
>   Complenynge and wepinge with sorow inwertlee,
> And wep bitter teres alle þe days of my life!
>   My vnstabille delinge is euer in myn ee.
>   I saide I wald not leve my master for to dee;
> He said I shuld forsak hym or þe cok crow thris.
> But I was presumptuose, vnware, and vnwise!   (358–64)

Physically overcome by his grief, he must be reminded by Andrew and John that they 'shalle haue gud tidinges! This is þe thrid day!' (403). Their anticipation of Christ's imminent Resurrection balances Peter's grief, providing an ahistorical assurance that heightens the meditative value of the play.

Such a certainty is absent for the characters in *The Winter's Tale*; indeed, it is absent for the audience, since Shakespeare has not given us any private glimpses of Hermione alive. Nonetheless, Camillo and Polixenes similarly attempt to comfort Leontes, whose sorrow is 'too sore laid on' (49). Leontes' own language expresses the spiritual experience of compunction – literally severe pricking or piercing of conscience – that both the Magdalene and Peter feel; the appearance of the statue is 'So much to [Leontes'] good comfort as it is / Now piercing to [his] soul' (33–4). He feels shame and rebuke for his failings, and those 'evils' are 'conjured to [his] remembrance' (37, 40). Even before his 'entrance' in Paulina's resurrection play, Leontes has been preparing for this role; Cleomenes observes that he has 'performed / A saint-like sorrow' (5.1.2–3), the kind of exemplary penitence that also characterizes Peter in *Christ's Resurrection*. There, John remarks of the apostle, 'This gret contrition of your hart, dowtlese, / To God is plesant sacrifice' (406–7). Cleomenes' word-play on 'perform' points to a penance so thorough that it constitutes a kind of impersonation of a remorseful saint like Peter.

Leontes' performance as Peter contrasts with less admirable roles he has played elsewhere in *The Winter's Tale*. 'Go play, boy, play,' he fumes in the first act, 'thy mother plays, and I / Play too, but so disgraced a part, whose issue / Will hiss me to my grave' (1.2.185–7). Leontes sees himself in the role of a stage cuckold, whose exit ('issue') will draw mockery from the audience. Michael O'Connell argues that the king's sexual jealousy here is informed by memories of the doubting figure of Joseph in the cycle plays.[45] Leontes also rages like a tyrant – his syntactically convoluted fury and impulse to infanticide out-Herod Herod. But in his final role as Peter, Leontes repents, and like the apostle he is eventually comforted by a post-resurrection reunion with his beloved. In two manuscripts of the Chester cycle and in the reformist play *The Resurrection of Our Lord*, Christ appears to the apostle alone.[46] These scenes restore a relationship that was maimed by Peter's faithless denial; they emphasize the apostle's second chance to live out his sacred calling. Similarly, Paulina cues Leontes' second chance: 'Do not shun her / Until you see her die again, for then / You kill her double' (5.3.105–7).

However, the sequence of events in 5.3 does not follow the episodic pattern of the Easter play, where both the Magdalene and Peter enter and confess their failings *after* the Resurrection occurs. Furthermore, neither of them actually witnesses Christ emerging from the tomb. In contrast, Hermione's awakening is itself observed by Leontes and his companions, in the midst of the exchanges I have detailed above. Shakespeare thus conflates two events typically kept separate in both liturgy and drama: the Resurrection moment and the *Visitatio sepulchri*. The music that Paulina calls for enhances the impression of a resurrection, since singing typically accompanied Christ's emergence from the tomb. The York, Towneley, and Chester texts include a music cue, with the latter two plays specifying the antiphon 'Christus resurgens' (Towneley 28/229+SD, Chester 18/153+SD). Records of Coventry's Cappers' guild, responsible for that city's Resurrection play from 1534 to 1579, include recurring payments to singers, and the Thame parish paid a minstrel for its 1530 Easter performance.[47] Though Shakespeare does not identify the kind of music that should accompany Hermione here, the Latin antiphon would reinforce those suggestions of 'the forbidden, other religion' that Robert Miola sees as 'as a potent fund of myth, ritual and concern' in Shakespeare's classical settings.[48] Music could also be interpreted as an accompaniment to witchcraft, a charge Paulina pre-emptively repudiates (5.3.90–1).

The interplay of speech and silence in Hermione's awakening also connects to variants within the Easter play tradition. Hermione herself remains surprisingly mute as she descends and embraces Leontes. Hermione's silence prolongs the awe and wonder of the 'resurrection,' as in those extra-liturgical plays that staged the Resurrection as a tableau vivant. The York pageant follows this example. In other plays, however, Christ speaks directly to the audience. In the Towneley, Chester, and N-Town plays, the risen Christ calls attention to his wounds and links his resurrected body to the Eucharistic sacrament (Towneley 26/230–350, Chester 18/156–85, N-Town 35/73–88). His speech is associated with the medieval *imago pietatis* of Christ as Man of Sorrows; as Pamela Sheingorn explains, the image depicts the '*Christus patiens* who suffered and continues to suffer for mankind.'[49] In *The Winter's Tale*, Hermione's aged appearance and Leontes' reaction to the 'magic' he is witnessing create effects similar to that speech. Though Hermione does not mention her sorrows in the last scene of *The Winter's Tale*, her wrinkles evince the years she has lost due to Leontes' sins, and testify to her suffering just as Christ's wounds do. And like those wounds, to which Renaissance aesthetics granted beauty otherwise denied to physical imperfections, Hermione's wrinkles are aestheticized by Paulina as evidence of artistic excellence and beauty (5.3.30–2).[50]

The Eucharistic theme of Christ's Resurrection speeches is here displaced onto Leontes, who exclaims his wonder at Hermione's warm, physical reality: 'If this be magic, let it be an art / Lawful as eating' (110–11). The phrase evokes the sacramentarian controversies of early modern England and invites similar debates about Hermione's body. Has it really undergone a mystical transformation from stone to flesh through Paulina's magical authority? Or does the communion that Leontes now enjoys depend instead on his own faith, a faith celebrated through her symbolic resurrection? Such questions about Christ's body resulted in two versions of his post-Resurrection speech in the Chester cycle. In the surviving texts of Chester's Resurrection pageant, all of which post-date the cycle's last performance, a rather Lutheran Christ explains that the bread 'becomes [his] fleshe through [our] beleeffe / and doth release [our] synfull band' (18/176–7). However, complaints of a Puritan citizen in 1572 reveal that these lines replaced others emphasizing the act of transubstantiation. In another version the bread had become '[Christ's] fleshe / throgh wordes 5 betwyxt the prestes handes.'[51] Leontes' words accommodate either of the understandings of the communion rite expressed in the Resurrection play tradition, since he does not specify what type of eating – memorial or physical – is 'lawful.' Shakespeare also keeps both interpretations of Hermione's body in play by framing her miraculous transformation within the metadramatic structure.

Paulina's authority informs her parts in this metadrama. The concern about lawful magic first emerges in her lines, and we can see that she takes multiple roles in this resurrection drama staged in her chapel. If the courtly company seeking the statue within her chapel resemble the visitors to the sepulchre, then Paulina takes the part of the angel who provides music for the moment of resurrection, displays the marvel of the empty tomb, and commands them to spread the news: 'Go together, / You precious winners all; your exultation / Partake to everyone' (5.3.130–2). Paulina is also a stage manager who controls, cues, and interprets this drama for her onstage and offstage audiences, anxious that they should not misread the performance as 'unlawful' or magical.[52] In these respects she resembles the expositor figures of two reformist resurrection plays, Grimald's *Christus Redivivus* and the anonymous *The Resurrection of Our Lord*. In the first play, the expositor opens each act by setting the scene and previewing the action; he tells the audience at the outset of act 1, 'I shall be a spectator of the play with you.'[53] The expositor in *The Resurrection of Our Lord*, delightfully named Appendix, interprets the episodes the audience is viewing in the light of reformist doctrine, legitimizing what the audience has seen with reference to the Word.[54] As she mediates her own play for her audience, Paulina is particularly anxious that her audience should not misread it as diabolical. Clerics such as Bishop John Hooper had condemned 'resuscitat[ing] dead bodies, or call[ing] spirits departed unto the body again' as 'nothing else but an illusion and craft of the devil to make men believe lies,' but she assures them that Hermione's actions are 'holy' and her own spell 'lawful' (5.3.105–6).[55] Paulina won't explain the performance at the expense of her stagecraft, however. When Polixenes expects her to explicate the scene – to 'make it manifest where [Hermione] has lived, / Or how stol'n from the dead' (114–15), she cites his inability to believe such an account. Unlike Appendix, Paulina initially offers only the evidence of the audience's eyes, rather than words: 'That she is living, / Were it but told you, should be hooted at / Like an old tale; but it appears she lives, / Though yet she speak not' (115–18). The remark reminds us that Paulina's witness has enjoyed a dubious reception elsewhere in the play, and it implicitly casts Polixenes as a sceptical disciple, one of those who disbelieved the holy women's news of the Resurrection. In the words of the King James Bible, the reports 'seemed to [the apostles] as idle tales, and they beleeued them not' (Luke 24:11), and some resurrection plays vigorously expanded the disciples' scriptural reaction.[56] Mary Magdalene's announcement of the Resurrection in the Towneley plays, for example, meets with over fifty lines of disbelief. Peter rebukes her, 'Do way, woman, thou carpys wast!' (28/7), and Paul supports him with misogynistic fervour.[57] Instead of questioning and doubting how this resurrection has been orchestrated, Paulina suggests Polixenes and Camillo '[m]ark a little while' (5:3.118), or pay attention to the performance. As angelic herald, expositor, or holy woman testifying to the Resurrection, she urges her audience to recognize Hermione as alive, and to wonder at the holy drama that has revealed that fact. 'The faith to be awakened,' suggests Kenneth Gross, 'is partly the faith that the ... stage trick was performed in good faith.'[58] Should we then assume that Polixenes and others in the audience must see to believe – that a kind of 'ocular proof' must remedy the harm done by ignoring oracular proof earlier in the play?

This apparent return to the visual sense as a means to discover truth leaves Paulina's play open to the criticism of iconoclasts. Leontes sees a statue of his wife come to life, an apparent resurrection, and trusts these events are actually happening. Many critics see in Paulina's line, 'It is required / You do awake your faith,' an invitation to iconoclastic criticism. Because of Leontes' faith, and ours as well, they argue, the statue comes to life. Michael O'Connell contends:

> The effect on the spectators would appear quite precisely analogous to religious experience in that an act of faith is required for the enactment of the seeming miracle. In its quasi-religious enactment, the scene realizes the worst fears also of the antitheatricalists, for it presses an audience into idolatry as it assents with Leontes to whatever reality the apparent statue may mysteriously possess. Insofar as their desires coalesce with those of the characters on stage, the viewers become complicit in worship of the statue and thus agents in whatever it is that brings about the statue's incarnation into full theatrical life. If the scene for the moment fully associates theatricality with idolatry, Shakespeare does not counter, but embraces the charge.[59]

Given the way the statue scene draws on episodes from the Resurrection play tradition and implicates Leontes in that performance, I am not convinced that Shakespeare embraces this charge of idolatry as thoroughly as O'Connell suggests. In the Easter plays, the belief of disciples like Peter and Mary Magdalene is not the power that raises Christ. However, that fact does not eliminate the requirement that they, like Leontes, awake their faith. For Leontes, as for Peter and the Magdalene, faith involves recognizing and accepting a miracle that *has already taken place*. In post-Resurrection appearances the apostles rarely recognize Christ at first. They cannot imagine that he is living again, but their sight is repaired by faith. That faith is not needed to legitimize the Resurrection, but to complete the process of their own repentance and heal their relationship with the risen one. This perspective on Peter's repentance had come into vogue among Elizabethan preachers.[60] In the second *Book of Homilies*, the sermon 'Of Repentance and of True Reconciliation unto God' contrasts Judas, who did penance 'as all the Schole men' or Catholics do, with Peter, who exemplifies reformed repentance.[61] This process of repentance includes the stages of contrition and confession, but replaces satisfaction by works of penance with faith, 'whereby we do apprehende and take holde vppon the promises of God, touchyng the free pardon and forgeuenes of our sinnes.'[62] Paulina has already told Leontes that penitent mortification of the body through fasting, exposure to the elements, and ten thousand years of prayers 'could not move the gods' (3.2.208–11), but by moving beyond his 'saint-like sorrow' he finds forgiveness and grace.[63]

As an actor in a resurrection play, Leontes experiences not the resurrection moment itself, but rather a post-resurrection appearance. While Paulina's drama seems to conflate the resurrection moment with the *Visitatio sepulchri*, Shakespeare has also suggested that Hermione has been alive all along, that she has sequestered herself for sixteen years with Paulina's help, awaiting the oracle's fulfilment. Her return to life in this scene thus is symbolic, not actual.[64] If we interpret Paulina's play as self-conscious theatre, like the Resurrection dramas performed by cities and parishes, households, cathedrals, and schools, then some of the anxieties about its supernatural power or deceptive illusions are lessened; a Resurrection play doesn't supernaturally grant life to a dead actor, but reminds its audience that 'Christ is risen.' And its dramaturgy provides a framework for Paulina to re-introduce Hermione to her loved ones and kingdom. Though Shakespeare seems to present a potentially idolatrous moment, he also offers an alternate interpretation that can allay that iconoclastic anxiety.

A metatheatrical allusion in the sheep-shearing scene might prepare us for the way Shakespeare will induce and then soothe anxieties about image, theatre, and deception in 5.3. Uneasy about the queenly role she has assumed for the sheep-shearing festival, Perdita remarks, 'Methinks I play as I have seen them do / In Whitsun pastorals – sure this robe of mine / Does change my disposition' (4.4.133–5). Her words highlight one concern of anti-theatricalists – the disrupted role of clothing as a social signifier. Perdita thinks her costume has led her to act above her station. However, we as an audience also recognize the emptiness of this fear, for

Perdita *is* royal. Similarly, the theatrical history behind the statue scene helps to modulate the impression that Paulina is bringing Hermione to life. To see the end of *The Winter's Tale* as resurrection metadrama is not to attribute a single confessional identity to Shakespeare, to his audience, or even to the characters in the play. While originally liturgical and Catholic, the Resurrection play tradition had already expanded to include both Protestant polemic and classical tragicomedy, and Shakespeare's version gestures towards each expression of the genre. It thus engages various positions on the spectrum of early modern religious belief, not by ignoring their differences, but by acknowledging particularities of multiple confessional identities. What remains constant, however, is the theatrical power and longevity of the Resurrection play tradition, and its ability to signal a new era of forgiveness for those who can awake their faith.

NOTES

I am grateful to the many scholars who commented on drafts of this article in the meetings of the Northfield Medieval and Renaissance Colloquium and in the 'Shakespeare and the Middle Ages' seminar at the SAA in 2004. Thanks also to Phebe Jensen, Paul Menzer, and David Klausner. My greatest debt is, of course, to Professor Alexandra F. Johnston.

1 All quotations will be taken from *The Winter's Tale*, ed. Stephen Orgel (Oxford: Clarendon Press, 1996).
2 Cynthia Marshall notes the stigma of source study, while examining 5.3 in light of the 'resurrection plays in surviving cycle texts'; see 'Appendix B: *The Winter's Tale* and the Corpus Christi Resurrection Plays,' in *Last Things and Last Plays: Shakespearean Eschatology* (Carbondale: Southern Illinois University Press, 1991), 122–9. Two related studies ranging more widely over the play as a whole are François Laroque, 'Pagan Ritual, Christian Imagery, and Folk Customs in *The Winter's Tale*,' *Cahiers Élisabéthains* 22 (1982): 25–33, and Darryll Grantley, '*The Winter's Tale* and Early Religious Drama,' *Comparative Drama* 20 (1986): 17–37. For readings focusing on the scene's iconoclastic tensions, see Phebe Jensen, 'Singing Psalms to Horn-Pipes: Festivity, Iconoclasm and Catholicism in *The Winter's Tale*,' *Shakespeare Quarterly* 55 (2004): 303–6; Michael O'Connell, *The Idolatrous Eye: Iconoclasm and Theater in Early-Modern England* (Oxford: Oxford University Press, 2000), 138–44; Julia Reinhard Lupton, *Afterlives of the Saints: Hagiography, Typol-*

ogy, and Renaissance Literature (Stanford: Stanford University Press, 1996), 175–218; and Ruth Vanita, 'Mariological Memory in *The Winter's Tale* and *Henry VIII*,' *Studies in English Literature* 40 (2000): 311–37.

3 Alexandra F. Johnston, 'The Emerging Pattern of the Easter Play in England,' *Medieval English Theatre* 20 (1998): 3–23.

4 These and other single-subject biblical dramas proliferated across the realm, and may represent the materials used by compilers of the N-Town and Towneley manuscripts. Many scholars now believe that these two collections are synthetic anthologies of pre-existing and purpose-written plays, perhaps never actually performed by any town; in fact, the 'persistent myth' that N-Town and Towneley are 'cycles' was one topic in a panel discussion sponsored by the Medieval and Renaissance Drama Society at the Thirty-Eighth International Medieval Congress on Medieval Studies at Western Michigan University, May 2003.

5 Johnston, 'Emerging Pattern,' 5.

6 Phebe Jensen sees the statue scene as a 'dramatic reincorporation of Catholic ritual' ('Singing Psalms,' 304) while Michael O'Connell follows Louis Montrose in reading it as 'displaced religious ritual' (*Idolatrous Eye*, 142). Stephen Orgel, editor of the Oxford edition, notes the religious allusions in the text, but concludes that Paulina's 'demand for a suspension of disbelief, her invocation of wonder, and most of all, her claims for the therapeutic quality of her performance sound much more like Renaissance apologias for theatre than like any Renaissance version of religious experience'; see Orgel, Introduction to *The Winter's Tale* (Oxford: Clarendon Press, 1996), 62. Stanley Cavell rejects the idea that the scene is a 'translated moment of religious resurrection,' but instead sees 'this theater as in competition with religion, as if declaring itself religion's successor'; see Cavell, *Disowning Knowledge in Seven Plays of Shakespeare* (Cambridge: Cambridge University Press, 2003), 218.

7 For example, Julia Reinhard Lupton finds that Shakespeare 'definitively undercuts the Catholic iconography the scene so powerfully evokes, enacting the movement from the Church to its Reform' (*Knowledge*, 216), while for Ruth Vanita, the statue scene expresses nostalgia for Mariological piety ('Mariological Memory'). Walter S.H. Lim does note that '[t]he idea of the icon is not something associated exclusively with Catholic thought and practice' and finds that the competing Catholic and Protestant meanings 'facilitate consideration of the distinctions, if any, between knowledge and opinion, faith and gullibility'; see Lim, 'Knowledge and Belief in *The Winter's Tale*,' *Studies in English Literature* 41 (2001): 320, 330.

8 For a description of the forms this structure took, see Pamela Sheingorn,

The Easter Sepulchre in England, Early Drama, Art, and Music Reference 5 (Kalamazoo, MI: Medieval Institute Publications, 1987), 33–45. A catalogue of churches known to have had sepulchres is found on pages 77–368, and plates 27–55 illustrate surviving examples.

9 For the *Regularis Concordia*'s texts of the *depositio* and *elevatio*, see Karl Young, *The Drama of the Medieval Church* (Oxford: Clarendon Press, 1933), 1:132–4. David Bevington also prints and translates the *depositio* in *Medieval Drama* (Boston: Houghton Mifflin, 1975), 16.

10 Young defines the trope 'in its broadest sense' as 'a verbal amplification of a passage in the authorized liturgy, in the form of an introduction, an interpolation, or a conclusion, or in the form of any combination of these'; see Young, *Drama of the Medieval Church*, 1:178.

11 Quotations of the Latin text are taken from Young, *Drama of the Medieval Church*, 1:249; English translations are from Bevington, *Medieval Drama*, 27–8.

12 Young, *Drama of the Medieval Church*, 1:271.

13 See Sheingorn, *Easter Sepulchre*, 60–2 for a description of sixteenth-century sepulchre observances, and for the 1565 Coventry and Lichfield injunctions, see her 'No Easter Sepulchre on Good Friday,' in *Iconoclasm vs. Art and Drama*, ed. Clifford Davidson and Ann Eljenholm Nichols, Early Drama, Art, and Music Monograph 11 (Kalamazoo, MI: Medieval Institute Publications, 1989), 161. Ronald Hutton observes that 'after Easter 1548 there is only one, very doubtful, mention of the existence of the custom anywhere in England as long as Edward lived'; see *The Rise and Fall of Merry England: The Ritual Year 1400–1700* (Oxford: Oxford University Press, 1994), 84. For an account of Cranmer's attacks on the sepulchre ritual in 1547 and 1548, see Eamon Duffy, *The Stripping of the Altars: Traditional Religion in England 1400–1580* (New Haven, NJ: Yale University Press, 1992) 461–2.

14 Barnabe Googe, trans., *The Popish Kingdom or Reigne of Antichrist, written in Latin verse, by Thomas Naogeorgus* [Kirchmeyer] *and englyshed by Barnabe Googe* (1570) (New York: Johnson Reprint, 1972), 52v.

15 Googe, *Popish Kingdom*, 51v.

16 Johnston, 'Emerging Pattern,' 5–6, 19.

17 Sheingorn, *Easter Sepulchre*, 34–5.

18 Johnston also includes the Anglo-Norman *La Seinte Resurrection* in this group; for the purposes of this study I am highlighting dramas composed or being performed in sixteenth-century England.

19 *The Shrewsbury Fragments* consist of parts and cues for one actor in three plays: the third shepherd in a Nativity play, the third Mary in an '*Officium Resurreccionis in die Pasche*,' and Cleophas in a *peregrini* play for Easter

288   Karen Sawyer Marsalek

Monday; see Norman Davis, ed., *Non-Cycle Plays and Fragments*, EETS ss 1 (Oxford: Oxford University Press, 1970), 1–7. For *Christ's Burial* and *Christ's Resurrection*, see Donald C. Baker, John L. Murphy, and Louis B. Hall, Jr, eds, *The Late Medieval Religious Plays of Bodleian MSS Digby 133 and e Museo 160*, EETS os 283 (Oxford: Oxford University Press, 1982), 141–93.

20 Baker, Murphy, and Hall, *Late Medieval Religious Plays*, 142.

21 The play survives in fragmentary form in Folger Shakespeare Library MS V.b.192. All quotations will be taken from Karen Sawyer (Marsalek), '*The Resurrection of Our Lord*: A Study and Dual-Text Edition' (PhD dissertation, University of Toronto, 2001); see 110–17 for discussion of the play's episodic content.

22 Johnston, 'Emerging Pattern,' 4–5.

23 For the Lichfield statutes, see Young, *Drama of the Medieval Church*, 2:522. Lincoln Cathedral records performances between 1321 and 69 and from 1383 to 91; see Stanley J. Kahrl, ed., *Records of Plays and Players in Lincolnshire, 1300–1585*, Malone Society *Collections* 8 (Oxford: Oxford University Press, 1974 for 1969), 24–5. At Wells, expenses for Easter plays are recorded in 1408–9, 1417–18, 1418–19, and 1470–1; see James Stokes with Robert J. Alexander, eds, *Somerset including Bath*, REED (Toronto: University of Toronto Press, 1996), 1:242, 243, 248–9; 2:834, 835, 838.

24 Records survive for 1495–6, 1509–10, 1517–18, and 1519–20. A play on Mary Magdalene, possibly the same as the Easter drama, is recorded in 1506–7. See John R. Elliot, Jr, Alan H. Nelson, Alexandra F. Johnston, and Diana Wyatt, eds, *Oxford: University and City*, REED (Toronto: University of Toronto Press, 2004), 1:38, 46, 52, 61, 63; 2:933, 940, 944, 949, 951.

25 Suzanne R. Westfall, *Patrons and Performance: Early Tudor Household Revels* (Oxford: Clarendon Press, 1990), 28.

26 At St Saviour's, Dartmouth (1494–5); see John M. Wasson, ed., *Devon*, REED (Toronto: University of Toronto Press, 1986), 62.

27 At St Mary Magdalene, Taunton; see Stokes and Alexander, *Somerset*, 1:227.

28 At Rye; see Cameron Louis, ed., *Sussex*, REED (Toronto, University of Toronto Press, 2000), 94, 97.

29 Johnston, 'Emerging Pattern,' 7–12, and '"What revels are in hand?"': Dramatic Activities Sponsored by the Parishes of the Thames Valley,' in *English Parish Drama*, ed. Alexandra F. Johnston and Wim Hüsken, Ludus 1 (Amsterdam: Rodopi, 1996), 98–9; and Alexandra F. Johnston and Sally-Beth MacLean, 'Reformation and Resistance in Thames/Severn Parishes: The Dramatic Witness,' in *The Parish in English Life, 1400–1600*, ed. Katherine L. French, Gary G. Gibbs, and Beat A. Kümin (Manchester: Manchester Uni-

versity Press, 1997), 178–200.

30 Rosin was used at St Laurence, Reading, in 1506–7; see Johnston, 'Emerging Pattern,' 11; the Kingston-upon-Thames parish used parchment and gunpowder; see Surrey Record Office KG 2/2/1, 1503–38, p. 100. I am grateful to Sally-Beth MacLean for giving me access to her unpublished research.

31 William Lambarde, *Dictionarium Angliae Topographicum et Historicum: An Alphabetical Description of the Chief Places in England and Wales* (London: Fletcher Gyles, 1730), 459. Lambarde began amassing material for this survey before 1570, but gave up the project in 1585 when he learned of Camden's work on *Britannia*.

32 Johnston, 'Emerging Pattern,' 9–10.

33 See Karen Sawyer Marsalek, '"Doctrine Evangelicall" and Erasmus's *Paraphrases* in *The Resurrection of Our Lord*,' in *Tudor Drama Before Shakespeare, 1485–1590: New Directions for Research, Criticism, and Pedagogy*, ed. Lloyd Edward Kermode, Jason Scott-Warren, and Martine Van Elk (New York: Palgrave Macmillan, 2004), 35–66.

34 Johnston, 'Emerging Pattern,' 19.

35 Lawrence M. Clopper, ed., *Chester*, REED (Toronto: University of Toronto Press, 1979), 110.

36 Michael O'Connell, 'Vital Cultural Practices: Shakespeare and the Mysteries,' *Journal of Medieval and Early Modern Studies* 29 (1999): 156.

37 Bale records these in his 1548 *Summarium*; see Peter Happé, Introduction to *The Complete Plays of John Bale* (Cambridge: D.S. Brewer, 1985), 1:8–9.

38 L.R. Merrill, ed., *The Life and Poems of Nicholas Grimald*, Yale Studies in English 69 (New Haven, CT: Yale University Press, 1925). All quotations from the play are taken from this edition and identified by page number. English translations are also Merrill's translation, and appear on facing pages with the Latin text. No records of an Oxford performance survive.

39 John Bale, *Scriptorum Illustrium Maioris Britannie ... Catalogus 701*, quoted and trans. in Merrill, *Life and Poems*, 15–19. However, Grimald's commitment to Protestantism proved less than firm. Evidence suggests that he betrayed the Protestant martyrs Cranmer, Latimer, and Ridley and recanted when he himself was imprisoned; see Merrill, *Life and Poems*, 36–51.

40 Leonard Barkan, 'Making Pictures Speak: Renaissance Art, Elizabethan Literature, Modern Scholarship,' *Renaissance Quarterly* 48 (1995): 343.

41 Lupton, *Afterlives of the Saints*, 206–18.

42 R.A. Foakes and R.T. Rickert, eds, *Henslowe's Diary* (Cambridge: Cambridge University Press, 1961), 319–20.

43 G.E. Bentley, *The Jacobean and Caroline Stage* (Oxford: Clarendon Press, 1949), 1:94.

44 Grantley, '*Winter's Tale*,' 33; Marshall, 'Appendix B,' 123–5; Cynthia [Marshall] Lewis, 'Soft Touch: On the Renaissance Staging and Meaning of the "Noli me tangere" Icon,' *Comparative Drama* 36 (2002): 68–70. For texts of the Towneley and York Resurrection plays, see Martin Stevens and A.C. Cawley, eds, *The Towneley Plays*, 2 vols, EETS ss 13–14 (Oxford: Oxford University Press, 1994), and Richard Beadle, ed., *The York Plays*, York Medieval Texts, 2nd series (London: Arnold, 1982).

45 O'Connell, 'Vital Cultural Practices,' 160–2.

46 See *The Chester Mystery Cycle*, ed. R.M.Lumiansky and David Mills, vd.1, EETS ss 3 (London: Oxford: University Press, 1974), Play 18/401–12 and Appendix 1D 60–80, as well as *The Resurrection of Our Lord*, 436–99.

47 R.W. Ingram, ed., *Coventry*, REED (Toronto: University of Toronto Press, 1981), 139–40; Sally-Beth MacLean, 'Festive Liturgy and the Dramatic Connection: A Study of Thames Valley Parishes,' *Medieval and Renaissance Drama in English* 8 (1996): 55. No other parishes include music among their Resurrection play expenditures, but this absence does not mean that musicians were not performing, only that they weren't reimbursed for doing so.

48 Robert S. Miola, '"An alien people clutching their gods"?: Shakespeare's Ancient Religions,' *Shakespeare Survey* 54 (2001): 45.

49 Pamela Sheingorn, 'The Moment of the Resurrection in the Corpus Christi Plays,' *Medievalia et Humanistica: Studies in Medieval and Renaissance Culture* 11 (1982): 122. The Towneley and Chester speeches both draw on a lyric associated with this image; see Stevens and Cawley, *Towneley Plays*, 2:605 note on lines 230–350. For the lyric, see #102 in *Religious Lyrics of the Fifteenth Century*, ed. Carleton Brown (Oxford: Clarendon Press, 1939), 151–6.

50 In a recent conference paper, Stephen Greenblatt distinguished the wounds of Christ and the martyrs' and soldiers' battle scars as the only kinds of physical 'marks' that could be beautiful. Stephen Greenblatt, 'The Mark of Beauty,' Shakespeare Association of America, Bermuda, April 2005.

51 David Mills, *Recycling the Cycle: The City of Chester and Its Whitsun Plays*, SEED 4 (Toronto: University of Toronto Press, 1998), 182. It is not clear that the reformist revisions were ever actually performed.

52 Jörg Hasler analyses Paulina's careful orchestration of the scene in 'Romance in the Theater: The Stagecraft of the "Statue Scene" in *The Winter's Tale*,' in *Shakespeare: Man of the Theater, Proceedings of the Second Congress of the International Shakespeare Association, 1981*, ed. Kenneth Muir, Jay Halio, and D.J. Palmer (Newark: University of Delaware Press, 1983), 205–9.

53 'Ego uobiscum unà spectator ero fabulæ'; Merrill, *Life and Poems*, 118–19.

54 For additional discussion of Appendix's work as an expositor, see K. Janet

Ritch's essay in this collection.

55 John Hooper, 'A Declaration of the Ten Holy Commandments of Almighty God' (1548, 1550), in *Early Writings of John Hooper*, ed. Samuel Carr, Parker Society 20 (Cambridge: Cambridge University Press, 1843), 326.

56 For additional discussion of 'womens witnes' in this play, see Garrett Epp's essay in this collection.

57 Though not crucial to my argument, an echo of the King James version is just possible here; the edition was published in the same year as the first account of *The Winter's Tale* performance.

58 Kenneth Gross, *The Dream of the Moving Statue* (Ithaca, NY: Cornell University Press, 1992), 109.

59 O'Connell, *The Idolatrous Eye*, 141.

60 Marjory E. Lange observes: 'Sermons on Peter's weeping ... belong to a moment of curious sensibility extending from the later years of Elizabeth's reign into the early part of James I's'; *Telling Tears In the English Renaissance* (New York: Brill, 1996), 136.

61 'An Homilie of Repentance, and of true reconciliation vnto God,' in *The second tome of homilees, of such matters as were promised, and intituled in the former part of homilees. Set out by the aucthoritie of the Queenes Maiestie: and to bee read in euery parishe church agreeably.* (London, 1571), 532–3.

62 'An Homilie of Repentance,' 531.

63 Discussing Leontes' 'Romanist penance,' Jensen argues that Paulina directs him in 'Catholic forms of atonement' in these lines, but I submit that Paulina is instead emphasizing their lack of efficacy. See Jensen, 'Singing Psalms,' 303.

64 Lupton, *Afterlives of the Saints*, 216.

One Hell of an Ending: Staging Last Judgment in the Towneley Plays and in *Doctor Faustus* A and B

DAVID BEVINGTON

A common and not inaccurate view is that Christopher Marlowe's *Doctor Faustus* owes an important debt to the Tudor morality play, even if it upends that dramatic tradition in ways that would no doubt have surprised William Wager and Thomas Lupton. ('I am shocked, sir, shocked!') Especially from Nathaniel Woodes's *The Conflict of Conscience*, with its two possible endings, one with the protagonist saved at the last moment and the other with the protagonist eternally damned, Marlowe could have learned a lot about the potential of English mid-century drama for a cliff-hanging account of spiritual struggle that could go either way right down to the last moment – and then, in one version at least, opts for failure.[1] Less has been said about *Doctor Faustus* and the biblical drama, despite the fact that the morality play does not normally portray on stage the terrors of hell, whereas the biblical drama does. The so-called A-text of *Doctor Faustus* (printed 1604) is visually restrained in its depiction of damnation, concentrating more on the spiritual terror of a man who realizes at last that he has no hope of escaping the very real terrors of hell, but the B-text (1616) has no such inhibitions. It goes back to P.F.'s English translation of the German *Faustbuch*, called *The History of the Damnable Life and Deserved Death of Doctor John Faustus* (1592), for all the macabre details it can muster as to what hell is physically like and what gory dismemberment Faustus's body must have suffered when the devils come to collect on Faustus's bad bargain. The differences between the A-text and the B-text have important theological as well as dramaturgical implications.[2] Perhaps we can gain some perspective on the striking differences between these two printed texts by examining those differences in the context of late medieval staging of damnation, as seen for example in the Wakefield Master's *Harrowing of Hell* and *Last Judgment* pageants from the Towneley plays.[3]

This essay proceeds from the assumption, based on research done by this author and Eric Rasmussen in 1993, that the 1604 A-text is substantially closer to what Marlowe wrote than is the B-text.[4] To be sure, the A-text did not show up in print until some eleven years after Marlowe died, and it appears to have been written collaboratively with another dramatist, possibly Henry Porter, who took responsibility chiefly for the comic scenes. Perhaps because various episodes from the *Faust Book* were parcelled out to two authors and then had to be interleaved in such a way as to alternate serious and comic scenes in more or less regular rotation, the chance for misordering of some episodes and flat loss of others was not inconsiderable. The A-text shows manifest signs of such textual distress. It is implausibly short for a London stage play ca. 1588–9, as compared, say, with either part of *Tamburlaine* or *The Jew of Malta* or *Edward II*. It contains a very long scene in Act 2 that seems to require separation into two scenes (as it is so divided in the B-text), which separation can conjecturally best be accomplished by moving the first comic scene between Robin and Rafe into this slot, thereby remedying also an awkward linking of two scenes of clownage in the A-text that would require the comic actors to exit from the first such scene and then immediately reappear. Yet despite these shortcomings, the A-text bears marked characteristics of having been set from an authorial manuscript. Quite plausibly, the Admiral's Men sold these authorial papers in 1601 (at a time when they were selling off four plays from their repertory to London publishers) because they had a theatrical prompt book in hand and were about to commission (in 1602) some additions from William Birde (or Borne) and Samuel Rowley. The acting company no longer needed the original authors' papers.

The 1616 B-text must surely be the result of the Admiral's Men's commissioning of new material. Rowley's imprint can be seen in certain stylistic tics and in the new material's fascination with John Foxe's *Acts and Monuments* (a.k.a. *The Book of Martyrs*), to which Rowley had devoted much attention in his dramatization of Lutheran intrigue in *When You See Me You Know Me* (1603–5). Another set of stylistic traits distinguishes those portions of the new material that were the work of someone other than Marlowe or Porter or Rowley, presumably William Birde. The B-text, based in part on the third quarto of the A-text, published in 1611 and with new scenes that show a particular interest in practical matters of staging, appears to be a revised version paid for by the Admiral's Men because they sensed that their audiences wanted more stage magic and popular Calvinist-slanted theology.

Another assumption of this essay is that the affinity of *Doctor Faustus*'s staging of damnation, especially in the B-text, to earlier biblical drama can hardly have been the result of first-hand theatrical experience. Biblical drama had been suppressed by the authorities of the English Reformation by the time Marlowe wrote. Quite possibly he, along with Shakespeare and others of his generation, might have seen some late survivors (like those at Coventry and Chester, for example), but then the visual staging of hell with which we are concerned in this essay does not really materialize in *Doctor Faustus* until the B-text. In the 1600s, when the B-text revision presumably took place, the great religious drama could only have been a distant memory. To what pictorial tradition, then, were Birde and Rowley indebted? The Reformation authorities had been busy whitewashing church murals of the Last Judgment and other vestiges of Catholic picture making, but doubtless some such representations still survived in churches and were certainly extant in the visual arts of painting and engraving. The intriguing question, perhaps, is why the B-text revisers, encouraged no doubt by the Admiral's Men's interest in financial success, reverted to a visual depiction of hell's pains that Protestant religious reformers were trying to eradicate. Thus, although Birde and Rowley are perhaps unlikely to have known the biblical drama at first hand, its central importance in the iconographic depiction of the afterlife, along with its use of the theatrical medium in which Marlowe and his revisers worked, offer that great religious drama as a kind of dramatic workshop in which to study the shifting stage conventions that materialize in Marlowe's great play.

The question as to why the B-text revisers of *Doctor Faustus* added such garish details of damnation becomes especially intriguing when we note that the A-text makes a special point of rejecting such visualization of hell as childish and superstitious. 'Come, I think hell's a fable,' declares Faustus, in response to Mephistopheles' description of hell as being 'Within the bowels of these elements, / Where we are tortured and remain for ever.' Faustus will hear none of Mephistopheles' argument that hell is real and that Faustus, having sold his soul to the devil in return for twenty-four years in which Faustus is to have Mephistopheles at his command to 'do for him and bring him whatsoever,' will dwell in hell for the rest of eternity.

> Think'st thou that Faustus is so fond
> To imagine that after this life there is any pain?
> Tush, these are trifles and mere old wives' tales.

When Mephistopheles reminds Faustus that he has 'given [his] soul to Lucifer,' Faustus pounces with his reply: 'Ay, and body too. But what of that?' (A-text, 2.1.98–138). Faustus is proud to be able to see through such infantile nonsense. After all, he is himself a famous scholar who, though of humble origins, has 'Gravelled the pastors of the German Church' with his 'concise syllogisms,' to such an extent that 'the flow'ring pride of Wittenberg' swarm to his 'problems' – that is, to his scholastic disputations and public lectures (1.1.114–16). His common talk has become the very stuff of 'sound aphorisms.' His medical discoveries are 'hung up as monuments, / Whereby whole cities have escaped the plague / And thousand desp'rate maladies been eased' (1.1.19–22). Long gone are the days when the writings of Aristotle, the medical wisdom of Galen, or the legal expertise of Justinian could have taught him anything. And is this man to tremble at naive legends about hell that even the Bible, a book he also regards with considerable scepticism, does not authenticate? Perish the thought.

Or, perhaps, perish Doctor Faustus. His big mistake, of course, is that he does not understand how to interpret correctly those stories about hell. He scorns their literalism, and rightly so, but does not listen to what Mephistopheles repeatedly cautions him about their deeper meaning. 'Hell hath no limits, nor is circumscribed / In one self place,' Mephistopheles tells him; 'for where we are is hell, / And where hell is must we ever be.' When the world dissolves, and the time of final purification has arrived, 'All places shall be hell that is not heaven' (2.1.124–9). What could be more plain? Hell is eternal absence from God. Eternity lasts for a very, very long time. When one reaches the first million years, one has not even fairly started to serve a sentence that is truly endless. Mephistopheles is excruciatingly aware of the fact: he is 'an instance to prove the contrary' of Faustus's glib assertion that hell is merely an old wives' tale. 'For,' as Mephistopheles confesses, 'I am damned and now in hell.' Why is Faustus unable to listen to such clear warnings, and why does Marlowe put such sad wisdom into the mouth of a devil?

Faustus's difficulty is in being too literal. Even before he signs the contract, he is devoured with curiosity to know the whereabouts of hell. 'Where are you damned?' is one of his first questions to Mephistopheles, prompted by that devil's account of how Lucifer, once dearly loved of God, became the prince of devils 'by aspiring pride and insolence, / For which God threw him from the face of heaven' (1.3.69–70). This account has a familiar ring to Faustus's ears, as to ours; it imagines Lucifer being thrown down from heaven to the pit of hell, as in Milton's *Paradise Lost*. This story of the fall of Lucifer was, as Marlowe may well have understood, a legendary accretion from the third century, entirely absent from Genesis 1 and based instead on an erroneous interpretation of Luke 10:15

and 18: 'And thou, Capernaum, which art exalted to heaven, shalt be thrust down to hell ... And he [Jesus] said unto them [his followers], "I beheld Satan as lightning fall from heaven."' Capernaum was a town on the shore of the Sea of Galilee whose impenitent people were judged by Jesus to be headed for destruction. The passage from Luke 10:18 cannot, in the opinion of most scholars, be seen as a reliable explanation of the famous lines from Isaiah 14:12: 'How art thou fallen from heaven, O Lucifer, son of the morning! How art thou cut down to the ground, which didst weaken the nations!' Conflating these two passages from Luke and Isaiah gave rise to the naming of Satan as Lucifer, albeit that name of Lucifer (Latin for 'light-bearer') was originally intended for the planet Venus as the morning (or evening) star, having nothing to do with the fall of the rebel angels – a story not even in the Bible in the first place. The point here is that Faustus's scepticism is nominally plausible, even if it is also fatally misguided.

What Faustus fails to understand is that being in hell is a state of mind and spirit. An understanding of its true nature need not and should not depend on the kinds of stories so widely associated with hell as depicted in much Western art from Dante to Brueghel and beyond: unimaginable physical tortures of thirst, hunger, and pain, devil figures running about with pitchforks impaling their sin-laden victims on torture racks above roaring flames, loathsome snakes and worms crawling in and out of the corrupting dead body or spewing forth from the mouth, and so on. Faustus seems confirmed in his impatient dismissal of such frivolous images by what he perceives of his conversations with Mephistopheles. If Mephistopheles is in hell, as he insists, what can be so bad about hell? 'How? Now in hell? Nay, an this be hell, / I'll willingly be damned here. What? Walking, disputing, etc.?' (2.1.141–3). The two of them are not only conversing in a congenial fashion, they are doing what Faustus loves most of all: disputing, arguing, debating. Hell seems to foster the life of the mind, as well as offering sybaritic pleasure. Indeed, Faustus embraces his new situation as one in which to pursue knowledge of geography, of ancient history and poetry, and especially of the celestial cosmos, though on this latter score he is frustrated by being shown no more of planetary motion than he has known for years. Faustus's hunch that more indeed is to be discovered about the cosmos adds to his scepticism when he is denied that knowledge, and perhaps to Marlowe's audience as well (since some of his spectators at least would have heard of Copernicus's as yet unproven hypothesis of a heliocentric universe). As a result, the audience may well empathize with Faustus's intellectual curiosity and his scornful dismissal of hell's physical pains, while at the same time shaking its collective head at his wilfulness in failing to listen to what the devil is telling him. It is as though Marlowe, by putting so much cautionary wisdom in the mouth of Mephistopheles, is creating a world in which Faustus is given fair warning. No one is to blame but Faustus himself, in his wilful misreading of the legendary accounts about hell.

If Faustus chooses to be wilfully ignorant in this matter, Marlowe as author had every reason to be more aware of what is at stake. As a student at Cambridge he had the opportunity to learn Calvinist theology by heart. And Calvin is very astute on this matter of the tactile images of hell, the little devils with pitchforks and all that. These are the stories we devise and tell one another, says Calvin, because the diseased imaginings of which we are barely capable are the inheritance of our fallen condition. We cannot begin to see God face to face; we can only hope to see him through a glass darkly, in the wonderful language of St Paul (1 Cor. 13:12), and even that much of a glimpse of eternal bliss is vouchsafed only to the chosen few. Being fallen creatures of appetite and mortal frailty, we can communicate our dreams and fears only through crude approximations, through stereotyped icons that tell more about us than about the thing intended. We pictorialize because we are children. To understand this is to acknowledge one's abysmal ignorance and to place one's trust in the great Unseen that can never be captured in images.[5]

We will come to the ending of the A-text shortly, in which the stage picture makes no attempt to literalize heaven and hell, and to the B-text, where the literalization is quite heavy-handed. Before we do so, we might do well to look at the Wakefield Master's depiction of the horrors of hellfire for insights as to how the subject of damnation was staged in the great medieval biblical plays. *The Harrowing of Hell* is perhaps a good place to begin, because it dramatizes an episode of divine history that is legendary in the sense of having no direct biblical authority. It is based on the apocryphal Gospel of Nicodemus, which in turn owes its inspiration to Psalm 24:9–10: 'Lift up your heads, O ye gates; even lift them up, ye everlasting doors; and the King of glory shall come in. / Who is this King of glory? The Lord of hosts, he is the King of glory.' The very concept of hell is shadowy in the Old and New Testaments, being originally a place of the dead, linguistically akin to the Hebrew 'Sheol' and the Greek 'Haides.' Equivalents of the word 'hell' only fleetingly appear in the scriptures (and depend on translation), as in Deut. 32:22, Psalm 55:15 ('Let death seize upon them, and let them go down quick into hell, for wickedness is in their dwellings, and among them'), Psalm 86:13 ('For great is thy mercy toward me: and thou hast delivered my soul from the lowest hell'); the concept is sometimes rendered as 'the grave' as in 1 Cor. 15:55 ('O death, where is thy sting? O grave, where is thy victory?').

Undeterred by such lack of biblical authority, exegetical and liturgical tradition created and greatly elaborated a vision of the so-called Harrowing of Hell as a visualized answer to the intriguing question, what did Christ do on Saturday of Holy Week? Having been crucified on Friday and being about the rise again on the third day (traditionally Sunday), Christ was imagined to have descended into hell in order to free the souls of those many long-suffering persons who had persevered in goodness, despite their weaknesses, and yet had had to await the Resurrection before they could be saved through Christ. The Wakefield Master, in his *Harrowing of Hell*, brings on Adam and Eve, Isaiah, Simeon, John the Baptist, and Moses as representative figures, though he might also have included Noah and his family, Abraham, Isaac, and many others. Importantly, such souls were not in hell as the place of eternal torment; church theology had devised another legend, of limbo, as a holding pattern for virtuous pagans, in answer to the vexed scholastic problem of what to do with all good people who surely cannot be damned for eternity and yet cannot be saved without having received Christian baptism. 'Limbo' is so splendidly apocryphal that it is not even listed in *The Westminster Dictionary of the Bible*.[6]

The Wakefield Master's *Harrowing of Hell* takes as gospel the narrative account of Jesus' arriving before hell's gates, his defiance of the devils within, his thrice challenging his enemy to open the gates to him as the King of glory, the bursting open of those gates, and the deliverance of hell's virtuous occupants. The episode had long been adopted into the liturgy, after all, as the basis of the ceremony for consecrating a church; as early as the ninth century, the bishop of Metz had used the rite as a means of exorcising any non-sacred presences by going in procession around the building and to its north portal, challenging the occupants to open, processing around the church again and repeating the challenge, then doing so once more, until, at the sound from within of the question, 'Quis est iste rex gloriae?' (Who is this King of glory?), the bishop responded, 'Dominus virtutem, ipse est rex gloriae' (The Lord of hosts, he is the King of glory), at which point the portal flung open to admit the entire procession, singing antiphons as they entered. The voice from within had been that of a cleric who had discreetly absented himself in order to be shut up within in the role of the devil; this same cleric took flight at the end, by way of demonstrating that evil spirits had indeed been exorcised. The text for the chanted ceremony was taken from Psalm 24:9–10: 'Lift up your heads, O ye gates; even lift them up, ye everlasting doors; and the King of glory shall come in.

Who is this King of glory? The Lord of hosts, he is the King of glory.'
Exegetical tradition interpreted this text as referring to the Harrowing of
Hell, as narrated in the Gospel of Nicodemus.[7]

Narrative and stage action in the Wakefield Master's *Harrowing of Hell*
are accordingly simple, but not without a plenitude of stage pictures
reproducing in action a series of images familiar to audiences from illus-
trated Bibles, wall paintings, and the like. The gates themselves, a central
stage property, undoubtedly must bear a resemblance to hell mouths depicted in medieval art as the gaping mouth of a leviathan. A glorious light
must be seen to shine from within, illuminated at Jesus' words, 'A light I
will thay have / To know I will com sone' (21–2). The rapturous occupants
perceive this 'glorious gleme' that has been brought 'to make us glad' (30).
They sing a verse of the hymn 'Salvator Mundi' to anticipate their imminent release. Meantime, the devils raise a din in the customary fashion of
dramatizing hell, by shouting accusations at one another in such a way that
the holy chant of Adam and his comrades is counterparted by cacophony.
The devils scurry about barricading the gates ('Go spar the yates!' 120) and
setting watches 'on the wall' (121), suggesting a structure not unlike that of
a besieged city in medieval warfare (or, later, in many an English history
play of the 1590s). Undoubtedly the devils in hell are 'Besegyd aboute'
(148). They are alternatively confident that their gates 'will last, / Thay ar
so strong' (202–3) and are terrified that this 'trature' (traitor) at the gates
'travesses us allway' (thwarts us in every way, 153).

The climactic action is of course the actual bursting asunder of the gates,
at which point the text calls for maximum effect. Jesus commands a third
time that the devils 'Open up, and let my pepill pas!' (206), and the
moment has arrived. 'Out, harro! Oure baill is broken, / And brusten ar all
our bandys of bras!' exclaims Ribald, at which point Belzabub fearfully
concurs: 'Harro! Oure yates begin to crak! / In sonder, I trow, they go, /
And hell, I trow, will all to-shak' (shake to pieces, 207–11). As staging of
this and similar plays at the University of Toronto over the last twenty-five
years has confirmed, much of it inspired by the leadership of Professor
Alexandra Johnston, stage action at such moments cannot be simply mimed
with actors' gestures; the dramatic medium plainly calls for the physical
effects of gates being torn down. 'Limbo is lorne, alas!' laments Ribald
(213), as he calls to Satan for assistance. Satan confronts Jesus in a scholastic debate about whether this Jesus' father was a mere carpenter (246) or
God Almighty, but Satan's protestations are of course to no avail. He is
commanded by Jesus to 'go downe / Into thy seate where thou shall sit'
(358), evidently some physical representation of the pit of hell. There Satan

must ignominiously remain, in the company of his defeated companions, while the souls of the saved are delivered. 'Com now furth, my childer all,' Jesus bids them. 'I forgif you youre mis' (362–3). They exit in procession, singing 'Te Deum laudamus.' In the spirit of the Sermon on the Mount, the last become the first; 'A prince of peasse' (195) has triumphed over the brutish and heavily defended forces of evil not through violence but by the power of his gospel.

For the purposes of this essay, the point is that once-apocryphal legends of hell are visualized on stage as living truths at the very heart of Christian teaching. They are as demonstrable as any part of the Creed or liturgy. Theatre reifies doctrine. Especially as graced with the comic genius of the Wakefield Master, hell is a place of obscene and grotesque humour, physical violence, and noise. The climactic moment of Jesus' triumph over the forces of evil occurs when he stands before the gates of hell and bursts them asunder. Any Christian inclining to doubt the existence of hell need only consider how central the concept of hell has become to the missionary purpose of Christianity, and how the theatrical representation of hell gives to that idea a tactile reality beyond the power of mere words.

The Wakefield Master's *Last Judgment* achieves much the same effect. It celebrates another central and definitive moment in Christian world history, and does so in a visual configuration that will turn up in the B-text of *Doctor Faustus* by antithetically juxtaposing a vision of heavenly bliss with that of eternal torment. The antithesis of such a design was of course integral to many a representation of Judgment, as for example in Jan van Eyck's fifteenth-century dyptich of the Crucifixion and Last Judgment, in the twelfth-century 'Weighing of Souls' at Autun Cathedral, and on many a west wall of a church facing the congregation as it turned to leave by the west door.

The Towneley *Last Judgment* illustrates how a staging design of antithesis is inherent in the play text. Christ, enthroned in heaven, dispatches his angels to earth to separate the good from the wicked as the play commences. (Some opening verses are missing, but their substance can be inferred from the closely related *Last Judgment* at York.) A trumpet of doom sounds, prompting the wicked to bewail their onrushing fate: 'Alas, I harde that horne that callys us to thy dome!' exclaims one (3). 'Alas, I am forlorne! A spitus blast here blawes!' says another (41). Their anguished utterances are like those of Faustus in Act 5 of Marlowe's play, even if the cadences are those of an earlier verse tradition:

Alas, carefull catifys may we rise,
Sore may we wring oure handys and wepe!
For cursid and sore covetise
Dampnyd be we in hell full depe.
Roght we never of Godys service;
His commaundementys wold we not kepe;
Bot oft times maide we sacrifice
To Sathanas when others can slepe.   (17–24)

Like Faustus, they cast their eyes aloft and behold Christ's bleeding wounds. 'To se his woundys bledande, this is a dulfull case,' one laments. 'Alas, how shall I stand or loke him in the face?' (53–4). (Compare *Doctor Faustus*, A-text: 'See, see where Christ's blood streams in the firmament! One drop would save my soul, half a drop. Ah, my Christ!' [5.2.78–9], simplified and impoverished in the B-text version to 'One drop of blood will save me. O, my Christ!' [5.2.151].)

The antithetical separation of the blessed from the damned is thus reinforced in stage picture by the vertical separation of heaven and earth, Christ and humanity. An angel armed *'cum gladio,'* with a sword, separates the good souls from the wicked, saying to the former, 'On his right hand ye good shall go,' while banishing the latter to stand 'On his left hand as none of his' (77–80). When Jesus thereupon descends to sit in judgment as both God and man, taking with him the body that humankind has tortured and desecrated (86–9), he sits enthroned. The devils in hell meanwhile roar in dismay at the terrifying sound of the trumpet of doom. They complain that hell has been emptied of all its former prisoners: 'all oure saules ar wente, and none ar in hell' (116). Yet they recall with roars of appreciative laughter the sinful ways of those former inmates, and chortle at the prospect that now hell will be given a new and double supply of damned souls as a result of Last Judgment: 'Now gett we dowbill store: of bodyss miscarid / To the soules where they wore, both same to be harrid' (181–2). That is, the doomed souls will be reunited in hell with their bodies, so that the devils will be able to torment body and soul together. This text does not entertain any doubt, then, that hell's torments will be physical and graphic. The devils extensively catalogue the sins of pride and of the flesh (fashions in long hair, expensively decorated robes with fur trim, elaborate headgear, ribbons, curls, padded shoulders, prominent codpieces, garments designed to accentuate the buttocks, etc.) in such a way as to justify the physical tortures that will be inflicted on those who have sinned thus.

The moment of judgment is theatrically composed in such a way that it could almost be an altarpiece. Coming as 'crownyd king,' Jesus is both God and man, wearing the crown of glory and yet clearly the son, sent down by 'My Fader of heven' to pronounce sentence (390). The stage directions are iconic: *Tunc expandit manus suas et ostendit eis vulnera sua* (Then he spreads apart his hands and shows them his wounds). His turning to right and left is explicit: *Tunc vertens se ad bonos, dicit illis* (Then turning to the good souls, he speaks to them), addressing them as 'My blissid barnes on my ryght hande' (433–4). He blesses the virtuous for having performed the so-called corporal works of mercy, feeding the hungry, clothing the naked, comforting the sick and sorrowful, offering shelter to those in need; as he explains in the familiar language of the New Testament and the liturgy, when good people have done these things on behalf of the poor they have done them as though to Jesus himself (442–73). Conversely, when he turns to the wicked on his left hand, addressing them as 'Ye cursid catifs, of Kames kin ' Jesus spells out in an approximately equal number of verse lines their failure to visit the poor and clothe the naked, etc., through which they have in effect repudiated Jesus' own flesh and blood: 'To the lest of mine when ye oght did, / To me ye did the self and the same' (474–523). This emphasis on good works as a means of earning a heavenly award, so anathematized by the Protestant reformers in Marlowe's day, is here in harmony with a theatre that physicalizes for its audience the issues of salvation and damnation. The play ends as the good souls on Jesus' right hand are led off to heaven while the devils gleefully herd their victims into hell, driving them as though they were teams of animals. 'Do now, furth go, trus! Go we hyne / Unto endles wo, ay-lastand pyne' (532–3). The wicked say nothing; they must endure the verbal and physical abuse of their tormentors.

When we return to *Doctor Faustus*, this time to the B-text written around 1602 and published in 1616, we can see that one of the adapters, perhaps William Birde, has used the Admiral's Men's commission as an opportunity to move Act 5 in a direction that is markedly more spectacular than the ending of the A-text and more fascinated by the physical nature of hell than Marlowe seems to have wished. Gone for the most part is the Calvinist idea that hell's physical torments are to be understood as grossly inadequate metaphors for the immeasurably greater spiritual torment of eternal absence from God. The B-text positively revels in the physicality of hell, and heaven too. Devils are added in profusion, first as diabolical servants *'with covered dishes'* tending to Faustus's last feast with his fellow scholars that Wagner mentions in both texts but is materialized by servants with dishes only in the later version. Then, at the beginning of what in the A-text is the final long and terrifying scene (5.2), the B-text inserts a gloating conference among Lucifer, Beelzebub, and Mephistopheles, to the accompaniment of thunder. Probably they enter above; 'Thus from infernal Dis do we ascend / To view the subjects of our monarchy,' Lucifer begins, and, whereas this could mean that they ascend from below the stage as representing hell, their determination to view Faustus's last hour is more in keeping with an acting station above. Moreover, they must not be physically in the way when the main stage is busily occupied with a descent of the heavenly throne and a 'discovery' of hell. The best place for the devils' wry choric observations is above.

Wherever they in fact locate themselves, they remain unobserved in turn by Faustus, Wagner, the three Scholars, and the Good and Bad Angels; they are present throughout, resolved not to miss anything. 'Here we'll stay / To mark how he doth demean himself,' says Beelzebub to his companions (B-text, 5.2.9–10). This is an amazing difference in staging from that of the A-text, where, in 5.2, Faustus is alone after the departure of his fellow scholars until the devils arrive right at the end, silently and ominously, to 'exeunt with him' to hell. That is the last thing that happens in the A-text except for the brief final chorus as epilogue. In the B-text, contrastingly, all of Faustus's agonizing final soliloquy is witnessed and heard by the devils. When he looks upward pleadingly to heaven, the B-text offers nothing to be seen 'above' other than the devils in the upper acting area, invisible to him though plainly visible to us. The presence throughout of the devils plainly signals a deterministic universe in which Faustus's doom is not only unavoidable but the direct consequence of the devils' having laid traps for him. Lucifer indeed claims just this sort of absolute diabolical power over his victim. When Faustus is about to enter onstage in this his final hour of life, Lucifer apostrophizes him in the following lines, absent from the A-text:

Faustus, we come to thee,
Bringing with us lasting damnation
To wait upon thy soul. The time is come
Which makes it forfeit.   (4–7)

These devils are thus more than a chorus, framing the scene and pacing our expectation of it; they are the controllers of Faustus's spiritual destiny.

None of these three devils addresses Faustus in the course of Act 5 except Mephistopheles. His brief exchange with Faustus, occurring once the scholars have left, is another confirmation of the B-text's deterministic view of diabolical control. No entrance is given here for Mephistopheles, confirming that he has been present all along. (Whether he addresses Faustus from above or by descending to the main stage is not clear.) Mephistopheles' present purpose is to taunt his victim with no longer having any hope of heaven and no prospect other than despair. When Faustus accusingly replies, 'O thou bewitching fiend, 'twas thy temptation / Hath robbed me of eternal happiness,' Mephistopheles is quick to claim credit:

> I do confess it, Faustus, and rejoice.
> 'Twas I that, when thou wert i'the way to heaven,
> Dammed up thy passage. When thou took'st the book
> To view the Scriptures, then I turned the leaves
> And led thine eye.   (B-text, 5.2.95–101)

This is a remarkable interpretation of the passage at the end of 2.1 where, in the A-text (not in the B-text), Mephistopheles does turn pages for Faustus in a book of spells and incantations, but without the least suggestion of leading him into a new and conclusive temptation; Faustus has already sold his soul to the devil. The interpolation at 5.2.95–101 in the B-text is thus gratuitous in its insistence that Faustus is the victim of a diabolical conspiracy. The idea goes against everything that the A-text stands for and that remains intact in much of the early scenes of the B-text as well, especially when Mephistopheles admits to Faustus that he has come not solely because of Faustus's ability to conjure (any fool can conjure the devil, as the clowns make clear) but because the devil is ready to come when a corrupted heart shows a willingness to heed evil counsel (A-text, 1.3.44–55, B-text, 1.3.41–52).

Earlier in the B-text, as well, in 1.3, Lucifer and four devils hover over the scene in which Faustus, unaware of their presence, conjures with his magic books and thus summons Mephistopheles. They appear to be above, as in 5.2, exerting an unheard but (for the audience) highly visible supernatural influence. The A-text begins instead by focusing on Faustus, alone, with his conjuring book, making his own decision to pursue his quest for secret knowledge and power.

A plausible concomitant of this emphasis on diabolical conspiracy in the B-text is the visual panorama brought on by the Good and Bad Angels in 5.2 to torment Faustus with a preview of what he has lost and won. Here the stage picture is markedly reminiscent of the biblical plays' dramatizations of judgment, and indeed of other medieval visualizations of that apocalyptic event. Once Mephistopheles has finished with his gloating claim of being the author of Faustus's tragedy in 5.2, the Good and Bad Angels enter '*at several doors*' to present the terrified protagonist with a picture show of heavenly and hellish rewards. The B-text reviser is determined not to leave Faustus alone on stage. Previously, the Good Angel has not given up hope that Faustus can be saved if he will repent; now he joins the Bad Angel chorically in rubbing it in that Faustus has wilfully turned down the precious offer of salvation that was extended to him. The only difference now of the two angels is that the Good Angel shows Faustus a picture of a lost heaven while the Bad Angel presides over a display of the hell that awaits. Staging is more elaborate than in the A-text, which of course has none of this panorama. First, '*Music while the throne descends.*' The stage direction does not specify what is visually presented, but the Good Angel's running commentary gives a pretty good idea:

> Hadst thou kept on that way, Faustus, behold
> In what resplendent glory thou hadst set
> In yonder throne, like those bright shining saints,
> And triumphed over hell. That hast thou lost.
> And now, poor soul, must thy good angel leave thee.
> The jaws of hell are open to receive thee.   (5.2.115–20)

The command to 'behold' calls Faustus's and our attention to the stage picture of a glorious heavenly throne and some representation of a host of 'shining saints.' Whether they are puppet figures, or painted images, or possibly actors in dumb show we do not know; perhaps puppets are the most likely. In any case, the stage picture is a conventional one of the heavenly host basking in its reward, as at the end of the Towneley *Last Judgment* and in similar depictions of the blessed standing on the right hand of God, though God/Christ are not mentioned in the B-text. Once it has made its presumably devastating impression on the mute Faustus, the throne ascends into the theatre's 'heavens' by means of ropes and pulleys and the Good Angel probably exits through the stage door that he used for his entrance, though he could remain on stage until line 137 if the '*Exit*' there in the B-text signals the departure of both angels. (The singular *exit* is often used for a multiple departure in early modern texts, though here it may refer to the Bad Angel alone.)

Once the heavenly throne has ascended, it is the Bad Angel's turn. First, '*Hell is discovered*,' presumably by the dropping or parting of a curtain that has concealed a 'discovery space' in the tiring house wall – the sort of discovery space that would have been suitable early in the play when, in both A- and B-texts, the opening chorus steps aside with a wave of the hand toward Faustus: 'And this the man that in his study sits' (28/27). At this point the B-text stage direction reads simply *'Faustus in his study.'* Whether the earlier A-text calls for a different stage arrangement with its *'Enter Faustus in his study'* is not clear, but in any case the B-text does perhaps suggest that Faustus's study is the 'discovery space' in which he is now 'discovered' and from which he then can emerge onto the main stage for the large remainder of the opening scene. In 5.2 the stage arrangement seems unambiguous in the B-text: Hell is *'discovered.'* This is indeed an ideal use for the 'discovery space' on the Elizabethan stage, since it is entirely visual and requires no dialogue or action within the limited space there provided.

The Bad Angel's description accompanying the tableau of hell is more specific than that accompanying the throne of heaven, and predictably so; depictions of hell are always more graphic than those of heaven. This is Calvin's point, that the human superstitious imagination more readily conceives of ugly violence than it does of bliss:

> Now, Faustus, let thine eyes with horror stare
> Into that vast perpetual torture-house.
> There are the Furies tossing damnèd souls
> On burning forks; there bodies boil in lead.
> There are live quarters broiling on the coals,
> That ne'er can die. This ever-burning chair
> Is for o'er-tortured souls to rest them in.
> These that are fed with sops of flaming fire
> Were gluttons, and loved only delicates,
> And laughed to see the poor starve at their gates.
> But yet all these are nothing. Thou shalt see
> Ten thousand tortures that more horrid be.   (5.2.121–32)

The images are familiar from the tradition of Van Eyck and Brueghel, with pitchforks, boiling lead, and never-ending fire. As in the Towneley *Last Judgment*, the indictable sins of those who are damned prominently include failure to perform the corporal works of mercy: here, gluttons have not fed the poor at their gates. The antithetical parallelism of the two tableaux is reinforced by the focus on a throne in each case. Faustus is invited to 'stare / Into that vast perpetual torture-house,' suggesting again that the spectacle is in a recessed 'discovery space.' Again, we cannot be sure whether puppet figures are used, or painted scenery, or even actors, but in any case the two pageants are antithetically symmetrical. The two angels, who entered '*at several* [i.e., separate] *doors*,' presumably leave as they came in. Interestingly, no stage direction specifies the closing or removing of the tableau of hell. Conceivably, then, it could remain in plain view throughout Faustus's last soliloquy. As we have speculated, Lucifer, Beelzebub, and Mephistopheles may also be visible to the audience throughout these last minutes; although the B-text specifies that '*the devils*' enter with '*thunder*' during Faustus's last four lines, more or less as in the A-text, such an entry could mean simply that the devils, present throughout in the upper acting area, descend at this point backstage and come on stage menacingly to collect their victim. The final stage direction for this scene in the B-text says simply, '*Exeunt.*'

Not content with these graphic and contrasted stage images depicting Faustus's terrible fate, the B-text then adds a final scene not in the original. The A-text leaves to our imagination the task of conceiving what Faustus's end will be like; all we are told is that devils '*enter*' at the last three lines of Faustus's final speech and then '*exeunt with him.*' The B-text reviser, curious to know and display more, goes back to the *Damnable Life*, where he finds this illuminating description of the scene awaiting Faustus's fellow scholars on the morning after his rendezvous with damnation: 'The hall lay besprinkled with blood, his brains cleaving to the wall, for the devil had beaten him from one wall against another. In one corner lay his eyes, in another his teeth ... They found his body lying in the horse dung, most monstrously torn and fearful to behold, for his head and all his joints were dashed in pieces' (chapter 63).

How is the B-text to capitalize on this piece of extravagant gore? The dialogue of the three Scholars plainly indicates that they see plenty. 'O, help us, heaven!' one exclaims. 'See, here are Faustus' limbs / All torn asunder by the hand of death.' Another Scholar has no doubt that

The devils whom Faustus served have torn him thus,
For, 'twixt the hours of twelve and one, methought
I heard him shriek and call aloud for help,
At which self time the house seemed all on fire
With dreadful horror of these damnèd fiends.   (5.3.6–12)

The Scholars resolve to 'give his mangled limbs due burial' (5.3.17). Whether they then carry off some dummy representing the mangled corpse we cannot be sure; perhaps all the acting company did was to 'discover' a painted scene backstage and then drop a curtain over the dismal spectacle at the end. A painted scene would afford an easier way to depict blood everywhere, brains cleaving to the wall, eyes and teeth scattered hither and yon, the decapitated and dissevered body lying in horse dung, etc., than would an actual staging of these horrors. But then you never know.

Why, finally, did the Admiral's Men and the B-text revisers wish to accentuate the very physicality of hell that the A-text went to such lengths to denounce as the very kind of superstitious thinking that has led Faustus into fatal error by his supposing that, since such childish pictures of hell are foolish, hell itself cannot be real? Part of the presumed answer is that such spectacle was good show biz – an appeal that the Admiral's Men never tried to resist. Other B-text revisions that are not germane to this current analysis show a fascination with duplicating and extending the kinds of stage tricks that audiences clearly loved: antler's heads placed ignominiously on the head of a knight having the effrontery to scoff at Faustus, severed limbs rejoined to the body, trees moving at Faustus's command, clownish figures transported by Faustus's magic from their tavern to the duke of Vanholt's court, devils proliferating at every turn, and still more. The dual displays of heaven and hell are of a piece with these popular shenanigans. The Admiral's Men were not wrong in supposing that such spin-offs would add to the stage life of this valuable property, the text of *Doctor Faustus*.

At the same time, part of that same popularity seems to have taken the form of belying the A-text's seriously Calvinist theology in favour of a more popular idea about salvation and damnation. The result is a kind of simplified mingle-mangle in which, on the one hand, the devil is to blame for Faustus's tragedy. Faustus is trapped, in the B-text version. The staging repeatedly enforces the impression that the devil is always on hand, gloating, directing, tempting, determining the outcome. This is a scary notion, well suited to a kind of tragic melodrama. It is not inconsistent with a popular view of Calvinist theology, which is that everything is predetermined since the cards are stacked against certain doomed individuals. If that view heretically implies in turn that heavenly providence itself is partner in a conspiracy seeking the ruin of certain predeterminately evil men, so be it. On the other hand, the implied theology of the B-text seems comfortable with the notion so prominent in the Towneley *Last Judgment* that good works are a necessary and efficacious step towards individual salvation. The Protestant reformers had done their best to eradicate what they regarded as an especially heinous heresy, but such ideas do not die easily. The B-text reviser or revisers, eager to entertain popular audiences, knew what they were doing.

NOTES

1 David Bevington, *From 'Mankind' to Marlowe: Growth of Structure in the Popular Drama of Tudor England* (Cambridge, MA: Harvard University Press, 1962).
2 David Bevington, 'Staging the A- and B-Texts of *Doctor Faustus*,' in *Marlowe's Empery: Expanding His Critical Contexts*, ed. Sara Munson Deats and Robert A. Logan (Newark: University of Delaware Press; London: Associated University Presses, 2002), 43–60.
3 Some scholars have recently challenged the concept of the Wakefield Master. John T. Sebastian did so in a presentation at the International Congress on Medieval Studies, Kalamazoo, MI, 2 May 2002, entitled 'The Birth and Death of the Author: The Case of the Wakefield Master.' In 2004, at the same conference, Warren Edminster made a strong argument that whoever was responsible for most of the so-called Wakefield Master plays did not write *Mactacio Abel* – the only play among the so-called Wakefield plays that explicitly links play to Wakefield itself. See also Garrett Epp, '"Corected & not playd": An Unproductive History of the Towneley Plays,' *Research Opportunities in Renaissance Drama* 43 (2004): 38–53, a paper originally presented at Kalamazoo in 2004. I nonetheless remain convinced that a single and distinctive genius is to be found in the works among the Towneley Plays customarily associated with the name of the Wakefield Master.
4 Christopher Marlowe, '*Doctor Faustus, A- and B-texts (1604, 1616)*,' ed. David Bevington and Eric Rasmussen. The Revels Plays (Manchester: University of Manchester Press, 1993), 62–70. Citations to the play in this essay, for both A- and B-texts, are from this edition. Early editors of the play took the B-text to be the primary one: these included C.W. Dilke, *Old English Plays* (1814–16), W. Oxberry, *The Tragicall Historie of the Life and Death of Doctor Faustus with New Additions* (1818), and George Robinson, *The Works of Christopher Marlowe* (1826). In later decades of the nineteenth century and in the early twentieth century, opinion swung in favour of the A-text, as in the editions of Alexander Dyce, *Works* (1850), Wilhelm Wagner (1877), Adolphus William Ward, *Old English Drama: Select Plays* (1878), A.H. Bullen, *Works* (1885), Havelock Ellis, *Christopher Marlowe*, Mermaid Series (1887), and C.F. Tucker Brooke, *Works* (1910). Francis Cunningham, *Works* (1870), based his edition on the B-text, though allowing the A-text to be closer to the Marlovian origi-

nal. Then a group of textual scholars returned to the B-text as purportedly the earlier version and thus closer to a Marlovian original: Frederick S. Boas, *The Tragical History of Doctor Faustus* (1932), Leo Kirschbaum, *The Plays of Christopher Marlowe* (1946 and 1962), W.W. Greg, *Marlowe's 'Doctor Faustus' 1604–1616: Parallel Texts* and *The Tragicall History of the Life and Death of Doctor Faustus by Christopher Marlowe: A Conjectural Reconstruction* (1950), John D. Jump, *Doctor Faustus*, Revels Plays (1962), Irving Ribner, *The Complete Plays of Christopher Marlowe* (1963), and Roma Gill, *Doctor Faustus*, New Mermaids (1965). Greg held that the A-text was a 'bad quarto,' memorially constructed. Fredson Bowers, *The Complete Works of Christopher Marlowe* (1973) saw the A-text as one that was memorially reconstructed by actors from the play as originally performed, with the B-text containing the Birde-Rowley additions. In recent years, editors have generally opted for the A-text: Gill (in her 1989 New Mermaid edition and 1990 Oxford University Press edition), David Ormerod and Christopher Wortham, *Christopher Marlowe, 'Dr Faustus': The A-Text* (1985), and Michael Keefer, *Christopher Marlowe's 'Doctor Faustus': A 1604–Version Edition* (1991).

5 John Calvin, *Institutes of the Christian Religion*, ed. John T. McNeill, trans. Ford Lewis Battles, 2 vols (Philadelphia and London: Westminster, 1960). See Pauline Honderich, 'John Calvin and Doctor Faustus,' *MLR* 68 (1973): 1–13; and Paul R. Sellin, 'The Hidden God: Reformation Awe in Renaissance English Literature,' in *The Darker Vision of the Renaissance: Beyond the Fields of Reason*, ed. Robert S. Kinsman (Berkeley and Los Angeles: University of California Press, 1974), 147–96.

6 John D. Davis, *The Westminster Dictionary of the Bible*, rev. Henry Snyder Gehman (Philadelphia: The Westminster Press, 1944).

7 M.R. James, trans. *The Apocryphal New Testament* (Oxford: Clarendon Press, 1924), 94–146. Citations from the bishop of Metz's Service for the Consecration of a Church, and, later in this essay, from the Towneley *Harrowing of Hell* and *The Last Judgment*, are from *Medieval Drama*, ed. David Bevington (Boston: Houghton Mifflin, 1975), 12–13, 594–607, 637–8.

A Bibliography of Alexandra F. Johnston's Publications, 1967–2006

Compiled by KAREN SAWYER MARSALEK

1967
'Medieval Drama in England – 1966,' *Queen's Quarterly* 74 (1967): 78–91.

1971
With Margaret Dorrell (Rogerson), 'The Doomsday Pageant of the York Mercers, 1433,' *Leeds Studies in English* ns 5 (1971): 29–34.

1972
With Margaret Dorrell (Rogerson), 'The York Mercers and Their Pageant of Doomsday, 1433–1526,' *Leeds Studies in English* ns 6 (1972): 10–35.

1973
'The Procession and Play of Corpus Christi in York after 1426,' *Leeds Studies in English* ns 7 (1973–4): 55–62.

1974
'A Medieval and Renaissance Dramatic Records Project,' *Research Opportunities in Renaissance Drama* 17 (1974): 105–6.

1975
'The Plays of the Religious Guilds of York: The Creed Play and the Pater Noster Play,' *Speculum* 50 (1975): 55–90.

'*The Medieval English Stage: Corpus Christi Pageants and Plays* by Alan H. Nelson; A Review Article,' *University of Toronto Quarterly* 44 (1975): 238–48.

1976
'The Guild of Corpus Christi and the Procession of Corpus Christi in York,'
Mediaeval Studies 38 (1976): 372–84.
'Yule in York,' *REED Newsletter* 1976.1: 3–10.
'York Notes,' *REED Newsletter* 1976.2: 9–11.

1977
'The York Cycle: 1977,' *University of Toronto Quarterly* 48 (1978): 1–9.

1979
Ed. with Margaret Rogerson, *York*. Records of Early English Drama (Toronto:
University of Toronto Press, 1979).
'*Records of Early English Drama* and Chaucer Studies,' *The Chaucer Newsletter*
1.2 (1979): 23–4.
With Audrey W. Douglas, Alice B. Hamilton, and David N. Klausner, 'Research
in Progress,' *REED Newsletter* 1979.1: 13–24.

1980
'Errata in *York*,' *REED Newsletter* 1980.1: 35–8.
'Medieval Drama in Modern Performance,' *Book Forum* 5 (1980): 300–3.

1981
With Sally-Beth MacLean and Cameron Louis, *Handbook for Editors* (Toronto:
Records of Early English Drama, 1981).
'Parish Entertainments in Berkshire,' in *Pathways to Medieval Peasants*, ed. J.A.
Raftis. Papers in Mediaeval Studies 2 (Toronto: Pontifical Institute of Mediae-
val Studies, 1981), 335–8.

1982
'York Pageant House: New Evidence,' *REED Newsletter* 1982.2: 24–5.

1984
'The Parliament of Heaven in Performance: The English Tradition,' in *Atti Del
IV Colloquio della Société Internationale pour l'Étude du Théâtre Médiéval*,
ed. M. Chiabo, F. Doglio, and M. Maymone (Viterbo: Privately printed, 1984),
373–8.

1985
'The York Corpus Christi Play: A Dramatic Structure Based on Performance
Practice,' in *The Theatre in the Middle Ages*, ed. Herman Braet, Johan Nowé,

and Gilbert Tournoy. Medieavalia Lovaniensia Series 1, Study 13 (Leuven: Leuven University Press, 1985), 362–73.

1986
'Wisdom and the Records: Is There a Moral?' in *The Wisdom Symposium: Papers From the Trinity College Medieval Festival*, ed. Milla Cozart Riggio (New York: AMS Press, 1986), 87–102.

1987
Ed., *Editing Early English Drama: Special Problems and New Directions: Papers Given at the Nineteenth Annual Conference on Editorial Problems, University of Toronto, 4–5 November 1983* (New York, AMS Press: 1987).
Introduction, in *Editing Early English Drama: Special Problems and New Directions: Papers Given at the Nineteenth Annual Conference on Editorial Problems, University of Toronto, 4–5 November 1983*, ed. A.F. Johnston (New York: AMS Press, 1987), 13–16
'The *York Cycle* and the *Chester Cycle*: What Do the Records Tell Us?' in *Editing Early English Drama: Special Problems and New Directions: Papers Given at the Nineteenth Annual Conference on Editorial Problems, University of Toronto, 4–5 November 1983*, ed. A.F. Johnston (New York: AMS Press, 1987), 121–43.
'The Churchwarden Accounts of Great Marlow, Buckinghamshire,' *REED Newsletter* 12.1 (1987): 9–12.
'Cycle Drama in the Sixteenth Century: Texts and Contexts,' in *Early Drama to 1600*, ed. Albert H. Tricomi, Acta 13 (Binghamton: Center for Medieval and Early Renaissance Studies, 1987), 1–15.

1988
'The Audience of the English Moral Play,' in *Le Théâtre et la Cité dans l'Europe médiévale: Actes du Véme colloque international de la Société Internationale pour l'Étude du Théâtre Médiéval*, ed. Edelgard E. Dubruck and William C. McDonald, *Fifteenth Century Studies* 13 (1988): 291–7.
'Chaucer's Records of Early English Drama,' *REED Newsletter* 13.2 (1988): 13–20.
' Lille: The External Evidence: An Analysis,' *Research Opportunities in Renaissance Drama* 30 (1988): 167–72.

1989
'Evil in the Towneley Cycle,' *Medieval English Theatre* 11 (1992 for 1989): 94–103.

'English Guilds and Municipal Authority,' *Renaissance and Reformation/Renaissance et Réforme* ns 13 (1989): 69–88.

'What If No Texts Survived? External Evidence for Early English Drama,' in *Contexts for Early English Drama*, ed. Marianne G. Briscoe and John C. Coldewey (Bloomington, IN; Indiana University Press, 1989), 1–19.

'York Plays,' in *Dictionary of the Middle Ages*, ed. Joseph R. Strayer (New York: Scribner, 1989), 12: 727–8.

'Pageant,' in *A Companion to the Medieval Theatre*, ed. R.W. Vince (New York: Greenwood, 1989), 271–9.

1990

'English Civic Ceremony,' in *Petrarch's Triumphs: Allegory and Spectacle*, ed. Konrad Eisenbichler and Amilcare A. Iannucci. University of Toronto Italian Studies 4 (Ottawa: Dovehouse, 1990), 395–401.

1991

'English Puritanism and Festive Custom,' *Renaissance and Reformation/Renaissance et Réforme* ns 15 (1991): 289–97.

'"All the World Was a Stage": Records of Early English Drama,' in *The Theatre of Medieval Europe: New Research in Early Drama*, ed. Eckehard Simon. Cambridge Studies in Medieval Literature 9 (Cambridge: Cambridge University Press, 1991), 117–29.

1992

'Four *York* Pageants Performed in the Streets of York: July 9, 1988,' *Research Opportunities in Renaissance Drama* 31 (1992): 101–4.

1993

'"Amys and Amylon" at Bicester Priory,' *REED Newsletter* 18:2 (1993): 15–18.

'Performance Practice Informed by Image: The Iconography of the Chester Pageants,' in *Spectacle and Image in Renaissance Europe: Selected Papers of the XXXIInd Conference at the Centre d'études supérieures de la Renaissance de Tours, 29 June–8 July 1989*, ed. André Lascombes (Leiden: Brill, 1993), 245–62.

'*The Word Made Flesh*: Augustinian Elements in the *York Cycle*,' in *The Centre and Its Compass: Studies in Medieval Literature in Honor of Professor John Leyerle*, ed. Robert Taylor et al. Studies in Medieval Culture 33 (Kalamazoo, MI: Medieval Institute Publications, 1993), 225–46.

'The *York Cycle* and the *Chester Cycle*: What Do the Records Tell Us?' (see above under 1987). Anthologized in *The Chester Mystery Cycle: A Casebook*, ed. Kevin J. Harty. Garland Medieval Casebooks (New York: Garland, 1993), 18–35.

1994

'Summer Festivals in the Thames Valley Counties,' in *Custom, Culture and Community in the Later Middle Ages: A Symposium*, ed. Thomas Pettitt and Leif Søndergaard (Odense, Denmark: Odense University Press, 1994), 37–56.

'The Inherited Tradition: The Legacy of Provincial Drama,' in *The Elizabethan Theatre XIII, Papers Given at the Thirteenth International Conference on Elizabethan Theatre Held at the University of Waterloo, Waterloo, Ontario, in July 1989*, ed. A.L. Magnusson and C.E. McGee (Toronto: Meany, 1994), 1–25.

1995

'Bicester Priory Revisited,' *REED Newsletter* 20.2 (1995): 16–17.

'Traders and Playmakers: English Guildsmen and the Low Countries,' in *England and the Low Countries in the Late Middle Ages*, ed. Caroline Barron and Nigel Saul (Stroud: Alan Sutton; New York: St Martin's, 1995), 99–114.

With Robert Tittler, '"To catch a thief" in Jacobean London,' in *The Salt of Common Life: Individuality and Choice in the Medieval Town, Countryside and Church: Essays Presented to J. Ambrose Raftis*, ed. Edwin Brezette DeWindt. Studies in Medieval Culture 36 (Kalamazoo, MI: Medieval Institute Publications, 1995), 233–69.

'Acting Mary: The Emotional Realism of the Mature Virgin in the N-Town Plays,' in *From Page to Performance: Essays in Early English Drama*, ed. John Alford (East Lansing, MI: Michigan State University Press, 1995), 85–98.

1996

Ed. with Wim Hüsken, *English Parish Drama*. Ludus 1 (Amsterdam and Atlanta: Rodopi, 1996).

Introduction, in *English Parish Drama*, ed. Alexandra F. Johnston and Wim Hüsken. Ludus 1 (Amsterdam and Atlanta: Rodopi, 1996), 7–14.

'"What revels are in hand?" Dramatic Activities Sponsored by the Parishes of the Thames Valley,' in *English Parish Drama*, ed. Alexandra F. Johnston and Wim Hüsken. Ludus 1 (Amsterdam and Atlanta: Rodopi, 1996), 95–106.

1997

Ed. with Wim Hüsken. *Civic Ritual and Drama*. Ludus 2 (Amsterdam and Atlanta: Rodopi), 1997.

Introduction, in *Civic Ritual and Drama*, ed. Alexandra F. Johnston and Wim Hüsken. Ludus 2 (Amsterdam and Atlanta: Rodopi, 1997), 7–14.

'The Continental Connection: A Reconsideration,' in *The Stage as Mirror: Civic Theatre in Late Medieval Europe*, ed. Alan Knight (Woodbridge, Suffolk: D.S. Brewer, 1997), 7–24.

'"At the still point of the turning world": Augustinian Roots of Medieval Dra-
maturgy,' in *European Medieval Drama 2, Papers from the Second Interna-
tional Conference on European Medieval Drama, Camerino, 4–6 July 1997*, ed.
Sydney Higgins (Camerino: Università degli studi di Camerino, Centro
linguistico di Ateneo, 1997), 5–24.
With Sally-Beth MacLean, 'Reformation and Resistance in Thames/Severn
Parishes: The Dramatic Witness,' in *The Parish in English Life, 1400–1600*, ed.
Katherine L. French, Gary G. Gibbs, and Beat A. Kümin (Manchester:
Manchester University Press, 1997), 178–200.

1998
'The Emerging Pattern of the Easter Play in England,' *Medieval English Theatre*
20 (1998): 3–23.
With David Parry, *The Castle of Perseverance: A Modernization*. Posted on the
internet December 1998. http://www.chass.utoronto.ca/~ajohnsto/
cascomp.html
'The Robin Hood of the Records,' in *Playing Robin Hood: The Legend as
Performance in Five Centuries*, ed. Lois Potter (Newark: University of Dela-
ware Press, 1998), 27–44.
'William Revetour, Chaplain and Clerk of York, Testator,' in *Essays in Honour of
Peter Meredith*, ed. Catherine J. Batt. *Leeds Studies in English* ns 29 (1998):
153–71.
'Vernacular Drama,' in *Medieval England: An Encyclopedia*, ed. Paul E.
Szarmach, M. Teresa Tavormina, and Joel T. Rosenthal (New York: Garland,
1998), 244–8.

1999
With Stanley J. Kahrl, *The N-Town Plays: A Modernization*. Posted on the
internet September 1999. http://www.chass.utoronto.ca/~ajohnsto/
frntmt.html.
'English Community Drama in Crisis: 1535–80,' in *Drama and Community:
People and Plays in Medieval Europe*, ed. Alan Hindley. Medieval Texts and
Cultures of Northern Europe I (Turnhout, Belgium: Brepols, 1999), 248–69.

2000
Ed. with Helen Ostovich. *The York Cycle Then and Now*. A special edition of
Early Theatre 3 (2000).
Introduction, to *Early Theatre* 3 (2000): 17–21.
'"His langage is lorne": The Silent Centre of the York Cycle,' *Early Theatre* 3
(2000): 185–95.

'York Cycle 1998: What We Learned,' *Early Theatre* 3 (2000): 199–203.

'York, 1998,' in *European Medieval Drama, 1999: Papers From the Fourth International Conference on Aspects of European Medieval Drama, Camerino, 5–8 August 1999*, ed. Sydney Higgins (Camerino : Università degli studi di Camerino, Centro linguistico di ateneo, 2000), 21–7.

2001

With Arleane Ralph and Abigail Anne Young, 'The Conundrum of the Label,' in *Shakespeare's Face*, ed. Stephanie Nolen (Toronto: Knopf, 2001), 274–9.

'"It pleased the Lord to discover his displeasure": The 1652 Performance of *Mucedorus* in Witney,' in *Porci ante Margaritam: Essays in Honour of Meg Twycross*, ed. Sarah Carpenter, Pamela King, and Peter Meredith. *Leeds Studies in English* ns 32 (2001): 195–209.

2002

'Gendering Abstractions: The Portrayal of Women in *The Castle of Perseverance*,' *European Medieval Drama* 5, *A Selection of Papers Presented at the Tenth Colloquium of the Société Internationale pour l'Étude du Théâtre Médiéval held in Groningen (Netherlands) 2–7 July 2001* (Turnhout, Belgium: Brepols, 2002), 123–34.

'"The Lady of the farme": The Context of Lady Russell's Entertainment of Elizabeth at Bisham, 1592,' *Early Theatre* 5.2 (2002): 71–85.

'The City as Patron: York,' in *Shakespeare and Theatrical Patronage in Early Modern England*, ed. Paul Whitfield White and Suzanne R. Westfall (Cambridge: Cambridge University Press, 2002), 150–75.

'The *York Cycle* and the Libraries of York,' in *The Church and Learning in Later Medieval Society: Essays in Honour of R.B. Dobson; Proceedings of the 1999 Harlaxton Symposium*, ed. Caroline M. Barron and Jenny Stratford. Harlaxton Medieval Studies 11 (Donnington, UK: Shaun Tyas, 2002), 355–70.

2003

'The Feast of Corpus Christi in the West Country,' *Early Theatre* 6.1 (2003): 15–34. (Winner of Martin Stevens Award for the Best New Essay in Early Drama Studies, 2004.)

'Biblical Plays,' 'Corpus Christi Plays,' 'Cornish Rounds,' 'Cycle Plays, Medieval,' 'Guilds,' 'Miracle Plays,' and 'Mystery Plays,' for *The Oxford Encyclopedia of Theatre and Performance*, ed. Dennis Kennedy (Oxford: Oxford University Press, 2003), 1:154–6, 315, 315–16, 342–3, 555–6, 2:861–2, 907.

2004
With John R. Elliott, Jr, Alan H. Nelson, and Diana Wyatt, *Oxford: University and City*, 2 vols. Records of Early English Drama (Toronto: University of Toronto Press), 2004.
'Fifteenth-Century Yorkshire Drama: A Hypothesis,' in *Music and Medieval Manuscripts: Paleography and Performance; Essays Dedicated to Andrew Hughes*, ed. John Haines and Randall Rosenfeld (Aldershot, Hants: Ashgate, 2004), 263–78.

2006
'Parish Playmaking before the Reformation,' in *The Late Medieval English Parish: Proceedings of the 2002 Harlaxton Symposium*, ed. Clive Burgess and Eamon Duffy. Harlaxton Medieval Studies 14 (Donington, Lincolnshire: Shaun Tyas/Paul Watkins, 2006), 325–41.
'The Audience of Early Drama: REED and the Techniques of Historical Fiction,' in *Teaching with the Records of Early English Drama*, ed. Elza Tiner. Studies in Early English Drama (Toronto: University of Toronto Press, 2006), 3–13.
'The Founding of Records of Early English Drama,' in *REED in Review: Essays in Celebration of the First Twenty-five Years*, ed. Audrey Douglas and Sally-Beth MacLean. Studies in Early English Drama (Toronto: University of Toronto Press, 2006), 21–38.

Forthcoming
Berkshire, Buckinghamshire, and Oxfordshire. Records of Early English Drama (Toronto: University of Toronto Press).
'Records of Early English Drama in Retrospect,' in *Toronto Edits*, ed. Gillian Fenwick (Toronto: University of Toronto Press).

Contributors

Caroline M. Barron is Professor of the History of London at Royal Holloway College, University of London.

David Bevington is Phyllis Fay Horton Distinguished Service Professor in the Humanities Emeritus, in the Departments of English and Comparative Literature, at the University of Chicago.

Garrett P.J. Epp is Professor of English and Film Studies at the University of Alberta.

David N. Klausner is Professor of English and Medieval Studies at the University of Toronto.

Sally-Beth MacLean is Professor of English at the University of Toronto and Executive Editor of Records of Early English Drama.

Karen Sawyer Marsalek is Associate Professor of English at St Olaf College.

Peter Meredith is Emeritus Professor of Medieval Drama in the School of English at the University of Leeds.

David Mills is Professor Emeritus of English in the School of English, University of Liverpool.

Barbara D. Palmer is Professor of English, retired, at the University of Mary Washington.

K. Janet Ritch is Adjunct Professor in the Department of the Humanities, York University and the Toronto School of Theology, University of Toronto.

Margaret Rogerson is Senior Lecturer in the Department of English at the University of Sydney.

Chester Scoville is Lecturer in the Department of English and Drama at the University of Toronto at Mississauga.

Alan Somerset is Professor of English at the University of Western Ontario.

Meg Twycross is Professor Emeritus of English and Medieval Studies in the Department of English and Creative Writing at Lancaster University.

Index

Le Mystère de la Passion (Amiens),
264–5
Le Mystère de la Passion (Château-
dun), 246
Le Mystère de la Passion (Mons),
252–4, 257, 264–5n46
*Le Mystère de la Passion Nostre
Seigneur* (*Le Mystère Sainte-
Geneviève*), 244, 249
Le Mystère de la Résurrection
(Angers), 244–5, 249

N-Town plays, 136, 160n49, 223, 232,
254, 286n4; banns, 111; 1: *The
Creation of Heaven*, 235; 9: *The
Presentation of Mary in the Temple*,
264n37; 10: *The Marriage of Mary
and Joseph*, 264n37; 14: *The Trial of
Mary and Joseph*, 264n37; 32: *The
Crucifixion*, 174; 35: *Christ's Appearance to Mary*, 180n30, 274, 281;
38: *The Appearance to Thomas*, 165,
178n9; 41: *Assumption of Mary*,
237–9; *The Mary Play*, 239, 241,
257, 264n37
Newdigate family, 84–5
Nichodemus, Gospel of, 297, 299

Oxford colleges. *See* Brasenose,
Magdalen

pantry accounts. *See under* Clifford
La Passion de Semur, 243–4, 249
patrons. *See* minstrels, players
patronage, 58–90
Pecham, John, archbishop of Canterbury, 257
Percy, Henry, duke of Northumberland, 274–5, 278; household accounts, 59

Perkins, William, 212–13
playing spaces, 12, 59–60, 64–6, 70–1,
83–4, 92, 192–3, 198, 303, 304–5, 308
plays, suppression of, 13–14, 18, 28
players, 18; Admiral's, 39–40n43, 278,
293–4, 302, 308; Children of the
Revels, 17; countess of Warwick's,
87; His Majesty's Revels, 13; Mr
Kempton's, 13; King and Queen of
Bohemia's, 88; King's Men, 13, 79,
86, 88, 278; Lord Admiral's, 13;
Lord Henry Berkeley's, 79; Lord
Chandos's, 13; Lord Darcy's, 13,
27; Lord Derby's, 13, 19, 21, 23–4,
32–3; Lord Dudley's, 16–19, 27–9,
87–9; Lord Essex's, 13; Lord Monteagle's, 17, 27, 39n42, 82; Lord
Morden's, 13; Lord Ogle's, 13;
Lord Strange's, 39–40n43; Lord
Vaux's, 39–40n43; Lord Wharton's,
21, 23, 24, 32–3, 82–3; Mr Parry's,
13; Prince's Men, 88; Queen's Men,
13, 67, 87; earl of Shrewsbury's, 18,
28–9; Mr Swinerton's, 13
Pomery family, 69
Porter, Henry, 293
printing of plays, 293
Priory House, Warw., 86, 88, 89n2
Puckering family, 84–5, 90n5;
household accounts, 86, 88; Sir
Thomas's household accounts, 86,
88–9
Puritans, 212–14, 218–21, 281

queens of England: Catherine of
Valois, 92–6; Elizabeth I, 43, 49,
212, 276; Mary, 42–3, 50, 53–4n1,
55nn9, 13, 218, 222, 273; — marriage to Philip of Spain, 42–3
Queen's College, Cambridge, 74n41

Reading, Berks.: St Laurence parish,
275
records, civic, 12, 23. *See also* Barn-
staple, Exeter, York
records, innkeepers', 12
recusancy, 214. *See also* Catholicism
Reformation, 229n34, 237, 242–3, 250,
254, 257, 259–60, 271–2, 277, 294,
308
Regularis Concordia, 271
The Resurrection of Our Lord, 237,
241, 243, 250, 274–5, 279–80, 282
Revetour, William, 123–4
rhetoric, 255
Rhetorica ad Herennium, 255
Robin Hood, 58, 70–1n3
Rogers, David, 214; 'Brevary of
Chester History,' 213
Rolle, Richard: *Novem Virtutes*, 190
Rowley, Samuel, 293–4; *When You
See Me You Know Me*, 293
rushbearings, 49

sacramentarian controversy, 281
St George, play of, 10
Sapcote, John, 69
La Seinte Resurrection, 287n18
Selby Abbey, 14–15; records of, 11, 26
Sermon Preached at Paul's Cross
(1578), 83
sermons, 256–60, 266–7n82
*Seuene Poyntes of Trewe Loue and
Euerlastynge Wisdome*, 184–5
Shakespeare, William, 9, 198, 234, 294;
Henry V, 243; *King Lear*, 16;
Pericles, 243; *Romeo and Juliet*, 243;
The Winter's Tale, 243, 271, 276–85
Sheldon family, 84–5
Shrewsbury, Shrops., 14; bailiffs'
accounts, 25–6

Shrewsbury Fragments, 274
Shrovetide, 20–2, 24, 28, 32–3, 47–8,
56n23, 61
singers and singing, 95, 97–8, 118,
182–3, 187, 190, 216
Somer, Will, 15, 36n24, 37n26
Southampton, Hants., 15; book of
fines, 25–6; stewards' accounts, 26
Stanley, Henry, 214
Stanley, Thomas, 214
Stanley, William, Baron Monteagle,
17, 27, 82
Stanzaic Life of Christ, 219, 224
summer games, 49
Suso, Heinrich: *Büchlein der Ewigen
Weisheit*, 184; *Orologium
Sapientiae*, 184–6
Swan Theatre, 74n42
Swinerton, Thomas, player, 13, 19

Talbot family, earls of Shrewsbury:
Edward, 8th earl, 18; Francis, 5th
earl, 19; Gilbert, 7th earl, 18
terminology for performers, 11,
35n12, 59
Thetford, Norf., 15; priory register,
25–6
Thomas of Elmham, 93
Tomlinson, William: account book of,
20–1
Towneley family, 10, 34, 166
Towneley plays, 10, 34n4, 160n49,
177–8n4, 197–9, 219, 235, 286n4; 4:
Abraham, 219; 7: *The Prophets*,
238; 8: *Pharaoh*, 235; 18: *Christ and
the Doctors*, 264n37; 23: *The Crucifixion*, 169; 24: *The Play of the
Dice*, 175; 25: *The Harrowing of
Hell*, 292, 297–300; 26: *The Resurrection*, 274, 278, 281; 27: *The*